European Union and its Neighbours in a Globalized World

Volume 31

The series publishes monographs and edited volumes in the field of European and international law and policy. A special focus is put on the European neighbourhood policy, current problems in European and international law and policy as well as the role of the European Union as a global actor. The series supports the publishing and distribution of research results of cross-border research consortia. Besides renowned scientists the series is also open for publication projects of young academics. The series emphasizes the interplay of the European Union and its neighbouring countries as well as the important role of the European Union as a key player in the international context of law, economics and politics.

Jenny Poon

Counteracting Containment Policies in the EU

Safeguarding the Non-Refoulement Principle

Springer

Jenny Poon
Western University, Faculty of Law
London, Ontario, Canada

ISSN 2524-8928 ISSN 2524-8936 (electronic)
European Union and its Neighbours in a Globalized World
ISBN 978-3-032-08350-0 ISBN 978-3-032-08351-7 (eBook)
https://doi.org/10.1007/978-3-032-08351-7

This Springer imprint is published by the registered company Springer Nature Switzerland AG.
The registered company address is: Gewerbestrasse 11, 6330 Cham, Switzerland

Preface

At the time of writing, the Syrian civil war has brought a large number of asylum claimants and refugees into and across the European Union (EU) in search of refuge.

At the EU level, negotiations for reforms to the Common European Asylum System (CEAS) have begun to take place, with proposed changes to the Dublin III Regulation, including recasting the current key instruments from 'directives' into binding 'regulations' to further promote compliance.

At the same time, various countries within the EU are adopting measures to cope with the mass influx. In the United Kingdom (UK), plans for exiting the CEAS, following Brexit, are underway. In Germany, the 'open door' policy under Chancellor Angela Merkel has seen diminishing support.

EU countries are continuing to sign bilateral and multilateral agreements with third countries with the aim of reducing secondary asylum claimant movements and preventing 'forum-shopping'. Measures to curtail irregular migration continue to take place daily, especially along the Mediterranean Sea route, where asylum claimants and refugees make perilous journeys to access asylum. During this time, the number of claimants being returned to non-EU countries deemed 'safe' continues to rise.

In addition to these developments, the use of migration control mechanisms is steadily increasing, with measures including the criminalization of migrants, securitization of borders, and the externalization of border control.

Against this backdrop, this book examines the protection of *non-refoulement* within the EU and its implications for the protection of those most at risk for serious human rights abuses.

The material in this book is current as of August 2025.

This publication is my own work and reflects my personal views, and it does not reflect the views of any of my former or current employers, including the Government of Canada, the Federal Public Service, or the Department of Justice Canada.

Acknowledgements To my mentors and faculty advisors, my spouse, family and friends, whose relentless belief, patience, and faith in me allowed me to see the doctoral project and subsequent editions come to fruition.

This book is dedicated to the stakeholders: those who had to overcome insurmountable difficulty and risk their lives to reach safety and to reunite with loved ones. They exemplify resilience and bravery at the highest level and are a true inspiration to me.

All views and any errors are my own.

Competing Interests The author has no competing interests to declare that are relevant to the content of this manuscript.

Contents

1 **Introduction: Setting the Stage** 1
1.1 Introduction 1
1.1.1 The Book's Structure 3
1.1.2 Concluding Remarks 5
References 6

2 ***Non-Refoulement* Protection Under International and European Refugee Law** 9
2.1 Introduction 9
2.1.1 History of Non-Refoulement 10
2.2 The Current Conception of Non-Refoulement Under International Refugee Law 16
2.3 Current Conception of Non-Refoulement Under International Human Rights Law 23
2.4 Non-Refoulement in European Law 28
2.5 Conclusions on the Principle of Non-Refoulement 35
References 36

3 **The Common European Asylum System and *Non-Refoulement*** 39
3.1 Introduction 39
3.2 The European Legal Order 41
3.2.1 EU Law 41
3.2.2 ECHR Law 50
3.3 Claiming Asylum in the EU 56
3.3.1 Dublin III Regulation and the Determination of the Member State Responsible 56
3.3.2 Qualifying for International Protection and Relevant Asylum Procedures 58
3.3.3 The New Pact on Migration and Asylum 60
3.4 Gaps Between Law and Practice with Respect to Non-Refoulement within the EU 61

3.4.1 The 'Margin of Discretion' and *Non-Refoulement* 62
3.4.2 The Presumption of Mutual Trust Within the EU 67
3.5 Concluding Remarks 70
References 72

4 Containment in Europe 77
4.1 Introduction 77
4.2 Theories of Containment 78
4.3 Containment in the Common European Asylum System 85
4.4 Containment and *Non-Refoulement* 95
4.5 Concluding Remarks 101
References 102

5 The United Kingdom and *Non-Refoulement* 107
5.1 Introduction 107
5.2 UK Refugee Law 109
5.3 The UK Domestic Asylum System: Institutional Structure 122
5.4 Claiming Asylum in the UK 124
5.5 Containment by the UK Through Procedural Methods and Evidentiary Thresholds 129
5.6 Concluding Remarks 142
References 144

6 Germany and *Non-Refoulement* 147
6.1 Introduction 147
6.2 German Refugee Law 149
6.3 The German Domestic Asylum System 156
6.4 Non-Refoulement in Germany 162
6.5 Containment in Germany as Illustrated by the Presumption of Mutual Trust 171
6.6 Concluding Remarks 176
References 177

7 Conclusion: Protecting *Non-Refoulement* 181
7.1 Introduction 181
7.1.1 Situating *Non-Refoulement* Within the Domestic: Comparing UK and German Practices 183
7.1.2 The Future of *Non-Refoulement* Protection in International Refugee Law 193
7.1.3 Conclusion: Future Directions for *Non-Refoulement* 212
References 213

Appendix: Bibliography 217

Glossary 277

Abbreviations

BAMF	Bundesamt für Migration und Flüchtlinge (Federal Office for Migration and Refugees of Germany)
BverG	Bundesverfassungsgericht (Federal Constitutional Court of Germany)
BverWG	Bundesverwaltungsgericht (Federal Administrative Court of Germany)
CAT	Convention Against Torture and Other Cruel, Inhuman or Degrading Treatment or Punishment
CEAS	Common European Asylum System
CJEU	Court of Justice of the European Union
ECHR	European Convention for the Protection of Human Rights and Fundamental Freedoms
EU	European Union
ECtHR	European Court of Human Rights
ICCPR	*International Covenant on Civil and Political Rights*
TEU	Treaty on the European Union (Treaty of Maastricht)
TFEU	Treaty on the Functioning of the European Union (Treaty of Rome)
UDHR	Universal Declaration of Human Rights
UK	United Kingdom
UN	United Nations
UNHCR	United Nations High Commissioner for Refugees
VCLT	Vienna Convention on the Law of Treaties

List of Figures

Fig. 3.1 Determining the Member State responsible under Dublin III 58
Fig. 5.1 UK asylum procedures 129
Fig. 6.1 Germany asylum procedures 162

List of Tables

Table 5.1 Dublin transfers by country in the order of outgoing requests (2018) 108
Table 7.1 Comparing United Kingdom and German Practices 192

Chapter 1
Introduction: Setting the Stage

1.1 Introduction

One person is forcibly displaced every two seconds as a result of conflict or persecution.[1] An unprecedented 79.5 million people are forcibly displaced around the world today, and 26 million of them, or almost 35%, are refugees.[2] In 2011, the Syrian armed conflict began.[3] That civil war has led to the forced displacement of millions of people into neighbouring countries and regions, including the European Union (EU).[4] As the United Nations High Commissioner for Refugees (UNHCR) has confirmed in official numbers, the situation is unprecedented: the number of people displaced as a result of the Syrian conflict has surpassed the number of people displaced in the post-World War II era.[5] The high number of forcibly displaced persons during this period has created an urgent need for a fair and efficient method of processing asylum applications and it has tested the limits of domestic asylum systems in EU Member States. In particular, the Common European Asylum System (CEAS), which aims to establish common asylum procedures within the EU, has been put under constant strain.[6]

At the same time, the protection of the human rights of those forcibly displaced, including asylum claimants and refugees, must be monitored and scrutinized, so that instances of ill-treatment are less likely to occur. While international law obliges States to comply with relevant international human rights law principles, including the prohibition against *refoulement*, States are nonetheless free to accept

[1] UNHCR (2020); See, also: Anadolu Agency (2020); UNHCR (2020).

[2] *Ibid.*

[3] BBC News (2018).

[4] UNHCR (2018).

[5] UNHCR (2017).

[6] European Commission, Migration and Home Affairs (2016).

J. Poon, *Counteracting Containment Policies in the EU*, European Union and its Neighbours in a Globalized World 31,
https://doi.org/10.1007/978-3-032-08351-7_1

or reject the granting of refugee status under their domestic laws and to set external border controls within the boundaries of these obligations.[7] Defined as the prohibition against forced return to persecution, *non-refoulement* is a cardinal principle of international refugee law.[8] A violation of *non-refoulement* means sending someone to face the risk of death, torture, or other forms of ill-treatment as well as returning them to territories where there are often consistent patterns of gross, flagrant, or mass violations of human rights.[9] Violations of *non-refoulement* not only take place when States send asylum claimants to a situation in which they are at risk of serious human rights abuses, they also occur when States cooperate internationally to deter or prevent asylum claimants and refugees from accessing the asylum-granting State's territory and its asylum procedures.[10]

There is an ongoing trend towards more restrictive migration controls in the EU and elsewhere. These controls are carried out through various tactics such as visa regimes, carrier sanctions, and 'pushback' operations by border authorities of EU Member States to discourage asylum claimants and refugees from entering into Member State territories to access asylum procedures.[11] These controls are also instituted through 'protection elsewhere' regimes.[12] 'Protection elsewhere' regimes send claimants elsewhere to seek international protection or involve measures which return them to other EU Member States, and which exclude and deter them from entering a Member State's territory to access territorial asylum.[13] For example, many EU Member States use 'safe' third country concepts—countries deemed 'safe' which asylum claimants have passed through and where the Member State believes they should have applied for asylum, but did not, and to which they may be returned.[14] 'Safe' third country concepts not only do not have a legal basis under international law, they also rely heavily upon blanket diplomatic assurances from receiving States that purport to guarantee that asylum procedures are in place to permit claimants to access international

---

[7] *Convention Relating to the Status of Refugees* (adopted 28 July 1951, entered into force 22 April 1954) at art 33(1) [Refugee Convention].

[8] *Ibid.*

[9] *Convention Against Torture or Other Cruel, Inhuman or Degrading Treatment or Punishment* 1465 UNTS 85 (adopted 10 December 1984; entered into force 26 June 1987) at art 3(2) [CAT].

[10] See, for example: Hathaway, James C., and Gammeltoft-Hansen, Thomas (2014).

[11] Hathaway and Gammeltoft-Hansen at 12; The term 'visa regimes' refers to 'a visa not being offered for the purpose of seeking refugee protection', the term 'carrier sanctions' refers to 'significant fines imposed on transporting persons without valid visas, and includes impounding aircraft or other vessels', and the phrase ''pushback' operations at sea' refers to 'the interception and push back of any migrant boat, regardless of whether it is in need of rescue', see: Migrants At Sea (2016); Davitti, Daria, and Fries, Marlene (2016).

[12] See, for example: Foster, Michelle (2007); Frelick, Bill, Kysel, Ian M., and Podkul, Jennifer (2016) at 193.

[13] *Ibid.*

[14] European Commission, Migration and Home Affairs, "Safe Third Country" (2016) [Europa STC].

protection for refugee status.[15] EU Member States misuse 'safe' third country concepts when they knowingly return claimants to countries where these claimants do not actually have adequate access to international protection for refugee status.[16] All of these migration control policies have the ultimate goal of 'containing migratory flows and tackling irregular migration through enhanced border management [as well as fighting] against smuggling and trafficking'.[17]

Containment policies represent a twofold failure: first, of EU Member States to put into practice the strong statements of law on *non-refoulement* they have adopted through various international and regional instruments, and second, of EU Member States to share responsibility for refugees. EU law and policy have been crafted to encourage a 'fair' distribution of responsibility for processing asylum applications and the sharing of 'burdens' among EU Member States in a cooperative manner when they implement the CEAS within domestic law, but this approach is not always reflected in actual practice.[18]

1.1.1 The Book's Structure

This book is structured so as to present building blocks of the overall book statement described above. While each chapter examines a discrete issue, it also serves a larger role: providing the underlying legal analysis required in order to consider the dissonance between the legal understanding of *non-refoulement* and the actual application of that principle within asylum systems. This section summarizes the approach of each chapter, in order to illustrate the interlinked nature of the book structure.

Chapter 2 introduces the international and regional EU law framework on *non-refoulement*. It begins with the drafting history of Article 33(1) of the 1951 Refugee Convention on *non-refoulement* protection, as well as the inclusion of a related provision in the ICCPR and the CAT. It explains the subsequent dual life of the *non-refoulement* norm, existing simultaneously in international refugee law and international human rights law. While the norm co-exists in both areas of law, its contours are different within each. For example, in refugee law, *non-refoulement* protection is provided to asylum claimants and refugees, while in human rights law, its scope is widened to include protection from torture for

[15] Note, however, that the reliance upon diplomatic assurances has been cautioned against by both the UNHCR and the Committee Against Torture; For UNHCR commentary, see: UNHCR (2006) at 12–15; For the Committee Against Torture, see: Committee Against Torture (2018) at paras 19–20.

[16] *TI v United Kingdom,* Application No 43844/98, (ECHR, 7 March 2000) at 18 [TI].

[17] See, for example: Buscaini, Annalisa (2018); For more on EU's agenda to tackle irregular migration and secondary movements such as smuggling activities, see: European Commission (2015).

[18] *Treaty on the Functioning of the European Union (Consolidated Version),* OJ C326/47, 26 October 2012 at art 80 [TFEU].

everyone. Under refugee law, the principle of *non-refoulement* is not guaranteed to everyone without limits: those who have been deemed to be a danger to the community of the country of refuge are excluded from its reach. However, this exception does not exist in international human rights law, as the prohibition against torture protects everyone regardless of their legal or political status. As well, within both international refugee and human rights law, the principle applies both territorially as well as outside of the territories of a State, including over persons or areas where the State can exercise its effective authority and control. This chapter also explains the codification of *non-refoulement* under the ECHR, the EU Charter, the Dublin III Regulation, and key directives. The law on *non-refoulement* within Europe is quite robust, reflecting the simultaneous application of both the international refugee law and international human rights law approaches. Additionally, *non-refoulement* protection under the ECHR has expanded to be applicable outside of a State's territory, including on the high seas, as well as in situations involving risk of harm to health. That said, the actual practice with respect to this norm has been constrained and contained. This is explored further in Chaps. 3 and 4.

Chapter 3 explains in more detail the EU law applicable to the principle of *non-refoulement*, including in treaties and other binding documents. The ECtHR and the CJEU have interpreted and applied the prohibition against *refoulement*, resulting in somewhat disparate case law. The legislative and jurisprudential picture that emerges shows that *non-refoulement* is a fundamental and widely protective norm under European law. However, this chapter also demonstrates that the actual practice of some EU Member States has been to adopt a narrower understanding of *non-refoulement*, one that is limited through domestic interpretation as a result of the 'margin of discretion' allowed to Member States when transposing directives, and limited through the presumption of mutual trust when transferring asylum claimants to other EU Member States.

Chapter 4 describes the theory of containment, derived from the fields of human and spatial geography and migration studies. Containment policies seek to control, divide, and discipline 'unruly' migration (as perceived by States). While rarely applied within public international law and specifically international refugee law, the theory of containment holds particular significance as an explanatory theory for these fields. The theory suggests that policies of containment are methods used by EU Member States to circumvent their international refugee law and human rights law obligations, including *non-refoulement*. Containment theory provides a rationale for the differences between the fulsome statements of *non-refoulement* law in, for example, treaties and the actual constricted interpretation and application of that law through EU policies such as Dublin transfers, 'safe' third country agreements, the interception of asylum seekers prior to reaching Europe, migrant tracking, narrow interpretations of the Refugee Convention, and deterrence policies.

Chapter 5 on the UK examines the domestic law and procedures for claiming asylum in the UK, how international protection is granted or withdrawn from these claimants, and the points in the system during which the possibilities of *refoulement* are considered. It also explores how the principle of *non-refoulement* has been interpreted in the UK in a restrictive manner, particularly with respect to the presumption of mutual trust among EU Member States and the burden placed on the claimant to rebut that presumption.

Chapter 6 on Germany describes domestic German refugee law, including on *non-refoulement*, and the procedures for claiming asylum in Germany. While German legislation appears to adopt a more liberal reading of *non-refoulement* than the UK (in line with international law), the mixed jurisprudence suggests that the application of *non-refoulement* requires refinement and modification for a more consistent approach to interpreting the norm. The final part of this chapter reviews evidence of containment theory at work in Germany, including Germany's interpretation of the presumption of mutual trust in Dublin transfers.

Chapter 7 is the concluding chapter. It reiterates the centrality of *non-refoulement* as a cardinal principle of refugee protection. It begins with a focus on the domestic level, comparing the UK and Germany's practices on *non-refoulement*, particularly with respect to 'safe' third country concepts and Dublin transfers. It then considers recommended changes at the regional level that would help to align the expansive norm on *non-refoulement* with the actual application of the principle at the domestic and regional levels. This book therefore proposes four main ways to address and to counteract containment policies in order to strengthen the implementation of the *non-refoulement* norm: strengthening procedural guarantees in order to ensure access to asylum justice; reshaping the determination of mutual trust; re-evaluating the use of diplomatic assurances in transfer cases; and the implementation of periodic review coupled with a judicial review mechanism.

In total, this book involves a 'critical analysis and synbook of the law' of *non-refoulement*, which is in line with the aims of legal doctrinal analysis.[19] In particular, it considers the contours and substance of the legal understanding of *non-refoulement*, compares and contrasts this understanding with the actual practice within the EU, and engages 'with issues of institutional design' to identify approaches to lessen the gap between the law and actual State practice regarding the principle.

1.1.2 Concluding Remarks

This chapter has outlined the objectives, methodology, structure and limitations of this book. This book is meant to contribute to the understanding of *non-refoulement* internationally and within the EU by highlighting the gap between the statement of the law and the practice of that law and proposing ways to bridge that gap. The principle of *non-refoulement* is absolutely central to international refugee law. Described as the cornerstone of international refugee protection, access to asylum

[19] Hutchinson, Terry (2015).

has little meaning without corresponding protection from *refoulement.* This centrality of the principle of *non-refoulement* requires that States do not send back claimants or refugees to frontiers of territories where they may face threats to life or freedom. This obligation is an *active* duty upon the Member State and incorporates the *essence* of international refugee law: to provide the widest protection available to those who deserve it. As well-respected international refugee law experts acknowledge, *non-refoulement* has shaped the current system of international protection by becoming the guiding principle for States to provide minimum protection for claimants.[20] This bare minimum protection offered for claimants in the form of the prohibition against torture or the prevention of being sent back to face the death penalty or other gross, massive or flagrant violation of human rights can mean the difference between life and death for some. While international refugee law and European refugee law codifies the principle, practice from Member States has shown that the domestic interpretation and implementation of this norm is far from consistent. This book highlights the divergence between Member States and their courts in applying the principle of *non-refoulement* through case law. The domestic law of the UK and Germany demonstrate that there is still room for improvement.

The following chapter sets the stage for the focus of the book by providing the history and current understanding of the principle of *non-refoulement* in international law. It illustrates the content of the norm, and how it is recognized both in international refugee and international human rights law. It is the fact of this dual recognition which provides the principle with its scope and wide applicability within the international legal system.

References

BBC News (2018) Syria profile—timeline. https://www.bbc.com/news/world-middle-east-14703995

Buscaini A (2018) When will the time be ripe for a european legal migration policy? https://eu.boell.org/en/2018/09/14/when-will-time-be-ripe-european-legal-migration-policy

Committee Against Torture (2018) General comment no. 4 (2017) on the implementation of article 3 of the Convention in the context of article 22. https://www.refworld.org/docid/5a903dc84.html

Davitti D, Fries M (2016) Offshore processing and complicity in current EU migration policies: parts 1 & 2 EJIL!Talk Blog. https://www.ejiltalk.org/offshore-processing-and-complicity-in-current-eu-migration-policies-part-2

European Commission, Migration and Home Affairs (2016) Common European asylum system. https://ec.europa.eu/home-affairs/what-we-do/policies/asylum_en

[20] Goodwin-Gill, Guy S (2014), which states: ‘Today, the principle of *non-refoulement* is not only the essential foundation for international refugee law, but also an integral part of human rights protection, implicit in the subject matter of many such rights, and a rule of customary international law’ [Goodwin-Gill].

European Commission (2015) Communication from the commission to the European parliament, the council, the European economic and social committee and the committee of the regions: a European agenda on migration, com(2015) 240 final

European Commission, Migration and Home Affairs (2016) Safe third country. https://ec.europa.eu/home-affairs/what-we-do/networks/european_migration_network/glossary_search/safe-third-country_en

Foster M (2007) Protection Elsewhere: the legal implications of requiring refugees to seek protection in another state. Mich J Intl Law 28(2):223–286

Frelick B, Kysel IM, Podkul J (2016) The impact of externalization of migration controls on the rights of asylum seekers and other migrants. J Migr Hum Secur 4(4):190–220

Goodwin-Gill GS (2014) The international law of refugee protection. In Fiddian-Qasmiyeh E, Loescher G, Long K, Sigona N (eds) The oxford handbook of refugee and forced migration studies. Oxford University Press, Oxford

Hathaway JC, Gammeltoft-Hansen T (2014). Non-Refoulement in a world of cooperative deterrence (2014) Law & Economics Working Papers, 1–64.

Hutchinson T (2015) The doctrinal method: incorporating interdisciplinary methods in reforming the law. Erasmus Law Rev 8(3):130

Migrants At Sea (2016) NATO expands aegean sea migrant patrols into Turkish and Greek territorial waters. https://migrantsatsea.org/tag/push-back-practice

UNHCR (2006) UNHCR note on diplomatic assurances and international refugee protection. https://www.refworld.org/docid/44dc81164.html

UNHCR (2018) Syria emergency. https://www.unhcr.org/syria-emergency.html

UNHCR (2017) Forced displacement worldwide at its highest in decades. http://www.unhcr.org/news/stories/2017/6/5941561f4/forced-displacement-worldwide-its-highest-decades.html

UNHCR (2020) Figures at a glance. https://www.unhcr.org/figures-at-a-glance.html; See also: Anadolu Agency (2020) World now has nearly 80 million refugees: UN. https://www.aa.com.tr/en/europe/world-now-has-nearly-80-million-refugees-un/1881306

UNHCR (2020) Global trends: forced Displacement in 2019. UNHCR Global Data Service, 2020, Denmark

Chapter 2
Non-Refoulement Protection Under International and European Refugee Law

2.1 Introduction

The principle of *non-refoulement* plays a vital role in the international refugee law regime. The principle is widely regarded as a cornerstone of international refugee law by the UNHCR, academic commentators, and States Parties of the Refugee Convention.[1] This doctrine protects asylum claimants and refugees from being returned to territories where their lives or freedom would be threatened.[2]

International and European law provide the standards that are to be implemented by national asylum systems within the European Union (EU) through domestic asylum procedures. Therefore, this chapter introduces the principle of *non-refoulement* as it is currently articulated in international and European law, in order to set the stage for the next chapter, which discusses how EU Member States interpret and apply the principle within the Common European Asylum System (CEAS). The first part of this chapter considers the history of the principle of *non-refoulement*. The second part of the chapter discusses the principle of *non-refoulement* under international refugee law and international human rights law. Next, the chapter situates the principle of *non-refoulement* in European law.

This book is centered around the foundational legal norm of *non-refoulement* and the ways in which it is meant to protect refugees and asylum seekers. Therefore, this chapter sketches out the parameters of the principle and concludes that there is a crucial difference between the way in which international and European refugee laws define the scope of the obligation of States not to *refoule* individuals versus the manner in which international and European human rights law articulate the right of individuals not to be *refouled*. In particular, international

[1] See, for example: Note on Non-Refoulement at A; *Németh v Canada* [2010] 3 SCR 281 at para 1; Gillard (2008) at 704.

[2] Refugee Convention at art 33(1).

J. Poon, *Counteracting Containment Policies in the EU*, European Union and its Neighbours in a Globalized World 31,
https://doi.org/10.1007/978-3-032-08351-7_2

and European human rights laws are absolute in their prohibition, while international and European refugee laws permit exceptions to *non-refoulement.* Some scholars therefore argue that the definition of *non-refoulement* in human rights law must displace the definition in refugee law because it is broader in nature (as it applies to all human being, regardless of their status) and bridges the gap that refugee rights may not cover.[3] However, others contend that human rights law and refugee law do not interact in this manner; that they are intrinsically intertwined and one does not act as a surrogate for the other.[4] This discussion and others on the principle of *non-refoulement* in this chapter sets the stage for the next chapter, which discusses how EU Member States interpret and apply the principle within the CEAS.

2.1.1 History of Non-Refoulement

A discussion of the principle of *non-refoulement* involves examining the origins of the principle in international refugee law. This section therefore provides the history of the principle of *non-refoulement*, beginning with a discussion of the originating sources of international refugee law and the development of *non-refoulement* through treaty law. In the 1920s, over one million Russian refugees were forcibly displaced and removed along the border of the former Russian empire.[5] Some countries surrounding the former Russian empire opened up their borders to accept these refugees but, generally, these refugees were not accepted by other countries.[6] In 1922, the High Commissioner for Russian Refugees appointed by the League of Nations, Fridtjof Nansen, was given the task of securing the assistance and legal protection of these refugees.[7] Governments gathered together in Geneva to unanimously accept the issuance of certificates to grant legal status to Russian refugees.[8] This arrangement was referred to as the Arrangement with Respect to the Issue of Certificates of Identity to Russian Refugees, also commonly known as the 1922 Arrangement.[9] These certificates were later known as the 'Nansen Passport', which

---

[3] Chetail (2012) at 22; Hathaway (2012), where James C. Hathaway argued that: "[. . .] general human rights norms do not address many refugee-specific concerns (such as non-rejection at the frontier, or non-penalisation for illegal entry)" in suggesting that human rights law norms are in general, broader than refugee rights, and sometimes do not encompass the specific concerns addressed by refugee law. A general overview of the discussion on the interaction between international refugee and human rights law is further explored in: Poon (2017) [Poon Cornell Article].

[4] See, generally: McAdam Research Paper.

[5] Skran (2011) at 6.

[6] *Ibid.*

[7] *Ibid* at 7.

[8] *Ibid.*

[9] League of Nations (1922) at 927.

acted as identity certificates for refugees to travel across international borders, and was the beginning of the international refugee law system.[10]

Following this development, the principle of *non-refoulement* was developed and amended through three significant treaties concerning refugee protection: the 1933 *Convention Relating to the International Status of Refugees* (1933 Convention), the 1938 *Convention Concerning the Status of Refugees coming from Germany* (1938 Convention), and the 1951 Refugee Convention.

The 1933 Convention represented the first explicit recognition of *non-refoulement* as a norm under international treaty law.[11] By the 1920s, the piecemeal approach of the Nansen Passport had become unreliable, which triggered the need for a more comprehensive approach to the issue of refugees.[12] The 1933 Convention formally codified the rights granted to refugees.[13] It was drafted as a result of the gathering of representatives from Belgium, Bulgaria, Egypt, France, and Norway under the framework of the League of Nations in response to the situation of Russian and Armenian refugees post World War I.[14] Article 3 of the 1933 Convention provides that:

> Each of the States Parties undertakes not to remove or keep from its territory by application of police measures, such as expulsions or non-admittance at the frontier (*refoulement*), refugees who have been authorized to reside there regularly, unless the said measures are dictated by reasons of national security or public order. It undertakes in any case not to refuse entry to refugees at the frontier of their countries of origin [. . .].[15]

The 1933 Convention was ratified by nine States, including France and the UK, which were the most powerful States of that time.[16] However, three of these States ratified the 1933 Convention with reservations and declarations.[17] Although the first of its kind and more comprehensive than the piecemeal approach of the

---

[10] Skran at 8; Weis (1982) at 28: 'The earliest international instruments dealing with refugees, established at the initiative of Dr. Nansen, therefore provided for the issuance of a travel document to refugees which has become known as the 'Nansen passport'' [Weis MJIL].

[11] Jaeger (2001) at 730 [Jaeger].

[12] Skran at 11.

[13] *Ibid.*

[14] *Convention Relating to the International Status of Refugees* CLIX LNTS 3663, 28 October 1933 at art 3 [1933 Convention]; Jaeger at 728–730; See, also: Beck (1999) [Beck].

[15] 1933 Convention at art 3; See, also: UNHCR (1997) at 14 [UNHCR on CSR51]: 'Article 3 of the 1933 Convention contained the rule of 'non-refoulement' to a country of persecution which is also set forth in Article 33(1) of the present Convention, but the former did not contain the exceptions to the rule which are found in Article 33(2) of the present Convention. It seems fair to imply that Article 33 of the present Convention does not impair the absolute right of non-refoulement which a person who qualified as a refugee under the terms of the 1933 Convention could claim by virtue of Article 3 of that Convention, which means that Article 33(2) is not applicable in his [or her] case'.

[16] Jaeger at 730.

[17] The reservations and declarations included an emphasis on the retention of sovereign competence in the matter of expulsion, with the United Kingdom expressly objecting to the principle of non-rejection at the frontier: Goodwin-Gill and McAdam (2007) at 202 [Goodwin-Gill and McAdam].

Nansen Passport of the 1920s, the 1933 Convention was limited in its scope of application.[18] For instance, the 1933 Convention did not apply to refugees outside of the interwar period (1918–1939).[19]

From 1933 until the beginning of World War II, about 400,000 refugees fled from Germany.[20] The 1938 *Convention Concerning the Status of Refugees coming from Germany* was created to arrange 'a system of legal protection' for these refugees.[21] This treaty incorporated key provisions and elements from the Nansen Passport system and the 1933 Convention.[22] Article 4(1) of the draft 1938 Convention contained a provision which stipulated that, in all cases, if a refugee is required to leave, 'he [or she] shall be granted a suitable period to make the necessary arrangements' and for those refugees given authorization to be in the country, Article 4(2) states that they should not be expelled unless required by 'national security or public order'.[23] Most importantly, a form of the principle of *non-refoulement* was incorporated in Article 4(3), which provided that even when expulsion or return at the frontier is warranted by reasons of national security or public order, 'refugees shall not be sent back across the frontier of the [German-occupied territory] unless they have been warned and have refused to make the arrangements necessary to proceed to another country'.[24] Together, the 1933 Convention and the 1938 Convention formed the basis for the drafting of the 1951 Refugee Convention.[25]

The aftermath of World War II produced over 30 million displaced persons, including refugees, who were forced to leave their homes in Europe.[26] By the end of the war, there were over 10 million refugees.[27] The mass influx of refugees to neighbouring countries led to the need for the creation of an international refugee convention which would solidify legal protections for refugees.[28] This situation prompted the process of drafting the 1951 Refugee Convention, which began with

---

[18] Skran at 24.

[19] *Ibid.*

[20] *Ibid*; League of Nations (1939) at 2.

[21] Skran at 27.

[22] *Ibid.*

[23] *Ibid.*

[24] *Ibid*; However, in Article 5(3)(a) of the 1938 Convention, the prohibition against 'reconduction' (referring to present day *non-refoulement* protection to a country of persecution) was qualified in certain respects, namely: 'The High Contracting Parties undertake not to reconduct refugees to German territory unless they have been warned and have refused, without just cause, to make the necessary arrangements to proceed to another territory or to take advantage of the arrangements made for them with that object' in UNHCR on CSR51 at 135.

[25] *Ibid*; The 1951 Refugee Convention has been described as 'at the universal level, the most comprehensive legally binding international instrument, defining standards for the treatment or refugees' in UNHCR, "The Refugee Convention, 1951: The Travaux Preparatoires Analysed with a Commentary by Dr Paul Weis" at 4 [Weis].

[26] Einarsen (2011) at 43.

[27] *Ibid.*

[28] *Ibid* at 48.

the United Nations General Assembly Resolution 8(I) of February 12, 1946, and concluded with the United Nations Conference of Plenipotentiaries adopting the treaty on July 28, 1951.[29] (This treaty was later supplemented with the 1967 *Protocol Relating to the Status of Refugees* (1967 Protocol).[30]

Most notably, the 1951 Refugee Convention defined the term 'refugee' as well as codified the cardinal principle of *non-refoulement*.[31] The principle of *non-refoulement* is defined under Article 33(1) of the 1951 Refugee Convention.[32] Article 33(1) is one of only two Articles within the Refugee Convention to which States Parties are not permitted to make reservations.[33] Article 33(1) of the Refugee Convention provides:

> No Contracting State shall expel or return ('*refouler*') a refugee in any manner whatsoever to the frontiers of territories where his [or her] life or freedom would be threatened on account of his [or her] race, religion, nationality, membership of a particular social group or political opinion.[34]

The preparatory works, or the *travaux préparatoires,* to the 1951 Refugee Convention reveal States Parties' intentions during drafting negotiations.[35] In 1946, the UN Ad Hoc Committee on Statelessness and Related Problems (Ad Hoc Committee) was tasked with drafting a convention relating to the international status of refugees and stateless persons.[36] It first proposed the incorporation of Article 3 of the 1933 Convention on *non-refoulement* based on a working paper

---

[29] *Ibid.*

[30] Refugee Convention; *Protocol Relating to the Status of Refugees* 606 UNTS 267 (adopted 31 January 1967, entered into force 4 October 1967) [Refugee Protocol].

[31] *Ibid*; Weis MJIL at 31: 'The most important principle of *non-refoulement* [. . .] This principle, enunciated in Article 33, can be regarded as the cornerstone of refugee law. It has acquired the character of a general principle of law or of a rule of customary international law; it is, by some, even considered as *jus cogens*'.

[32] Refugee Convention at art 33(1).

[33] Long (2010) at paras 58 and 61, http://www.unhcr.org/4c207bd59.pdf [Long]; This point is important because reservations for a treaty permits a State, 'when signing, ratifying, accepting, approving or acceding to a treaty [. . .] to exclude or to modify the legal effect of certain provisions of the treaty in their application to that State' in *Vienna Convention on the Law of Treaties,* 1155 UNTS 331 (adopted 23 May 1969, entered into force 27 January 1980) at art 2(1)(d) [VCLT].

[34] Refugee Convention at art 33(1).

[35] Under the VCLT, the preparatory works during treaty negotiations may be a supplementary means of determining the intention of drafters, see: VCLT at art 32: 'Recourse may be had to supplementary means of interpretation, including the preparatory work of the treaty and the circumstances of its conclusion, in order to confirm the meaning resulting from the application of article 31, or to determine the meaning when the interpretation according to article 31: (a) Leaves the meaning ambiguous or obscure; or (b) Leads to a result which is manifestly absurd or unreasonable'.

[36] Kälin et al. (2011) at 1338 [Kälin]; United Nations Economic and Social Council, "Resolution 248 (IX) B of 8 August 1949".

drafted by the UN Secretary-General.[37] The result was that the first iteration of the 1951 Refugee Convention incorporated the principle in draft Article 24(3), which stated:

> Each of the High Contracting Parties undertakes in any case not to turn back refugees to the frontiers of their country of origin, or to territories where their life or freedom would be threatened on account of their race, religion, nationality or political opinions.[38]

This absolute prohibition on *refoulement* was proposed in 1950.[39] The provision, which was slightly amended,[40] became present-day Article 33(1) of the 1951 Refugee Convention and was adopted by a vote of 21 in favour and none against, with two abstentions.[41]

During a meeting of the Ad Hoc committee, the representative from the UK suggested that an exception be added on the grounds of national security.[42] In the end, the Ad Hoc Committee accepted the draft of Article 24(3) without the amendment suggested by the UK.[43] Then, in 1951, at the Conference of Plenipotentiaries, the representative of the UK, Sir Leslie Brass, expressed his concern over the potential absoluteness of the *non-refoulement* principle and again proposed an amendment.[44] This proposal was supported by Switzerland, with the United States, France and Denmark arguing against.[45] Despite the proposal not initially gaining traction, the representatives from France and the UK suggested adding this new paragraph:

> The benefit of the present provision may not, however, be claimed by a refugee whom there are reasonable grounds for regarding as a danger to the security of the country in which he [or she] is residing, or who, having been lawfully convicted in that country of particularly serious crimes or offences, constitutes a danger to the community thereof.[46]

---

[37] Skran at para 10; Ad Hoc Committee on Statelessness and Related Problems (1950a) UN Doc E/AC.32/2 Annex at 45.

[38] *Ibid.*

[39] United Nations Economic and Social Council, "Summary Record of the Twentieth Meeting: Ad Hoc Committee on Statelessness and Related Problems, First Session", UN Doc E/AC.32/SR.20, 1950 at paras 54 and 55; See, also: Goodwin-Gill (2008) at 5.

[40] As mentioned above, the text of Article 33(1) reads: 'No Contracting State shall expel or return ("*refouler*") a refugee in any manner whatsoever to the frontiers of territories where his life or freedom would be threatened on account of his race, religion, nationality, membership of a particular social group or political opinion': Refugee Convention at art 33(1).

[41] Conference of Plenipotentiaries (1951) UN Doc A/CONF.2/SR.35 at 25.

[42] Sir Leslie proposed to add the words 'unless the said measures are dictated by reasons of national security' at the end of the paragraph for Article 24(3) in Ad Hoc Committee on Statelessness and Related Problems (1950b) UN Doc E/AC.32/SR.20 at paras 10–12; See, also: Kälin at 1338.

[43] Ad Hoc Committee on Statelessness and Related Problems (1950c) UN Doc E/AC.32/L.32 at 12.

[44] Goodwin-Gill at 204; See also: Skran at para 11.

[45] Ad Hoc Committee on Refugees and Stateless Persons (1950d) UN Doc E/AC.32/SR.40 at 30.

[46] Conference of Plenipotentiaries, 1951 UN Doc A/CONF.2/69; See, also: Kälin at 1340.

This amendment, which was slightly changed,[47] was adopted by 19 votes to none, with three abstentions, and incorporated in the Refugee Convention as Article 33(2).[48] Thus, the prohibition against *refoulement* is not absolute under international refugee law.[49] Note, however, that this exception has since been interpreted even more narrowly than drafted in Article 33(2): in 2007, the UNHCR issued an advisory opinion indicating that this exception must be read in conjunction with international human rights law's prohibition on *refoulement* to torture, discussed further below.[50]

The Conference of Plenipotentiaries also discussed the concepts of 'expel' and 'return'.[51] The representative from Switzerland opined that the text of the *non-refoulement* prohibition covered only refugees who had already entered a country and States were accordingly not obliged to admit large groups of persons claiming refugee status at the border.[52] It argued that the word 'expel' seems to refer to refugees residing lawfully in the country, while the word 'return' seems to refer to refugees who had already entered the country but were not yet resident there.[53] The representatives from France, the Netherlands, Italy, Sweden, Germany, and Belgium all agreed with this interpretation, with France and Belgium stressing that situations of mass influx of refugees were not covered by the provision.[54] This debate shows that the text of the principle of *non-refoulement* was not easily ascertained and brings the discussion to the present day dilemma surrounding the question of *lex specialis* between international refugee and human rights law.

---

[47] Article 33(2) states: 'The benefit of the present provision may not, however, be claimed by a refugee whom there are reasonable grounds for regarding as a danger to the security of the country in which he is, or who, having been convicted by a final judgement of a particularly serious crime, constitutes a danger to the community of that country': Refugee Convention at art 33(2).

[48] The abstentions were not recorded in the original document; Statement by Chance (Canada) and Hoeg (Denmark) (1951) UN Doc A/CONF.2/SR.16 at 8.

[49] This exception to *non-refoulement* must be applied with great caution, however, and this provision is to be read restrictively, see: UNHCR NR Note at para 14; More discussion on the connection between *non-refoulement* and the national security exception provided for under Article 33(2) is further explored in: Poon (2019) [Poon PKI Journal].

[50] UNHCR (2007) at para 11: 'the host State would be barred from removing a refugee if this would result in exposing him or her, for example, to a substantial risk of torture' [UNHCR Advisory Opinion].

[51] Kälin at 1341.

[52] *Ibid.*

[53] *Ibid.*

[54] Note, however, that subsequently in 1981, it is the view of the UNHCR Executive Committee that: 'In situations of large-scale influx, asylum seekers should be admitted to the State in which they first seek refuge and if that State is unable to admit them on a durable basis, it should always admit them at least on a temporary basis ... In all cases the fundamental principle of non-refoulement—including non-rejection at the frontier—must be scrupulously observed' in UNHCR, Executive Committee, "Conclusion No. 22", 1981 at paras II.A.1-II.A.2; See, also: Statements of Chance (Canada) and Hoeg (Denmark) (1951) UN Doc A/CONF.2/SR.16 at 6.

Another item that was debated during the drafting of Article 33 was the issue of non-admittance of refugees at the border. The Secretariat of the League of Nations at the time of translating (unofficially) the text of the 1933 Convention was quite clear that the prohibition against *refoulement* did not cover 'non-admittance at the frontier' (meaning the 'refusal of leave to land', and 'exclusion').[55] Thus, during the negotiation of the 1951 Refugee Convention, the Swiss representative was of the opinion that Article 33 'could not [...] be applied to a refugee who had not yet entered the territory of a country. The word 'return' used in the English text, gave that idea exactly [...] That Article 33 forbids return and not 'non-admittance' is also made clear by the words 'to the frontiers of territories' in the English text and even more so by the words 'sur les frontiers des territories' in the French text'.[56] This controversy is still present today as the question of whether *non-refoulement* applies extraterritorially has been a matter of debate among scholars.

As can be seen in the historical development of *non-refoulement*, the development of Article 33 is not without controversy and debate among the States. The next section discusses the current understanding of the principle of *non-refoulement*.

2.2 The Current Conception of Non-Refoulement Under International Refugee Law

The current meaning of Article 33(1) of the Refugee Convention is best understood by understanding the phrases used in that provision. A textual analysis of the provision—'No Contracting State shall expel or return ('*refouler*') a refugee in any manner whatsoever to the frontiers of territories where his life or freedom would be threatened on account of his race, religion, nationality, membership of a particular social group or political opinion—reveals the scope, temporal requirements and jurisdictional application of the principle of *non-refoulement*.

The first phrase in the article is 'no Contracting State', which refers to States Parties that have ratified the Refugee Convention.[57] The Refugee Convention is a widely-ratified international human rights instrument, currently with 146 ratifications.[58] States Parties to the 1967 Protocol[59] that are not parties to the Refugee

[55] UNHCR on CSR51 at 136.

[56] McNamara (1997) at 136 [McNamara]; Weis MJIL at 37 and 38: 'The Convention is unclear on the question of whether the principle of *non-refoulement* applies to refugees who have not yet been admitted into a country of asylum [...] Other countries have provisions in their aliens' legislation that either explicitly or *de facto,* as a result of the prohibition of *refoulement*, including rejection at the frontier, establish a right to asylum'.

[57] Kälin at 1357.

[58] Status as at June 2020; United Nations Treaty Collection (1951) [UNTS CSR51].

[59] There are 147 States Parties to the Protocol as of June 2020: United Nations Treaty Collection (1967) [UNTS Protocol].

Convention (namely the United States, Cabo Verde, and Venezuela) are also bound by the principle of *non-refoulement*, as paragraph 1 of the Protocol requires all States Parties to the Protocol to apply Articles 2–34 of the Refugee Convention.[60] Therefore, Article 33 binds the vast majority of States in the world. It should be mentioned that States that are not States Parties to either the Refugee Convention or the Protocol will nonetheless be obliged not to *refoule* under customary international law, regional refugee law instruments, other international human rights law instruments, international humanitarian law, and extradition law.[61] Thus, while they are not legally bound under the treaty phrase 'no Contracting State', they cannot avoid the norm as a result.

The Refugee Convention uses the phrase 'shall expel or return' to explain '*refouler*', but does not otherwise define the term. The term '*refouler*' is also not defined in any of the other treaties discussed above. Therefore, the meaning of the term must be determined using the rules for the interpretation of international treaties found in the *Vienna Convention on the Law of Treaties* (VCLT).[62] Under the VCLT, there are two ways of ascertaining the meaning of a treaty provision. The general rules of interpreting the meaning of a treaty provision is by its ordinary meaning and through the object and purpose of the provision as determined by the preamble and annexes of an international treaty.[63]

The term '*refoulement*' is derived from the French word '*refouler*' meaning, in its ordinary meaning, 'to drive back' or 'to repel'.[64] In a number of jurisdictions such as the UK, the United States, and Australia, dictionaries have been used to determine the plain meaning of certain terms within the Refugee Convention.[65] For instance, the dictionary definition of the term '*refouler*' as used in Article 33(1) has been interpreted to mean 'repulse', 'repel', and 'drive back'.[66] The word '*refouler*' has also been described to mean 'the act of returning refugees to a place where they may be persecuted'.[67] . The United States Supreme Court, in the case of *Sale v. Haitian Centers Council Inc,* held that the repatriation of Haitian asylum claimants back to

[60] Refugee Protocol at art 1; See also: Lauterpacht at 87 and 108.

[61] For international humanitarian law, see: *Geneva Convention Relative to the Protection of Civilian Persons in Time of War* (Geneva Convention IV) 75 UNTS 287 (adopted 12 August 1949, entered into force 21 October 1950) at art 45(4); For extradition law, see: *European Convention on Extradition* ETS 24 (adopted 13 December 1957, entered into force 18 April 1960); *Inter-American Convention on Extradition* (adopted 25 February 1981, entered into force 28 March 1992).

[62] VCLT at art 31.

[63] *Ibid* at art 31(1). As a supplementary means of treaty interpretation, the meaning of a treaty provision may be ascertained by the preparatory works or the *travaux préparatoires* during negotiations as well as the circumstances of its conclusion: *Ibid* at art 32. The negotiation history is discussed above.

[64] Goodwin-Gill and McAdam at 201.

[65] McAdam (2011) at 87 [McAdam CSR51 Interpretation].

[66] *Sale v Haitian Centers Council Inc* 509 US 155 (US) at 191 [Sale].

[67] Pirie (1986) at 187; Pizor (1993) at 1063 [Pizor].

Haiti by the United States Coast Guard on the high seas was clearly prohibited by the ordinary understanding of the term 'return' under Article 33(1).[68] The case concerned vessels traveling with passengers from Haiti to the United States that were intercepted on the high seas.[69] The passengers were forced to flee Haiti as a result of a military coup in 1991.[70] The United States Coast Guard interdicted over 34,000 Haitians who were then sent to be detained at the Guantanamo Bay United States military base.[71] The Respondents in the case, an organization representing the interdicted Haitians, argued that the word 'return' referred to the destination to which the refugee would be removed or sent back.[72] However, the Supreme Court did not accept this approach, holding that that this definition of the word 'return' was expansive and would make the word 'deport' redundant.[73]

The meaning of '*refouler*' can also be ascertained pursuant to the object and purpose of the treaty as found in the preamble.[74] The preamble of the Refugee Convention states that:

> Considering that the United Nations has, on various occasions, manifested its profound concern for refugees and *endeavoured to assure refugees the widest possible exercise of these fundamental rights and freedoms* (emphasis added).[75]

According to the preamble, the purpose of the 1951 Refugee Convention is to ensure the widest possible protection for refugees.[76] The word '*refouler*' refers to States' obligation to protect refugees from being returned to territories where they may experience persecution.[77] Reading the two together, 'offering the widest possible' protection may involve not only protection from being sent back to persecution, but corresponding access to asylum procedures, including the right to seek asylum as enshrined in Article 14 of the *Universal Declaration on Human Rights*.[78]

Thus, the ordinary meaning of the term '*refouler*' includes 'return' ('to send back' or 'to bring, send, or put back to a former or proper place'), 'repulse', 'repel', and 'drive back'.[79] This understanding is uncontroversial. An approach to defining

---

[68] McAdam CSR51 Interpretation at 87.

[69] Sale at 162.

[70] *Ibid.*

[71] *Ibid* at 166.

[72] Jones (1994) at 120.

[73] Sale at 174; Pizor at 1093: 'The [US] government relied on the plain meaning of the 1951 Convention's text. The government argued that the word 'expel' in Article 33(1) referred to aliens in the territory of a States Party, and that 'expel' is one translation of 'refouler'. The government concluded that the phrase 'return ('refouler')' merely refers to its territorial use'.

[74] VCLT at art 31(1).

[75] Refugee Convention at preamble.

[76] *Ibid* at preamble.

[77] *Ibid* at art 33(1).

[78] UDHR at art 14.

[79] Merriam-Webster Online Dictionary, 10th Edition; *Sale v Haitian Ctr Council, Inc,* 509 US 155 (1993).

'*refouler*' based on the object and purpose of the Refugee Convention is less well-developed, but indicates that *non-refoulement* may include a negative obligation on States not to send individuals back to certain situations,[80] logically coupled with a positive duty on States to determine whether the individual in question is at risk of serious human rights violations on return, plus an additional positive duty to ensure access of asylum seekers to asylum procedures.

In contrast to the widespread understanding of 'return' and '*refouler*' as synonyms, there is some debate over the meaning of the word 'expel'. During treaty negotiations, the Swiss Government was of the view that the term 'expel' applied to a refugee who had already been admitted to the territory of a country, while the term '*refouler*' could not be applied to a refugee who had not yet entered the territory of a country.[81] The French representative also agreed with the Swiss Government's view.[82] While this view has been challenged, the Swiss and French interpretation has since been revived in response to the mass influx of refugees into Europe prompted by the Syrian armed conflict.[83]

Article 33 uses the term 'refugee', which is defined in Article 1A of the Refugee Convention. As described in Chap. 1, this is an individual with a well-founded fear of persecution who, for reasons of race, religion, nationality, 'membership of a particular social group' or political opinion is outside of his or her country of nationality, is unable or unwilling to avail him or herself of State protection, and owing to such fear is unable or unwilling to return to his or her country of origin.[84] However, the definition of 'refugee' in Article 1A does not apply to those who have committed a 'crime against peace, a war crime, or a crime against humanity', 'a serious non-political crime in the country of refuge', and/or 'acts contrary to the purposes and principles of the United Nations' under Article 1F.[85] Additionally, the protection against *refoulement* also does not apply to refugees who fall under the cessation clauses (Article 1C) (defining when protection is no longer needed), those who receive protection and assistance from United Nations organs and agencies

[80] However, this would logically coupled with a positive duty on States to determine whether the individual in question is at risk of serious human rights violations on return.

[81] Weis MJIL at 236.

[82] Ibid.

[83] The Swiss Government's view was that the term '*refouler*' could not apply to a refugee who had not yet entered the territory of a country and would only be applicable to refugees who have already been admitted to the territory of a country. From the viewpoint of the States, the provision implied that there were two categories of refugees: "refugees who were liable to be expelled, and those who were liable to be returned". This is controversial at the time because the Swiss Government took the viewpoint that the meaning of the word "return" "applied solely to refugees who had already entered a country, but were not yet resident there". The reason for adopting this definition was unknown, see Weis MJIL at 236.

[84] Refugee Convention at art 1A.

[85] *Ibid* at art 1F.

other than the UNHCR (Article 1D), and individuals who are recognized by the country of refuge as its nationals (Article 1E).[86] Therefore, under the Refugee Convention there is a specifically delimited category of people who are endowed with *non-refoulement* protection. Despite these restrictions, individuals falling outside of the protection scope of Article 33(1) may invoke human rights law protection offered by the *Convention Against Torture* and the *International Covenant on Civil and Political Rights*, as explained below.[87] The human rights protection offered by these instruments protect everyone—not only refugees—from being deprived of the right to life and freedom from torture.[88]

The words 'in any manner whatsoever' clarify the breadth of the prohibition on *refouling* refugees: Contracting States cannot use non-admittance at the frontier of territories or extradition as alternative means of sending refugees back to situations of serious personal danger.[89] However, the words 'in any manner whatsoever' do not translate to a right to be granted asylum for the individual claiming asylum and do not preclude instances where the admitting State may decide to expel the claimant to another State willing to accept him or her.[90] The *travaux préparatoires* are also clear in that the Refugee Convention provision supersedes any previous extradition agreements concluded privately between States Parties to the Refugee Convention.[91] Therefore, *non-refoulement* protection entails protecting the asylum claimant or refugee from being returned to territories where his or her life or freedom is threatened, regardless of any extradition agreements previously agreed upon between States Parties of the Refugee Convention. Further, the phrase 'to expel or return a refugee in any manner whatsoever' indicates that *non-refoulement* obligations arise regardless of the State's conduct or where the expelling or return occurs.[92]

The phrase 'frontiers of territories' means the territory of the country of origin or last habitual residence.[93] The term not only includes territories where the refugee may face a future risk of *refoulement* but also the territory of a State where authorities of concern, such as security service or military personnel, are present.[94]

---

[86] *Ibid* at art 1C, 1D, and 1E.

[87] Kälin at 1350–1352.

[88] CAT at art 3; ICCPR at arts 6 and 7.

[89] Weis MJIL at 245; See, also: Wouters at 99: 'The premise of protection from refoulement is an evaluation of a future threat to life or freedom. Consequently, every time a State wants to remove a refugee in any manner whatsoever the State must evaluate the risk of his [or her] being persecuted after removal, thereby taking into account all relevant information, including new or previously unrecognised facts'; See, also: Hathaway (2005) at 320.

[90] *Ibid.*

[91] *Ibid.*

[92] Wouters at 50.

[93] Kälin at 1380.

[94] *Ibid* at 1381.

An example of this is in the context of an occupation where one part of the territory of a State may be occupied by enemy forces.[95] Also, the legal status of the place to which the refugee may be sent is not material in considering whether Article 33(1) protection applies, given that the word 'territories' was used by the drafters of the Refugee Convention rather than 'countries' or 'States'.[96]

The phrase 'frontiers of territories' also denotes territorial scope.[97] There has been some debate over the meaning of this phrase.[98] Some States argue that *non-refoulement* obligations and corresponding responsibility for the claimant only trigger when the individual concerned is *within* the territory of the State deemed responsible (as mentioned above).[99] However, academic commentators interpret the phrase to mean that it is exercised wherever the State has 'effective authority and control' over the individual, including on the high seas.[100] The latter approach is supported by a plain language reading of the term, as per the VCLT.[101] This idea is supported by the ECtHR, the Human Rights Committee, the International Court of Justice, and the Committee Against Torture.[102] Moreover, the UNHCR is of the view that the principle of *non-refoulement* applies wherever a State exercises its jurisdiction.[103]

The words 'where his [or her] life or freedom would be threatened' have the same meaning as the phrase 'well-founded fear of persecution' under Article 1A(2) of the Refugee Convention.[104] This threat to life or freedom is an anticipation of a

---

95 *Ibid.*

96 *Ibid*; See, also: Wouters at 134.

97 Refugee Convention at art 33(1).

98 UNHCR Advisory Opinion at paras 34 and 35.

99 Kim (2017) at 50 [Kim]: 'Regrettably, major refugee-intake countries have denied [the principle of non-refoulement's] extraterritorial applicability in the conduct of external migration controls such as interdiction or interception of refugees on the high seas'.

100 *Ibid* at 69–70.

101 VCLT at art 31(1).

102 *Hirsi Jamaa and Others v. Italy* App no 27765/09 (ECHR, 23 February 2012) [Hirsi]; By analogy to the ICCPR: Human Rights Committee, "Concluding Observations of the Human Rights Committee, United States of America", 3 October 1995, UN Doc CCPR/C/79/Add.50 at para 284; Human Rights Committee, "Concluding Observations of the Human Rights Committee, United States of America", 18 December 2006, UN Doc CCPR/C/USA/CO/3/Rev.1 at para 10; By analogy to the *International Covenant on Civil and Political Rights*: International Court of Justice, *Legal Consequences of the Construction of a Wall in the Occupied Palestinian Territory*, Advisory Opinion, ICJ Gen List No 131, 9 July 2004 at para 109 and 111; International Court of Justice, *Case Concerning Armed Activities on the Territory of the Congo (DRC v Uganda)*, ICJ Gen List No 116, 19 December 2005 at para 216; Committee Against Torture, "Conclusions and Recommendations of the Committee Against Torture concerning the Second Report of the United States of America", 25 July 2006, UN Doc CAT/C/USA/CO/2 at para 14; Pursuant to the VCLT, where the meaning of the provision within a treaty is ambiguous or otherwise bring the meaning of the treaty into absurdity, the *travaux préparatories* may also be used as supplementary means of interpretation, see: VCLT at art 32.

103 UNHCR Advisory Opinion at para 9.

104 Wouters at 245; Refugee Convention at 1A(2): 'As a result of events occurring before 1 January 1951 and owing to well-founded fear of being persecuted for reasons of race, religion,

future threat, so that every time a State wishes to remove a refugee, the removing State must evaluate the risk of the refugee being persecuted after removal, by taking into account all relevant information including any new or previously unrecognized facts.[105] The obligation of *non-refoulement* is designed to protect certain human rights violations from occurring and is therefore prospective in nature, rather than an obligation to right past wrongs.[106] Further, the obligation on the prohibition against *refoulement* applies regardless of whether or not the threat to life or freedom materializes.[107] For instance, the prohibition against *refoulement* applies regardless of whether or not certain human rights are violated in actuality.[108]

In sum, the current understanding of the prohibition on *refoulement* under international refugee law is multifaceted, and is reflected not only in treaty law, but also in customary international law.[109] Individuals cannot be *refouled* (returned) by Contracting States back to the territory of the country or entity of origin or last habitual residence if they satisfy the definition of 'refugee' and do not fall into any of the exceptions to that definition. Extradition or non-admittance cannot be used by States in an attempt to avoid the duty not to *refoule*. The prohibition on *refoulement* applies to States acting both within and outside of their own territory, where they exercise effective authority and control. Finally, the evaluation of the threat to the refugee if returned is forward-looking in time.

nationality, membership of a particular social group or political opinion, is outside the country of his nationality and is unable or, owing to such fear, is unwilling to avail himself of the protection of that country; or who, not having a nationality and being outside the country of his former habitual residence as a result of such events, is unable or, owing to such fear, is unwilling to return to it. In the case of a person who has more than one nationality, the term 'the country of his nationality' shall mean each of the countries of which he is a national, and a person shall not be deemed to be lacking the protection of the country of his nationality if, without any valid reason based on well-founded fear, he has not availed himself of the protection of one of the countries of which he is a national'.

[105] *Ibid* at 119; Hathaway(2005) at 320 [Hathaway].

[106] Miller (2003) at 303.

[107] Wouters at 25.

[108] *Ibid*; An example is the argument that *non-refoulement* itself is an independent human right and should not depend on whether the removing State has violated the human rights of the person being removed, see: Wouters at 25; This issue was further explored in: Poon (2017).

[109] This is the view of the UNHCR, see: UNHCR NR Note at A: 'The principle of non-refoulement is the cornerstone of asylum and of international refugee law. Following from the right to seek and to enjoy in other countries asylum from persecution, as set forth in Article 14 of the Universal Declaration of Human Rights, this principle reflects the commitment of the international community to ensure to all persons the enjoyment of human rights, including the rights to life, to freedom from torture or cruel, inhuman or degrading treatment or punishment, and to liberty and security of person. These and other rights are threatened when a refugee is returned to persecution or danger'; In interpreting whether *non-refoulement* obligations are binding upon all States, the view of the UNHCR is that *non-refoulement* is a customary norm which is binding upon all States regardless of whether they are States Parties to the Refugee Convention; This view has been criticized by a small number of academic commentators, see: Costello and Foster (2016) [Costello and Foster].

2.3 Current Conception of Non-Refoulement Under International Human Rights Law

While the principle of *non-refoulement* originated in international refugee law, as outlined above, it has since evolved to simultaneously have meaning within international human rights law. This section explains this joint existence by explaining *non-refoulement* under international human rights law.

Both the *Convention Against Torture* and the *International Covenant on Civil and Political Rights* codify *non-refoulement* protection in their respective treaties. For the CAT, the prohibition against *refoulement* is formulated as the prohibition against torture under Article 3, while for the ICCPR, the prohibition against *refoulement* is codified as both the prohibition against torture and the prohibition on denying an individual his or her right to life respectively under Articles 6 and 7.[110]

Article 3 of the CAT states that:

1. No State Party shall expel, return (*'refouler'*) or extradite a person to another State where there are substantial grounds for believing that they would be in danger of being subjected to torture.
2. For the purpose of determining whether there are such grounds, the competent authorities shall take into account all relevant considerations including, where applicable, the existence in the State concerned of a consistent pattern of gross, flagrant or mass violations of human rights.[111]

Article 3 explicitly prohibits States from *refouling* an individual to another State when there is a serious risk of torture in that State, and this prohibition has been confirmed by the Committee Against Torture, the CAT treaty monitoring body.[112] The definition of 'torture' for the purpose of Article 3 is codified under Article 1 of the CAT.[113] The prohibition against torture under Article 3 does not include an obligation upon States Parties of the CAT to prohibit other forms of cruel treatment.[114] Instead, the prohibition against cruel treatment is found under Article 16, which obliges States 'to prevent in any territory under its jurisdiction other acts of

[110] CAT at art 3; ICCPR at arts 6 and 7.

[111] CAT at art 3.

[112] Wouters at 425.

[113] CAT at art 1: 'the term 'torture' means any act by which severe pain or suffering, whether physical or mental, is intentionally inflicted on a person for such purposes as obtaining from him or a third person information or a confession, punishing him for an act he or a third person has committed or is suspected of having committed, or intimidating or coercing him or a third person, or for any reason based on discrimination of any kind, when such pain or suffering is inflicted by or at the instigation of or with the consent or acquiescence of a public official or other person acting in an official capacity. It does not include pain or suffering arising only from, inherent in or incidental to lawful sanctions'.

[114] Wouters at 438.

cruel, inhuman or degrading treatment or punishment which do not amount to torture as defined in Article 1'.[115]

The Committee Against Torture has indicated that the prohibition against torture is a right which cannot be taken away or compromised.[116] The Committee stated that the principle of *non-refoulement* is a core concept and fundamental principle of international refugee law, and, in the form of human rights law, there is no derogation from such right as the prohibition against torture.[117] Further, the Committee is of the view that the principle of *non-refoulement* should not be used as a loophole to circumvent international refugee law protection, especially in the instances of diplomatic assurances.[118] In such instances, sending States are cautioned against the use of political undertakings from receiving States to guarantee the human rights of individuals being received.[119]

Unlike the CAT's explicit reference to *non-refoulement*, the ICCPR contains implicit references to the principle. Article 6 of the ICCPR declares that "Every human being has the inherent right to life. This right shall be protected by law. No one shall be arbitrarily deprived of his life".[120] In similarly absolute language, Article 7 says "No one shall be subjected to torture or to cruel, inhuman or degrading treatment or punishment. In particular, no one shall be subjected without his free consent to medical or scientific experimentation".[121] While both provisions do not refer specifically to *non-refoulement,* they have been interpreted as prohibiting *refoulement* to situations in which life may be deprived or in which torture may occur. For example, the United Nations Human Rights Committee—the treaty-monitoring body of the ICCPR—commented on the *jus cogens* nature of *non-refoulement.*[122]

---

[115] *Ibid* at 518; CAT at art 16: 'Each State Party shall undertake to prevent in any territory under its jurisdiction other acts of cruel, inhuman or degrading treatment or punishment which do not amount to torture as defined in article I, when such acts are committed by or at the instigation of or with the consent or acquiescence of a public official or other person acting in an official capacity. In particular, the obligations contained in articles 10, 11, 12 and 13 shall apply with the substitution for references to torture of references to other forms of cruel, inhuman or degrading treatment or punishment'.

[116] Committee Against Torture (2018) at para 8 [CAT NR Comment]: "The Committee recalls that the prohibition of torture, as defined in article1 of the Convention, is absolute. Article 2(2) of the Convention provides that "no exceptional circumstances whatsoever, whether a state of war or a threat of war, internal political instability or any other public emergency, may be invoked as a justification of torture". The Committee further recalls that other acts of ill-treatment are equally prohibited and that the prohibition of ill-treatment is likewise non-derogable".

[117] *Ibid* at para 8.

[118] *Ibid* at para 20.

[119] *Ibid.*

[120] ICCPR at art 6.

[121] *Ibid* at art 7.

[122] United Nations, Human Rights Committee (1994) "General Comment No. 24 (52)" UN Doc CCPR/C/21/Rev.1/Add.6, 2 November 1994 at para 10: "this underlines the great importance of non-derogable rights. But not all rights of profound importance, such as articles 9 and 27 of the

Some scholars argue that the principle of *non-refoulement* is a *jus cogens* norm, from which no derogation is permitted.[123] The first mention of *non-refoulement* as a *jus cogens* norm is from the Executive Committee of the UNHCR in 1982.[124] Along the same lines, in 1996, the UNHCR's Executive Committee concluded that the 'principle of *non-refoulement* is not subject to derogation', and thus had achieved *jus cogens* status.[125] Others do not go this far, maintaining that *non-refoulement* is not necessarily a *jus cogens* norm at present, but that it is in the midst of crystallizing in that direction. They posit that *non-refoulement* is steadily acquiring the status of *jus cogens* over time, and recognition of this has been affirmed by State practice, particularly within Latin America on the basis of the 1984 *Cartagena Declaration on Refugees.*[126] The approach of the scholars suggesting that *non-refoulement* is progressing towards the status of *jus cogens* is more persuasive as the status of the principle as a peremptory norm is still lacking consensus among scholars and States.

In sum, international human rights law takes an activity-specific approach to defining who cannot be *refouled*: anyone who faces torture or deprivation of life on return to another State where that individual is under serious threat. In contrast, refugee law examines the rights of those forcibly displaced by protecting asylum seekers or refugees from being returned to places where they may be subjected to

Covenant, have in fact been made non-derogable. One reason for certain rights being made non-derogable is because their suspension is irrelevant to the legitimate control of the state of national emergency (for example, no imprisonment for debt, in article 11). Another reason is that derogation may indeed be impossible (as, for example, freedom of conscience). At the same time, some provisions are non-derogable exactly because without them there would be no rule of law. A reservation to the provisions of article 4 itself, which precisely stipulates the balance to be struck between the interests of the State and the rights of the individual in times of emergency, would fall in this category. And some non-derogable rights, which in any event cannot be reserved because of their status as peremptory norms, are also of this character—the prohibition of torture and arbitrary deprivation of life are examples".

[123] Costello and Foster (2016); Allain (2001) at 538, which states: 'What remains uncertain is whether that norm [of *non-refoulement*] has achieved the status of *jus cogens*' [Allain].

[124] Allain at 539; UNHCR, Executive Committee (1982) at para (b), which states: 'Reaffirmed the importance of the basic principles of international protection and in particular the principle of non-refoulement which was *progressively acquiring* the character of a peremptory rule of international law' (emphasis added).

[125] Allain at 539; UNHCR, Executive Committee (1996) at para (i), which states: 'Distressed at the widespread violations of the principle of non-refoulement and of the rights of refugees, in some cases resulting in loss of refugee lives, and seriously disturbed at reports indicating that large numbers of refugees and asylum-seekers have been refouled and expelled in highly dangerous situations; *recalls that the principle of non-refoulement is not subject to deroation*' (emphasis added).

[126] Allain at 539–540; *Cartagena Declaration on Refugees* (adopted on 19 November 1984; entered into force 22 November 1984), which states, at para 5: '[. . .] the importance and meaning of the principle of *non-refoulement* (including the prohibition of rejection at the frontier) as a corner-stone of the international protection of refugees. This principle is imperative in regard to refugees and in the present state of international law *should be acknowledged and observed as a rule of jus cogens*'.

threats of death or persecution *linked to a Convention ground.* In other words, while human rights law can be said to be activity-specific in setting the parameters for *non-refoulement,* refugee law is concerned with the civil and political rights of the refugees. Further, refugee law is limiting in that it applies to only asylum seekers and refugees.[127] As well, *non-refoulement* as interpreted under refugee law is narrower than human rights law as a result of exceptions to the principle. For instance, the exception to *non-refoulement* found under Article 33(2) of the Refugee Convention provides that refugees who otherwise are protected from *refoulement* cannot be granted such protection where they are deemed to have committed a serious crime or would endanger the community of the country of refuge.[128]

The dual existence of *non-refoulement* within international refugee and human rights law, and the different levels of protection under each strand of law, raise the question of which approach to *non-refoulement* applies and when. On this, there are differing views and no clear resolution. McAdams argues that this lack of clarity is due to the 'general reluctance by States, academics and institutions to view human rights law, refugee law and humanitarian law as branches of an interconnected, holistic regime'.[129] Some scholars have argued that the wider human rights law definition of *non-refoulement* displaces the narrower refugee law definition of *non-refoulement.*[130] In other words, they posit that the definition of *non-refoulement* in human rights law must set aside or override the definition in refugee law because it is broader in nature (as it applies to all human beings, regardless of their status, without exception) and bridges the gap that refugee rights may not cover.[131] Under this conception, the human rights version of the prohibition on *refoulement* is the central version. However, others contend that human rights law and refugee law do not interact in this manner; that they are intrinsically intertwined and one does not act as a surrogate for the other.[132] They maintain that the refugee and human rights law definitions of *non-refoulement* do not displace

[127] Refugee Convention at art 33(1).

[128] *Ibid* at art 33(2): "The benefit of the present provision may not, however, be claimed by a refugee whom there are reasonable grounds for regarding as a danger to the security of the country in which he is, or who, having been convicted by a final judgment of a particular serious crime, constitutes a danger to the community of that country"; For a more in-depth discussion of the exception to *non-refoulement* and national security issues, see: Poon PKI Journal.

[129] McAdam Research Paper at 1.

[130] Chetail (2014) [Chetail].

[131] *Ibid* at 22; Hathaway (2012) at 190, where James Hathaway argued that: '[. . .] general human rights norms do not address many refugee-specific concerns (such as non-rejection at the frontier, or non-penalisation for illegal entry)' in suggesting that human rights law norms are in general, broader than refugee rights, and sometimes do not encompass the specific concerns addressed by refugee law. A general overview of the discussion on the interaction between international refugee and human rights law is further explored in: Poon Cornell Article.

[132] McAdam Research Paper.

one another, but instead work to complement the protection offered by the two regimes.[133] As one commentator indicates, the two regimes operate and develop together, with each area of the law informing the other: 'The framers' unambiguous reference in the Preamble of the 1951 Convention to the UDHR indicates a desire for the refugee definition to evolve *in tandem* with human rights principles' (emphasis added).[134] Lauterpacht and Bethlehem state that this co-existence means that international human rights law is 'an essential part of [the Refugee Convention's] framework'.[135] For the norm of *non-refoulement*, this means that the interpretation in the Refugee Convention is accompanied by the human rights law interpretation, so they are applied together when considering the risk to asylum claimants. A branch of this approach argues for refugee law to be viewed as *lex specialis*.[136] In this view, refugee law, as the specialized law (*lex specialis*) applying to asylum claimants and refugees, normally prevails, taking priority over the generalist rule (*lex generalis*). However, when there is a conflict of norms between international refugee and human rights law, 'such a conflict is resolved in favour of the most protective treatment essentially provided by human rights law, without regard to the alleged speciality of the prevailing norm'.[137] This is because refugee law does not exist in a 'normative vacuum' and 'no legal regime is fully self-contained'.[138]

The ambiguous nature of the roles of refugee law and human rights law means that privileging certain interpretations may create a normative conflict or a normative gap in situations where an individual's protection is at stake. Norm conflicts arise when the same issues are governed by two different set of rules, and there is a potential for different outcomes for the refugee claimant based on how those different sets of rules are interpreted and applied by States. For instance, a norm conflict can arise in the situation where the individual in question is being faced with a return to a territory where the endangerment is greater than persecution but does not rise to the level of a threat to life or a threat of torture or inhuman or degrading treatment.[139] In this situation, some states may argue that refugee law is the primary law applicable because it is *lex specialis* over human rights law, which is *lex generalis*.[140] In this example, this refugee would not be able to be *refouled*, but under a pure primacy approach for international human rights law, the same refugee may be returned since the individual being contemplated for return is

[133] *Ibid* at 4.

[134] Sternberg von (2002) at 314, as cited in McAdam Research Paper at 8.

[135] Lauterpacht at 75.

[136] The International Law Commission considers the relationship between *lex specialis* and general law in International Law Commission (2006); The issue of *lex specialis* and non-refoulement law is further explored in: Poon (2017).

[137] Chetail (2014) at 2.

[138] International Law Commission (2006) at 7 and 10.

[139] See CAT NR Comment at para 8.

[140] See, Poon Cornell Article at 33.

not facing a risk to life or of torture, inhuman or degrading treatment or punishment. On the other hand, normative gaps can occur when a State interprets either refugee law or human rights law in a manner to exclude protection, without resorting to the other area of law to see if protection might apply. Normative conflicts and normative gaps can be eliminated by adopting an approach in which both areas of law are considered to apply at all times. Under this approach, one set of rules complements and adds onto the other such that return to persecution *or* threat of life *or* torture, inhumane or degrading treatment or punishment are all considered to violate the norm of *non-refoulement*, an approach considered in more detail in subsequent chapters.

Despite the fact that there is no single agreed approach on the interaction between international refugee law and international human rights law on *non-refoulement*, this debate does not impact upon the analysis in this book: this is because EU law adopts the approach that both forms of *non-refoulement* exist together, and that the widest approach envelops the narrower approach, thus avoiding both norm conflicts and gaps, as explained in the next section and more fully in Chap. 3.

2.4 Non-Refoulement in European Law

The principle of *non-refoulement* is also found in European law, namely EU law and *European Convention on Human Rights* (ECHR) law. While Chap. 3 provides a detailed explanation of the European asylum system and its relation to *non-refoulement*, this section briefly describes the presence of *non-refoulement* law within the EU, in order to compare it to the international law explained above. Therefore, this section explains where the principle of *non-refoulement* is found under EU law and ECHR law.

EU law is the corpus of law that binds EU Member States.[141] The EU *acquis* is 'the body of common rights and obligations that are binding on all EU countries'.[142] The EU *acquis* is comprised of EU primary and secondary law.[143] EU primary law consists of treaties, which form the basis or ground rules for all EU action.[144] EU secondary law includes regulations, directives, and decisions, and are derived from the principles and objectives set out in the treaties.[145] Examples of EU

[141] The EU is comprised of 27 Member States. The UK withdrew from the EU on January 31, 2020: European Union (2016) "Countries".

[142] European Commission, European Neighbourhood Policy and Enlargement Negotiations (2016) "Acquis".

[143] The *acquis* refers to 'the body of common rights and obligations that is binding on all the EU members [. . .] it is constantly evolving', see: European Commission (2016) "European Neighbourhood Policy and Enlargement Negotiations".

[144] European Union, "EU Law" (2019).

[145] *Ibid.*

primary law relevant to *non-refoulement* include the *Treaty on the Functioning of the EU* (TFEU) and the *Charter of Fundamental Rights of the EU* (EU Charter).[146] Examples of EU secondary law relevant to *non-refoulement* include the Dublin III Regulation and its key directives, namely: the Qualification Directive, Asylum Procedures Directive, and the Reception Conditions Directive.[147] (Each of these secondary laws are discussed further in Chap. 3.)

Although the EU is itself not a State Party to the Refugee Convention, EU primary law—namely Article 78 of the TFEU—requires that the EU establish a common asylum policy which is in compliance with the Refugee Convention, including the principle of *non-refoulement.*[148] As primary law, all EU Member States are obliged to follow this treaty regardless of their pre-existing domestic asylum procedures.[149] The EU Charter is also primary law. It does not have an explicit provision mentioning the term '*non-refoulement*'; instead, an iteration of the principle is formulated as the right to life and the prohibition against torture under Articles 2 and 4 respectively and Article 19 on protection from removal.[150] Article 2 of the EU Charter states: '1. Everyone has the right to life. 2. No one shall be condemned to the death penalty, or executed'.[151] Article 4 says: 'No one shall be subjected to torture or to inhuman or degrading treatment or punishment'.[152] Article 19 indicates that '[n]o one may be removed, expelled or extradited to a State where there is a serious risk that he or she would be subjected to the death penalty, torture or other inhuman or degrading treatment or punishment'.[153] Further, Article 18 of the EU Charter guarantees the right to asylum with 'due respect for the rules of the [Refugee] Convention', which includes *non-refoulement.*[154] While the prohibition on *refoulement* is implicitly included in Articles 2, 4, and 19, both the UNHCR and the CJEU also view Article 18 as incorporating protection from *refoulement,* and that this protection sets the com-

[146] TEFU; EU Charter.

[147] Directive 2011/95/EU of the European Parliament and of the Council of 13 December 2011 on standards for the qualification of third-country nationals or stateless persons as beneficiaries of international protection, for a uniform status for refugees or for persons eligible for subsidiary protection, and for the content of the protection granted (recast) (2011) OJ L337/9 [Qualification Directive]; Asylum Procedures Directive; Directive 2013/33/EU of the European Parliament and of the Council of 26 June 2013 laying down standards for the reception of applicants for international protection (recast), OJ L180/96, 29 June 2013 [Reception Conditions Directive].

[148] TFEU at art 78.

[149] EU primary law is comprised of treaties concluded at the international level.

[150] EU Charter at arts 2 and 4.

[151] *Ibid.*

[152] *Ibid* at art 4.

[153] EU Charter at art 19.

[154] *Ibid* at art 18.

mon minimum standard which EU Member States are to follow.[155] Thus, both the international refugee law and international human rights law conceptions of *non-refoulement* are included in EU primary law, through the TFEU and the EU Charter. They co-exist, creating a combined—and therefore robust—legal norm.

Under EU secondary law, the recital of the Dublin III Regulation mentions the importance of safeguarding the principle of *non-refoulement.*[156] Recital 3 of the Reception Conditions Directive mirrors this provision, reiterating that Member States are to follow and respect the principle of *non-refoulement.*[157] Additionally, Article 21(1) of the Qualification Directive has a specific provision on the protection from *refoulement.*[158] Article 21(1) states: 'Member States shall respect the principle of *non-refoulement* in accordance with their international obligations'.[159] Article 21(2) of the Qualification Directive mirrors Article 33(2) of the Refugee Convention, providing an exception to the prohibition on *refoulement.*[160] The Asylum Procedures Directive also addresses an aspect of *non-refoulement*, particularly in Article 38, which provides for the 'safe' third country concept.[161] Under

---

[155] UNHCR, Executive Committee, "Conclusion No. 82 (XLVIII)", 1997 at para d; *HT v Land Baden-Württemberg,* C-373/13 at paras 65–68.

[156] Dublin III Regulation at recital 3: 'The European Council, at its special meeting in Tampere on 15 and 16 October 1999, agreed to work towards establishing the CEAS, based on the full and inclusive application of the Geneva Convention Relating to the Status of Refugees of 28 July 1951, as supplemented by the New York Protocol of 31 January 1967 ('the Geneva Convention'), thus ensuring that nobody is sent back to persecution, i.e. maintaining the principle of *non-refoulement.* In this respect, and without the responsibility criteria laid down in this Regulation being affected, Member States, all respecting the principle of *non-refoulement*, are considered as safe countries for third-country nationals'.

[157] Reception Conditions Directive at recital 3: 'At its special meeting in Tampere on 15 and 16 October 1999, the European Council agreed to work towards establishing a Common European Asylum System, based on the full and inclusive application of the Geneva Convention Relating to the Status of Refugees of 28 July 1951, as supplemented by the New York Protocol of 31 January 1967 ('the Geneva Convention'), thus affirming the principle of *non-refoulement.* The first phase of a Common European Asylum System was achieved through the adoption of relevant legal instruments, including Directive 2003/9/EC, provided for in the Treaties'.

[158] Qualification Directive at art 21.

[159] *Ibid* at art 21(1).

[160] *Ibid* at art 21(2): 'Where not prohibited by the international obligations mentioned in paragraph 1, Member States may *refoule* a refugee, whether formally recognised or not, when: (a) there are reasonable grounds for considering him or her as a danger to the security of the Member State in which he or she is present; or (b) he or she, having been convicted by a final judgment of a particularly serious crime, constitutes a danger to the community of that Member State'.

[161] Asylum Procedures Directive at art 38: '1. Member States may apply the safe third country concept only where the competent authorities are satisfied that a person seeking international protection will be treated in accordance with the following principles in the third country concerned: (a) life and liberty are not threatened on account of race, religion, nationality, membership of a particular social group or political opinion; (b) there is no risk of serious harm as defined in Directive 2011/95/EU; (c) the principle of *non-refoulement* in accordance with the Geneva Convention is respected; (d) the prohibition of removal, in violation of the right to freedom from torture and cruel, inhuman or degrading treatment as laid down in international

Article 38, the Directive indicates that procedural safeguards must be in place for a non-EU (or 'third') country to be deemed 'safe', so that claimants who have demonstrated a 'sufficient connection' with the 'safe' third country may be returned without contravening the principle of *non-refoulement*.[162]

The principle of *non-refoulement* as reflected in these primary and secondary laws has been litigated before the Court of Justice of the EU, based in Luxembourg. The CJEU is tasked with monitoring Member States' application of EU law and to ensure that EU law has been applied uniformly throughout the EU.[163] The CJEU comprises two courts, namely the Court of Justice and the General Court.[164] The Court of Justice handles requests for preliminary rulings from domestic courts of EU Member States, and is therefore the tribunal handling *non-refoulement* cases from individuals,[165] while the General Court is tasked with ruling on actions dealing mainly with competition law, State aid, trade, agriculture, and trademarks.[166] The CJEU has indicated that the CEAS is based on, *inter alia*, the guarantee that no one will be sent back to a territory where that person is at risk of being persecuted.[167] The CJEU has waded directly into the debate about how the refugee and human rights law conceptions of *non-refoulement* fit together. The Court recognized that the Refugee Convention permits States to derogate from the principle of *non-refoulement* in cases in which a refugee has committed a serious crime and presents a threat to the nation, or if the refugee presents a serious threat to society and that EU law transposed this, therefore permitting *refoulement* in these circumstances.[168] At the same time, the Court found that EU law must conform with the EU Charter, which prohibits exposure to torture and inhuman or degrading punishment or treatment.[169] Therefore, Member States cannot return refugees to their home States if there is a possibility that they will face such treatment.[170] In this way, the CJEU has reaffirmed the dual and simultaneous application of the refugee and human rights approaches within the EU to *non-refoulement*, thereby providing claimants with the widest possible protections.

ECHR law has two strands: the content of the ECHR itself, and the jurisprudence created by the ECtHR in its interpretation and application of the ECHR. The ECHR does not contain a specific provision on *non-refoulement*. Like the ICCPR

law, is respected; and (e) the possibility exists to request refugee status and, if found to be a refugee, to receive protection in accordance with the Geneva Convention'.

[162] *Ibid* at art 38(2)(a).

[163] European Union (2019).

[164] *Ibid.*

[165] *Ibid.*

[166] *Ibid.*

[167] *NS v Secretary of State for the Home Department and ME and Others v Refugee Applications Commissioner and Minister for Justice, Equality and Law Reform*, 21 December 2011 at para. 75 [NS/ME].

[168] *M, X and X*, C-391/16, C-77/17, C-78/17, Judgment of 14 May 2019 at para 110.

[169] *Ibid* at para 110.

[170] *Ibid.*

and the CAT, however, it contains the right to life in Article 2 and a prohibition on torture in Article 3. The prohibition against torture under Article 3 of the ECHR is absolute and without derogation, exclusion, or exception, even if there are concerns on national security grounds, unlike the Refugee Convention.[171] The ECHR applies to all persons falling under the jurisdiction of any State Party to the ECHR, regardless of the nationality or legal status of the person in question.[172] Therefore, unlike the Refugee Convention, the ECHR also applies to persons who have not yet left their country of origin or habitual residence.[173] Thus, and perhaps not surprisingly, the conception of *non-refoulement* under the ECHR reflects international human rights law.

The ECtHR is a court that monitors and scrutinizes the Council of Europe Member States' implementation of the ECHR and is based in Strasbourg.[174] The Council of Europe, an international organization and a separate entity from the EU, is comprised of 47 Member States, including the current 27 EU Member States that are a part of, and have acceded to, the ECHR.[175] All 27 EU Member States are, as a result of their membership within the Council of Europe, also members of the ECtHR.[176] Parties to a case before the ECtHR must abide by the judgments of the ECtHR and take necessary measures to comply with them.[177]

The ECtHR has developed a significant body of *non-refoulement* case law based on the prohibition of torture and inhuman or degrading treatment or punishment under Article 3 of the ECHR,[178] which it has indicated is an absolute, non-derogable right.[179] Broader than the *non-refoulement* protection offered by the Refugee Convention, and in line with international human rights law, the ECtHR

---

[171] *Saadi v Italy,* App No 37201/06 (ECHR, 28 February 2008) [Saadi].

[172] ECHR at art 1.

[173] *Fadele v the United Kingdom,* App No 13,078/87 (ECHR, 12 February 1990).

[174] Council of Europe (2016) "Convention for the Protection of Human Rights and Fundamental Freedoms".

[175] Council of Europe (2016) "Our Member States".

[176] *Ibid.*

[177] ECHR at art 1.

[178] Klug (2011) at 124 [Klug]; UNHCR, *The Case Law of the European Regional Courts: the Court of Justice of the European Union and the European Court of Human Rights—Refugees, Asylum-seekers, and Stateless Persons* (June 2015); Some examples of this case law are: *Soering v the United Kingdom,* No. 14038/88, Judgment of 7 July 1989 [Soering]; *Cruz Varaz and others v Sweden,* Series A, No 201 [Cruz]; *Vilvarajah and Others v the United Kingdom,* Nos. 13163/87, 13164/87, 13165/87, 13447/87 and 13448/87, Judgment of 30 October 1991 [Vilvarajah]; *Chahal v the United Kingdom,* No. 22414/93, Judgment [GC] of 15 November 1996 at 1831–1874 [Chahal].

[179] Soering at para 88; *Chahal v the United Kingdom,* No. 22414/93, Judgment [Grand Chamber] of 15 November 1996 at paras 80–81; *D v the United Kingdom,* No. 30240/96, Judgment of 2 May 1997 at para 47; *Saadi* at para 138; *Auad v Bulgaria,* No. 46390/10, Judgment of 11 October 2011, at para 101; *MSS v Belgium and Greece,* No. 30696/09, 21 January 2011 at paras 126–127 [MSS]; *Babar Ahmed and Others v the United Kingdom,* Nos. 24027/07, 11949/08, 36742/08, 66911/09 and 67354/09, Judgment of 10 April 2012 at paras 167–175 [Ahmed].

has interpreted Article 3 of the ECHR to be applicable to both State and non-State actors, to cover indirect *refoulement*, and to apply to all forms of removal from the host State to another State (to countries inside and outside of the CEAS).[180] Importantly, the returning State (and not only the receiving State) are considered to be responsible for *refoulement* where there are substantial grounds for believing that the person concerned faces a real risk of torture or inhuman or degrading treatment or punishment upon return or extradition.[181] In terms of evaluating the risk of harm, the ECtHR has held that the harm may come from both State and non-State actors, and that, while the risk is usually intentionally inflicted, it could also arise in other circumstances (including in poor living conditions).[182] The claimant only needs to be exposed to a 'real risk' of ill-treatment, but it must be higher than a 'mere possibility' and lower than 'more likely than not'.[183] The Court noted the particular vulnerability of asylum claimants as a factor to be considered when assessing the risk and severity of ill-treatment.[184] Notably, the Court has indicated that assurances by the third State that the claimant will not be ill-treated are not, on their own, sufficient to demonstrate lack of risk: the quality and reliability of these assurances must be evaluated.[185] The Court has also held that *non-refoulement* applies in cases involving returns to countries in which a substantial and

---

[180] *Salah Sheekh v the Netherlands*, App No 1948/04 (ECHR, 11 January 2007); Cruz at paras 69–70; Vilvarajah at para 103; Ahmed at para 168; Hirsi at paras 114 and 156; TI at 15*; KRS v the United Kingdom*, No. 32733/08, Decision of 2 December 2008 [KRS]; MSS at para 347; *Abdolkhani and Karimnia v Turkey*, No. 30471/08, Judgment of 22 September 2009, at para 88. The ECtHR has indicated that, where a State is aware, or ought to be aware, of a 'real and immediate risk' of a person being exposed to ill-treatment through being forcibly transferred by any person to another State, it has an obligation to take 'within the scope of [its] powers, such preventive operational measures that, judged reasonably, might be expected to avoid that risk': *Savriddin Dzhurayev v Russia*, No. 71386/10, Judgment of 25 April 2013, at paras 177–185; *Nizomkhon Dzhurayev v Russia*, no. 31890/11, Judgment of 03 October 2013 at paras 136–139; *Ermakov v Russia*, no. 43165/10, Judgment of 07 November 2013 at paras 208–211; *Kasymakhunov v Russia*, no. 29604/12, Judgment of 14 November 2013 at paras 134–141.

[181] Soering at para 91; Vilvarajah at para 107ff. The Court has defined categories of ill-treatment and the levels of severity of that ill-treatment that fall within these terms in, for example: *Selmouni v. France*, No. 25803/94, Judgment [GC] of 28 July 1999 at para 101; *A. and Others v the United Kingdom*, No. 3455/05, Judgment [GC] of 19 February 2009 at para 127; *Ireland v the United Kingdom*, No. 5310/71, Judgment (Plenary) of 18 January 1978 at para 162; *Raninen v Finland*, No. 20972/92, Judgment of 16 December 1997 at para 55; *Hilal v the United Kingdom*, No. 45276/99, Judgment of 6 March 2001, at para 60.

[182] *HLR v France*, No. 24573/94, Judgment [GC] of 29 April 1997 at para 40; *Salah Sheekh v the Netherlands*, No. 1948/04, Judgment of 11 January 2007 at para 147; *D v the United Kingdom*, No. 30240/96, Judgment of 2 May 1997 at para 49; MSS at paras 367 and 254.

[183] Vilvarajah at para 111; *Saad i* at para 140.

[184] MSS at para 232.

[185] *Othman (Abu Qatada) v the United Kingdom*, No. 8139/09, Judgment of 17 January 2012 at paras 187 and 189 [Othman]; Chahal at para 105; *Baysakov and Others v Ukraine*, No. 54131/08, Judgment of 18 February 2010 at paras 51–52.

foreseeable risk of the death penalty or execution exists.[186] As well, the ECtHR has also held in its decisions that the ECHR takes precedence over other EU law obligations for EU Member States,[187] thus reinforcing the human rights lens of *non-refoulement* and essentially confirming the widest protection approach of the CJEU.

The ECtHR has indicated that *non-refoulement* protections are incorporated into ECHR rights other than Article 3. As mentioned above, the ECHR contains, in Article 2, a provision on the right to life. Since applicants have often argued *non-refoulement* concerns under both Article 2 and 3, the ECtHR has generally opted to examine the merits of the complaint under Article 3.[188] However, in recent years, the Court has pronounced itself on *non-refoulement* considerations under Article 2, finding that returning to a serious risk of 'a flagrant denial of a fair trial ... the outcome of which was or is likely to be the death penalty' is a violation of that principle.[189] Other cases have considered the link between *non-refoulement* and Article 5, on the right to liberty and security of person, finding that, in principle, 'a flagrant breach of Article 5 would occur only if, for example, the receiving State arbitrarily detained an applicant for many years without any intention of bringing him or her to trial ... or if an applicant would be at risk of being imprisoned for a substantial period in the receiving State, having previously been convicted after a flagrantly unfair trial'.[190] Similarly, cases have found a link between *non-refoulement* and Article 6, on the right to a fair trial for similar reasons: when there are 'substantial grounds for believing that ... [the applicant] would be exposed to a real risk of being subjected to a flagrant denial of justice'.[191]

The full contours of the European understanding of *non-refoulement* are explored in Chap. 3, but this summary indicates the extent to which the EU

---

[186] *Bader and Kanbor v Sweden,* App No 13284/04 (ECHR, 8 November 2005) [Bader and Kanbor]; *Al Nashiri v Poland, No. 28761/11, 24 July 2014; AL (XW) v Russia*, App No 44095/14 (ECHR, 29 October 2015).

[187] TI; See, also: Klug at 125.

[188] See, for example: *Said v Netherlands*, No. 2345/02, Decision of 5 October 2004 and Judgment of 5 July 2005; *NA v The United Kingdom*, No. 25904/07, Judgment of 17 July 2008.

[189] Bader and Kanbor at para 42. See also *Al-Saadoon and Mufdhi v The United Kingdom*, No. 61498/08, Judgment of 2 March 2010 at paras 118 and 123; and *Öcalan v Turkey*, No. 46221/99, Judgment of Grand Chamber of 12 May 2005 at para 166, which required a risk of an unfair trial, not a trial that was flagrantly unfair. The case of *Kaboulov v The Ukraine*, No. 41015/04, Judgment of 19 November 2009 indicated that the test was whether 'there are substantial grounds to believe that the person in question, if extradited, would face a real risk of being liable to capital punishment in the receiving country' or whether the sending State 'knowingly puts the person concerned at such high risk of losing his life as for the outcome to be a near certainty' at para 99.

[190] Othman at para 233.

[191] *Ibid* at para 261.

conception reflects the international human rights law approach, and the intertwining of the principle as stated in the Refugee Convention with that approach.

2.5 Conclusions on the Principle of Non-Refoulement

International and European refugee law protects asylum seekers and refugees against *refoulement* while international and European human rights law protects all human beings regardless of their legal or political status against *refoulement*.[192] The activities that are prohibited under refugee law include return to a place where persecution or death or where the asylum seeker or refugee's life or freedom would be threatened, while in human rights law, the individual is protected against return to torture, inhuman or degrading treatment or punishment.[193] The obligation to protect asylum seekers, refugees, and other individuals from *refoulement* triggers both within a State's territory and outside of the State's territory. For example, the obligation of *non-refoulement* can trigger when an individual has not yet arrived in the territory of a State and has not yet been subjected to individual refugee status determination processes.[194]

Despite the distinctive nature of refugee law and human rights law in their application to asylum seekers, refugees, and individuals, the two branches of international law are clearly intrinsically intertwined. However, the exact manner of that interaction is still ambiguous. Refugee law protects a specific group of individuals, namely asylum seekers and refugees, and human rights law either fills in the legal gap by protecting those who do not fall under the definition of a refugee or protects everyone, including refugees. Some scholars argue that refugee law acts as a surrogate in the sense that it protects refugees who are unable to obtain protection from their host State.[195] Other scholars argue that human rights law

[192] See analysis by Vincent Chetail and James Hathaway on the discussion regarding the distinction between refugee law and human rights law.

[193] *Ibid*; For refugee law, see: Refugee Convention at art 33(1); For human rights law, see: ICCPR at arts 6 and 7; CAT at art 3; Poon Cornell Article at 32–33.

[194] This topic is explored further in: Poon (2020) [Poon Refugee Review]; Hirsi at 69; The test to determine State responsibility for protecting individuals from *refoulement* entails examining whether the State exercises effective authority and control over the individual: *Hirsi* at 69: "under international law concerning the protection of refugees, the decisive test in establishing the responsibility of a State was not whether the person being returned was on the territory of a State but whether that person fell under the effective control and authority of that State"; In the context of the high seas, once it can be shown that a State is exercising effective authority and control, by extension through the actions or omissions of that State's agents, over the asylum claimants arriving in boats towards the shore of a State's territory, *non-refoulement* obligations are triggered: For the test of effective authority and control, see: *Bankovic et al v. Belgium and 16 Other Contracting States* App no 52207/99 (ECHR, 12 December 2001) (Admissibility Decision) at 37–38 [Bankovic].

[195] Hathaway (2012) "Refugees and Asylum" in B Opeskin, R Perruchoud, and J Redpath-Cross (eds) *Foundations of International Migration Law* (Cambridge: Cambridge University Press) at 7.2.6 [Hathaway Refugees and Asylum].

acts as complementary protection to refugee law instead of displacing the latter.[196] Yet others argue that the role of human rights law is not merely complementary to refugee law, but is normatively superior to refugee law.[197] While this debate has relevance at the international level, it is of less concern at the EU level due to the simultaneous application of both refugee law and human rights law conceptions of *non-refoulement* for asylum claimants and refugees.

The principle of *non-refoulement* is a principle of central importance to refugee and human rights law given that its role is to protect those who are at risk of being returned to situations where their life or bodily integrity may be threatened. Given the complexity of the norm of *non-refoulement* and its application within Europe, the next chapter therefore explores the CEAS, also referred to as the Dublin System, in more detail. It highlights the history and challenges of the Dublin System, in particular how EU Member States' *non-refoulement* obligations are undermined as a result of certain policies implemented within the EU to contain and control the flow of refugees.

References

Ad Hoc Committee on Refugees and Stateless Persons (1950d) UN Doc E/AC.32/SR.40

Ad Hoc Committee on Statelessness and Related Problems (1950a) UN Doc E/AC.32/2 Annex

Ad Hoc Committee on Statelessness and Related Problems (1950b) UN Doc E/AC.32/SR.20

Ad Hoc Committee on Statelessness and Related Problems (1950c) UN Doc E/AC.32/L.32

Allain J (2001) The *jus cogens* Nature of non-refoulement. Int J Refug Law 13(4):533–558

Beck RJ (1999) Britain and the 1933 refugee convention: national or state sovereignty? Int J Refug Law 11(4):597–624

Chetail V (2012) Are refugee rights human rights? An unorthodox questioning of the relations between refugee law and human rights law. In: Rubio-Marin R (ed) Human rights and immigration. Oxford Scholarship Online

Chetail V (2014) Armed conflict and forced migration: a systematic approach to international humanitarian law, refugee law, and international human rights law. In: Clapham A, Gaeta P (eds) The Oxford handbook of international law in armed conflict. Oxford University Press, Oxford

Committee Against Torture (2006) Conclusions and recommendations of the committee against torture concerning the second report of the United States of Americ UN Doc CAT/C/USA/CO/2

Committee Against Torture (2018) General comment no. 4 (2017) on the implementation of article 3 of the convention in the context of article 22, UN Doc CAT/C/GC/4

Conference of Plenipotentiaries (1951) UN Doc A/CONF 2.69

Conference of Plenipotentiaries (1951) UN Doc A/CONF.2/SR.35.

Costello C, Foster M (2016) Non-refoulement as custom and Jus Cogens? Putting the prohibition to the test. Neth Yearb Int Law 46:273–327

Council of Europe (2016) Convention for the protection of human rights and fundamental freedoms. https://www.coe.int/en/web/conventions/full-list/-/conventions/treaty/005

[196] See more on this: McAdam Research Paper.

[197] See Chetail.

Einarsen T (2011) Background, drafting history of the 1951 convention and the 1967 protocol. In: Zimmermann A (ed) The 1951 convention relating to the status of refugees and its 1967 protocol: a commentary. Oxford University Press. Oxford

European Commission (2016) Acquis. https://ec.europa.eu/neighbourhood-enlargement/policy/glossary/terms/acquis_en

European Commission (2016) European neighbourhood policy and enlargement negotiations. https://ec.europa.eu/neighbourhood-enlargement/policy/glossary/terms/acquis_en

European Union (2016) Countries. https://europa.eu/european-union/about-eu/countries_en

European Union (2019) Court of justice of the European Union (CJEU). https://europa.eu/european-union/about-eu/institutions-bodies/court-justice_en#what-does-the-cjeu-do

European Union (2019) EU law. https://europa.eu/european-union/law_en

Gillard E-C (2008) There's no place like home: states' obligations in relation to transfers of persons. Int Rev Red Cross 90 871.

Goodwin-Gill GS (2008) Convention relating to the status of refugees, protocol relating to the status of refugees. United Nations Audiovisual Library of International Law.

Goodwin-Gill GS, McAdam J (2007) The refugee in international law, 3rd edn. Oxford University Press.

Hathaway JC (2005) The rights of refugees under international law. Cambridge University Press, Cambridge

Hathaway JC (2012) Refugees and asylum. In: Opeskin B, Perruchoud R, Redpath-Cross J (eds) Foundations of international migration law. Cambridge University Press, Cambridge

Human Rights Committee (1994) General Comment No. 24 (52) (1994), UN Doc CCPR/C/21/Rev.1/Add.6

Human Rights Committee (1995) Concluding observations of the human rights committee, United States of America, UN Doc CCPR/C/79/Add.50

Human Rights Committee (2006) Concluding observations of the human rights committee, United States of America, UN Doc CCPR/C/USA/CO/3/Rev.1

International Law Commission (2006) Fragmentation of international law: difficulties arising from the diversification and expansion of international law: report of the study group of the international law commission: finalized by Martti Koskenniemi, A/CN.4/L.682

Jaeger G (2001) On the history of the international protection of refugees. Int Rev Red Cross 83(843):727–736.

Jones TD (1994) Sale v. Haitian Centers Council, Inc. Am J Int Law 114–126.

Kälin W, Caroni M, Heim, L (2011) Article 33, para. 1 (Prohibition of expulsion or return ('*Refoulement*'). In: Zimmermann A (ed) The 1951 convention relating to the status of refugees and its 1967 protocol: a commentary. Oxford University Press, Oxford

Kim S (2017) Non-refoulement and extraterritorial jurisdiction: state sovereignty and migration controls at sea in the european context. Leiden J Int Law 30, 49–70

Klug A (2011) Regional developments: Europe. In: Zimmermann A (ed) The 1951 convention relating to the status of refugees and its 1967 protocol: a commentary. Oxford University Press, Oxford

League of Nations (1922) Russian refugees: report by Dr. Nansen, high commissioner of the league of nations 1922 LNOJ

League of Nations (1939) Supplementary report: submitted to the twentieth ordinary session of the assembly of the league of nations by Sir Herbert Emerson, GCIE, KCSI, CBE, High Commissioner for Refugees. LN Doc A18(a)

Long K (2010) No entry! A review of UNHCR's response to border closures in situations of mass refugee influx. http://www.unhcr.org/4c207bd59.pdf

McAdam J (2011) Interpretation of the 1951 Convention. In: Zimmermann A (ed) The 1951 convention relating to the status of refugees and its 1967 protocol: a commentary. Oxford University Press, Oxford

McNamara D (1997) Commentary on the refugee convention 1951 Articles 2-11, 13-37 published by the division of international protection of the united nations high commissioner for refugees. https://www.unhcr.org/3d4ab5fb9.pdf
Merriam-Webster Online Dictionary, 10th Edition
Miller DJ (2003) Holding states to their convention obligations: The United Nations convention against torture and the need for a broad interpretation of state action. Geo Immigration Law J 17:299–323
Pirie SH (1986) Note: the need for a codified definition of 'Persecution' in United States Refugee Law. Stanford Law Rev 39(1):187–234
Pizor AG (1993) Sale v. Haitian centres council: the return of Haitian refugees. Fordham Int Law J 17(4):1062–1114
Poon J (2017) Non-refoulement in the international refugee law regime: a lex specialis? Cornell Int Law J Online 3:31–33
Poon J (2017) Non-refoulement as lex specialis? London School of Economics and Political Science Human Rights Blog. https://blogs.lse.ac.uk/humanrights/2017/07/07/non-refoulement-as-lex-specialis
Poon J (2019) The protection nexus between non-penalisation and national security exception under the refugee convention. Philippe Kirsch Inst Glob Just J 3:37
Poon J (2020) Extraterritorial application of non-refoulement: triggering the prohibition on the high seas. Refug Rev 4:114–128
Skran CM (2011) Background, historical development of international refugee law. In: Zimmermann A (ed) 1951 convention relating to the status of refugees and its 1967 protocol: a commentary. Oxford University Press, Oxford
Statement by Chance (Canada) and Hoeg (Denmark) (1951) UN Doc A/CONF.2/SR.16
Sternberg von MR (2002) The grounds of refugee protection in the context of international human rights and humanitarian law: Canadian and United States Case law compared. The Hague, Martinus Nijhoff
UNHCR (1951) The refugee convention, 1951: The travaux preparatoires analysed with a commentary by Dr Paul Weis
UNHCR (1997) Commentary on the refugee convention 1951. Articles 2–11:13–37
UNHCR (2007) Advisory opinion the extraterritorial application of non-refoulement obligations under the 1951 convention relating to the status of refugees and its 1967 protocol
UNHCR (2015) The case law of the European regional courts: the court of justice of the European Union and the European Court of human rights—Refugees, Asylum-seekers, and Stateless Persons. https://www.refworld.org/pdfid/558803c44.pdf
UNHCR, Executive Committee (1981) Conclusion no. 22
UNHCR, Executive Committee (1982) General conclusion on international protection no. 25 (XXXIII)–1982
UNHCR, Executive Committee (1996) General conclusion on international protection no. 79 (XVLII)—1996, 11 Oct 1996
UNHCR, Executive Committee (2017) Conclusion no. 82 (XLVIII)
United Nations Economic and Social Council (1949) Resolution 248 (IX) B of 8 August 1949
United Nations Economic and Social Council (1950) Summary record of the twentieth meeting: ad Hoc committee on statelessness and related problems, first session. UN Doc E/AC.32/SR.20
United Nations Treaty Collection (1951) Chapter V: refugees and stateless persons, 2. Convention relating to the status of refugees, Geneva, 28 July 1951. https://treaties.un.org/Pages/ViewDetailsII.aspx?src=IND&mtdsg_no=V-2&chapter=5&Temp=mtdsg2&clang=_en
United Nations Treaty Collection (1967) Chapter V: refugees and stateless persons, 5. Protocol relating to the status of refugees. New York, 31 January 1967. https://treaties.un.org/Pages/ViewDetails.aspx?src=IND&mtdsg_no=V-5&chapter=5&clang=_en
Weis P (1982) The development of refugee law. Michigan J Int Law 3(1):27–42

Chapter 3
The Common European Asylum System and *Non-Refoulement*

3.1 Introduction

The European Union (EU) is a destination region for many asylum claimants, with over 600,000 asylum applicants arriving in EU Member States in 2019.[1] Germany is currently the EU country with the most asylum applicants, with roughly 473,000 first-time asylum applications filed between January and September 2019.[2] The mass influx of refugees into Europe began with the Syrian conflict in 2011, peaked in 2015–2016, and has shifted over time, but the issue of mass influx is still a European reality and a source of contention.[3] This is evident in recent developments at the EU-Turkey border, when Turkey announced that it will 'no longer be preventing refugees and migrants from crossing the border into Europe. [However] Greek authorities have responded by announcing that they will not allow people to seek asylum and will be sending people back to Turkey'.[4]

The purpose of the Common European Asylum System (CEAS) is to harmonize asylum standards across the EU and to create efficient access to asylum

---

[1] Eurostat (2020).

[2] InfoMigrants (2019).

[3] Collett and Le Coz summarize it this way: "In late 2013, governments were alerted to increasing flows and significant loss of life along the central Mediterranean route. After a particularly notable tragedy in which at least 800 migrants drowned, and emergency European Summit was held in April 2015 ... the impact at this stage was largely confined to a single EU Member State: Italy. However, during the summer of 2015, the number of sea arrivals from Turkey and Greece rose exponentially, followed by a mass movement of asylum seekers and migrants through the Western Balkans and onwards to a wide range of EU Member States [totaling 1 million in 2015]. This shift in flow changed the nature of the crisis, and its depth ... the scale of the phenomenon in the eastern Mediterranean challenged the European Union's ability to respond on multiple fronts." Collett, Elizabeth and Le Coz, Camille (2018) at 4.

[4] Norwegian Refugee Council (2020) "Q&A: What does the Turkish border situation mean for Europe?".

J. Poon, *Counteracting Containment Policies in the EU*, European Union and its Neighbours in a Globalized World 31,
https://doi.org/10.1007/978-3-032-08351-7_3

procedures.[5] Despite established EU law specifying the minimum standards of procedural safeguards for these applicants—including on *non-refoulement*—the Dublin System[6] has been critiqued by academic commentators, the UNHCR, nongovernmental organizations, and Member States as ineffective and deficient.[7]

This chapter aims to explain the law—written law, case law, and procedural law—applied in the EU regarding the refugee law principle of *non-refoulement*. It does so in order to illustrate the obligations EU Member States are meant to implement with respect to *non-refoulement*, and the gap that exists between obligations and actual practice. Therefore, this chapter begins by examining the sources and hierarchy of EU law and ECHR law in order to provide a background as to the where *non-refoulement* is derived under European law. Given the discussion in Chap. 2 of the relationship between international refugee law and international human rights law, the interrelationship between EU law and ECHR law is crucial and, as will be seen, results in a relatively robust norm prohibiting *refoulement*. The chapter then discusses the asylum process within the CEAS, followed by an exploration of gaps between the way the norm of *non-refoulement* is articulated in EU legal documents and how it is observed in practice, particularly as a result of the EU's 'margin of discretion' when implementing refugee law at the domestic level and the presumption of mutual trust between EU Member States.[8] Finally, it ends with concluding remarks on the meaning of these gaps.

---

[5] European Commission, Migration and Home Affairs (2019) "Common European Asylum System" [CEAS].

[6] While often used interchangeably with the term 'CEAS' in this book, the Dublin System refers to a particular part of the CEAS: the Dublin III Regulation of 2013, which replaced the earlier Dublin II Regulation of 2003 and the original Dublin Convention of 1990. Essentially, the Dublin System is a mechanism in the EU which identifies which EU country is responsible for processing the asylum application of someone belonging to a non-EU country or a stateless person. Usually, this is the first EU member state that the claimant enters. The Regulation also strives to ensure that each application gets a fair examination in one EU country. Signatories to the Dublin III Regulation include the EU's 27 Member States, and Liechtenstein, Norway, Iceland and Switzerland.

[7] For example: Sidorenko, Olga Ferguson (2007) at 16 [Olga]; Goodwin-Gill, Guy S., and McAdam, Jane (2007) [Goodwin-Gill]; UNHCR (2013); See also: *MSS* and *TI*; French President Francois Hollade has publicly condemned the Dublin System: "Frankly, the Dublin process, in its present form, is obsolete" in Thym, Daniel (2015); Foreign Minister Peter Szijjarto of Hungary stated: "The Dublin system is dead" in Marton Dunai, "Hungary says EU's Dublin rules 'dead'; won't leg migrants come back", Ruth Pitchford (ed), Thomson Reuters UK, 11 November 2015.

[8] Note that the 'margin of discretion' is similar but not the same as the 'margin of appreciation', which is a concept created by the European Court of Human Rights. The 'margin of discretion' is the discretionary room of EU Member States when interpreting and applying legal norms under EU law. The 'margin of appreciation' is the discretionary room of Council of Europe Member States when they interpret and apply legal norms under ECHR law. The distinction between the 'margin of discretion' under EU law and the 'margin of appreciation' under ECHR law is an important one, as, although similar, the 'margin of appreciation' is a well-developed doctrine in ECHR law that has a body of jurisprudence signaling its application. On the other hand, the 'margin of discretion' concerns an EU Member State's discretionary room when interpreting and

3.2 The European Legal Order

EU law and ECHR law establish the obligations of EU Member States with respect to refugee law and, more specifically, the principle of *non-refoulement*. This subsection therefore begins by explaining the sources and hierarchy of EU law, before launching into a discussion of the scope and content of EU law as it relates to *non-refoulement*. Next, it examines the sources, hierarchy, scope and content of ECHR law in the same manner. Both discussions illustrate the multi-layered nature of refugee law within Europe, particularly as it relates to *non-refoulement*.

3.2.1 EU Law

EU law is comprised of both primary and secondary law.[9] The EU was established by a number of treaties, namely: The *Treaty of Maastricht*, the *Treaty of Amsterdam*, and the *Treaty of Lisbon*. The *Treaty of Maastricht* (or, formally, the *Treaty on European Union*) officially established the EU, and subsequent treaty amendments, detailed below, expanded the powers of the EU in its relations with Member States.[10] The *Treaty of Maastricht* was adopted on February 7, 1992, which also created a single European currency, the Euro.[11] The *Treaty of Amsterdam* (or, formally, the *Treaty of Amsterdam amending the Treaty of the European Union, the Treaties establishing the European Communities and certain related acts*) was signed on October 2, 1997 and made substantive changes to the *Treaty of Maastricht*, in which EU Member States agreed to defer certain powers under immigration, civil and criminal laws, and foreign security policies, to the European Parliament.[12] The *Treaty of Lisbon* (or, formally, the *Treaty of Lisbon Amending the Treaty on European Union and the Treaty Establishing the*

applying a provision of EU law and is within the purview of the Court of Justice; For more on the 'margin of discretion' in EU law, see, generally: *TB v Bevándorlási és Menekültügyi Hivatal* (Case C-519/18), CJEU, 5 September 2019; For more on the 'margin of appreciation' in ECHR law, see: Steven Greer (2000) *The Margin of Appreciation: Interpretation and Discretion under the European Convention on Human Rights* (Strasbourg: Council of Europe Publishing), 1–60.

[9] European Union (2016) "Sources and Scope of European Union Law: Fact Sheets on the European Union—2016" at 1 [EU Sources].

[10] European Union (2016) "The History of the European Union".

[11] *Ibid*; See also: *Treaty on European Union (Consolidated Version), Treaty of Maastricht*, 7 February 1992, OJ C325/5, 24 December 2002, http://www.refworld.org/docid/3ae6b39218.html [TEU].

[12] European Parliament, "Fact Sheets on the European Union: The Maastricht and Amsterdam Treaties", October 2016, http://www.europarl.europa.eu/atyourservice/en/displayFtu.html?ftuId=FTU_1.1.3.html; See also: *Treaty on European Union (Consolidated Version), Treaty of Amsterdam* (adopted 2 October 1997, entered into force 1 May 1999), http://www.refworld.org/docid/3dec906d4.html.

European Community, Treaty of Lisbon) was signed on December 13, 2007. This treaty amended the *Treaty of Maastricht* and the *Treaty of Rome* (the treaty which created the European Economic Community, the precursor to the EU).[13]

The sources of EU law are primary and secondary legislation. Examples of primary legislation are: the *Treaty of the EU* (TEU), *Treaty on the Functioning of the EU* (TFEU), and international agreements.[14] EU treaties and general principles of EU law are known as primary legislation and are at the top of the legal EU hierarchy.[15] Examples of primary EU treaties that are relevant to this book include: the TEU, TFEU, and the EU Charter.[16] Next in the legal hierarchy are international agreements concluded by the EU, which are subordinate to primary legislation.[17] At the bottom of the legal hierarchy of the EU is secondary legislation.[18] Primary legislation supersedes secondary legislation, and secondary legislation is only valid if it is consistent with the acts and agreements which have precedence over it.[19]

Secondary legislation is made up of legislative acts, delegated acts, and implementing acts.[20] Legislative acts are 'legal acts which are adopted through the ordinary or a special legislative procedure'.[21] Delegated acts are 'non-legislative acts of general application which supplement or amend certain non-essential elements of a legislative act'.[22] Implementing acts are 'generally adopted by the Commission [...] Implementing acts are a matter for the Council only in specific cases which are duly justified and in areas of common foreign and security policy'.[23]

Legislative acts include regulations, directives, decisions, recommendations, and opinions.[24] Regulations are binding legislative acts that must be applied in their entirety across the EU.[25] Directives, on the other hand, are legislative acts that set out a goal that all EU Member States must achieve, but it is up to the individual

---

[13] *Treaty of Lisbon Amending the Treaty on European Union and the Treaty Establishing the European Community, Treaty of Lisbon,* 13 December 2007, 2007 C306/01, http://www.refworld.org/docid/476258d32.html.

[14] EU sources at 1.

[15] *Ibid.*

[16] *Ibid.*

[17] *Ibid*; See, also: *Kadi II,* C-584/10P, C-593/10P, C-595/10P, Judgment of 18 July 2013 at para 119 [Kadi II]: 'the Court of Justice thus seems to have regarded the constitutional framework created by the EC Treaty as a wholly autonomous legal order, not subject to the higher rules of international law—in this case the law deriving from the Charter of the United Nations' (emphasis added).

[18] *Ibid.*

[19] *Ibid.*

[20] EU Sources at 2.

[21] *Ibid.*

[22] *Ibid.*

[23] *Ibid.*

[24] *Ibid.*

[25] Europa (2016a) "Regulations, Directives and Other Acts".

Member States to devise their own laws on how to achieve these goals.[26] Decisions are binding on only those to whom they are addressed, including EU Member States and natural or legal persons, and are directly applicable.[27] Recommendations are not binding, but allow the EU institutions to make their views known and suggest a line of action without imposing any legal obligation on EU Member States.[28] Opinions are instruments that allow EU institutions to make a statement in a non-binding fashion without imposing any legal obligation on those to whom they are addressed.[29]

The EU is comprised of a number of institutions. The most important EU institutions are the EU Parliament, the EU Commission, and the EU Council. The EU Parliament is a directly-elected EU body with legislative, supervisory, and budgetary responsibilities.[30] The EU Commission promotes the general interests of the EU by proposing and enforcing legislation and implementing policies and the EU budget.[31] The EU Council defines the general political direction and priorities of the EU.[32]

Now that the general structure of EU law has been explained, it is important to explain EU law on the principle of *non-refoulement*. The scope of EU law on *non-refoulement* is evident in the relevant EU primary and secondary legislation on asylum, the legally-binding force of these pieces of legislation, and the application of the Schengen Area in relation to the freedom of movement of non-EU nationals.

Primary and secondary legislation such as the TFEU, EU Charter, and the Qualification Directive (recast) define the scope of the application of *non-refoulement* in EU law. Although the EU is itself not a States Party to the Refugee Convention or the Protocol, all of the EU Member States are signatories to, and have ratified, both treaties and the EU itself is bound by the TFEU.[33] Article 78 of the TFEU provides the legal basis for the EU to comply with the principle of *non-refoulement*: this Article obliges EU Member States to establish a common European asylum policy which complies with the Refugee Convention and the Protocol. Additionally, the principle of *non-refoulement* articulated as the prohibition against return to torture is found under Article 19(2) of the EU Charter, which states that:

> no one may be removed, expelled or extradited to a State where there is a serious risk that he or she would be subjected to the death penalty, torture or other inhuman or degrading treatment or punishment.[34]

---

[26] *Ibid.*

[27] *Ibid.*

[28] *Ibid.*

[29] *Ibid.*

[30] Europa (2016a) "EU Institutions and Other Bodies".

[31] *Ibid.*

[32] *Ibid.*

[33] European Parliament (2013) at 6; TFEU at art 78.

[34] EU Charter at art 19(2).

The principle of *non-refoulement* is therefore violated when an EU Member State removes a person if there is a real risk of ill-treatment in the receiving State, whether or not the removed person is actually ill-treated in the receiving State.[35] Article 15(b) of the Qualification Directive (recast) similarly recognizes the importance of the principle of *non-refoulement* and extends 'subsidiary protection'—in other words, complementary protection—for asylum claimants who do not meet the definition of 'refugee' under Article 1A of the Refugee Convention.[36] Under Article 15(b), 'subsidiary protection' may be provided to those facing 'serious harm', consisting of 'torture or inhuman or degrading treatment or punishment of an applicant in the country of origin'.[37]

The legally-binding nature of EU primary and secondary legislation determines how this legislation is applied in the EU. For example, EU Member States are automatically bound by EU regulations and decisions on the date they take effect.[38] Directives, however, must first be incorporated into domestic legislation by EU Member States.[39] The EU Commission monitors whether EU Member States have correctly applied EU law and the CJEU ensures that EU laws are interpreted and applied uniformly across all EU Member States.[40] The clauses concerning *non-refoulement* in both primary and secondary EU law all use the terms 'no one', 'any person', or 'no person', so that asylum claimants, refugees *and* all Third-Country Nationals are protected under those provisions.[41] (A 'Third-Country National' is an individual who is a non-EU citizen who is also not a person enjoying the EU right to free movement).[42]

The Schengen Area and its application to freedom of movement define the scope of EU law as it is applied to Third-Country Nationals. Under EU law, States have the sovereign right to control the entry and presence of non-nationals in their territories.[43] However, EU law and the ECHR impose certain limitations on this sovereignty, namely, that rejections at the border of individuals at risk of persecution or other serious harm in contravention of the principle of *non-refoulement* is not permitted.[44] The Schengen *acquis* establishes 'a unified system for maintaining external border controls and allows individuals to travel freely across borders

[35] Hamdan, Eman (2016) at 16 [Hamdan].

[36] See, generally: McAdam, Jane (2007); Qualification Directive at art 15(b); Refugee Convention at art 1A; See, also: McAdam, Jane (2007) at chp 2 [McAdam Complementary Protection].

[37] Qualification Directive at art 15(b).

[38] European Commission, "Applying EU Law".

[39] *Ibid*; However, it is up to the Member State in question to incorporate the directors into their domestic law.

[40] European Union (2016) "Court of Justice of the European Union (CJEU)".

[41] Moreno-Lax, Violeta (2017a) at 289 [Moreno-Lax]; See, also: EU Charter at arts 4 and 19(2).

[42] European Commission, Migration and Home Affairs (2016) "Third-Country National".

[43] Council of Europe (2014) at 26 [EU Handbook].

[44] *Ibid;* For the protection from *refoulement* under EU law, see: Qualification Directive at art 15(b); For the Council of Europe, see: ECHR at art 3.

within the Schengen Area'.[45] The Schengen Area guarantees freedom of movement for EU nationals and those who are legally present.[46] The Schengen Area was established in 1985 when the Governments of the States of Benelux Economic Union, the Federal Republic of Germany, and the French Republic signed the *Convention Implementing the Schengen Agreement* of 1985.[47] The Schengen Area 'entitles every EU citizen to travel, work and live in any EU country without special formalities'.[48] The Schengen Area encompasses the very idea of freedom of movement as guaranteed under Article 45 of the EU Charter.[49] The Schengen Area applies to most EU Member States except for Iceland, Liechtenstein, Norway, and Switzerland.[50] As a result of Brexit, the United Kingdom has reached an agreement with the Council of the European Union and the EU Parliament to include the United Kingdom in Part 1 Annex II of Regulation 2018/1806 on possession of visas for third country nationals.[51] This means that, although after Brexit, 'the Treaties and Directive 2004/38/EC, along with the right to enter the territory of the Member States without a visa or equivalent formalities, will cease to apply to nationals of the United Kingdom who are British citizens', including the United Kingdom in the annex of Regulation 2018/1806, British citizens will be exempt from the visa requirement.[52] Article 21 of the *Convention Implementing the Schengen Agreement* provides that Third-Country Nationals who hold 'uniform visas and who have legally entered the territory of a Schengen state may freely move within the whole Schengen Area while their visas are still valid'.[53] The Schengen Area was at risk of collapse due to the mass influx of asylum claimants into and across Europe since the beginning of the Syrian war in 2011, leading to the temporary reinstatement of border controls by some EU Member States within the Schengen Area.[54] This is examined in more detail in the next chapter.

---

[45] EU Handbook at 27.

[46] European Commission, Migration and Home Affairs (2016) [Schengen Area].

[47] *Convention implementing the Schengen Agreement of 14 June 1985 between the Governments of States of the Benelux Economic Union, the Federal Republic of Germany and the French Republic on the gradual abolition of checks at their common borders*, OJ 2000 L249/19.

[48] Schengen Area.

[49] EU Charter at art 45.

[50] EU Handbook at 27.

[51] Council of the European Union (2019) "Proposal for a Regulation of the European Parliament and of the Council amending Council Regulation (EC) No 539/2001 listing the third countries whose nationals must be in possession of visas when crossing the external borders and those whose nationals are exempt from that requirement, as regards the withdrawal of the United Kingdom from the Union—Confirmation of the final compromise text with a view to agreement", 2018/0390(COD) at 6, para 3.

[52] *Ibid.*

[53] EU Handbook at 29; Third Country Nationals are defined as 'anyone who is not a citizen of an EU country' in EUR-Lex (2016).

[54] Library of Congress (2016) "Refugee Law and Policy: European Union".

The content of EU law in the asylum context is found in the key instruments comprising the CEAS and its procedures. The history of the CEAS began in 1999 when the European Commission started working with Member States to create a common asylum policy.[55] The central aim of the CEAS is to establish a harmonized, fair, and effective asylum procedure to process asylum claims across EU Member States, while complying with international law obligations to protect asylum claimants fleeing from persecution.[56] The CEAS was established under Article 78 of the TFEU, which provides that the CEAS must respect EU Member States' obligations under the Refugee Convention and Protocol (which includes the prohibition on *refoulement*).[57] The CEAS also has related aims, expressed in different ways. For example, the European Council indicates that the CEAS is meant to assist with the development of the EU as 'an area of freedom, security and justice'.[58] Additionally, the European Commission's *Policy Plan on Asylum* in 2008 stated that the CEAS is meant to: harmonize the standards of protection by aligning EU Member States' asylum legislation; enhance effectiveness and support practical cooperation among EU Member States on matters relating to asylum; and increase solidarity and responsibility-sharing among EU Member States and between EU and non-EU Member States.[59] With all of these goals in mind, the instruments comprising the CEAS are meant to create clarity in determining the EU Member State responsible for processing asylum applications, set common standards for a fair and efficient asylum procedure, indicate common minimum conditions of reception of asylum applicants, and establish the rules on recognition and granting of refugee status.[60] They create a minimum standard for EU Member States, although the instruments provide room for State interpretation as to how substantive and procedural CEAS rules are implemented into domestic legislation.[61]

The CEAS has been reformed in three phases. Phase I of the CEAS, from 1999 to 2003, focused on the adoption of legislation necessary to implement common minimum standards for asylum,[62] including on the reception of asylum claimants, qualification of claimants for international protection, the content of the protection granted, and procedures for granting and withdrawing refugee status.[63] The first phase involved the drafting and adoption of the Qualification Directive, the Asylum Procedures Directive, the Reception Conditions Directive, the Dublin Convention, the Eurodac Regulation, the Temporary Protection Directive and the Family

[55] CEAS at 331.

[56] Refugee Convention at art 1A; CEAS.

[57] TFEU at art 78.

[58] EUR-Lex (2016) "Justice, Freedom and Security".

[59] *Ibid;* See also: Commission of the European Communities (2018) at 4.

[60] *Ibid.*

[61] *Ibid* at 31; TEU at arts 63(1) and (2)(a).

[62] CEAS.

[63] European Asylum Support Office (2016) at 15.

Reunification Directive.[64] The second phase took place from 2004 to 2013.[65] Phase II reformed Phase I of the CEAS and involved five main measures: recasting the Qualification Directive from 2004 to 2011/95/EU, recasting the Asylum Procedures Directive from 2005 to 2013/32/EU, recasting the Reception Conditions Directive from 2003 to 2013/33/EU, recasting the Dublin II Regulation from 2003 to Dublin III Regulation (604/2013), and recasting the Eurodac Regulation from 2000 to 2013.[66] The CEAS is currently in its third phase, and is now being discussed before the European Council.[67] The first package of the third phase to reform the CEAS was presented in May 2018, which included a proposal to recast the Qualification Directive and the Asylum Procedures Directive from directives into binding regulations, a recast of the Reception Conditions Directive, and a 'Dublin IV' Proposal.[68] This work is still ongoing.

Of all of the instruments mentioned, the central instruments of the CEAS are the Dublin Convention (1990), the Dublin II Regulation (2003), the Dublin III Regulation (2013), and three key directives: Qualification Directive (2011/95/EU), the Asylum Procedures Directive (2013/32/EU), and the Reception Conditions Directive (2013/33/EU), which together are known as the 'Dublin System'.[69] The Dublin III Regulation is an instrument which sets out the criteria which determines the Member State responsible for determining asylum applications for Third-Country Nationals and stateless persons.[70] Under the Dublin III Regulation, Article 3(2) allows Member States to send the asylum claimant back to the Member State responsible as determined by the Regulation based on a set criterion (termed 'Dublin transfer').[71] For instance, the practice in some Member States such as Germany is that, a 'personal conversation' takes place to allow the asylum claimant to explain to the asylum official any reasons why a deportation to

---

64 Statewatch (2013a) "Analysis: The second phase of the Common European Asylum System: A Brave New World—or lipstick on a pig?" at 2–3; See, also: Council Directive 2001/55/EC of 20 July 2001 on minimum standards for giving temporary protection in the event of a mass influx of displaced persons and on measures promoting a balance of efforts between Member States in receiving such persons and bearing the consequences thereof, OJ L212/12, 7 August 2001; Council Directive 2003/86/EC of 22 September 2003 on the right to family reunification, OJ L251/12, 3 October 2003.

65 *Ibid* at 16.

66 *Ibid.*

67 *Ibid.*

68 European Council (2016) "Timeline: Reform of EU Asylum Rules".

69 Dublin III Regulation at 25; Qualification Directive at art 15(b); Asylum Procedures Directive at recital 12; Reception Conditions Directive at art 1.

70 *Ibid;* The UK has opted into the Dublin III Regulation, see, for example: Costello, Cathryn (2014a) at 5, which states: 'the UK has opted in to the Dublin III Regulation, which purports to address some of the problems outlined above. In particular, the reform provides for crisis-prevention and cooperation measures between Member States, places limits on detention of asylum seekers, and prevents transfer of a person where there is a real risk of violating a fundamental right' [Costello Policy Primer].

71 Dublin III Regulation at art 3(2).

another Dublin State could be impeded, such as the existence of relatives in Germany. The Qualification Directive sets out the procedures for determining Third-Country Nationals and stateless persons who qualify for international protection and for subsidiary protection.[72] The Asylum Procedures Directive sets out the standards which Member States are to follow in the granting and withdrawing of international protection.[73] Finally, the Reception Conditions Directive sets out the standards which Member States are to follow for the reception conditions—the conditions under which applicants for international protection live within the host state.[74]

Of these CEAS documents, as mentioned earlier, Article 15(b) of the Qualification Directive (recast) directly recognizes the importance of the principle of *non-refoulement*. As well, *non-refoulement* is also formulated under Articles 28(2), 35(b), 39(4), 41, and Annex I (c) of the Asylum Procedures Directive.[75] The recitals of the three key directives of the CEAS, although non-binding as they are not the operative provisions of the directive, also reiterate some form of *non-refoulement*.[76] Apart from these explicit references to *non-refoulement*, the common procedures created by the Dublin System are meant to provide a shared framework which fulfills EU Member States' obligations under the Refugee Convention and protect claimants against violations of their rights, including the right not to be *refouled*.

[72] Qualification Directive.

[73] Asylum Procedures Directive.

[74] Reception Conditions Directive.

[75] Asylum Procedures Directive at art 28(2) states: 'Member States shall ensure that such a person is not removed contrary to the principle of non-refoulement'; Article 35(b) states: 'he or she otherwise enjoys sufficient protection in that country, including benefiting from the principle of non- refoulement [. . .]'; Article 38 states: 'the principle of non-refoulement in accordance with the Geneva Convention is respected'; Article 39(4) states: 'The Member States concerned shall lay down in national law the modalities for implementing the provisions of paragraph 1 and the consequences of decisions pursuant to those provisions in accordance with the principle of non-refoulement, including providing for exceptions from the application of this Article for humanitarian or political reasons or for reasons of public international law'; Article 41 states: 'Member States may make such an exception only where the determining authority considers that a return decision will not lead to direct or indirect refoulement in violation of that Member State's international and Union obligations'; Annex I (c) states: 'respect for the non-refoulement principle in accordance with the Geneva Convention'.

[76] See, for example: Asylum Procedures Directive at recital para 3, which states: 'The European Council, at its special meeting in Tampere on 15 and 16 October 1999, agreed to work towards establishing a Common European Asylum System, based on the full and inclusive application of the *Geneva Convention Relating to the Status of Refugees* of 28 July 1951, as amended by the *New York Protocol* of 31 January 1967 ('the Geneva Convention'), thus affirming the principle of non-refoulement and ensuring that nobody is sent back to persecution'; For the binding nature of EU directives, see: Case C-162/97, *Nilsson* [1998] ECR I-7477 at para 54: 'the preamble to a Community act has no binding legal force and cannot be relied on as a ground for derogating from the actual provisions of the act in question'; See, also: Baratta, Robert (2014).

The above-mentioned ongoing negotiations for Phase III of the reforms of the CEAS include proposals to recast the Qualification Directive and the Asylum Procedures Directive from directives into regulations; this phase also includes the proposal to reform the Dublin III Regulation into 'Dublin IV'.[77] Both proposals could be a positive step towards deeper respect for the principle of *non-refoulement*. A 'directive' of the EU is a legislative act establishing a goal that all EU countries must achieve, but requires domestic legislation in order to transpose the provisions within each EU country.[78] A 'regulation' of the EU, on the other hand, is a binding legislative act, which must be applied in its entirety across the EU.[79] Recasting the key instruments of the CEAS from directives to regulations results in directly imposing asylum policies of the EU upon Member States, rather than requiring Member States to transpose them into domestic legislation. Requiring Member States to transpose their EU law obligations into domestic law through directives potentially leaves each country a wide 'margin of appreciation' or 'margin of discretion' in the transposition of such provisions and could lead to the circumvention of international law, including *non-refoulement* obligations, in instances when a Member State's interpretation of *non-refoulement* obligations are overly narrow.[80] Thus, the Phase III reforms could help to eliminate the variability in EU Member States' interpretations of the prohibition against *refoulement*.

The proposal to improve the Dublin III Regulation, termed 'Dublin IV', is currently underway, but the proposal has already received criticism from various academic commentators and nongovernmental organizations.[81] Among the critiques is the claim that the 'Dublin IV' proposal, in contrast with the Dublin III Regulation, intends to determine responsibility for examining asylum applications based on a formula calculated using the Member States' population size as well as Gross Domestic Product.[82] The problem with this formula is that the uneven

---

[77] See, generally: Costello, Cathryn (2014a) [Costello Migration Observatory]; European Parliament (2017) "The Common European Asylum System—Third Reform".

[78] European Union (2018).

[79] *Ibid.*

[80] This issue was explored in more detail in: Poon, Jenny (2016b) [Poon MOA]; See above for an explanation of the distinctions between a 'margin of appreciation' and a 'margin of discretion'.

[81] See, for example: Peers, Steve (2016); Di Filippo, Marcello (2016); International Commission of Jurists (2016); European Council on Refugee and Exiles (2016).

[82] The formula variables are: the population, total Gross Domestic Product (GDP), the average number of asylum applications over the 5 preceding years per million inhabitants with a cap of 30% of the population and GDP, and the unemployment rate with a cap of 30% of the population and GDP of the EU Member State in European Commission, "Proposal for a Regulation of the European Parliament and of the Council establishing a crisis relocation mechanism and amending Regulation (EU) No 604/2013 of the European Parliament and of the Council of 26 June 2013 establishing the criteria and mechanisms for determining the Member State responsible for examining an application for international protection lodged in one of the Member States by a third country national or a stateless person", 2015/0208 (COD), Brussels, 9 September 2015 at 10–13.

'burden' faced by Member States geographically situated near the external borders of the EU, including the burden of ensuring individuals are not *refouled*, is not considered.[83]

In sum, EU law contains several important protections against *refoulement* of individuals. Article 78 of the TFEU obliges EU Member States to establish a common European asylum policy which complies with the Refugee Convention and the Protocol, including the prohibition on *refoulement*. Article 19(2) of the EU Charter prohibits an individual being sent to a country where there is a serious risk that he or she would be subjected to the death penalty, torture or other inhuman or degrading treatment or punishment. Article 15(b) of the Qualification Directive (recast) also recognizes the importance of the principle of *non-refoulement*. Another direct mention of *non-refoulement* within the EU Directives is found in paragraph 3 of the recital of the Reception Conditions Directive (recast).[84] The CEAS itself also creates the framework of agreed rules which establish common procedures for asylum across the EU—procedures which are meant to more generally assist EU Member States in meeting their refugee law obligations, including protection against *non-refoulement*.[85] Although heavily referenced within key EU directives of the CEAS, the practice of EU law often reveals procedural and substantive gaps within the interpretation and implementation of *non-refoulement* in reality. Given the centrality of the principle of *non-refoulement* in international refugee law, it is important that the interpretation and implementation of *non-refoulement* in EU law is in line with the minimum international standards set by the Refugee Convention.

EU law and the CEAS framework co-exist with ECHR law, described in the next subsection. When considering the content of the principle of *non-refoulement* within Europe, it is important to consider both EU law and ECHR law together.

3.2.2 ECHR Law

The Council of Europe is a separate entity from the EU and is an international organization focused on human rights, democracy, and the rule of law, comprised of the 47 Member States that acceded to the ECHR.[86] All current 27 EU Member

[83] This issue is further explored in: Poon, Jeny (2016b).

[84] Reception Conditions Directive at recital para 3: 'At its special meeting in Tampere on 15 and 16 October 1999, the European Council agreed to work towards establishing a Common European Asylum System, based on the full and inclusive application of the *Geneva Convention Relating to the Status of Refugees* of 28 July 1951, as supplemented by the *New York Protocol* of 31 January 1967 ('the Geneva Convention'), thus affirming the principle of non-refoulement. The first phase of a Common European Asylum System was achieved through the adoption of relevant legal instruments, including Directive 2003/9/EC, provided for in the Treaties'.

[85] CEAS.

[86] Council of Europe (2016) "Values: Human Rights, Democracy, and Rule of Law".

States are members of the Council of Europe.[87] A main body of the Council of Europe is the ECtHR, located in Strasbourg, which is tasked with monitoring Council of Europe Member States' compliance with the ECHR.[88]

The ECtHR creates jurisprudence stemming from interpretations of the ECHR. Article 3 of the ECHR is important in the asylum context because it codifies *non-refoulement* protection in the form of the prohibition against torture in ECHR law.[89] Article 3 states: 'no one shall be subjected to torture or to inhuman or degrading treatment or punishment'.[90] The ECtHR has been 'characterized as the vanguard institution on *non-refoulement* [. . .] substantively leading the development of international law' on this principle.[91] A foundational case in this respect is *Soering v. the United Kingdom,* in which the Strasbourg court decided that, although States Parties to the ECHR have the right to control the entry, residence, and expulsion of aliens through domestic legislation, this right is not absolute and is restricted by their obligations under the ECHR, such as the requirement to comply with the prohibition against torture under Article 3.[92] This prohibition against torture is an absolute prohibition, as indicated by the ECtHR in other cases such as *Ireland v. the United Kingdom.*[93] It has also been held by the ECtHR that the obligation of *non-refoulement* under Article 3 of the ECHR extends to cases where there is a real risk of cruel treatment in the receiving State.[94] The ECtHR has interpreted Article 3 to include acts that may give rise to potential future breaches of the principle upon removal to another country.[95]

As determined by the case law of the ECtHR, Article 3 involves interpreting two prohibited acts, namely: 'torture' and 'inhuman and degrading treatment or punishment'.[96] In *The Greek Case,* the European Commission on Human Rights held that:

> All torture must be inhuman and degrading treatment, and inhuman treatment [is] also degrading. The notion of inhuman treatment covers at least such treatment as deliberately [causing] severe suffering, mental or physical, which, in the particular situation, is [unjustifiable. Torture] has a purpose, such as the obtaining of information or confessions, or the infliction of punishment, and it is generally an aggravated form of inhuman

[87] Europe in Strasbourg (2016) "Member States of the European Union and the Council of Europe".

[88] Council of Europe (2016).

[89] ECHR at art 3.

[90] *Ibid.*

[91] Cali, Basak, Costello, Cathryn, and Cunningham, Stewart (2020) at 357 [Cali et al].

[92] Soering at para 85.

[93] *Ireland v the United Kingdom,* Application No 5310/71, Council of Europe: European Court of Human Rights, 18 January 1978 at para 163.

[94] Soering at para 88 and 91.

[95] Moreno-Lax at 267.

[96] See, for example: Long, Debra (2002) [Debra Long].

> treatment. Treatment or punishment of an individual may be said to be degrading if it grossly humiliates him [or her] before others or drives him [or her] to act against his [or her] will or conscience.[97]

According to *The Greek Case*, therefore, the distinction between 'torture' and 'inhuman and degrading treatment or punishment' is that the former is 'an aggravated form of inhuman treatment', while the latter would involve deliberately causing treatment that may not amount to 'torture' but is nonetheless unjustifiable in the particular situation.[98]

The judgments from the ECtHR are binding upon the States Parties concerned.[99] Some EU Member States have directly incorporated provisions of the ECHR within their domestic law or have added provisions within their domestic law to enforce rights provided under the ECHR.[100]

The scope of ECHR law, especially Article 3 on *non-refoulement* protection in the form of the prohibition against return to torture, includes the application of the provision both territorially and extraterritorially. The obligation of *non-refoulement* arises at the moment in time when an asylum claimant is at the border of an EU Member State, which includes both territorial waters and transit zones.[101] However, this obligation does not arise unless the State exercises jurisdiction.[102] A State may exercise its jurisdiction over a person or a territory.[103] With respect to exercising jurisdiction over a person, Article 1 of the ECHR guarantees its rights and freedoms to 'everyone'.[104] The protection against *refoulement* therefore is guaranteed to *all* individuals regardless of their status under the law, in contrast with Article 33(1) of the Refugee Convention, which protects only asylum claimants and refugees.[105] ECHR case law and the UN Committee Against Torture both apply the principle to protect those without status under the law, including

---

97 European Commission of Human Rights, *The Greek Case*, App nos 3321/67, 3322/67, 3323/67 and 3344/67 (1969) *Yearbook of European Convention on Human Rights* at 186; See, also: Debra Long at 14.

98 *Ibid.*

99 ECHR at art 46(1); See, also: European Court of Human Rights (2014) at 9.

100 See, for example: *Human Rights Act* [1998] c 42 at s 2(1): 'A court or tribunal determining a question which has arisen in connection with a Convention right must take into account any [...] judgment, decision, declaration or advisory opinion of the European Court of Human Rights [...] whenever made or given, so far as, in the opinion of the court or tribunal, it is relevant to the proceedings in which that question has arisen'; Durham University, "Are UK Courts bound by the European Court of Human Rights?", *Law School Research Briefing No 10* at 1.

101 Council of Europe (2014) *Handbook on European Law relating to Asylum, Borders and Immigration* (Strasbourg: Council of Europe Publishing) at 35 [COE Handbook].

102 Hamdan at 35.

103 Crawford, James (2012) at 462 [Crawford].

104 ECHR at art 1.

105 Hamdan at 36–37.

refused asylum claimants and those deprived of protection under Article 1F of the Refugee Convention.[106]

Extraterritorial application of *non-refoulement* under Article 3 of the ECHR has been affirmed by ECHR case law, particularly in *Bankovic* et al *v. Belgium and 16 Other Contracting States*.[107] In that case, the ECtHR held that there are two grounds for extraterritorial application of *non-refoulement*, namely: the State, through its agents, over an individual outside of its territory, and the State over an area outside of its national territory.[108] The jurisdiction clause under Article 1 of the ECHR is the norm, which states that 'the High States Parties shall secure to everyone *within their jurisdiction* the rights and freedoms defined in Section 1 of this Convention' (emphasis added).[109] There are three exceptions to the norm as interpreted by the ECtHR. First, a State exercises jurisdiction extraterritorially through its diplomatic and consular agents.[110] Where a State's diplomatic and consular agents exercise authority and control over individuals, that State then has jurisdiction over those individuals, through the acts or omissions of the State's agents.[111] Whether the act or omission of a State's agent constitutes effective control is a matter of fact, determined in light of the circumstances of each case.[112] Second, in some cases, the use of force by a State's agents outside of the State's territory may bring an individual under the control of these agents into the State's jurisdiction.[113] For instance, where an individual is in the custody of a State's agent extraterritorially, the State's jurisdiction extends to the acts of the State's agent, so that the State is under an obligation not to *refoule* the individual in custody to torture or other cruel treatment.[114] Third, through consent, invitation or acquiescence of a foreign State's government, a State may exercise all or some of the public powers normally exercised by that foreign State's government.[115] For example, the jurisdiction of the State will extend to the acts or omissions of

---

[106] See, for example: Committee Against Torture, *SV et al v Canada,* Communication No 48/1996, 15 May 2001; *Jabari v Turkey,* Application No 40035/98, Council of Europe: European Court of Human Rights, 11 July 2000.

[107] Bankovic at para 132; This view is supported by the UNHCR, for more, see: UNHCR Advisory Opinion.

[108] *Ibid;* See also: Wilde, Ralph (2010) at 324.

[109] ECHR at art 1.

[110] *WM v Denmark,* Application No 17392/90, Council of Europe: European Court of Human Rights, 14 October 1992.

[111] Bankovic at para 73; *Al-Skeini and Others v the United Kingdom,* Application No 55721/07, Council of Europe: European Court of Human Rights, 7 July 2011 at para 134 [Al-Skeini].

[112] Hirsi at para 73.

[113] Al-Skeini at para 134.

[114] Hamdan at 48; See also: *Ocalan v Turkey* Application No 6221/99, Council of Europe: European Court of Human Rights, 12 May 2005 at para 88.

[115] Bankovic at para 71.

immigration border officers checking travel documents for asylum claimants outside the State's territory.[116]

Relevant to the consideration of jurisdiction as envisioned by Article 1 of the ECHR, are three conceptual models examined by scholars.[117] First, scholars contend that the first such conceptual model is the Spatial Model, which sees the exercise of 'public powers' as, in its entirety, amounting to jurisdiction. For example, where there is exercise of 'public powers', the State exercises jurisdiction. The exercise of 'public powers' is not a factor to consider nor is it a prerequisite to State jurisdiction—rather, it is automatic in that, once it can be established that 'public powers' are exercised by the Government of a Member State, such Member State *has* jurisdiction over the territory and individuals in question.[118] The second conceptual model regarding State jurisdiction pondered by Article 1 of the ECHR is the Personal Model. In this model, scholars maintain that the exercise of 'public powers' is *relevant* to the consideration of State jurisdiction. For instance, the exercise of 'public powers' is a *factor to consider* when determining jurisdiction and is not in itself conclusive. Even in situations where an official or State agent exercises 'public powers', the State may or may not exercise jurisdiction.[119] In the third conceptual model when considering State jurisdiction as contemplated by Article 1 of the ECHR, scholars suggest that the exercise of 'public powers' is a *prerequisite* to the consideration of State jurisdiction. As a requirement, there must be an exercise of 'public powers' *before* a determination can be made with regards to jurisdiction. Hence, if the official or State agent does *not* exercise 'public powers' over the individual or territory, the State does *not* exercise jurisdiction.[120]

The protection against *refoulement* under Article 3 of the ECHR as developed by Strasbourg case law is wider than that provided by Article 33(1) of the Refugee Convention.[121] Subsequent expulsion cases by the ECtHR have reaffirmed this position.[122] The protection from *refoulement* guaranteed under Article 3 of the ECHR is also wider than the protection against torture as required under Article 3 of the *Convention Against Torture*, in that Article 3 of the ECHR not only protects individuals from being returned where a real risk of torture exists, but also offers individuals protection from being expelled where there is a real risk of cruel treatment.[123]

---

[116] Hamdan at 50.

[117] Ryngaert, Cedric (2012) at 58–59.

[118] *Bankovic.*

[119] *Al-Skeini.*

[120] *MN and Others v Belgium,* Application No 3599/18, Council of Europe: European Court of Human Rights, 5 May 2020 [MN]; For analysis on *MN,* see: Stoyanova, Vladislava (2020).

[121] *Ahmed v Austria,* Application No 25964/94, Council of Europe: European Court of Human Rights, 17 December 1996 at para 41; *N v Finland,* Application No 38,885/02, Council of Europe: European Court of Human Rights, 26 July 2005 at para 159.

[122] *D v the United Kingdom,* Application No 30240/96, Council of Europe: European Court of Human Rights, 2 May 1997 at para 48.

[123] Weissbrodt and Hörtreiter (1999) at 50 [Weissbrodt and Hörtreiter]; Duffy, A (2008) at 379.

Additionally, the ECtHR has recognized that *non-refoulement* applies in a wider number of circumstances than identified in the Refugee Convention. For instance, the return of claimants to situations where they may not be able to access the right to fair trial, situations where the return would cause material deprivations due to scarce resources, or situations in which the claimants will suffer from severe and targeted discrimination (for example, against persons with disabilities), all constitute a violation of *non-refoulement* under EU law and ECHR law.[124] Where a low recognition rate means a lesser likelihood for an individual claimant to be recognized as a refugee, the result may lead to unfairness rising to the level of a 'flagrant denial of justice'.[125] Although the phrase 'flagrant denial of justice' has not been precisely defined by the ECtHR, the ECtHR has indicated that certain forms of unfairness could amount to a 'flagrant denial of justice'.[126] These forms of unfairness include conviction *in absentia* with no subsequent possibility of a fresh determination of the merits of the charge, detention without any access to an independent and impartial tribunal to have the legality of the detention reviewed, and deliberate and systematic refusal of access to a lawyer.[127]

A discussion of the content of ECHR law includes examining the burden and standard of proof of establishing treatment that is contrary to Article 3. The burden of proof is upon the individual asylum claimant to establish individualized or particularized risk of treatment contrary to the prohibition against torture upon expulsion.[128] The standard of proof for the individual asylum claimant to prove is substantial grounds for believing that he or she would be exposed to a real risk of inhuman or degrading treatment or punishment on return, contrary to Article 3 of the ECHR.[129] The nature of 'risk' to be proven by the asylum claimant is that of 'risk of inhuman or degrading treatment or punishment'.[130] As mentioned earlier, *non-refoulement* in the form of the prohibition against torture is an absolute prohibition, so that even where the individual claimant is found to have been guilty of committing any of the remunerated crimes under Article 1 F of the Refugee Convention, the claimant cannot be returned to face torture.[131] Under the ECHR,

---

[124] See, for example: Costello (2016b) [Costello Outer Edges]; EU Charter at art 47; ECHR at art 6.

[125] See Othman; *D v United Kingdom* App no App no 30240/96 (ECHR, 2 May 1997); *SHH v United Kingdom* App no 60367/10 (ECHR, 29 January 2013).

[126] European Court of Human Rights (2018) at para 498.

[127] *Einhorn v France* App no 71555/01 (ECHR, 16 October 2001) at para 33; *Al-Moayad v Germany* App no 35865/03 (ECHR, 20 February 2007) at para 101.

[128] COE Handbook at Chapter 3.

[129] *Ibid* at 75.

[130] *Ibid.*

[131] On the absolute prohibition against torture, see: *Saadi v Italy,* Application No 37201/06, Council of Europe: European Court of Human Rights, 28 February 2008 at para 138 and Committee Against Torture, *MBB v Sweden,* Application No 104/1998 at para 6.4; For exclusion of international protection for persons who do not deserve it, see: Qualification Directive at arts 12 and 17.

any individual who wishes to make a claim for protection under Article 3 of the ECHR can do so at the ECtHR, regardless of that individual's legal status, which means the individual need not be seeking asylum or be recognized as a refugee to benefit from this protection.[132]

In sum, the principle of *non-refoulement* under EU law and ECHR law, formulated as the prohibition against return to torture, is absolute in nature such that no derogation from the principle is permitted. The principle of *non-refoulement* is also applicable both within the territory of the sending State, as well as extraterritorially, as an exception to the general rule provided for under Article 1 of the ECHR.

3.3 Claiming Asylum in the EU

The above subsections examined the structure and content of EU law and ECHR law as well as the jurisprudence of the CJEU and the ECtHR courts relevant to the principle of *non-refoulement*. In order to understand the context in which the principle of *non-refoulement* arises in the EU context, it is vital to understand the procedures involved in claiming asylum within the EU. This section therefore details the procedures for claiming asylum within the EU. It begins by introducing the Dublin III Regulation, the current instrument for determining the Member State responsible for processing asylum applications. It then discusses the process for qualifying for international protection. Next, it explains the procedures and standards for the granting and withdrawing of international protection. Finally, it ends by exploring the standards for reception conditions for applicants of international protection. The application of the principle of *non-refoulement* is discussed at each stage.

3.3.1 Dublin III Regulation and the Determination of the Member State Responsible

The Dublin III Regulation (604/2013) is the current CEAS instrument determining the Member State responsible for the processing of asylum applications.[133] It sets out the criteria and mechanisms for making such a determination.[134] It provides that a single Member State is responsible for processing an asylum application when it is deemed responsible.[135] Where no Member State is designated as responsible for

[132] ECHR at art 1.

[133] Dublin III Regulation.

[134] *Ibid.*

[135] *Ibid* at art 3(1).

the processing of the asylum application on the basis of the criteria listed in the Dublin III Regulation, the Member State responsible shall be the first Member State in which the application for international protection has been lodged.[136]

The criteria for determining the Member State responsible for the processing of asylum applications are set out based on a hierarchy.[137] First, where the applicant is an unaccompanied minor, the Member State responsible shall be the Member State where a family member or a sibling of the unaccompanied minor is legally present.[138] In the absence of a family member or a sibling or relative, the Member State responsible shall be the Member State where the unaccompanied minor has lodged his or her application for international protection, provided that it is in the best interests of the child.[139] Second, where the applicant is in possession of a valid residence document, the Member State which issued the residency document shall be responsible for the examination of the asylum application.[140] Where the applicant is in possession of a valid visa, the Member State responsible for the processing of the asylum application shall be the Member State which issued the visa.[141] Where the applicant is in possession of more than one valid residence document or visa issued by more than one Member State, the Member State responsible shall be the Member State which issued the residence document or visa having the latest expiry date.[142] Third, where the applicant has irregularly crossed the border into a Member State by land, sea or air having come from a third country, the Member State deemed responsible for the processing of the asylum application shall be the Member State he or she first entered.[143] Fourth, where the applicant made the application for international protection in the international transit area of an airport of a Member State, that Member State where the application was made shall be responsible for the processing of the asylum application.[144] The responsible EU Member State identified through this process is the Member State bearing the responsibility to enforce the principle of *non-refoulement*.

Figure 3.1 depicts the above description of the Dublin III process for determining the Member State responsible for processing asylum applications.

The section below examines the process for qualifying for international protection and the asylum procedures involved.

---

[136] *Ibid* at art 3(2).

[137] *Ibid* at chp III.

[138] *Ibid* at art 8; This is to be done in accordance with the best interests of the child international standard.

[139] *Ibid* at art 8(4).

[140] *Ibid* at art 12(1).

[141] *Ibid* at art 12(2).

[142] *Ibid* at arts 12(3)(a) and 12(3)(b).

[143] *Ibid* at art 13(1).

[144] *Ibid* at art 15.

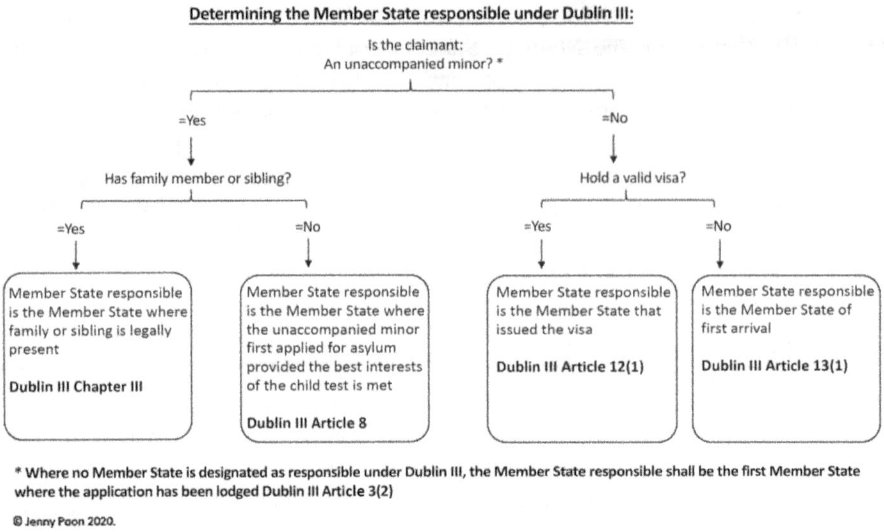

Fig. 3.1 Determining the Member State responsible under Dublin III

3.3.2 *Qualifying for International Protection and Relevant Asylum Procedures*

Once the responsible Member State is designated, the Qualification Directive (2011/95/EU) requires that Member State to ensure minimum common standards for applicants of international protection to qualify for refugee and subsidiary protection.[145] The Asylum Procedures Directive (2013/32/EU) also determines the common minimum standards and procedures for the granting and—crucially for the principle of *non-refoulement*—withdrawing of international protection.[146] The minimum common standards referenced in the Qualification Directive and the Asylum Procedures Directive are the bare minimum standards which EU Member States are to follow when they implement relevant EU law in domestic practice.[147] Therefore, it is important to first ascertain what the common minimum standards

[145] Qualification Directive. Subsidiary protection is protection that is complementary in nature to refugee status for individuals who cannot meet the refugee definition under Article 1A of the Refugee Convention: McAdam at chp 2.

[146] Asylum Procedures Directive.

[147] See, for example: CEAS, which states: 'Asylum is a fundamental right and granting it is an international obligation, stemming from the 1951 Geneva Convention on the protection of refugees. Those who seek, or have been granted, protection do not have the right to choose in which Member State they want to settle. To this end, the Common European Asylum System (CEAS) provides common minimum standards for the treatment of all asylum seekers and applications".

are before turning to the core *non-refoulement* rights granted by both directives under EU law.

In order to understand the points at which the principle of *non-refoulement* may become an issue, it is important to first ascertain the different stages from registration to appeal for an asylum application under the Asylum Procedures Directive (recast).

At the first stage of the asylum process, EU Member States are obliged to assess the relevant elements of each application for international protection, which consists of: 'documentation regarding the applicant's age, background including relatives, identity, nationality(ies), country(ies) and place(s) of previous residence, previous asylum applications, travel routes, travel documents and the reasons for applying for international protection'.[148] At the second stage of the asylum process, applicants are triaged into caseload streams, and analysis is begun based on country of origin information.[149] As the application of these processes at Stages 1 and 2 do not contemplate return of the individuals, the principle of *non-refoulement* is not engaged. However, proper fulfilment of information collection at both stages is crucial, as incorrect information collection can heighten the chances of an applicant later being denied protection and therefore the risk of being *refouled* based on flawed assumptions. The standardized process within the CEAS is therefore designed with the aim of ensuring adequate information collection.

Stages 3 and 4 are central to the asylum determination process. During Stage 3, an initial assessment is conducted to determine whether the asylum claimant is admissible. During this stage, and depending on the specific situation of where the asylum claimant has applied for asylum (i.e. at the border or in the territory), a specific procedure will be used.[150] During Stage 4, the asylum application is assessed and a decision is made with a list of possible outcomes.[151] In order for an applicant to qualify for refugee status, an act of persecution must 'be sufficiently serious by its nature or repetition as to constitute a severe violation of basic human rights' and 'be an accumulation of various measures, including violations of human

[148] *Ibid* at art 4(2).

[149] European Asylum Support Office, "EASO Report on Asylum Procedures Directive and Non-Refoulement" at 23, which states: 'The first stage relates to the Dublin procedure for determining the Member State responsible for examining an application which may, if applicable, be a precondition for access to asylum procedures at the administrative level', https://www.easo.europa.eu/sites/default/files/asylum-procedures-ja_en.pdf [EASO Report].

[150] *Ibid* at 22–23, which states: 'The second stage refers to the actual examination procedure, which can be preceded by an initial admissibility procedure, at the administrative level. The APD (recast) permits Member States to operate two types of examination procedure. The examination procedure may take the form of a regular procedure (Article 31 APD (recast)) or an accelerated procedure (Article 31(8) APD (recast)). Both of these procedures may comprise an initial admissibility procedure, based on Articles 33 and 34 APD (recast), to determine the admissibility of the application; that is, whether the Member State is required to examine qualification for international protection. The accelerated procedure may be conducted in-territory or at the border'.

[151] *Ibid* at 23.

rights which is sufficiently severe as to affect an individual'.[152] If an applicant does not meet that test, the individual may instead qualify for subsidiary protection if serious harm is present.[153] Serious harm consists of: '(a) the death penalty or execution; or (b) torture or inhuman or degrading treatment or punishment of an applicant in the country of origin; or (c) serious and individual threat to a civilian's life or person by reason of indiscriminate violence in situations of international or internal armed conflict'.[154] If a person is found not to qualify for refugee status and is not granted subsidiary protection, whether at an accelerated border procedure or through a regular procedure, the potential for *refoulement* arises, because the applicant does not have a legal right to remain.

Applicants who are unsuccessful at Stage 4 may appeal at Stage 5. The appeal process concerns applications that have been denied at the procedural stage. Once an appeal process has begun, suspensive effect takes place, meaning that the asylum claimant has a right under EU law to stay in the territory of the EU pending the results of the appeal proceedings without being subjected to removal.[155] Again, if they are unsuccessful on appeal, the potential for *refoulement* arises as the individuals are usually deported. This is why 'most of the *non-refoulement* cases [brought under EU and human rights tribunals] are brought by rejected asylum-seekers'[156]: The risk of *refoulement* crystallizes at the point of exhaustion of domestic decision-making and appeals. However, *non-refoulement* is considered as a result of the automatic suspensive effect as discussed above requiring Member States to permit asylum claimants to remain in their territory pending the results of the appeal.[157]

3.3.3 *The New Pact on Migration and Asylum*

Since September 2020, the European Commission has adopted the New Pact on Migration and Asylum.[158] This new pact claims to offer a 'fresh start' to address the growing problems of free movement in the Schengen area, while addressing

---

[152] *Ibid* at art 9(1).

[153] *Ibid* at art 15.

[154] *Ibid.*

[155] EASO Report at 137, which states: 'The APD (recast) regulates the minimum standard concerning the right to remain in the ter-ritory during the appeals phase (Article 46(5)-(9)). In cases where derogations are pos-sible from the automatic suspensive effect of appeal Member States shall as a minimum allow applicants to remain in the territory pending the outcome of the procedure to rule whether or not the applicant may remain on the territory' (Article 46(8)).

[156] Cali et al at 358.

[157] EASO Report at 157, which states: 'the right to remain during the appeals procedure is a corollary of states' international obligation to comply with the principle of *non-refoulement*, which is reflected in Article 21 QD (recast)'.

[158] European Commission (2020).

urgent needs, such as the challenge of external border management, large-scale arrivals by land or sea, overpopulated reception centres, and unauthorized movements of migrants.[159] The new pact 'build[s] on progress made since 2016 but will also introduce a common European framework and better governance of migration and asylum management, as well as a new solidarity mechanism'.[160]

Some new mechanisms proposed by the new pact includes: pre-entry screening, where all third-country nationals who cross the external border without authorization are screened prior to entry in to the EU.[161] The screening will include identification, health and security checks, and fingerprinting using the Eurodac database.[162] Another mechanism is the border procedure, which proposes to fast-track applications from certain categories of third-country nationals such as those who are from 'safe' third countries.[163] Yet another new mechanism is the implementation of the EU return border procedure, which takes place immediately after a third-country national whose claim has been refused based on the asylum procedure.[164] These new mechanism are established based on the presumption of mutual trust amongst EU countries, and as will be discussed later, the presumption itself is problematic, which relies on the idea that diplomatic assurances should serve as a safe way to assume the said EU country has robust implementation of international and EU human rights law, including *non-refoulement* protection.

In sum, consideration of the potential for, and steps to avoid, *refoulement* are intended to be built into all stages of the standardized CEAS asylum process. However, the adequacy of these safeguards has been questioned, as explained in the next section.

3.4 Gaps Between Law and Practice with Respect to Non-Refoulement within the EU

The 'compliance pull of norms [such as *non-refoulement*] depends in some measure on their coherence and clarity'.[165] Despite clear statements of the applicable EU law on *non-refoulement*—such as in Article 19(2) of the EU Charter and Article 15(b) of the Qualification Directive—many EU Member States interpret the principle differently, including very narrowly, thus affecting compliance. This section will provide two overarching and interlinked examples of how the 'compliance

[159] *Ibid* at 1.

[160] *Ibid* at 4.

[161] *Ibid* at 5.

[162] *Ibid.*

[163] *Ibid* at 6.

[164] *Ibid.*

[165] *Ibid* at 357.

pull' of *non-refoulement* is weakened through practice within the EU that undermines the norm: first, through negative exercise of the 'margin of discretion' within EU asylum processes and, second, through the presumption of mutual trust relied upon by the EU Member States.

3.4.1 The 'Margin of Discretion' and Non-Refoulement

In the application of EU law in the context of asylum policies in the CEAS, EU Member States are given a wide 'margin of discretion' by the regional courts, such as the CJEU, when implementing EU law norms.[166] Application of this 'margin of discretion' by EU Member States has resulted in disparate practices in the national implementation of EU asylum policies, resulting in widely varying interpretations of the *non-refoulement* obligation. One significant reason for these differing practices stems from the difference within the EU between 'regulations' and 'directives'. When a piece of EU legislation is in the form of a regulation, such as the Dublin III Regulation, the Member State must directly apply the regulation in its entirety at the domestic level without change or re-interpretation. On the other hand, an EU directive, such as the Qualification Directive (recast) (which recognizes the importance of the principle of *non-refoulement* in Article 15b), only becomes effective when transposed into domestic law. EU Member States exercise their margin of discretion when they conduct domestic transpositions of EU law.[167] The transposing process has resulted in different EU Member States adopting widely varying understandings of directives or failing to transpose at all. Where the domestic transposition of directives does not take place, or does not adequately take place, the procedural safeguards required by the directives may not be effective in providing protection for asylum claimants and refugees against *refoulement*.[168] The problem of ineffective transposition has been recognized by the European Commission.[169]

The reality is that the 'margin of discretion' has led some countries to bend the principle of *non-refoulement* "to their will and choose the more convenient

[166] Poon MOA.

[167] European Commission (2008) at explanatory memorandum.

[168] In particular, the 'safe' third country concept as defined under Article 28 of the Asylum Procedures Directive (recast) has not been transposed into German law; See, for example: UNHCR (2010) "Section 12: The Safe Third Country Concept"; For example, in the case of Germany, where the current Asylum Procedures Directive (recast) has not yet been transposed into its national legislation [UNHCR STC].

[169] For example, the European Commission's proposal for the Reception Conditions Directive (recast) tabled to the European Parliament and European Council stated that 'the level of reception conditions for asylum seekers [...] mainly results from the fact that the Directive currently allows Member States a wide margin of discretion concerning the establishment of reception conditions at the national level'; *Ibid.*

interpretation".[170] EU Member States have done so in a number of ways, often by creating various barriers to successfully claiming asylum. One such barrier results from external border and immigration controls, which may involve a combination of strict visa regimes, carrier sanctions, 'pushback' operations at sea, and cooperation with third countries through bilateral or multilateral agreements (jointly referred to as 'migration controls').[171] These State practices, which will be explored in more detail in Chap. 4, prevent asylum claimants and refugees from reaching the shores of the EU in search of safety, thus disallowing these individuals from accessing territorial asylum—the principle that asylum may be sought and granted when the claimant is on the territory of the asylum-granting State.[172] These EU migration control mechanisms have been critiqued because they have resulted in *refoulement.*[173]

Some Member States create legally unwarranted barriers for asylum claimants and refugees seeking international protection by enacting certain procedural requirements.[174] For example, some countries add a procedural requirement to require the asylum claimant to rebut the presumption of mutual trust—the presumption that EU Member States are 'safe' destinations to which claimants can return simply because they are Member States of the EU—that is above and beyond the onus to prove a 'well-founded fear of persecution'.[175] This additional procedural requirement increases the burden placed upon individual claimants to bear the onus of proof, making the recognition of refugee status a more onerous process.[176] Unnecessarily onerous processes result in more unnecessarily rejected

---

[170] Costello (2016b) at 357 [Costello Monograph].

[171] Hathaway and Gammeltoft-Hansen at 9.

[172] Davitti, Daria, and Fries, Marlene (2017) [Davitti and Fries].

[173] See, for example: Gammeltoft-Hansen, Thomas, and Feith Tan, Nikolas (2017) "The End of the Deterrence Paradigm? Future Directions for Global Refugee Policy" *Journal on Migration and Human Security* 28–56, which provides a comprehensive overview of shifts in paradigm on deterrence policies relevant to migration control, for example, at 41, citing the EU-Turkey Statement: 'Given the number of reports suggesting violations of both the non-refoulement principle and fundamental shortcomings in the implementation of other refugee rights, legal challenges seem unavoidable'.

[174] See, for example: Proposal for a Regulation of the European Parliament and of the Council establishing the criteria and mechanisms for determining the Member State responsible for examining an application for international protection lodged in one of the Member States by a third-country national or a stateless person (recast), COM(2016) 270 final, 2016/0133 (COD), Brussels, 4 May 2016 at art 4 [Dublin IV Proposal], where an additional procedural requirement for asylum claimants is required, such as requiring them to adhere to strict deadlines.

[175] For a definition of the 'presumption of mutual trust', see: Prechal, Sacha (2017) at 76 [Prechal], which states: '[the presumption of mutual trust is] based on mutual confidence and a presumption of compliance, by other Member States, with European Union law and, in particular, fundamental rights'; See, also: NS/ME at para 83.

[176] Strict deadlines for asylum claimants are not encouraged, as stated in the UNHCR Handbook, which noted that asylum officials, in their substantive evaluation of refugee status, should weigh the 'general credibility' of the claimant where the information (such as a passport) cannot be obtained within a reasonable time, see: UNHCR Handbook at para 93.

applicants and therefore an increased potential for returns and *refoulement*. It is therefore concerning that a proposed addition in the 'Dublin IV' proposal allows such an additional procedural requirement.[177]

A second example of a legally unwarranted barrier is the expectation that an asylum claimant possesses proper documentation to establish identity.[178] This requirement is not realistic for individuals fleeing from a 'well-founded fear of persecution', and also potentially permits Member States to evade their responsibility to process asylum applications by rejecting applications on the basis of insufficient documentation.[179] Moreover, Article 31(1) of the Refugee Convention precludes asylum claimants from being penalized for their irregular entry, such as through means other than at regular border crossings.[180] The UNHCR's position regarding asylum claimants without proper documentation is that claimants need not prove every element of their case and they are to be given the 'benefit of the doubt' when officers assess their asylum applications.[181] When asylum applications are rejected on technical grounds, such as on the basis of insufficient identity documentation, this raises the risk that they will be returned to their country of origin without a proper evaluation of their claim or the potential for *refoulement*.

In a similar vein, some countries create barriers to asylum claimants by removing (as opposed to adding) procedural safeguards. For example, prior to being transferred from one EU country to another under the Dublin procedure (also known as 'Dublin transfers'), some claimants are not provided with an opportunity to be heard, even though an interview would allow the claimant to provide reasons for why a deportation should be impeded.[182] This is despite the fact that the UNHCR's *Handbook on Refugee Status Determination* states that an individual interview is *required* for the asylum officer to properly assess the applicant's

---

[177] Dublin IV Proposal at art 4.

[178] For example, in EU law, documentation is required otherwise entry will be unauthorized until formally authorized by the asylum official regarding entry to EU territory for asylum seekers, see: European Agency for Fundamental Rights (2016) "Handbook on European law relating to asylum, borders and immigration" at 41.

[179] *Ibid.*

[180] Refugee Convention at art 31(1), which states: 'Contracting States shall not impose penalties, on account of their illegal entry or presence, on refugees who, coming directly from a territory where their life or freedom was threatened in the sense of article 1, enter or are present in their territory without authorization, provided they present themselves without delay to the authorities and show good cause for their illegal entry or presence'.

[181] UNHCR Handbook at para 203–204: 'after the applicant has made a genuine effort to substantiate his story there may still be a lack of evidence for some of his statements. As explained above (paragraph 196), it is hardly possible for a refugee to "prove" every part of his case and, indeed, if this were a requirement the majority of refugees would not be recognized. it is therefore frequently necessary to give the applicant the benefit of the doubt'.

[182] Dublin III Regulation at art 3(2).

eligibility for refugee status.[183] This barrier is particularly of concern where claimants are subjected to transfer to EU countries with less developed asylum systems lacking fundamental safeguards for claimants or extremely high rejection rates.[184] Where the asylum claimant is not given an opportunity to be heard, the claimant may be prevented from challenging a transfer decision, contrary to established EU case law, potentially resulting in *refoulement*.[185] These Dublin transfer practices evidence EU Member States' strategy to 'contain' unruly migrants and refugees in an attempt to shift responsibility outward, away from the EU, and to third countries deemed 'safe'.

An additional concern is that, in these transfer cases, EU Member States often rely upon diplomatic assurances from the receiving country (the 'responsible' EU Member State) that the individual will not be subject to *refoulement*.[186] This is particular worrisome when EU Member States rely upon blanket assurances that third countries are 'safe', even when these countries do not have procedural safeguards to ensure that claimants are able to access international protection for refugee status.[187] The UN Committee Against Torture is 'highly resistant' to the

---

[183] UNHCR Handbook at para 200. Although not legally binding, UNHCR commentaries and guidelines are considered authoritative by States Parties to the Refugee Convention. Further, States Parties to the Refugee Convention are required to cooperate with the office of the UNHCR in the implementation of provisions of the Refugee Convention, see: Refugee Convention at art 35(1). The UNHCR Handbook states that where asylum claimants provide basic information 'in the first instance, by completing a standard questionnaire ... [s]uch basic information will normally *not* be sufficient to enable the examiner to reach a decision, and *one or more personal interviews will be required*' (emphasis added): UNHCR Handbook at para 200.

[184] Discrepancies in recognition rates are problematic in that, regardless of the factors leading to a high or a low recognition rate, variations occur frequently even for claimants originating from refugee-producing countries such as Afghanistan, Iran, and Iraq: *Ibid* at 8. In fact, the divergencies for recognition rates from EU Member States for claimants originating from these countries ranged between 0 and 100%: *Ibid.* Variation in recognition rates of refugee status may also be due to a lack of harmonization in decision-making practices among Member States, which may be a result of differences in the assessment of country of origin situations, differences in interpretation of legal concepts, and/or differences in national jurisprudence: *Ibid.* Since low recognition rates of refugee status in any given Member State may mean that the individual claimant seeking refugee status is less likely to receive a positive decision for their application for international protection, a large variance in recognition rates from Member State to Member State may potentially result in situations where the claimant is not likely to be recognized as a refugee in certain Member States while very likely to be recognized as a refugee in others. While many factors may combine to contribute towards low recognition rates, including those aforementioned, low recognition rates in a certain Member State may potentially encourage claimants to apply for international protection elsewhere, thus increasing instances of forum-shopping and other secondary movements such as smuggling activities, contrary to the stated aim of the CEAS: CEAS.

[185] *Mehrdad Ghezelbash v Staatssecretaris van Veiligheid en Justitie,* C-63/15, CJEU, 7 June 2016 at paras 46 and 61 [Ghezelbash].

[186] Brouwer (2013) at 145.

[187] The use of diplomatic assurances can also be found in some countries' 'safe' third country practices, see, for example: *MH v Serbia,* App No 62410/17, 4 March 2019, "Written Submissions on behalf of the Interveners (Advice on Individual Rights in Europe), Dutch Council for Refugees, and European Council on Refugees and Exiles)" at para 23, which states: 'The

acceptance of diplomatic assurances, and does not 'accept them as effective risk mitigation' against *refoulement*.[188] The Committee has warned against relying on diplomatic assurances:

> *diplomatic assurances* from a State party to the Convention to which a person is to be deported *should not be used as a loophole to undermine the principle of non-refoulement* as set out in Article 3 of the Convention, where there are substantial grounds for believing that he/she would be in danger of being subjected to torture in that State (emphasis added).[189]

Both the UK and Germany have been warned against the usage of and reliance upon diplomatic assurances in their practice of returning claimants to another EU Member State. For the UK, the Committee Against Torture 'notes with concern the [UK's] reliance on diplomatic assurances to justify the deportation of foreign nationals suspected of terrorism related offences to countries in which the widespread practice of torture is alleged' contrary to Articles 3 and 13 of the CAT'.[190] The Committee Against Torture further cautioned the UK that:

> The more widespread the practice of torture or cruel, inhuman or degrading treatment is, the less likely it will be that a real risk of such treatment can be avoided by diplomatic assurances, however stringent any agreed follow-up procedure may be. Therefore, the Committee considers that diplomatic assurances are unreliable and ineffective and should not be used as an instrument to modify the determination of the Convention.[191]

The Committee Against Torture recommends that the UK 'recognize that diplomatic assurances and monitoring arrangements will not be relied upon to justify

---

interveners submit that in the situations where reliance on diplomatic assurances is appropriate and may secure a person's rights guaranteed by the Convention, these assurances must not only be tested against detailed and reliable information but also examined in light of the context in which such assurances are given. Importantly, for such assurances to be reliable they should be individualised, precise and cover the particular needs of the person whose Convention rights may be violated. The interveners consider that in countries where conditions rapidly change, where numbers of people in need of protection are higher than the capacity of the asylum system may handle, inadequate reception conditions and deficiencies in an asylum system, general assurances cannot be relied upon at all. Any assurances given by a State with a domestic system which has reported shortcomings and previous violations of Convention rights will inevitably struggle to satisfy the requirements of specificity or practicality'; See, also: Poon (2020); One needs to look no further than the judgment of *MSS v Belgium and Greece* to see that the Dublin II Regulation allows EU Member States to exercise their discretion as 'a way out' of the Regulation by evading responsibility to process asylum applications. A similar issue seems to persist in the Dublin III Regulation, whereby EU Member States are permitted to exercise their discretion to interpret specific terms within the Regulation which are purposely left ambiguous.

[188] Cali et al at 372.

[189] CAT NR Comment at para 20.

[190] Committee Against Torture, "Concluding observations on the fifth periodic report of the United Kingdom, adopted by the Committee at its fiftieth session (6–31 May 2013)—Advance Unedited Version" at para 18.

[191] *Ibid.*

transfers when such substantial risk of torture exists'.[192] For Germany, the Committee Against Torture specifically requested Germany to 'clarify to the Committee [the] steps taken to ensure that the use of diplomatic assurances is only employed in exceptional cases'.[193] In contrast, the UN Human Rights Committee accepts that EU Member States might use diplomatic assurances, but must ensure a thorough assessment of their quality and reliability, coupled with a robust monitoring mechanism within both states.[194] The issue has been that not all EU Member States undertake thorough assessments of the quality and reliability of the diplomatic assurances and do not possess robust monitoring mechanisms, thereby increasing the risk of *refoulement* resulting from the Dublin transfers.[195] Thus, they rely on diplomatic assurances to solve their asylum issues, without ensuring adequate protection against *refoulement.*

In sum, the 'margin of discretion' afforded to EU Member States has resulted in differing approaches to asylum procedures. That margin has been used in some cases to limit the ability of individuals to make asylum claims, or to limit procedures with the outcome of reducing successful asylum cases. The different approaches not only undermine the CEAS' goal of harmonization, they also widen the possibility of *refoulement.* Interlinked with this outcome is another EU policy, the presumption of mutual trust.

3.4.2 The Presumption of Mutual Trust Within the EU

The presumption of mutual trust is a well-recognized principle in EU law which presumes that all EU Member States comply with relevant EU and international law obligations in their exercise of EU law obligations, particularly concerning fundamental rights.[196] The Dublin System is founded on the presumption of mutual trust, where the system is 'grounded on the presumption that all Member States and the States bound by the regulation by virtue of bilateral agreements observe EU law, particularly EU fundamental rights and freedoms'.[197] As a fundamental right, this presumption applies to the principle of *non-refoulement*: the Dublin III Regulation prevents the transfer of an individual back to the responsible Member State where there are 'substantial grounds for believing that there are systemic flaws in the asylum procedure and in the reception conditions' of the Member

192 *Ibid* at para 19.

193 Committee Against Torture, "List of issues to be considered during the examination of the fifth periodic report of Germany", 23 June 2011, UN Doc CAT/C/DEU/5 at para 19.

194 Cali et al at 373.

195 For EU Member States and their practices on applying the principle of *non-refoulement* in the context of Dublin Transfers, see: International Commission of Jurists (2011).

196 Prechal.

197 *Ibid* at 55.

State, resulting in a risk of that individual being exposed to inhuman or degrading treatment.[198] The presumption of mutual trust assumes that EU Member States will or have already complied with relevant EU and international law norms without requiring a sending State to examine the merits of an individual's application before returning that individual.[199]

The ECtHR and the CJEU have both examined the presumption of mutual trust in the context of Dublin transfers and the principle of *non-refoulement.* This has resulted in contradictory interpretations of the principle, in particular regarding when the presumption might be rebutted and the consequences of this rebuttal.[200] These contradictions are important. When an EU Member State does not respect or ensure the fundamental guarantee to *non-refoulement*, 'Member States cannot safely return an asylum seeker to its territory'.[201] In other words, the 'return cannot be executed even though the Dublin regulation designates such State as the only Member State competent to assess his/her asylum claim'.[202] While the ECtHR and the CJEU agree that this is the outcome, they differ in how to evaluate whether or not a Member State does not respect or ensure the fundamental principle.

The CJEU has adopted a test of 'systemic deficiencies' as a precondition for opposing a Dublin transfer, or, in other words, a precondition for rebutting the presumption of mutual trust.[203] The CJEU requires claimants to prove that there are 'systemic deficiencies' existing in the asylum procedures and reception conditions of the Member State in order to rebut the presumption of mutual trust to prevent a removal under the Dublin transfer procedures. In the case of *N.S.*, it held that a Member State should be aware of the 'systemic deficiencies' before transferring an individual asylum claimant to the Member State responsible under the Dublin transfer procedure:

> Article 4 of the Charter of Fundamental Rights of the European Union must be interpreted as meaning that the Member States, including the national courts, may not transfer an asylum seeker to the 'Member State responsible' within the meaning of Regulation No 343/2003 *where they cannot be unaware that systemic deficiencies in the asylum procedure and in the reception conditions of asylum seekers in that Member State* amount to substantial grounds for believing that the asylum seeker would face a real risk of being subjected to inhuman or degrading treatment within the meaning of that provision (emphasis added).[204]

Although the case of *N.S.* introduced the concept of 'systemic deficiencies', the concept was not further elaborated upon in that judgment. However, 'systemic deficiencies' may imply that 'various flaws that cause an individual risk to a human

---

198 Vicini (2015) at 55 [Vicini]; Dublin III Regulation at art 3(2).

199 *Ibid.*

200 *Ibid* at 51.

201 Vicini at 52.

202 *Ibid.*

203 Lübbe (2015) at 135 [Lübbe].

204 NS/ME at para 106.

being within the asylum process have to reach a point of becoming conceptually one flaw that makes the whole system deficient'.[205] Other proposals have suggested that 'systemic flaw' may mean 'a lack of a structure, a structural void—that, for cases passing through this part of the system, leads to an error'. [206] Alternatively, 'systemic flaws' may mean flaws which are produced regularly and can be 'averted by changes in the regular procedures of the system'.[207]

The ECtHR, on the other hand, requires claimants to rebut the presumption of mutual trust on the threshold of 'individual assessments', so that the applicant's claim in view of the specific situation of the applicant is considered rather than the existence of deficiencies in the system. The ECtHR formulated the test of 'individual assessments' in the case of *Tarakhel v. Switzerland*. The case concerned eight Afghan nationals, who alleged that, if they were returned to Italy, they would be exposed to inhuman and degrading treatment which would violate, *inter alia,* Article 3 of the ECHR.[208] In citing the decision by the CJEU in the case of *N.S.*, which established the criterion for 'systemic deficiencies', the ECtHR held that:

> In the present case the Court must therefore ascertain whether, *in view of the overall situation with regard to the reception arrangements for asylum seekers in Italy and the applicants' specific situation*, substantial grounds have been shown for believing that the applicants would be at risk of treatment contrary to Article 3 if they were returned to Italy (emphasis added).[209]

Therefore, the ECtHR has deviated from the approach taken by the CJEU to consider the applicant's claim in view of the specific situation of the applicant, rather than the presence of 'systemic deficiencies' within Italy's asylum as the primary consideration. The ECtHR decision in *Tarakhal* was referred to in another case, *A.M.E. v. the Netherlands*, in which the ECtHR held that the applicant was not able to establish 'a sufficiently real and imminent risk of hardship severe enough to fall within the scope of Article 3', which concluded in the applicant's claim being held to be unfounded.[210]

The difference between the CJEU and ECtHR approaches to the rebuttal of the presumption of mutual trust in *non-refoulement* cases is important: The CJEU approach gives more prominence to systemic deficiencies in the asylum procedures and reception conditions of the asylum-receiving Member State, while the ECtHR approach considers the individual's circumstances as having more importance.[211] This difference illustrates a gap between the law on *non-refoulement* and the actual practice within the EU.

---

[205] Barrera and Vetter (2013).

[206] Lübbe at 137.

[207] *Ibid* at 138.

[208] *Tarakhel v Switzerland,* App No 29,217/12 (ECHR, 4 November 2014) at paras 2 and 3 [Tarakhel].

[209] *Ibid* at para 105.

[210] *AME v the Netherlands,* App no 51,428/10 (ECHR, 5 February 2015) at paras 28 and 35.

[211] Vicini.

The UK courts have adopted a compromise between the two different approaches of the Luxembourg and Strasbourg courts. In *E.M. and M.A.*, the UK Court of Appeal held that: 'the assessment of risk on return is seen by the Strasbourg court as depending on a combination of personal experience and systemic shortcomings which in total may suffice to rebut the presumption of compliance'.[212] The compromise of the UK Court of Appeal may be a way to reconcile the different approaches taken by the CJEU and the ECtHR on the threshold to rebut the presumption of mutual trust, and still adequately ensure protection against *refoulement*.

3.5 Concluding Remarks

This chapter has explained the EU law applicable to the principle of *non-refoulement*, including its multi-layered aspects. It has also examined how the ECHR and two European courts—the ECtHR and the CJEU—interpret and apply the prohibition against *refoulement.* The legislative and jurisprudential picture that emerges is of a relatively robust norm. Under EU law, *non-refoulement* applies within the EU Charter, as well as within the framework of the CEAS, specifically within the key directives: the Qualification Directive, Asylum Procedures Directive, and Reception Conditions Directive. Under ECHR law, *non-refoulement* applies extraterritorially as reaffirmed by case law from the ECtHR. The prohibition against *non-refoulement* under EU law is applicable based on the territorial scope of the EU Charter, which is governed by Article 51(1).[213] The EU Charter applies 'whenever the institutions, bodies, offices, and agencies of the Union exercise their powers'.[214]

However, this chapter has also indicated that the actual practice of some EU Member States has been to adopt a narrower understanding of *non-refoulement*, one that is limited through domestic interpretation as a result of the 'margin of discretion' allowed to Member States when transposing directives, and limited through the presumption of mutual trust when transferring asylum claimants to other ('responsible') States. Shortcomings of relying upon the presumption of mutual trust in Dublin transfers include the assumption that all EU Member States are in compliance with relevant international and European law obligations, including the protection against *refoulement*. Often, State practice has shown that

[212] *EM and MA* [2013] 1 WLR 576 at para 39 [EM/MA].

[213] EU Charter at art 51(1), which states: 'The provisions of this Charter are addressed to the institutions, bodies, offices and agencies of the Union with due regard for the principle of subsidiarity and to the Member States only when they are implementing Union law. They shall therefore respect the rights, observe the principles and promote the application thereof in accordance with their respective powers and respecting the limits of the powers of the Union as conferred on it in the Treaties'.

[214] *Ibid;* See, also: Moreno-Lax (2017b) at 290 [Violeta Monograph].

the reliance upon diplomatic assurances and the presumption of mutual trust do not translate into actual protection for claimants, but instead have the countereffect of permitting EU Member States to shift their responsibility for processing asylum applications elsewhere—outside of the EU to third countries deemed 'safe', or to another Member State within the EU. The shifting of responsibility outside of the EU to third States deemed 'safe' as a destination for the asylum claimant is not in itself a violation of international law.[215] However, the curtailment of human rights of the claimants when adequate procedural safeguards such as access to individual assessments prior to being transferred is a violation.

Unfortunately, these gaps between law and practice are likely to continue for the foreseeable future: the use of the words 'should' instead of 'shall' in the 'Dublin IV' Proposal may result in the implementation of minimum procedural guarantees, or less.[216] For example, one key recital provides that there *should* be personal interviews for the asylum claimants (recital 23), while another recital provides that there *should* be legal safeguards and the right to effective remedy (recital 24).[217] This approach arguably leave too much room for Member States to interpret the clauses as they wish, basing their discretion on State interests.[218] This wide 'margin of discretion' is likely to translate into more difficulties for asylum claimants to have their applications properly processed on their merits, resulting in a higher likelihood of rejection, and potentially increasing the possibility of *refoulement*.[219]

The next chapter considers an explanation for the actions of EU Member States in limiting, in practice, the principle of *non-refoulement*: the theory of containment.

---

[215] It should be noted, however, that 'safe' third country practices are derived from the omission of the Refugee Convention to include it as permissible or prohibited. The UNHCR does not oppose to its use, however, the concept of 'safe' third country has no legal basis under international law, see, for example: UNHCR (2018).

[216] Dublin IV Proposal at recitals 23 and 24.

[217] *Ibid;* In these examples, the word 'should' is used instead of 'shall', which permits the member state discretion in decision-making. It is important to note also, that, while the Dublin III Regulation determines which EU member state is responsible for examining individual asylum applications, in some member states such as Germany, the Dublin procedure does not refer to a separate procedure in domestic German law. Rather, in the German context, the Dublin procedure refers to the shifting of responsibility for an asylum application within the administration, for instance, the assumption of responsibility by the 'Dublin units' of the Federal Office for Migration and Refugees (BAMF) of Germany; See, for example: Asylum Information Database (2016) "Dublin: Germany" [AIDA].

[218] See, for example: *Institute for Human Rights and Development in Africa (on behalf of Sierra Leonean refugees in Guinea) v Guinea,* African Commission on Human and Peoples' Rights, Communication No 240/02, December 2004.

[219] Refugee Convention at art 33(1).

References

Asylum Information Database (2016) Dublin: Germany. http://www.asylumineurope.org/reports/country/germany/asylum-procedure/procedures/dublin

Baratta R (2014) EU legislative drafting: views from those applying EU law in the member states, 19th quality of legislation seminar, Brussels. https://ec.europa.eu/dgs/legal_service/seminars/20140703_baratta_speech.pdf

Barrera E, Vetter F (2013) 'Systemic deficiency': legal standard setting, human rights, and its effect on the individual in the Common European Asylum System. Spectra J 2(2)

Brouwer E (2013) Mutual trust and the Dublin Regulation: protection of fundamental rights in the EU and the burden of proof. Utrecht Law Rev 9(1):135–147

Cali B, Costello C, Cunningham S (2020) Hard protection through soft courts? non-refoulement before the United Nations treaty bodies. Ger Law J 21:355–384

Collett E, Le Coz C (2018) After the storm: learning from the EU response to the migration crisis (Migration Policy Institute Europe)

Commission of the European Communities, communication from the commission to the European parliament, the council, the European economic and social committee and the committee of regions: policy plan on asylum, Brussels, 17 June 2008, COM(2008) 360 Final. http://eur-lex.europa.eu/LexUriServ/LexUriServ.do?uri=COM:2008:0360:FIN:EN:PDF

Committee Against Torture, concluding observations on the fifth periodic report of the United Kingdom, adopted by the committee at its fiftieth session (6-31 May 2013) – Advance Unedited Version

Committee Against Torture, List of issues to be considered during the examination of the fifth periodic report of Germany, 23 June 2011, UN Doc CAT/C/DEU/5

Costello C (2014a) Policy primer: the UK, the Common European Asylum System and EU immigration law

Costello C (2014b) The UK, the Common European Asylum System and EU immigration law. https://migrationobservatory.ox.ac.uk/resources/primers/the-uk-the-common-european-asylum-system-and-eu-immigrat

Costello C (2016a) The search for the outer edges of non-refoulement in Europe: exceptionality and flagrant breaches. In Burson B, Cantor J (eds) Human rights and the refugee definition. Brill, Netherlands, pp 180–209

Costello C (2016b) The human rights of migrants and refugees in European law. Oxford, Oxford University Press

Council Directive 2001/55/EC of 20 July 2001 on minimum standards for giving temporary protection in the event of a mass influx of displaced persons and on measures promoting a balance of efforts between Member States in receiving such persons and bearing the consequences thereof, OJ L212/12, 7 August 2001

Council Directive 2003/86/EC of 22 September 2003 on the right to family reunification, OJ L251/12, 3 October 2003

Council of Europe (2014) Handbook on European law relating to asylum, borders and immigration. http://fra.europa.eu/sites/default/files/handbook-law-asylum-migration-borders-2nded_en.pdf

Council of Europe. Values: human rights, democracy, and rule of law. http://www.coe.int/en/web/about-us/values

Council of Europe. Migration and human rights European Court of Human Rights. http://www.coe.int/t/democracy/migration/bodies/echr_en.asp

Council of the European Union (2019) Proposal for a regulation of the European Parliament and of the Council amending Council Regulation (EC) No 539/2001, 2018/0390(COD)

Crawford J (2012) Brownlie's principles of public international law, 8th edn. Oxford University Press

Davitti D, Fries M (2017) Offshore processing and complicity in current EU migration policies: parts 1 & 2. EJIL!Talk Blog. https://www.ejiltalk.org/offshore-processing-and-complicity-in-current-eu-migration-policies-part-2

Development, Refugee studies centre. https://www.rethinkingrefuge.org/articles/rethinking-emergency-and-crisis

Duffy A (2008) Expulsion to face torture? *non-refoulement* in international law. Int J Refugee Law 20(3):373–390

Dunai M (2015) Hungary says EU's Dublin rules 'dead'; won't leg migrants come back (ed: Pitchford R). Thomson Reuters UK

Durham University. Are UK Courts bound by the European Court of Human Rights?, Law School Research Briefing No 10. https://www.dur.ac.uk/resources/law/research/AreUKCourtsboundbytheEuropeanCourtofHumanRights.pdf

Eman Hamdan (2016) The principle of Non-refoulement under the ECHR and the UN Convention against Torture. Brill, Leiden

EUR-Le (2016) Non-EU nationals—rules for long-term residence. http://eur-lex.europa.eu/legal-content/EN/TXT/?uri=URISERV%3Al23034

EUR-Lex (2016) Justice, freedom and security. http://eur-lex.europa.eu/summary/chapter/justice_freedom_security.html?root_default=SUM_1_CODED=23

Europa (2016a) Regulations, directives and other acts. https://europa.eu/european-union/law/legal-acts_en

Europa (2016b) EU institutions and other bodies. https://europa.eu/european-union/about-eu/institutions-bodies_en

Europe in Strasbourg (2016) Member states of the European Union and the Council of Europe (2016) http://en.strasbourg-europe.eu/member-states,44987,en.html

European Agency for Fundamental Rights (2016) Handbook on European law relating to asylum, borders and immigration. https://www.europarl.europa.eu/greece/resource/static/files/handbook-on-european-law-relating-to-asylum–borders-and-immigration.pdf

European Asylum Support Office (2016) An introduction to the Common European Asylum System for courts and tribunals

European Asylum Support Office, EASO report on asylum procedures directive and non-refoulement. https://www.easo.europa.eu/sites/default/files/asylum-procedures-ja_en.pdf

European Commission (2008) Proposal for a Directive of the European Parliament and of the Council laying down minimum standards for the reception of asylum seekers (recast), COM (2008) 815 final, 2008/0244 (COD), 3 December 2008 at explanatory memorandum

European Commission, Applying EU Law. https://ec.europa.eu/info/law/law-making-process/applying-eu-law_en

European Commission (2020) Communication from the Commission on a new pact on migration and asylum, COM (2020) 609 final, Brussels

European Commission, Migration and home affairs (2016) Schengen Area. http://ec.europa.eu/dgs/home-affairs/what-we-do/policies/borders-and-visas/schengen/index_en.htm

European Commission, Migration and home affairs (2019) Common European Asylum System

European Commission, Migration and home affairs. Third-Country National. https://ec.europa.eu/home-affairs/content/third-country-national_en

European Council, Timeline: reform of EU asylum rules. http://www.consilium.europa.eu/en/policies/ceas-reform/ceas-reform-timeline

European Council on Refugee and Exiles (2016) ECRE comments on the Commission Proposal for a Dublin IV Regulation, COM (2016) 270. http://www.ecre.org/wp-content/uploads/2016/10/ECRE-Comments-Dublin-IV.pdf

European Court of Human Rights (2014) The ECHR in 50 questions. https://www.echr.coe.int/Documents/50Questions_ENG.pdf

European Court of Human Rights (2018) Guide on Article 6 of the Convention – right to a fair trial (criminal limb). https://www.echr.coe.int/Documents/Guide_Art_6_criminal_ENG.pdf.

European Parliament (2016) Fact Sheets on the European Union: the Maastricht and Amsterdam treaties. http://www.europarl.europa.eu/atyourservice/en/displayFtu.html?ftuId=FTU_1.1.3.html
European Parliament (2017) The Common European Asylum System – Third reform. http://www.europarl.europa.eu/RegData/etudes/PERI/2017/580866/IPOL_PERI(2017)580866_EN.pdf
European Parliament (2013) Directorate-General for External Policies of the Union: Directorate B, Policy Department, Briefing Paper: current challenges for International Refugee Law, with a focus on EU Policies and EU Co-operation with the UNHCR. http://www.europarl.europa.eu/RegData/etudes/note/join/2013/433711/EXPO-DROI_NT(2013)433711_EN.pdf
European Union (2016) The history of the European Union. https://europa.eu/european-union/about-eu/history_en
European Union (2018) Regulations, directives and other Acts. https://europa.eu/european-union/eu-law/legal-acts_en
European Union, Court of Justice of the European Union (CJEU). https://europa.eu/european-union/about-eu/institutions-bodies/court-justice_en
European Union, Sources and scope of European Union law: fact Sheets on the European Union – 2016. http://www.europarl.europa.eu/ftu/pdf/en/FTU_1.2.1.pdf
Eurostat (2020) Asylum and first time asylum applicants by citizenship, age and sex: monthly data (rounded). https://appsso.eurostat.ec.europa.eu/nui/show.do?dataset=migr_asyappctzm&lang=en
Filippo MD (2016) Dublin 'reloaded' or time for ambitious pragmatism? http://eumigrationlawblog.eu/dublin-reloaded
Gammeltoft-Hansen T, Feith Tan N (2017) The end of the deterrence paradigm? Future directions for global refugee policy. J Migration Hum Security 28–56
Goodwin-Gill GS, McAdam J (2007) The Refugee in International Law, 3rd edn. Oxford University Press Inc.), New York
Greer S (2000) The margin of appreciation: interpretation and discretion under the European Convention on Human Rights. Council of Europe Publishing, Strasbourg
InfoMigrants (2019) Seeking asylum in Europe in 2019: facts and figures. https://www.infomigrants.net/en/post/21810/seeking-asylum-in-europe-in-2019-facts-and-figures
International Commission of Jurists (2011) Non-refoulement in Europe after M.S.S. v. Belgium and Greece. http://www.icj.org/wp-content/uploads/2012/06/Non-refoulement-Europe-summary-of-the-workshop-event-2011-.pdf
International Commission of Jurists (2016) Procedural rights in the proposed Dublin IV Regulation. http://www.icj.org/wp-content/uploads/2016/09/EU-Dublin-IV-Regulation_Comment-Advocacy-Analysis-Brief-2016-ENG.pdf
Library of Congress (2016) Refugee law and policy: European Union. https://www.loc.gov/law/help/refugee-law/europeanunion.php
Long D (2002) Guide to jurisprudence on torture And Ill-treatment: article 3 of the European Convention for the Protection of Human Rights. https://www.apt.ch/content/files_res/Article3_en.pdf
Lübbe A (2015) 'Systemic flaws' and Dublin transfers: incompatible tests before the CJEU and the ECtHR? Int J Refugee Law 27(1):135–140
McAdam J (2007) Complementary protection in international refugee law. Oxford University Press), Oxford
Moreno-Lax V (2017a) Accessing asylum in Europe: extraterritorial border controls and refugee rights under EU law. Oxford University Press), Oxford
Moreno-Lax V (2017b) EU non-refoulement (the irrelevance of) territoriality and pre-border controls. In Accessing asylum in Europe: extraterritorial border controls and refugee rights under EU Law. Oxford University Press), Oxford
Norwegian Refugee Council (2020) Q&A: what does the Turkish border situation mean for Europe? https://www.nrc.no/news/2020/march/q–a-refugees-and-migrants-to-europe

Peers S (2016) The Orbanisation of EU asylum law: the latest EU asylum proposals. http://eulawanalysis.blogspot.ca/2016/05/the-orbanisation-of-eu-asylum-law.html

Poon J (2016a) ESIL Reflection: the EU Commission on 'Dublin IV': sufficient safeguards for asylum claimants? Eur Soc Int Law Reflections 5(9):1–10. http://esil-sedi.eu/wp-content/uploads/2016/10/ESIL-Reflections-Jenny-Poon-Nov-2016-Revision-20161109-clean_1.pdf

Poon J (2016b) Is the margin of appreciation accorded to European Union member states too wide, permitting violations of international law? *Opinio Juris*. http://opiniojuris.org/2016/08/16/emerging-voices-is-the-margin-of-appreciation-accorded-to-european-union-member-states-too-wide-permitting-violation-of-international-law

Poon J (2020) Rethinking the Common European Asylum System: protection or containment? University of Oxford, Department of International: *Rethinking Refuge*

Prechal S (2017) Mutual Trust before the Court of Justice of the European Union. Eur Papers 1(2):75–92

Proposal for a regulation of the European parliament and of the council establishing the criteria and mechanisms for determining the member state responsible for examining an application for international protection lodged in one of the member states by a third-country national or a stateless person (recast), COM(2016) 270 final, 2016/0133 (COD), Brussels, 4 May 2016

Ryngaert C (2012) Clarifying the extraterritorial application of the European Convention on Human rights. Utrecht J Int Eur Law 28(74):57–60

Sidorenko OF (2007) The Common European Asylum System: background, current state of affairs, future direction. TMC Asser Press, The Hague

Statewatch (2013a) Analysis: the second phase of the Common European Asylum System: a brave new world – or lipstick on a pig? http://www.statewatch.org/analyses/no-220-ceas-second-phase.pdf

Statewatch (2013b) Analysis: the second phase of the Common European Asylum System: a brave new world—or lipstick on a pig? http://www.statewatch.org/analyses/no-220-ceas-second-phase.pdf

Stoyanova V (2020) MN and others v Belgium: no ECHR protection from refoulement by issuing visas. http://ejiltalk.org/m-n-and-others-v-belgium-no-echr-protection-from-refoulement-by-issuing-visas.

Thym D (2015) Beyond Dublin – merkel's vision of EU asylum policy. EU Immigration and Asylum Law and Policy

UNHCR (2010) Section 12: the safe third country concept, 1–39. https://www.refworld.org/cgi-bin/texis/vtx/rwmain/opendocpdf.pdf?reldoc=y&docid=4bab55e22

UNHCR (2018) Legal considerations regarding access to protection and a connection between the refugee and the third country in the context of return or transfer to safe third countries. https://www.refworld.org/pdfid/5acb33ad4.pdf

Vicini G (2015) The Dublin Regulation between Strasbourg and Luxembourg: reshaping non-refoulement in the name of mutual trust? Eur J Legal Stud 8(2):50–72. https://cadmus.eui.eu/bitstream/handle/1814/38608/EJLS_2015_Vicini.pdf?sequence=1&isAllowed=y

Weissbrodt D, Hörtreiter I (1999) The principle of *non-refoulement*: Article 3 of the Convention against Torture and Other Cruel, Inhuman or Degrading Treatment or Punishment in comparison with the *non-refoulement* provisions of other international human rights treaties. Buffalo Hum Rights Law Rev 5(1):1–74

Wilde R (2010) Compliance with human rights norms extraterritorially: 'human rights imperialism'? In: Chazournes L, Kohen M (eds) International law and the quest for its implementation. Brill, Boston

Chapter 4
Containment in Europe

4.1 Introduction

Chapters 2 and 3 outlined the international and regional law governing *non-refoulement* within the European Union (EU). They demonstrated that the principle prohibiting *refoulement* is quite robust, particularly when one considers the norm in a complementary manner taking into account its meaning and application under international refugee law *and* international human rights law. At the same time, Chap. 3 indicated that the full content of the principle is not always respected in practice within the EU. For example, some EU Member States restrict procedural safeguards, add procedural barriers, or adopt overly narrow interpretations of *non-refoulement* in domestic law when exercising the 'margin of discretion' they are permitted under EU law, thereby weakening the underlying safeguards that help to protect against *refoulement*. Some EU Member States rely upon the presumption of mutual trust to transfer responsibility for asylum seekers without ensuring adequate processes exist in the other Member States to prevent *refoulement*. These actions result in a gap between the written and customary international and regional law of *non-refoulement* and actual practices regarding the norm. This Chapter proposes an explanation of why this gap exists: the theory of containment and the adoption of containment policies. The goal of examining the theory of containment is to provide crucial context for the recommendations articulated in Chap. 7.

The theory of containment is exactly what it sounds like: a theory on how States contain or control the mobility or immobility of migrants within or outside of their borders.[1] The theory of containment is not exclusive to the field of international,

[1] Dartmouth College Library, "A Short Definition for Migration Studies", which states: 'The movement of groups and individuals from one place to another, involving a change of usual residence. Migration is usually distinguished from mobility in general by conventions of spatial and temporal scale. For example, by convention international migration requires crossing a national boundary for an actual or intended period of at least

J. Poon, *Counteracting Containment Policies in the EU*, European Union and its Neighbours in a Globalized World 31,
https://doi.org/10.1007/978-3-032-08351-7_4

regional and domestic refugee law or to the field of international human rights law. In fact, this theory originated outside of the legal sphere, and in recent years has been applied within the fields of spatial and human geography and migration studies. This chapter begins by explaining containment theories in these two fields. Next, it demonstrates that the theory of containment is applicable to certain policies and practices within the Common European Asylum System (CEAS), such as Dublin transfers and 'safe' third country agreements. The chapter turns to a discussion of how containment policies and practices in the EU affect the protection of asylum seekers from *refoulement*. Finally, the chapter ends with concluding remarks on the place of containment theory within the field of refugee law and international law. This chapter shows that, while the law of containment itself is not a violation of international law, the policies and practices surrounding the application of that law are of concern: containment arises not because of the law itself, but in the misuse and misapplication of that law.

4.2 Theories of Containment

There is not one single unified theory of containment, as the theory has emerged from a number of different disciplines. Rather, there are multiple theories of containment. For example, in the field of political science, the term 'containment' or 'strategies of containment' was used in the past to describe 'the appropriate American strategy to counter the threat of Soviet expansionism in the aftermath of World War II and the advent of the Cold War'.[2] This chapter focuses on theories of containment in two specific areas: geography and migration studies.[3] Migration studies can be categorized—at least in part—as a subset of the field of human and spatial geography, and therefore the theories of containment in both geography and migration studies intersect.

The field of spatial and human geography involves the study of human populations and their interactions with spaces and the environment.[4] For example, the geography of migration has been described as 'a spatio-temporal process that evolves over space and time[;] [it] involves the continual reshaping of places as persons move between various origins and destinations'.[5] In the field of spatial and

---

one year', https://researchguides.dartmouth.edu/human_geography/migration; See, also: Castree, Noel, Kitchin, Rob, and Rogers, Alisdair (2013) at 315–316.

[2] Litwak, Robert S (2004).

[3] Tazzioli, Martina (2017) [Tazzioli].

[4] Dartmouth College Library (2022), which states: 'The study of the interrelationships between people, place, and environment, and how these vary spatially and temporally across and between locations'.

[5] Li, Wei, Skop, Emily, and Morken, Adriana (2017), which states: 'Geographers are especially interested in the process because of the interconnections and spatial linkages that are formed when people move. The numbers of flows and channels that are created as a result of migration have

human geography, the term 'containment' is used to refer to 'discourse[s], laws or policies, and technologies of control—such as detention—[. . .] as global disciplinary strategies attempting to differentially shape migrant mobility'.[6] The theory of containment, as expressed in the field of spatial and human geography, has two main characteristics. First, the theory of containment suggests that migrants are kept on the move.[7] Mobility of migrants is restricted, contained, and confined to a specific sphere of movement. This can be done through refugee camps, transfers between detention facilities, and regulating the movement of asylum claimants and refugees through biometric data collection by border authorities.[8] Second, the theory suggests that migratory movements are contained.[9] Scholars have also asserted that 'the borders of the European Union are conceptualized as both tightening and filtering, employing biometric and passport technologies to select individuals to be detained or deported.[10] In other words, containment is possible where migrants are simultaneously kept on the move and contained outside of the countries where they are seeking asylum, rather than being contained within a specific, confined area.[11] Scholars have maintained that mobility can also be highly regulated through the transfers of those detained to and from detention centres, which is also a method of regulating, restricting, and controlling migratory movement through containment strategies.[12] 'Containment' can also be achieved through detention of migrants.[13] For instance, scholars have argued that containment may 'also be a consequence of other restrictions on refugees' movement

---

risen dramatically in the past two centuries, and the result is the constant transformation both of sending and receiving areas. The patterns, causes, and consequences of migration are innumerable and include complicated, multiscalar economic, political, cultural, and demographic effects, all of which are studied by geographers'.

[6] Mountz, Alison, Coddington, Kate, Catania, R Tina, and Loyd, Jenna M (2013) at 526 [Mountz].

[7] *Ibid.*

[8] *Ibid;* See, also: Houtum, Henk Van (2010) at 958–959, which states: 'at the external borders of the EU [there] consists of waiting zones, camps, new fences, and new biometric methods of patrol. Hence, an EU scape with increasingly defensive external borders is being erected' [Houtum].

[9] *Ibid.*

[10] *Ibid;* See, also: Houtum at 971, which states: 'For the EU, then, the installation of camps is a form of concentration and containment, of 'stocking' the people without papers in order to facilitate and manage more efficiently the daily biopolitical *control* of their whereabouts' (emphasis added).

[11] Tazzioli.

[12] Mountz at 528–530, which states: 'Even as detention contains migrant bodies, it simultaneously makes those same bodies more mobile in controlled ways through dispersal, transfers, and deportation. Rationales for detention often assert that detention is necessary to prevent migrants from absconding, yet, in order to prevent migrants from moving (or removing themselves from state oversight), detention continuously moves them around. Frequent transfers among detention facilities are common in the United States, Australia, Italy, and other countries'; see, also: Majcher, Izabella (2017).

[13] Mountz at 522, which states: 'processes of detention and confinement have been relatively neglected by geographers. This is surprising because these social practices of immobilization are

(including, but by no means limited to, border security, visa controls, and immigration detention), or a failure to facilitate lasting durable solutions that enable refugees and [internally displaced persons] to escape their conditions'.[14] Scholars have also contended that containment refers to:

> any effort to localize or internalize forced migration in countries or regions of origin. Visa requirements, carrier sanctions, return of asylum seekers to 'countries of first asylum', the creation of 'safe havens', and 'humanitarian' intervention are among the methods of containment.[15]

Containment, therefore, is a practice of *control* of the movement, or lack of movement, of migrants—of the geographic spaces in which they reside.

Strategies of geographic containment are often facilitated by law. One example of this is through the use of national deterrence laws.[16] National deterrence laws include laws that create barriers, whether politically or legally, which reduce, restrict, or deter the movement of asylum claimants and refugees into and across that State's territory.[17] Another example can be seen in 'refugees in orbit' situations, where refugees find themselves in legal limbo: rejected from the country where they are seeking refuge, yet not able to or unwilling to return to their country of origin.[18] While laws—or, specifically, narrow or self-serving interpretations of law by States—can create 'refugees in orbit' situations, it should be noted that such situations are against the established intention of the drafters of the Refugee Convention and contrary to the purpose of the institution of asylum, which seeks

---

fundamental reliant on spatial tactics, or the use of space to control people, objects, and their movement'.

[14] McConnachie, Kirsten (2016) at 398, which states: 'containment has been used to describe a shift from asylum predicated on protecting mobility to asylum predicated on managing mobility, with the latter goal primarily achieved by containment in migrants' region or even country of origin'; See, also: Shacknove, Andrew (1993) at 527, which states: 'Containment takes many forms and serves many purposes. For example, visa requirements and carrier sanctions are intended primarily to regulate illegal immigration [. . .] A policy of containing forced migration is likely to erode further the political and legal justification for distinguishing between refugees and the internally displaced [. . .] A second justification for a sustained commitment to asylum is that efforts to contain victims of human rights abuses within zones of conflict, even where doing so is possible, may be contrary to international stability' [Shacknove].

[15] Shacknove at 516, the author concludes with: 'A preference for containment, in itself or coupled with other forms of intervention, must proceed with caution [. . .] Containment is justifiable only under limited conditions. A policy of good governance worthy of its name entails commitments from both donors and aid-receiving States'.

[16] Mountz at 526.

[17] *Ibid;* For example, these laws and policies may use detention and deportation as tools and methods to regulate migration and to deter those who may not have legal status within the country from entering the territories of the State to claim asylum; Mountz at 527, which states: 'while detention serves to contain and isolate individual detainees, it simultaneously reconstitutes contained individuals as mobile collective threats'.

[18] Refugee Convention at preamble; Moreover, it must be clear that the denial of entry does not lead to a situation of refugees in orbit who cannot find protection because every State relies on the potential protection by another State.

to safeguard the right to seek asylum from persecution and *non-refoulement* protection.[19] This is explored further below.

Migration studies examines the movement of people, including the study of both mobility and immobility, and therefore uses a somewhat different lens than the one described above for the field of spatial and human geography.[20] Geographers who study migration question the containment efforts by the EU in their research. For example, scholars have argued that the EU has utilized geographies of exclusion as a method of containing asylum claimants and refugees including by:

> isolating migrants in remote locations, States restrict access to territories where they might make refugee claims or take up residency illegally. Articulated sequentially, these trends suggest an exclusionary series of maneuvers on the part of nation-states to *exercise control* (emphasis added).[21]

Experts on the Common European Asylum System have also cited the practices and policies of refugee containment. For instance, some scholars have contended that the CEAS is 'destined to remain a policy failure, an ethical sore, and political tinderbox' if refugee containment is not properly addressed.[22] However, these studies have focused mainly on the *costs* of containment rather than on the *causes* of containment and the sources and origin of the concept in refugee law.[23] Other experts have asserted the role of containment theories in public emergencies which threaten the life of the nation.[24] The main arguments of these scholars suggest that a theory of containment can explain the extent of the powers, and its limits, of a nation in a state of emergency to constrain and contain external threats.[25]

Within migration studies, one area of containment theory focus is on European 'hotspots': places at the external borders of Europe where large numbers of

---

[19] Also see *Travaux Préprаratories* of the Refugee Convention, See also: Weis.

[20] Dartmouth College Library (2021), which states: 'The movement of groups and individuals from one place to another, involving a change of usual residence. Migration is usually distinguished from mobility in general by conventions of spatial and temporal scale. For example, by convention international migration requires crossing a national boundary for an actual or intended period of at least one year'; See also: Tazzioli.

[21] Hyndman, Jennifer, and Mountz, Alison (2007) at 85, which states: 'Acknowledging international legal commitments but generating non-sovereign spaces of exception to them. Those fleeing spaces of political violence in their home countries are consistently conflated with those who represent a security threat elsewhere, creating new spaces of political violence in the form of exclusion, detention, and the suspension of civil and human rights'.

[22] Costello Containment at 17 and 22.

[23] For example, Costello mentions in her article that: 'Refugee containment is not only a European practice, but many of the policies and practices that are central to refugee containment are of fairly recent European origin [...] Containment contributed to the events styled as the 2015 refugee crisis in Europe, yet the crisis has generated a more intensified set of containment practices, also likely to backfire', and further, that: 'This Article identifies the costs of this refugee containment, not only for refugees and asylum-seekers, but also for Europe itself, its politics, and its adherence to the rule of law in particular', see Costello Containment at 17.

[24] Loevy, Karin (2016).

[25] *Ibid* at 6.

migrants arrive, such as the islands of Greece and Italy.[26] The geographical position of these hotspots along the Mediterranean Sea route serves to control the entry of migrants and to contain them away from the mainland.[27] Within these hotspots, a so-called EU 'hotspot approach' has evolved,

> where the European Asylum Support Office (EASO), the European Border and Coast Guard Agency (Frontex), Europol and Eurojust work on the ground with the authorities of frontline EU Member States which are facing disproportionate migratory pressures at the EU's external borders to help to fulfill their obligations under EU law and swiftly identify, register and fingerprint incoming migrants.[28]

The EU's hotspot approach on the islands of Greece and Italy has been described as 'the 'immediate response' to increased arrivals into Europe of refugees crossing the Mediterranean Sea'.[29] Frontline EU Member States assume a heavier share of responsibility to process asylum applications and use island hotspot infrastructures in order to enforce migration containment.[30] This very fact of hotspots as places where containment approaches are put under strain results in frontline EU Member States bearing the heaviest responsibility, contrary to the legally-binding principle of responsibility sharing among EU Member States.[31] The European Commission emphasized that:

> the experience of recent years has shown that, especially in situations of mass influx along specific migratory routes, the current system places responsibility, in law, for the vast majority of asylum seekers on a limited number of individual Member States, a situation which would stretch the capacities of any Member State.[32]

Amnesty International has critiqued the use of island hotspots because these areas also are areas where multiple abuses of force take place and maltreatment of asylum claimants occurs.[33] Since these island hotspots are part of the EU's strategy of containing migratory movement away from the mainland, some scholars have labeled the EU's hotspot approach as 'shrinking spaces of asylum'.[34] They do so

[26] Tazzioli, Martina, and Garelli, Glenda (2018), 2 [Tazzioli and Garelli].

[27] *Ibid.*

[28] European Commission, Migration and Home Affairs, "Hotspot Approach", https://ec.europa.eu/home-affairs/content/hotspot-approach_en.

[29] Garelli, Glenda, and Tazzioli, Martina (2016) at 4 [Beyond Detention].

[30] *Ibid* at 2765.

[31] TFEU at art 80.

[32] *Ibid.*

[33] Amnesty International (2016), which states: 'Amnesty International is deeply concerned that the procedures applied by Italian authorities to issue expulsion orders [. . .] were not in line with international law, including European human rights law, and that they may have therefore breached the principle of non-refoulement and the prohibition of collective expulsions'.

[34] Mountz (2011) at 126.

because migration is essentially funnelled to these hotspots, such as on the Lesbos Islands in Greece, where the movements of asylum seekers are restricted due to geography.[35] Further, island hotspots function as isolated mechanisms to exclude those who are 'unwanted', while allowing only those who are considered eligible for asylum claims into the system.[36] The 'unwanted' are often individuals who are deemed to be 'outsiders' or 'the other': those who do not have legal documentation or who otherwise arrived on the territories of the Member State through irregular means.[37] Those labeled 'unwanted' are often coerced to stay behind in detention or worse—deported to third country destinations deemed 'safe' but that often do not have adequate procedural safeguards for claimants to access international protection.[38] The hotspot approach is also a method of migration control, whereby entry to the mainland (as opposed to island hotspots) to claim asylum is obstructed.[39] The movements of these claimants are often obstructed through administrative detention, or through highly regularized travel restraints such as police checkpoints where identity papers are sought.[40]

As observed above in the field of spatial and human geography, there is also a link between law and containment in migration studies. Scholars have observed that strategies related to making and keeping migrants mobile or immobile are often facilitated by laws: for example, Tazzioli observes that States take *legal* terrain away from migrants in the same way they restrict access to physical terrain.[41] Sometimes the legal and physical terrains coincide, such as with laws restricting the movements of migrants into, within, and from a State.[42]

[35] Transnational Institute (2018) "The shrinking space for solidarity with migrants and refugees" September 2018, which states: 'Premised on providing support for member states dealing with large influxes of people, it is primarily designed to ensure that identification, registration and fingerprinting is systematically implemented, with security screening if necessary [. . .] Hotspots like the one in Moria on Lesbos effectively turned into long-term detention centres where people waited to be returned to Turkey, in pitiful conditions and with severe overcrowding', at 12 [TI Report].

[36] Beyond Detention at 4.

[37] TI Report at 16, which states: 'It is important to stress the rupture being forced upon Italian society by policies implemented within the framework of the European Agenda on Migration. Italy is in the difficult position of having to deal with the EU's unwanted migrants with little more than coercion and deportation'.

[38] *Ibid.*

[39] *Ibid.*

[40] Tazzioli, Martina (2018) at 2766: 'hotspots [work] as a lens for analysing modes of migration control through mobility and for bringing attention to migrants's *[sic]* spatial disobediences against the restrictions imposed by the EU policies of asylum'; See, also: TI Report at 25, which states: '[there are] unprecedented restrictions, including threats and acts of violence, criticism in the media and criminalization' [Tazzioli Journal].

[41] Tazzioli.

[42] Oxford Dictionary of Economics (2017); Where primary policies and laws refer to the stated goals of the CEAS—to harmonize asylum policies across the EU and to enhance efficiency in the processing of asylum applications.

Containment through law can occur through administrative or legislative measures by the government to regulate and create barriers for migratory movements.[43]

Together, spatial and human geography and migration studies explore the interactions and movements of human populations with spaces and places—both in the form of mobility and immobility. The theories of containment expressed in both spatial and human geography and migration studies are clearly interlinked. That said, Tazzioli notes that: 'the notion of "containment" has surprisingly remained quite under-theorised both in the field of migration studies and in geography scholarship', requiring further conceptualization.[44] Given the linkages to law, it can also be said that containment theory in legal analysis is also under-theorized, though there has been some recognition by scholars such as Costello.[45]

As a type of control theory which explicates spatial confinement, the containment theory applied in the migration context is an *explanatory* theory: it explains exclusion or inclusion of migrants through tactics to keep them out (migration control policies) or lock them in (detention policies).[46] However, the theory of containment need not be binary in nature, explaining only exclusion and inclusion, or mobility and immobility.[47] Containment policies may also involve tactics to keep migrants on the move, creating the 'refugees in orbit' situation. A warning, however: as an explanatory theory, containment theory should not be viewed 'as an overarching analytical grid' toward which countries should aim.[48] Rather, it is

---

[43] Tazzioli Journal at 2765, 'migration movements are obstructed in their autonomy not only by generating immobility and conditions of strandedness, nor through constant surveillance but through administrative, political and legal measures that use (forced) mobility as a technique of government. Containment refers to the ways in which migrants' movements and presence are troubled, subjected to convoluted or hectic movements and to protracted moment of strandedness. Thus, containment can involve both spatial and temporal hindrances that end up in troubling migrants' stay and mobility'.

[44] Tazzioli and Garelli at 3; See, also: Tazzioli.

[45] Costello Containment at 17–20, which states: 'Refugee containment is not only a European practice, but many of the policies and practices that are central to refugee containment are of fairly recent European origin [...] Containment contributed to the events styled as the 2015 refugee crisis in Europe, yet the crisis has generated a more intensified set of containment policies, also likely to backfire'; Further, that: 'Containment evidently has an immense cost in human lives [...] The EU now supports a network of places of detention and containment at the EU's periphery in order to prevent would-be refugees from seeking asylum beyond'; Also: 'Europe had several years to address the potential of that Syrians would seek protection in Europe, and it effectively chose to hope that containment would work [...] Due to containment practices, refugee arrivals are unpredictable and invariably look like a crisis'.

[46] Tazzioli; The Oxford English Dictionary defines 'control' as 'the power to influence or direct people's behaviour or the course of events', 'the restriction of an activity, tendency, or phenomenon', and 'a means of limiting or regulating something', as applied to the migration context of the EU, a theory about control involves a theory which explains EU's power to influence, direct, restrict, limit, and regulate migratory movements, see: "Control".

[47] *Ibid.*

[48] Tazzioli.

a geographical concept with spatial effects (physical, social, economic, and legal) that States generally try to avoid admitting they fulfill. Instead, they use obfuscatory language to indicate otherwise, such as when the EU justifies its secondary policies and laws as having the ultimate goal of 'containing migratory flows and tackling irregular migration through enhanced border management and the *fight against smuggling and trafficking'* (emphasis added).[49] At its core, containment is a theory about control.[50]

Having explained containment theory as developed in the fields of spatial and human geography and migration studies, the next section will examine how containment in the broadest sense—not only limited to confinement or detention, but also including calculated movement of migrants—is evident in the CEAS in a legal and policy sense.

4.3 Containment in the Common European Asylum System

The aims of the CEAS are to harmonize the standards of protection by aligning the EU Member States' asylum legislation, support cooperation among EU Member States on the implementation of asylum policies, and to increase solidarity and responsibility among EU Member States.[51] These aims exist uneasily beside certain practices within the CEAS that amount to forms of containment of migrants, including asylum seekers. The EU's asylum policies have been described as:

[49] Buscaini; The term 'irregular' is used rather than 'illegal' because the latter term connotates criminality, when there are many reasons and factors contributing to asylum claimants' decisions to enter the EU through irregular means. For example, incentives for irregular migration may include the inability to access legal and safe routes through migration control mechanisms, see: See, for example: UNHCR (2018) "Desperate Journeys: Refugees and Migrants Arriving in Europe and at Europe's Borders", at 15: 'Measures this year to try to further reduce the number of arrivals in Europe, in addition to the limited access to Italian ports for refugees and migrants rescued at sea since June, included further restrictions on the work of NGOs involved in search and rescue off the Libyan coast, and additional support to Libyan authorities to prevent sea crossings to Europe. These are in addition to other existing measures, such as the provisions of the EU-Turkey Statement concerning those crossing the sea from Turkey to Greece'; Moreover, an individual's choice (or lack of choice) to enter a State's territory to claim asylum through irregular means should not be penalized; this requirement is found in Article 31(1) of the Refugee Convention; There are many negative consequences which may result from the prevention of irregular migration into Europe. Most notably, individuals who are unable to enter the EU through regular, legal routes are often forced to make perilous journeys across the Mediterranean Sea or through other routes in order to seek safety. However, some scholars have made the argument that it is the operation of law-enabled *non-entrée* (non-admission) restrictions which sometimes incentivizes the use of *irregular* routes to reach safety, see: Wilde, Ralph (2017).

[50] *Ibid*; For example, hotspots in Greece evidence EU's attempt to regain control over migration movements.

[51] CEAS.

> actions directed at both attenuating causes of departure and reducing cross-border movements [including the use of] 'source control' measures, such as conflict prevention, development assistance, trade partnerships and political dialogue[,] increasingly deployed in order to lessen the migration pressure towards the EU.[52]

In other words, the EU actively endeavours to prevent the departure of individuals wishing to migrate to Europe, and to reduce cross-border movements toward Europe through actions in the countries or regions of origin for migrants. The activities of the EU's High Level Working Group on Asylum and Migration (Working Group) are crucial in this regard. The Working Group is a central forum set up in 1998 for strategic discussions with the aim of '[establishing] a common, integrated, cross-pillar approach targeted at the situation in the most important countries of origin of asylum-seekers and migrants'.[53] The significance of this High Level Working Group is that it marks the 'most concrete manifestation of the attempt to institutionalize centralized responsibility and a concerted framework of action for all relevant EU institutions dealing with asylum and migration policies'.[54] The usage of the term 'containment' to describe or explain the EU's asylum policies is therefore not new.[55]

Key CEAS containment policies include the use of Dublin transfers, 'safe' third country agreements, the interception of asylum seekers prior to reaching Europe, migrant tracking, narrow interpretations of the Refugee Convention, and deterrence policies. Each of these approaches will be discussed in turn.

As explained in Chap. 3, Dublin transfers are transfers of asylum seekers from one EU country to another EU country deemed 'responsible' for those asylum seekers. Responsibility is determined based on a hierarchy of considerations summarized in that chapter. The goal of the Dublin transfer regime 'not to spread refugees equitably among Contracting Parties, but to introduce a set of criteria to *swiftly assign* responsibility among them' (emphasis added).[56] These transfers take place on the presumption of mutual trust, also explained in Chap. 3:

> The system is based on the fundamental assumption that member states may be considered 'safe' countries for asylum seekers, and for that reason, it is presumed that transfers from one member state to another do not violate the principle of non-refoulement.[57]

This approach reduces the 'refugees in orbit' problem, but it also reinforces the control and containment of migrants at the external borders of the EU, particularly in the hotspots described above. As well, as described in Chap. 3, Dublin transfers based on the presumption of mutual trust can also return asylum seekers to EU

---

[52] *Ibid.*

[53] European Union (1999) at 1.

[54] See, for example: Channe Lindstrøm (2005) at 595 [Lindstrøm].

[55] Lindstrøm at 593.

[56] Cortinovis, Roberto (2018) at 4 [Cortinovis].

[57] *Ibid.*

countries that do not have, in actuality, adequate refugee processing systems and therefore adequate protections against *refoulement*.[58]

A related strategy with the aim of restricting migratory movements is related to registration and the notion of 'first country of asylum'. The Dublin III Regulation restricts movements of claimants and refugees who are in search of international protection by requiring them to register at the first EU Member State of arrival.[59] Where the claimant is found to have already registered in an EU Member State in which international protection for claiming refugee status is sought, but subsequently moved onward to another Member State, the individual will be sent back to the Member State responsible for processing the asylum application through the Dublin III Regulation.[60] This shifts the responsibility for processing the asylum application from one EU Member State to another Member State (via Dublin transfers).[61]

EU Member States' use of 'safe' third country agreements provides another example of containment policies in action. Like Dublin transfers, 'safe' third country agreements are diversion policies 'designed to shift to other States the responsibility for those asylum-seekers who manage to arrive at the borders of the European Union'.[62] 'Safe' third country are agreements in which an EU Member State provides another country (outside of the EU) with an overarching, or blanket, recognition of that country as a safe place to which to send asylum claimants. 'The safe third country notion rests on the assumption that an asylum applicant could have obtained international protection in another country and therefore the receiving state is entitled to reject responsibility for the protection claim'.[63] If the responsible country is deemed 'safe', then the transfer can happen efficiently without an inquiry into the specific situation of each asylum claimant. Where the claimant or refugee is found to have passed through a 'safe' non-EU country, that individual will be returned to that third country, as the country deemed to be responsible for processing the asylum application.[64] 'Safe' third country recognition and Dublin transfers are provided for under the Asylum Procedures Directive (recast) and the Dublin III Regulation respectively.[65]

---

[58] For example, nongovernment organizations have raised concerns about asylum laws, policies and practices in Serbia, Macedonia, Croatia, Hungary and Bulgaria: 'Rather than being places of safety, countries on the Western Balkan route have failed to offer protection or due process to many new arrivals and instead have pushed them back to their previous country of transit or even another country, without giving them a chance to claim asylum' thereby raising serious concerns about *refoulement*, see: Oxfam (2017) at 2, 9, and 12.

[59] Dublin III Regulation at art 3(1) and 3(2); A further discussion of the hierarchy of criteria which determines the Member State responsible for processing the asylum application is in Chap. 4.

[60] Dublin III Regulation at art 3(2).

[61] Court of Justice of the EU, "Opinion 2/13", 18 December 2014 at para 191; See also: Prechal.

[62] *Ibid* at 19(ii).

[63] Cortinovis at 3.

[64] Asylum Procedures Directive at art 38.

[65] *Ibid*; Dublin III Regulation at chp VI.

EU Member States use the 'safe' third country concept to shift the responsibility for processing asylum applications elsewhere, that is, from the Member State deemed responsible for examining the application based on the Dublin III Regulation, to a non-EU country deemed 'safe'.[66] At the same time, claimants who have been sent back to non-EU countries deemed 'safe' pursuant to the Asylum Procedures Directive (recast) are not allowed to re-enter the Member State that returned the claimant to the third country.[67] This approach keeps claimants from returning to the EU, and therefore contains migrants outside of the EU. For example, under Article 46(5) of the Asylum Procedures Directive (recast), EU Member States are allowed to not grant suspensive recourse (the right to remain in the country of asylum pending outcome of appeal) to persons whose application was initially considered unfounded or manifestly unfounded.[68] An 'unfounded' application for international protection means that the applicant does not qualify for international protection, while a 'manifestly unfounded' application means that the applicant for international protection does not qualify for refugee status due to reasons including fraud or deception during the application process.[69] This means that asylum claimants whose applications were initially considered unfounded or manifestly unfounded may be forced to return to their country of origin or forced to leave the territory of the Member State, without the possibility of return. One result of 'safe' third country policies is an increased chance of *refoulement*: in the event of an unfounded or manifestly unfounded asylum application, the claimant will be without any recourse against a rejected asylum application, thus the claimant's *non-refoulement* protection may be violated if he or she is returned without the ability to appeal against a wrongful determination.[70]

EU Member States also facilitate the use of 'safe' third country lists, which are lists of countries which the EU has predetermined to be 'safe' for claimants.[71] The use of predetermined 'safe' third country lists is problematic because it may

---

[66] *Ibid.*

[67] European Association for the Defence of Human Rights, International Federation for Human Rights, and EuroMed Rights (2016) at 9 [FIDH].

[68] Asylum Procedures Directive at art 46(5).

[69] European Commission, Migration and Home Affairs, "Manifestly Unfounded Application for International Protection": 'In the EU context, an unfounded application for international protection that is considered under national legislation of EU Member States to manifestly unfounded in one of the following circumstances: the applicant has only raised issues that are not relevant for the qualification as beneficiary of international protection; the applicant is from a safe country of origin; the applicant is, for serious reasons, considered a danger to the national security or public order or the application is based on deliberate deception or an abuse of the procedure for international protection'.

[70] For a discussion on how the use of 'safe' third country concepts may lower standards of protection including violating the principle of *non-refoulement*, see generally: Arribas, Gloria Fernandez (2016) [Arribas].

[71] 'As regards the EU list of safe third countries, the latest Presidency compromise provides that it is to be adopted via a Regulation modifying the Asylum Procedure Regulation (Article 46(1)) and that national lists may continue to exist in parallel (a sunset clause for such lists existed in the original Commission proposal)' in Council of the European Union (2018) at 4.

potentially increase instances of *refoulement*. First, predetermined 'safe' third country lists do not take into account the changing political situation and human rights record in the third country.[72] Therefore, the use of predetermined 'safe' third country lists may increase the potential for *refoulement* in situations where claimants are returned to territories with unstable or rapidly-changing political or human rights situations, where their lives or freedom would be threatened.[73] Second, predetermined 'safe' third country lists accelerate the asylum procedure for the claimant by sending him or her back to the third country deemed responsible for processing the claimant's application.[74] In practice, access to asylum procedures in the third country may not be adequate and may not meet international law standards, including the requirement to provide the claimant with fair and efficient access to those procedures.[75] As the UNHCR stated, *non-refoulement* is violated when the country of asylum denies the claimant's access to fair and efficient asylum procedures, for example, by not examining his or her particular circumstances and refusing the claimant an opportunity to rebut the presumption of safety.[76] The UNHCR has cautioned against the use of predetermined 'safe' third country lists and has requested that 'procedures in such cases should explicitly provide for return to be effected only if the individual will be readmitted to the ['safe' third] country, will be able to access fair asylum procedures and, if recognized, will be able to enjoy effective protection there'.[77]

Another containment strategy adopted by the EU is the prevention of certain migrants from reaching Europe's external borders, albeit often with State discourse 'about protecting migrants from traffickers and from dangerous crossing'.[78] These are termed 'non-arrival policies': policies 'aimed at preventing, interrupting or stopping improperly documented aliens, including potential asylum-seekers, from ever reaching Europe'.[79] In 2015, the European Commission to the European Parliament, the European Council, and the European Economic and Social

---

[72] For example, the UNHCR has reiterated that 'best practice involves an assessment that is indeed a repeated application in which there are no significant substantive changes to the asylum-seeker's individual situation or *to the circumstances in the country of origin*' (emphasis added) in UNHCR (2001) at para 31 [UNHCR Asylum Procedures].

[73] *Ibid.*

[74] The concept of 'safe' third country is defined as 'a non-EU country through which the asylum seeker has transited and to which h/she may be returned, as the Member State considers the asylum application should have been lodged there. The application for asylum is therefore examined not by the Member State but by the 'safe' third country in question' in FIDH at 5.

[75] UNHCR Asylum Procedures at 611.

[76] *Ibid* at paras 13 and 14: 'The third State needs actually to implement appropriate asylum procedures and systems fairly. Any list-based general assessment of safety of the third country needs to be applied flexibly, and ensure due consideration of that country's safety for the individual asylum-seeker'.

[77] *Ibid* at para 15; See, also: UNHCR, Executive Committee, "Note on International Protection", UN Doc A/AC.96/914 at para 19.

[78] Tazzioli at 542.

[79] *Ibid* at 19(i).

Committee and the Committee of the Regions tabled a report that initiated the use of the language of securitization and reliance on efforts to reduce irregular migration, including through the increase of border management.[80] Titled 'A European Agenda on Migration', the 22-page document details the EU's efforts to respond to the increase in the number of individuals crossing the Mediterranean Sea in search of safety and a better life.[81] This Agenda was presented by the European Commission to the European Parliament, the European Council, and the European Economic and Social Committee and the Committee of the Regions to 'address immediate challenges and equip the EU with the tools to better manage migration'.[82] This policy was later adopted by European heads of State and governments in the European Council on June 25–26, 2015, and since then has become the basis for the European policy on irregular migration.[83] The term 'irregular migration' refers to migration through routes that are not at authorized checkpoints such as border crossings by boat, on foot, or through other means.[84]

Some nongovernmental organizations such as Oxfam asserted that the European Agenda on Migration's main aim is to curtail or deter irregular migration into Europe, so that individuals arriving irregularly by boat or on foot are prevented from entering into EU Member State territories.[85] Scholars have contended that the underlying rationale and belief of deterrence paradigms—that is, policies to deter migrants from entering sovereign territories to claim asylum—such as the European Agenda on Migration is to allow 'developing states can successfully insulate themselves from taking on a substantive and proportional responsibility in

[80] European Commission (2015) [European Agenda on Migration]. For example, the Agenda states: 'The robust fight against irregular migration, traffickers and smugglers, and securing Europe's external borders must be paired with a strong common asylum policy as well as a new European policy on legal migration. … A clear and well implemented framework for legal pathways to entrance in the EU (both through an efficient asylum and visa system) will reduce push factors towards irregular stay and entry, contributing to enhance security of European borders as well as safety of migratory flows', at 6. It also discusses fighting criminal networks of smugglers and traffickers abroad as a form of border management, at 2 and 8.

[81] *Ibid* at 2; Oxfam (2017) at 2 [Oxfam].

[82] *Ibid;* See, also: European Commission, "European Agenda on Migration", https://ec.europa.eu/home-affairs/what-we-do/policies/european-agenda-migration_en.

[83] Oxfam at 2.

[84] The term irregular migration has no universal definition, but one definition is formulated by the International Organization for Migration as: 'Movement that takes place outside the regulatory norms of the sending, transit and receiving countries. There is no clear or universally accepted definition of irregular migration. From the perspective of destination countries it is entry, stay or work in a country without the necessary authorization or documents required under immigration regulations. From the perspective of the sending country, the irregularity is for example seen in cases in which a person crosses an international boundary without a valid passport or travel document or does not fulfil the administrative requirements for leaving the country. There is, however, a tendency to restrict the use of the term "illegal migration" to cases of smuggling of migrants and trafficking in persons' in International Organization for Migration, "Key Migration Terms", https://www.iom.int/key-migration-terms.

[85] *Ibid;* See, also: Human Rights Watch (2018).

regard to refugee protection', in essence, permitting 'wealthy states to have their cake and eat it too: maintaining a formal commitment to international refugee law, while at the same time largely being spared the associated burdens'.[86] The UNHCR is worried that the use of 'non-arrival' policies by EU Member States may lead to a general practice of not distinguishing between forced migrants (i.e. refugees and asylum claimants) and other migrants (i.e. economic migrants).[87] Such policies may 'inhibit the entry and access to asylum procedures of persons who would otherwise seek and enjoy asylum from persecution in their country'.[88] In sum, the European Commission's European Agenda on Migration aims to curtail migration into and across Europe, while the UNHCR and other nongovernmental organizations are concerned that the continuing trend with migration control in the EU can potentially infringe on the human rights of those seeking to gain access to international protection in EU Member States.

Non arrival strategies include shifting of the national borders outward, so that migrants are kept out of national territories of the EU.[89] One example of this is 'pushback' operations on the high seas to prevent claimants from reaching the territories of Member States.[90] For instance, on the Mediterranean Sea route, migrants on boats (including asylum claimants and refugees) are intercepted on the high seas by Libyan coastguard officials and pushed back toward their place of origin or otherwise are sent to Libyan detention facilities for further processing.[91] Another example of a non arrival strategy used by EU Member States is the use of offshore processing facilities to contain migrants outside of the EU.[92] Offshore detention facilities have been used by the EU in which 'thousands of migrants are languishing in detention centers in Libya, nominally run by the government there. Many of them were intercepted by Libya's EU-backed coast guard while attempting to cross the Mediterranean'.[93] Another example of externalization of migration control is the use of 'consensual containment', which is a practice by third countries on behalf of, or for the benefit of, EU Member States to reduce the

---

[86] Gammeltoft-Hansen, Thomas, and Feith Tan, Nikolas (2017) at 31, which states: 'It allows wealthy states to have their cake and eat it too: maintaining a formal commitment to international refugee law, while at the same time largely being spared the associated burdens' [Gammeltoft-Hansen and Tan].

[87] *Ibid* at para 27.

[88] *Ibid.*

[89] Bialasiewicz, Luiza (2012); Ashutosh, I., and Mountz, A. (2012a, 2012b); Collyer, M., and King, R. (2015).

[90] Hathaway and Gammeltoft-Hansen.

[91] For example, see: Gammeltoft-Hansen and Tan at 37, which states: 'In 2015, the European Union thus launched a military operation to seize and dispose boats used for human smuggling in international waters off the Libyan Coast' in an effort to prevent secondary movement such as migrant smuggling and trafficking.

[92] This issue is further explored in: Poon, Jenny (2018).

[93] Brandt, Jessica, and Higgins, Claire (2018); See, also: European Council (2018) at para 3.

number of arrivals to Europe.[94] These types of 'consensual containment' practices include collaborations between the third country and the EU to discourage departures, carry out effective exit controls, and halt new arrivals on EU Member State territory.[95] Examples of the collaboration between the EU and a third country to deter migrants include the Italy-Libya Memorandum of Understanding and the EU-Turkey statement.[96] The former agreement between Italy and Libya involves the collaboration between Italy and Libya in order to 'ensure the reduction of illegal migratory flows.[97] The latter agreement is a statement of collaboration between the EU and Turkey, a non-EU country, which aims to take back a Syrian from Turkey for every Syrian Turkey admits from the Greek Islands (termed the 1:1 scheme).[98]

It should be noted that non arrival strategies have had unintended consequences. Although one aim of the CEAS is to reduce secondary movements such as smuggling activities, non arrival strategies make access to international protection for claiming refugee status more difficult and actually incentivize human smuggling in the absence of safe and regular pathways.[99] This is because such policies make access to crossing borders contingent upon resources and means, and push more people to use covert and more dangerous routes in the search for protection.[100]

Another way in which EU Member States attempt to control migrant access to EU countries is through the restrictive application of the Refugee Convention. In particular, some countries 'define away' from the scope of the refugee definition certain categories of refugee claimants, such as victims of non-State agents of persecution, gender-related persecution, or localised persecution.[101] Scholars have argued that containment policies have 'in effect contributed to further blurring the distinction between refugee and economic migrant, a phenomenon for which the terms "asylum—migration nexus" or "mixed migration" have been coined'.[102]

Control of migrants is also enforced through infrastructures or systems designed to contain, partition, and discipline mobility.[103] The implementation of the Eurodac Regulation established new and enhanced measures to monitor and track claimants

---

[94] Moreno-Lax, Violeta, and Giuffré, Mariagiulia (2016) at 15 [Moreno-Lax and Giuffré].

[95] *Ibid.*

[96] This topic is explored further in: Poon, Jenny (2017); See, also: Poon, Jenny (2016).

[97] Memorandum of understanding on cooperation in the fields of development, the fight against illegal immigration, human trafficking and fuel smuggling and on reinforcing the security of borders between the State of Libya and the Italian Republic (English translated version), Odysseus Network, translated by: Sandra Uselli, revised by Filippo, Marcello Di, Marati, Elena, and Palm, Anja http://eumigrationlawblog.eu/wp-content/uploads/2017/10/MEMORANDUM_translation_finalversion.doc.pdf.

[98] European Council (2016).

[99] *Ibid* at 5.

[100] *Ibid.*

[101] *Ibid* at 19(iii).

[102] See, for example: Feller, Erika (2006) at 515; See, also: Hurwitz, Agnes G. (2009) at 19.

[103] Mezzadra, Sandro, and Neilson, Brent (2013).

and refugees who have entered the EU through irregular means as a method of containment.[104] First, claimants and refugees are required to be fingerprinted through the Eurodac Regulation.[105] Second, the Eurodac database which stores fingerprint information is connected with local law enforcement authorities and EUROPOL, which share data with each other.[106] These methods and practices of fingerprint collection forced upon claimants and refugees lead to instances of criminalizing irregular migration as well as penalizing irregular entry, which is against the protection standards codified under international law.[107]

One final example of containment theory in action in the EU is the use by some EU Member States of post-arrival dissuasion policies. These are policies 'such as detention, denial of or [provision of] inadequate means of subsistence, and restrictions on family reunification even after granting refugee status'.[108] In practice, the UK Home Office uses detention to 'effect removal; initially to establish a person's identity or basis of claim; or where there are reasons to believe that the person will fail to comply with any condition attached to the grant of temporary admission or release'.[109] Despite these reasons for detaining asylum claimants and refugees, there are 'problems with age assessment or identification of specific groups such as victims of trafficking or torture'.[110] For example, women who are pregnant and those who have severe mental health problems have been detained by the UK despite being identified as part of a vulnerable group.[111]

The UNHCR has expressed concern over the EU's use of non-arrival policies, diversion policies, restrictive applications of the Refugee Convention, and deterrence policies.[112] It has warned that the use of these strategies of containment has 'served to seriously undermine the foundations of the refugee protection regime'.[113] It is

---

[104] Regulation (EU) No 603/2013 of the European Parliament and of the Council of 26 June 2013 on the establishment of Eurodac for the comparison of fingerprints for effective application of Regulation (EU) No 604/2013 establishing the criteria and mechanisms for determining the Member State responsible for examining an application for international protection lodged in one of the Member States by a third-country national or a stateless person and on request for the comparison with Eurodac data by Member States' law enforcement authorities and Europol for law enforcement purposes, and amending Regulation (EU) No 1077/2011 establishing a European agency for the operational management of large-scale IT systems in the area of freedom, security and justice (recast), OJ L180/1, 29 June 2013 [Eurodac Regulation].

[105] *Ibid;* See, also: Tazzioli Journal at 2771.

[106] Eurodac Regulation.

[107] Contrary to the prohibition against non-penalization under the Refugee Convention, see: Refugee Convention at art 31(1).

[108] *Ibid* at 19(iv).

[109] See, for example: Bruycker, Philippe De, Bloomfield, Alice, Tsourdi, Evangelia (Lilian), and Petin, Joanna (eds) (2015) at 148.

[110] *Ibid* at 149–150.

[111] *Ibid.*

[112] UNHCR "Asylum in the Industrialized World", https://www.unhcr.org/3ebf9bb10.pdf at 161 [UNHCR Asylum].

[113] *Ibid.*

concerned that the EU's containment policies circumvent international law obligations such as *non-refoulement* and evade responsibilities owed to refugees pursuant to treaty and customary international law.[114] Filippo Grandi, the United Nations High Commissioner for Refugees, stated in a speech to an audience at the European Policy Centre in Brussels that:

> The failure of [the EU] to implement a humane, organised, collective response to the large-scale arrivals in 2015, and the resort to *policies of containment* rather than shared responsibility, with even the relevance of the 1951 Convention being called into question by some, has already set a negative example – there is certainly a link between recent policies by industrialised states and more restrictive refugee policies in the developing world (emphasis added).[115]

More specifically, Grandi commented on the EU's 'narrowing of access to Europe [. . .] with measures restricting entry by Syrians, for example, to neighbouring countries, leaving them displaced and trapped inside Syria as conflict intensifies'.[116] The UNHCR's concerns, therefore, illustrate the consequences of containment policies within Europe as well as the importance of addressing these policies at the macro-level, with European governments working together in solidarity to adopt a proper strategy to address refugee flows.[117]

In sum, EU containment policies not only exclude, deter, dissuade and contain, they also keep migrants on the move.[118] Moving migrants back and moving refugees around seem to be the two main methods which the EU is employing in order to retain control over migrants.[119] Another way to conceive of containment strategies is as a way for the EU to physically try to confine migrants to spaces that are beyond official detention facilities.[120] These strategies of containment are imposed upon claimants and refugees in the name of fighting against smuggling and trafficking.[121]

---

[114] UNHCR Asylum at para 49.

[115] Grandi, Filippo (2016).

[116] *Ibid;* See, also: Trauner, Florian (2016) at 319, which states: 'With the gap between the legal EU asylum regime and the actual practices of member states becoming wider, the EU has been compelled to engage in a process of policy reform. In May and September 2015, the European Commission proposed a series of measures under the title 'European Agenda on Migration'. The agenda includes a common list of 'safe countries of origin', plans to install a more efficient EU return policy, and strategies to tackle the root causes for migration in Africa and to solve the conflict causing people to flee'. Further, Trauner states in her article that: 'the Dublin system builds upon the assumption that comparable rules and procedures exist throughout the EU. Regardless of the EU's efforts to harmonise these rules in the Common European Asylum System, national asylum systems and procedures have continued to exhibit substantial differences'.

[117] *Ibid.*

[118] Tazzioli and Garelli.

[119] *Ibid.*

[120] *Ibid.*

[121] Moreno-Lax and Giuffré at 14.

4.4 Containment and *Non-Refoulement*

International refugee law is premised upon the protection against *refoulement.*[122] *Non-refoulement* is the bare minimum standard with which States Parties to the Refugee Convention must comply in order to fulfill their international law obligations.[123] Although relevant international human rights law norms such as the prohibition against torture and the prohibition against ill-treatment are also relevant customary and *jus cogens* norms with which States Parties must comply, *non-refoulement* is the most crucial standard of international protection under refugee law.[124] The UNHCR has confirmed the principle's status as the minimum standard for the treatment of refugees and thus constitutes the cornerstone of international protection for claiming refugee status.[125] The explanatory theory of containment is closely linked with the principle of *non-refoulement* and this link is a significant one with important implications for asylum claimants and refugees. This section describes how the theory of containment is related to the principle of *non-refoulement* by using the examples of the 'safe' third country concept and the use of the Eurodac Regulation to contain and to enforce migrant entries and exits.

As described above, 'safe' third country agreements are used by EU Member States to send migrants back to those countries in certain circumstances. This is also knowns as a 'protection elsewhere' regime.[126] Under international refugee law, countries to which claimants are sent should permit them to have adequate access to international protection for claiming refugee status, including having access to fair and efficient asylum procedures as well as access to the asylum country's territory.[127] The access to the asylum country's territory may be temporary, but nonetheless must be available under international law, so that the process of claiming and examining one's asylum application is possible.[128] In practice, however, claimants sent back to third States to access international protection for claiming refugee status there often cannot do so for a number of reasons.[129] These reasons may include poor asylum systems in the third States, such as not having fair and timely access to asylum procedures.[130] As well, when claimants are screened through accelerated procedures which do not consider the merits of their applications before they are returned to a third country deemed 'safe', they

[122] Refugee Convention at introductory note.

[123] *Ibid.*

[124] *Ibid;* CAT at art 3; ICCPR at arts 6 and 7; Committee Against Torture (2008) at para 1.

[125] *Ibid.*

[126] See, for example: Foster, Michelle (2007) [Foster MJIL].

[127] See, for example: UNHCR (2001) at para 25.

[128] Chetail, Vincent (2019) at 192.

[129] *Ibid* at para 11.

[130] *Ibid* at para 5.

are not provided the chance to argue that return to their originating state will amount to *refoulement*.[131] In third States with poor human rights records, claimants are especially vulnerable to having their human rights curtailed, and, without due process, to being sent onward to countries in which they may be persecuted or tortured.[132]

The 'safe' third country concept under Article 38 of the Asylum Procedures Directive (recast) works in the following way: first, there are procedural safeguards which seek to ensure that the competent authorities are satisfied that a person seeking international protection for claiming refugee status will be treated in accordance with those procedures. Second, the Asylum Procedures Directive (recast) requires a connection between the person seeking asylum and the third country to which this claimant is to be sent on the basis that it would be reasonable for that person to go to that third country.[133] In the view of the UNHCR, this connection means a 'meaningful link' based on having 'comparable asylum systems and standards' as the sending State.[134] Links that would be considered to fulfill the requirement of a 'meaningful link' would include family links or links to the broader community, previous residence such as previous long-term visits or studies, and linguistic or cultural links, in addition to simple transit through the country.[135] Additionally, the Danish Refugee Council calls for the use of 'safe' third country concepts to be based on 'a genuine assessment of the capacity and willingness of receiving countries to adhere to international and European human rights safeguards'.[136] Amnesty International makes a similar point, specifically warning that the application of Article 38 of the Asylum Procedures Directive:

> requires an individual assessment of whether the previous state will readmit the person, grant the person access to a fair and efficient procedure, and accord the person standards of treatment commensurate with the Refugee Convention and international human rights standards, including protection from *non-refoulement*.[137]

Moreover, Amnesty International is of the view that the individual being considered for return through 'safe' third country agreements should be given the right to be heard and the ability to rebut the presumption that he or she will be treated with relevant international human rights standards of protection upon return.[138]

The establishment of rules pursuant to the Asylum Procedures Directive (recast) is subject to national legislation and 'on the methodology by which the competent authorities satisfy themselves that the safe third country concept may be applied to

[131] Asylum Procedures Directive at art 38.

[132] *Ibid* at para 50(p).

[133] Asylum Procedures Directive at art 38; Refworld (2016) at 18 [Refworld].

[134] Refworld at 18.

[135] *Ibid.*

[136] *Ibid.*

[137] Amnesty International, European Institutions Office (2016) at 2 [Amnesty International Report].

[138] *Ibid.*

a particular country or particular applicant' on a case-by-case basis consideration 'of the safety of the country for a particular applicant and/or national designation of countries considered to be generally safe'.[139] Despite these procedural safeguards codified within the Asylum Procedures Directive (recast), in practice, Member States may not comply with these provisions when they are not transposed into domestic legislation.[140]

The sending State's reliance upon the diplomatic assurances which the receiving third State undertakes to commit is sometimes based on erroneous assurances, leading to instances where there is no guarantee that the undertaking in the form of diplomatic assurances is in fact complied with by the receiving State.[141] Where such undertaking has not been complied with, there is a potential that *non-refoulement* may be breached, especially when the receiving third State does not have proper asylum procedures in place or has a poor human rights record.[142] The UNHCR has specifically stated that the onus is upon the sending State:

> to establish, prior to implementing any removal measure, that the person whom it intends to remove from its territory or jurisdiction would not be exposed to a danger of serious human rights violations [. . .] Where the receiving State has given diplomatic assurances with regard to a particular individual [. . .] [s]uch assurances do not, however, affect the sending State's obligations under customary international law as well as international and regional human rights treaties to which it is party.[143]

When Member States do not heed the UNHCR's direction on diplomatic assurances, the risk of violating *non-refoulement* upon return of the claimant rises.

Additionally, specific 'safe' third country agreements raise concern, particularly the agreement with Turkey described above. The European Council on Refugees and Exiles (ECRE) critiqued the EU-Turkey statement on its adoption as an example of 'the approach taken [by the EU] which, if implemented, risks violating international refugee law, EU asylum law and the EU Charter of Fundamental Rights, and would lead to a policy of containment and chain *refoulement* of persons in need of protection'.[144] First, the ECRE cautioned that the policy put in place *vis-à-vis* the EU-Turkey statement involving the return of all 'irregular migrants

---

[139] *Ibid* at 12.

[140] For example, in the case of Germany, the Asylum Procedures Directive is not transposed into domestic German law, leading to instances where these provisions are not followed.

[141] The Committee Against Torture has specifically warned against the misuse of diplomatic assurances and to avoid using them as a 'loophole' to circumvent *non-refoulement* obligations in: at para 20; See also the discussion of this topic in Chap. 3.

[142] See, for example: Human Rights Watch, "'Diplomatic Assurances' against Torture—Questions and Answers" at 7, where it was emphasized that 'receiving states that provide diplomatic assurances are already under a duty not to torture or ill-treat detainees, and most have ratified legally binding treaties promising to refrain from such abuse. In light of this, the UN special rapporteur on torture stated in August 2005 that diplomatic assurances 'therefore do not provide additional protection to the deportees'".

[143] UNHCR (2006) at para 19.

[144] *Ibid.*

arriving in Greece' is incompatible with established international and EU law and is in complete dereliction of the principle of *non-refoulement*.[145] Further, its expressed concern that the EU-Turkey statement does not comply with the procedural safeguards laid down in Article 38 of the Asylum Procedures Directive, which requires that applicants must be protected from *refoulement* in the 'safe' third country and that the possibility exists to request and receive protection in accordance with the Refugee Convention.[146] The ECRE warns that the *Joint EU-Turkey Action Plan* reveals 'a policy of containment in Turkey on behalf of the EU, which can trigger the complicity of Member States in chain *refoulement*'.[147]

While the practice of containment itself is not a violation of *non-refoulement*, the curtailment of the human rights of those seeking refuge through the use of these containment policies can lead to *refoulement*, for the reasons outlined above.[148] In addition, Article 3(2) of the *Convention Against Torture* states that the consistent pattern of gross, flagrant or mass violations of human rights would constitute a breach of the prohibition of torture and the principle of *non-refoulement*.[149] Therefore, as demonstrated, the use of containment policies within the CEAS by EU Member States lead to human rights concerns, including the potential for *non-refoulement* obligations to be violated by these countries. First, the obligation of *non-refoulement* is the bare minimum safeguard for which all asylum claimants and refugees should be protected under international human rights law. Second, the misuse or abuse of the 'safe' third country concept by sending claimants to third countries outside of the EU to contain or constrain their movements has the potential to violate *non-refoulement* where adequate procedural mechanisms are not in place to ensure their safety.

The use of the Eurodac Regulation to force irregular migrants to provide their fingerprints wherever they enter an EU Member State may potentially increase the risk of *refoulement* when the claimant refuses to be fingerprinted and thus faces a removal order.[150] Some nongovernmental organizations and human rights organizations in Europe are concerned with the mandatory requirement imposed by the

---

[145] *Ibid.*

[146] *Ibid* at 1–2; European Council on Refugees and Exiles (2016) [ECRE EU-Turkey] .

[147] ECRE EU-Turkey at 2.

[148] See also Gowlland-Debbas, Vera (ed) (1994) at 66 [Gowlland-Debbas].

[149] CAT at art 3(2).

[150] See, also: Redress, "Mass Refugee Influxes, Refoulement and the Prohibition Against Torture", 3–50, https://www.refworld.org/pdfid/5800ecd14.pdf at 45, which states: 'Eurodac regulations requiring fingerprinting of persons arriving within the EU, when considered alongside the Dublin regulation has resulted in ill-treatment. Several reports and a study based on interviews with asylum seekers have highlighted the excessive use of force by personnel seeking to take fingerprints which may amount to ill-treatment [. . .] While the regulations make clear that states are bound to apply them in accordance with their relevant human rights obligations, the regulations lack specific guidance on the use of force'.

Eurodac Regulation on asylum seekers and refugees to provide their fingerprints or risk removal.[151] Fundamental rights are implicated when asylum seekers and refugees are forced to either provide fingerprints or risk removal: in particular, their *non-refoulement* protection and their right against being deprived of their liberty.[152] On the protection against being *refouled,* the European Agency for Fundamental Rights is concerned that the actions taken by EU Member States to require and to enforce the taking of fingerprints at the border to identify asylum seekers and refugees may interfere with a number of rights guaranteed under the EU Charter.[153] Regarding the deprivation of liberty, EU Member States' use of detention as a tool to force asylum claimants and refugees to provide fingerprints at the border is a major interference with the right to liberty set forth in Article 6 of the EU Charter and Article 5 of the ECHR.[154] Most importantly, the ECHR warrants that an individual cannot be punished for refusing to provide their fingerprints at the border nor can the person be coerced in giving their fingerprints to authorities as enumerated under Article 5(1)(b) of the ECHR.[155]

The UNHCR is concerned that the requirement laid down under the Eurodac Regulation, which obliges EU Member States to collect and store fingerprint data from all irregular migrants including asylum claimants, creates significant pressure among the Member States.[156] These Member States may face challenges of a technical nature to collect, store, and remit fingerprint data in the Eurodac database while complying with fundamental rights obligations such as the 'best interests of the child' international standard.[157] The UNHCR cautions that the

---

[151] See, for example: European Union Agency for Fundamental Rights, "Fundamental Rights Implications of the Obligations to Provide Fingerprints for Eurodac", https://fra.europa.eu/sites/default/files/fra_uploads/fra-2015-fingerprinting-focus-paper_en.pdf at 1 [FRA Eurodac].

[152] *Ibid* at 1, which states: '[there is a concern that the] deprivation of liberty to pressure persons to give their fingerprints must be an exceptional measure which should not be used against vulnerable people'.

[153] *Ibid* at 4, which states: 'Interferences may involve absolute rights—such as the principle of *non-refoulement* and the prohibition of torture, inhuman or degrading treatment of *[sic]* punishment—form which no derogations are possible'; Further, that: 'Interferences can, however, also involve rights that can be limited, for example, the right to liberty (Article 6 of the Charter and Article 5 of the European Convention on Human Rights (ECHR) or the protection of personal data and private life set forth in Articles 7 and 8 of the Charter and in Article 8 of the ECHR'.

[154] *Ibid* at 6, which states: 'Under EU law, any limitation on the right to liberty must be in line with the requirements of Article 52(1) of the Charter, namely: limitations must be provided for by law, must genuinely meet objectives of general interest recognised by the Union or the need to protect the rights and freedoms of others, respect the essence of the right, and be proportionate'; Further, it states: 'Taken together, under EU law and the ECHR, deprivation of liberty for immigration-related reasons can only be a measure of last resort, and an assessment needs to be made in each individual case to determine whether all pre-conditions required to prevent arbitrary detention are fulfilled'.

[155] *Ibid* at 6; See, also: *A and Others v the United Kingdom,* Application No 3455/05, 19 February 2009 at para 171.

[156] *Ibid;* See, also: Eurodac Regulation.

[157] See, generally: UNHCR (2004).

requirement to register the fingerprint of all irregular arrivals, including children, through the Eurodac database should 'be coupled with sufficient procedural safeguards to ensure compliance with fundamental rights and international protection obligations, including respect of the principle of *non-refoulement*'.[158]

The EU Agency for Fundamental Rights also cautions that EU Member States' patrolling vessels do not, in principle, have jurisdiction to 'stop other vessels in third-country territorial waters or to intercept migrants who want to leave the third state'.[159] Where an EU Member State knows, or should have known, that the intercepted migrants face a real risk of ill-treatment once they are returned to the third country or are handed over to third-country authorities, it would result in a violation of the principle of *non-refoulement*.[160] The requirement of *non-refoulement* is such that it places a positive duty upon the sending EU Member State to 'be aware of the situation in the host country and [must] assess the risks the intercepted people face in the host country'.[161] In assessing that future-oriented risk posed to the returnee, the EU Member State must ascertain whether such a risk may consist of the absence of a well-functioning asylum system in the third State and whether there is a real risk of ill-treatment or onward removal in the third State upon return.[162]

The principle of *non-refoulement* is a cornerstone of international refugee law. The principle is also safeguarded under international human rights law as the prohibition against torture, inhuman or cruel treatment or punishment, and is codified in a number of European law instruments such as the EU Charter and the ECHR. This principle must be rigorously observed by EU Member States including in their interpretation and implementation of European obligations within the CEAS. This chapter has demonstrated that several concerns have been raised by leading scholars and nongovernmental organizations in the asylum law field, including the use of 'safe' third country concepts and the Eurodac Regulation to enforce fingerprints against claimants as a policy of containment. The use of containment strategies to contain, restrict, and prevent the movement of asylum claimants and refugees has been shown to heighten breaches of the principle of *non-refoulement*. In particular, under international law, *non-refoulement* can be circumvented when 'safe' third country concepts are misused or abused by EU Member States to deflect their responsibility to process asylum applicants to third countries where procedural safeguards are not necessarily in place to permit claimants to access procedures and international protection. Finally, enforcement of the Eurodac Regulation requiring fingerprints from claimants and refugees at the border cannot also be used as a *non-refoulement* 'loophole' through forcible removal of those who refuse.

---

[158] *Ibid.*

[159] *Ibid* at 30.

[160] *Ibid.*

[161] *Ibid.*

[162] *Ibid;* See, also: Heijer, Maarten Den (2012) at 243–244.

4.5 Concluding Remarks

Containment through migration control seeks to control, divide, and discipline 'unruly' migration.[163] 'Unruly' migration, as perceived by States, occurs when migrants try to manage where they seek asylum, including by irregular means to evade the requirement to register their fingerprints under the Eurodac Regulation.[164] Techniques to identify and select migrants by categorizing, partitioning, and channeling them serve as methods to dominate and constrain the 'disobedience' of migrants.[165]

While rarely applied within public international law and specifically international refugee law, the theory of containment holds particular significance as an explanatory theory for these fields today. First, the theory suggests that policies of containment are methods used by EU Member States to elude their international refugee law and human rights law obligations. Second, the theory suggests that containment provides the underlying rationale for violations of *non-refoulement* by EU Member States. Thus, containment theory highlights the gaps between the law, such as the robust conception of the principle of *non-refoulement* under international and regional refugee and human rights law, and the interpretation and application of that law through policies within the EU.

This chapter explained the relevance of the theory of containment as an explanatory theory of EU migration policies and practices. The first part of this chapter outlined the contours of the theory of containment, particularly as it is articulated in the fields of human and spatial geography and migration studies. It explained that containment theory is a theory of control: control of mobility and immobility within a particular space, and that this space could be legal as well as being physical. The second section of the chapter explained containment theory in action within the CEAS, through several means: use of Dublin transfers, 'safe' third country agreements, the interception of asylum seekers prior to reaching Europe, migrant tracking, narrow interpretations of the Refugee Convention, and deterrence policies. The third part of this chapter considered the connection between CEAS containment policies as the principle of *non-refoulement*. All together, these explanations show that, while containment may be facilitated by law, containment occurs not because of the law itself, but because of the policies and practices around the application of that law.

The theory of containment provides a framework of explanation for the rest of the book, including the doctrinal analysis that takes place in the following chapters. In particular, it provides crucial context for the recommendations articulated in Chap. 7. The following chapter details the evidence for containment policies within the CEAS as demonstrated by practice within the United Kingdom. Chap. 5 explains the UK's domestic asylum system and shows how certain aspects of that asylum system are premised upon policies of containment, leading to negative implications for the principle of *non-refoulement* and its compliance.

---

[163] Tazzioli Journal at 2765.

[164] *Ibid;* See, generally: Eurodac Regulation at 1.

[165] Tazzioli Journal at 2765, 2770–2771.

References

Amnesty International (2016) Hotspot Italy: how EU's flagship approach leads to violations of refugee and migrant rights. https://www.amnesty.org/download/Documents/EUR3050042016ENGLISH.PDF

Amnesty International, European Institutions Office (2016) "The proposed Dublin reform"

Arribas GF (2016) The EU-Turkey agreement: a controversial attempt at patching up a major problem. European Papers 1(3):1097–1104

Ashutosh I, Mountz A (2012a) Migration management for the benefit of whom? interrogating the work of the international organization for migration. Citizenship Stud 15:21–38

Ashutosh I, Mountz A (2012b) The geopolitics of migrant mobility: tracing state relations through refugee claims, boats, and discourses. Geopolitics 17:335–354

Bialasiewicz L (2012) Off-shoring and out-sourcing the borders of Europe: Libya and EU border work in the mediterranean. Geopolitics 17:843–866

Brandt J, Higgins C (2018) Europe wants to process asylum seekers offshore—the lessons it should learn from Australia. *Brookings Institute, Order from Chaos*. https://www.brookings.edu/blog/order-from-chaos/2018/08/31/europe-wants-to-process-asylum-seekers-offshore-the-lessons-it-should-learn-from-australia

Bruycker PD, Bloomfield A, Tsourdi EL, Petin J eds (2015) Alternatives to Immigration and Asylum detention in the EU: time for implementation. Brussels, Odysseus Academic Network Publishing

Castree N, Kitchin R, Rogers A (2013) Migration. In A dictionary of human geography. Oxford University Press, Oxford, 315–316

Chetail V (2019) International migration law. Oxford University Press, Oxford

Collyer M, King R (2015) Producing transnational space: international migration and the extra-territorial reach of state power. Prog Hum Geogr 39:185–204

Committee Against Torture (2008) Convention against torture and other cruel, inhuman or degrading treatment or punishment. General Comment No 2". UN Doc CAT/C/GC/2

Cortinovis R (2018) Asylum: the role and limits of the safe third country concept in EU Asylum

Council E (2018) Note from the general secretariat of the council to delegations, conclusions of the European Council meeting on 28 June 2018. Brussels. https://www.consilium.europa.eu/media/35936/28-euco-final-conclusions-en.pdf

Council of the European Union (2018) Reform of the Common European Asylum System – the Safe Countries Concept. http://www.statewatch.org/news/2018/may/eu-council-safe-countries-concept-8735-18.pdf

Court of Justice of the EU, Opinion 2/13, 18 December 2014

Dartmouth College Library. A Short Definition of Human Geography. https://researchguides.dartmouth.edu/human_geography/main

Dartmouth College Library. A Short Definition for Migration Studies. https://researchguides.dartmouth.edu/human_geography/migration

Dartmouth College Library (2022). https://researchguides.dartmouth.edu/human_geography#:~:text=A_short_definition_for_Human,temporally_across_and_between_locations

European Association for the Defence of Human Rights, International Federation for Human Rights, and EuroMed Rights (2016) Safe' countries: a Denial of the right of Asylum. https://www.ohchr.org/Documents/Issues/MHR/ReportLargeMovements/FIDH2%20.pdf

European Commission, Migration and Home Affairs. Manifestly Unfounded Application for International Protection

European Commission (2015) Communication from the commission to the European parliament, the council, the European economic and social committee and the committee of the regions: a European agenda on migration, COM(2015) 240 final. https://ec.europa.eu/home-affairs/sites/homeaffairs/files/what-we-do/policies/european-agenda-migration/background-information/docs/communication_on_the_european_agenda_on_migration_en.pdf

European Commission, European agenda on migration. https://ec.europa.eu/home-affairs/what-we-do/policies/european-agenda-migration_en
European commission, migration and home affairs. Hotspot approach. https://ec.europa.eu/home-affairs/content/hotspot-approach_en
European Council (2016) Statement of the EU heads of state or government. https://www.consilium.europa.eu/en/press/press-releases/2016/03/08/eu-turkey-meeting-statement
European Council on Refugees and Exiles (2016) ECRE strongly opposes legitimising push-backs by declaring Turkey a 'safe third country'. https://www.ecre.org/ecre-strongly-opposes-legitimising-push-backs-by-declaring-turkey-a-safe-third-country
European Union Agency for Fundamental Rights. Fundamental Rights Implications of the Obligations to Provide Fingerprints for Eurodac. https://fra.europa.eu/sites/default/files/fra_uploads/fra-2015-fingerprinting-focus-paper_en.pdf
European Union, The Council (1999) "Terms of reference of the High Level Working Group on Asylum and Migration; preparation of action plans for the most important countries of origin and transit of asylum-seekers and migrants. http://data.consilium.europa.eu/doc/document/ST-5264-1999-INIT/en/pdf
Feller E (2006) Asylum, Migration and refugee protection: realities, myths and the promise of things to come. Int J Refugee Law 18(3):509–536 at 515
Foster M (2007) Protection elsewhere: the legal implications of requiring refugees to seek protection in another state. Michigan J Int Law 28(2):223–286
Gammeltoft-Hansen T, Tan Nikolas F (2017) The end of the deterrence paradigm? Future directions for global refugee policy. J Migration Hum Secur 5(1):28–56 at 31
Garelli G, Tazzioli M (2016) Beyond detention: spatial strategies of dispersal and channels of forced transfer. Society and Space https://www.societyandspace.org/articles/beyond-detention-spatial-strategies-of-dispersal-and-channels-of-forced-transfer
Gowlland-Debbas V (ed) (1994) The problem of refugees in the light of contemporary international law issues. Martinus Nijhoff Publishers
Grandi F (2016) Protecting refugees in Europe and beyond: can the eu rise to the challenge? European Policy Centre, Brussels. https://www.unhcr.org/admin/hcspeeches/58456ec34/protecting-refugees-europe-beyond-eu-rise-challenge.html
Heijer MD (2012) Europe and extraterritorial Asylum. Hart Publishing, Oxford
Houtum HV (2010) Human Blacklisting: the global apartheid of the EU's external border regime. Environ Plann D Soc Space 28(6):957–976 at 958–959
Human Rights Watch (2018) "Towards an effective and principled EU migration policy: recommendations for reform. https://www.hrw.org/sites/default/files/supporting_resources/hrw_eu_migration_policy_memo_0.pdf
Hurwitz AG (2009) The Collective responsibility of states to protect refugees. Oxford University Press. Oxford
Hyndman J, Mountz A (2007) Refuge or refusal: the geography of exclusion. In Gregory D, Pred A (eds) Violent geographies: fear, terror, and political violence. Routledge, New York, 77–92
International Organization for Migration. Key Migration Terms. https://www.iom.int/key-migration-terms
Library DC. A short definition of human geography. https://researchguides.dartmouth.edu/human_geography/main.
Library DC. A short definition for migration studies. https://researchguides.dartmouth.edu/human_geography/migration
Lindstrøm C (2005) European Union policy on asylum and immigration. addressing the root causes of forced migration: a justice and home affairs policy of freedom, security and justice? Soc Policy Admin 39(6):587–605
Litwak RS (2004) Containment. In Krieger J (ed) The Oxford companion to politics of the World. Oxford University Press, Oxford
Loevy K (2016) Emergencies in public law: the legal politics of containment. Cambridge University Press, Cambridge

Majcher I (2017) Border securitization and containment vs. fundamental rights: the European Union's 'Refugee Crisis'. Georgetown J Int Aff. https://www.georgetownjournalofinternationalaffairs.org/border-securitization-and-containment-vs-fundamental-rights-the-european-unions-refugee-crisis. *Conflict and Security Blog*

McConnachie K (2016) Camps of containment: a genealogy of the refugee camp. Human: Int J Hum Rights Human Develop 7(3):397–412 at 398

Mezzadra S, Neilson B (2013) Border as method, or, the multiplication of labor. Duke University Press, Durham

Moreno-Lax V, Giuffré M (2016) The raise of consensual containment: from 'contactless control' to 'contactless responsibility' for forced migration flows. In Juss S (ed) Research handbook on international refugee law. Edward Elgar

Mountz A (2011) The enforcement archipelago: detention, haunting, and asylum on islands. Political Geo 30(3):118–128at126

Mountz A, Coddington K, Catania T, Loyd JM (2013) Conceptualizing detention: mobility, containment, bordering, and exclusion. Prog Hum Geogr 37(4):522–541

Odysseus Network. Memorandum of understanding on cooperation in the fields of development, the fight against illegal immigration, human trafficking and fuel smuggling and on reinforcing the security of borders between the State of Libya and the Italian Republic (English translated version), translated by: Sandra Uselli, revised by Di Filippo, Marcello, Marati, Elena, and Palm, Anja, http://eumigrationlawblog.eu/wp-content/uploads/2017/10/MEMORANDUM_translation_finalversion.doc.pdf

Oxfam (2017) Beyond 'Fortress Europe': principles for a Humane EU Migration Policy. https://d1tn3vj7xz9fdh.cloudfront.net/s3fs-public/file_attachments/bp-principles-humane-eu-migration-policy-111017-en.pdf

Oxfam B Centre for Human Rights and Macedonian Young Lawyers Association (2017) Dangerous 'Game': the Pushback of migrants, including Refugees, at Europe's Borders. https://www-cdn.oxfam.org/s3fs-public/file_attachments/bp-dangerous-game-pushback-migrants-refugees-060417-en_0.pdf

Oxford Dictionary of Economics (2017) Immobile factors. Oxford University Press, Oxford

Oxford English Dictionary. Control. https://en.oxforddictionaries.com/definition/control

Poon J (2016) EU-Turkey Deal: violation of, or consistency with, international law? Euro Papers (Forum) 1(3):1195–1203. http://europeanpapers.eu/en/system/files/pdf_version/EP_EF_2016_I_054_Jenny_Poon.pdf

Poon J (2017) Libya-EU memorandum of understanding: implications for non-refoulement and compliance with international human rights law? Cambridge Int Law J Blog. http://cilj.co.uk/2017/12/02/libya-eu-memorandum-of-understanding-implications-for-non-refoulement-and-compliance-with-international-human-rights-law

Poon J (2018) Non-refoulement obligations in offshore detention facilities. E-International Relations Blog. https://www.e-ir.info/2018/10/16/non-refoulement-obligations-in-offshore-detention-facilities

Redress, Mass refugee influxes, refoulement and the prohibition against torture, 3-50, https://www.refworld.org/pdfid/5800ecd14.pdf

Refworld (2016) The safe third country concept (Article 27)" https://www.refworld.org/cgi-bin/texis/vtx/rwmain/opendocpdf.pdf?reldoc=y&docid=4bab55e22

Shacknove A (1993) From Asylum to containment. Int J Refugee Law 5(4):516–533

Tazzioli M (2017) Rethinking containment through the EU-Libya migration deal. Völkerrechtsblog. https://voelkerrechtsblog.org/rethinking-containment-through-the-eu-libya-migration-deal [Tazzioli]

Tazzioli M (2018) Containment through mobility: migrants' spatial disobediences and the reshaping of control through the hotspot system. J Ethnic Migrat Stud 44(16):2764–2779

Tazzioli M, Garelli G (2018) Containment beyond detention: the hotspot system and the disrupted migration movements across Europe. Soc Space 1–19

Transnational Institute (2018) The shrinking space for solidarity with migrants and refugees. https://www.tni.org/files/publication-downloads/web_theshrinkingspace.pdf

Trauner F (2016) Asylum Policy: the EU's 'crises' and the looming policy regime failure. J Euro Integr 38(3):311–325. https://www.tandfonline.com/doi/full/10.1080/07036337.2016.1140756

UNHCR (2001) Asylum Processes (Fair and Efficient Asylum Procedures). UN Doc EC/GC/01/12. https://www.unhcr.org/protection/globalconsult/3b389254a/asylum-processes-fair-efficient-asylum-procedures.html

UNHCR (2004) Separated children in europe programme: statement of good practice, Third Edition. https://www.unhcr.org/4d9474399.pdf

UNHCR (2006) UNHCR Note on diplomatic assurances and international refugee protection

UNHCR (2018) Desperate journeys: refugees and migrants arriving in Europe and at Europe's borders. https://data2.unhcr.org/en/documents/download/65373#_ga=2.259362563.824522296.1546209771-1257371235.1536847062

UNHCR, Asylum in the Industrialized World. https://www.unhcr.org/3ebf9bb10.pdf.

UNHCR EC, Note on International Protection. UN Doc A/AC.96/914

Watch HR, 'Diplomatic Assurances' against torture—questions and answers

Wei L, Skop E, Morken A (2017) Geography of migration. Oxford Bibliographies. https://www.oxfordbibliographies.com/view/document/obo-9780199874002/obo-9780199874002-0038.xml

Wilde R (2017) 'Let Them Drown': rescuing migrants at sea and the *non-refoulement* obligation as a case study of international law's relationship to 'crisis': part I & II *EJIL:Talk! Blog*. https://www.ejiltalk.org/let-them-drown-rescuing-migrants-at-sea-and-the-non-refoulement-obligation-as-a-case-study-of-international-laws-relationship-to-crisis-part-i

Chapter 5
The United Kingdom and *Non-Refoulement*

5.1 Introduction

The previous chapters detailed how international law is standard-setting, while regional asylum systems such as the Common European Asylum System (CEAS) in the EU implement those international law norms and have their own regional variations in qualification standards, asylum procedures, and reception conditions for applicants claiming international protection for refugee status. Domestic asylum systems interpret and implement these international and European law standards according to applicable national law. In the United Kingdom (UK), the interpretation and implementation of important norms such as the principle of *non-refoulement* greatly affect the lives of those who are in search of refuge within the country. Despite common minimum standards set by both international and European law, a worrying trend has developed: a narrower interpretation of *non-refoulement*, revealing policies of containment.

In 2018, the UK received 37,730 asylum applications for international protection. Around 15% of this number (5510) constituted Dublin transfers.[1] That means, in at least 15% of the cases when transfers outside of the UK take place, there may be *non-refoulement* concerns, depending on the destination country. This chapter therefore considers the UK's law and practice with respect to the principle of *non-refoulement*. The UK exited the EU on January 31, 2020. While it is no longer officially a part of the EU, the UK is currently in a transition period until December 31, 2020, during which time the CEAS rules and Dublin transfers still apply.[2] As well, the UK remains part of the Council of Europe and is therefore bound by the ECHR, which addresses *non-refoulement*. Until it left the EU, the UK

---

[1] See Table 5.1 below with specific data on UK's Dublin transfers.

[2] *Agreement on the Withdrawal of the United Kingdom of Great Britain and Northern Ireland from the European Union and the European Atomic Energy Community*, at Article 32 and Chap. 6, https://eur-lex.europa.eu/legal-content/EN/TXT/PDF/?uri = CELEX:12019 W/TXT(02)&from = EN.

J. Poon, *Counteracting Containment Policies in the EU*, European Union and its Neighbours in a Globalized World 31,
https://doi.org/10.1007/978-3-032-08351-7_5

was one of the top recipients of asylum applicants in the EU. Among EU countries in 2018, Germany received the most asylum seekers: 184,180 applicants or 29% of the EU total.[3] France (120,425, 19%), Greece (66,965, 10%), Italy (59,950, 9%), Spain (54,050, 8%) and the United Kingdom (37,730, 6%) followed.[4] Together, these countries received 81% of all asylum applications across the EU.[5] By examining Germany in the next chapter, and the UK in this chapter, it is possible to identify domestic trends on the law and practice of *non-refoulement* within two powerful countries with significant refugee inflows—that is, the highest and the sixth highest refugee-receiving countries in Europe and the highest civil and common law refugee-receiving countries.[6] These trends are important: even though they come from two different legal systems, common and civil law, both countries have adopted interpretations of the principle of *non-refoulement* that narrow the protections available to asylum claimants.

Table 5.1 illustrates the data gathered by EuroStat on the number of Dublin transfers under the Dublin III Regulation in 2018 by the top six countries in the order of outgoing transfers (Table 5.1).

Table 5.1 Dublin transfers by country in the order of outgoing requests (2018)[7]

Dublin Transfers by Country (2018)						
	Incoming requests	Implemented	Percentage accepted	Outgoing requests	Implemented	Percentage Returned
Germany	25,005	7580	30%	54,906	9209	17%
France	8744	1837	21%	45,358	3533	8%
Netherlands	5042	835	17%	8619	1849	21%
Belgium	3871	678	18%	8384	897	11%
Switzerland	6054	1292	21%	5941	1313	22%
United Kingdom	**1940**	**1215**	**63%**	**5510**	**209**	**4%**

[3] The Migration Observatory at the University of Oxford (analyzing Eurostat data), 8 November 2019 https://migrationobservatory.ox.ac.uk/resources/briefings/migration-to-the-uk-asylum/#kp7.

[4] *Ibid;* In comparison to the countries listed, 6% is still a significant number as it represents over 37,000 asylum applications and of those applications, around 15% constitute Dublin transfers—a situation in which concerns about *non-refoulement* are heightened.

[5] *Ibid.*

[6] While the UK was within the EU, it and Germany were both considered to be politically and economically influential: they both have strong economies, significant Gross Domestic Products, and significant political clout on the regional and world stage.

[7] House of Commons Library, "What is Dublin III Regulation? Will it be affected by Brexit?", https://commonslibrary.parliament.uk/home-affairs/immigration/what-is-the-dublin-iii-regulation-will-it-be-affected-by-brexit; See, also: EuroStat, "Dublin III Transfers 2018 by Country", 2018; The statistics were current as of 2018, taken from House of Commons Library, with reference to Eurostat numbers.

As Table 5.1 shows, the outgoing requests in the United Kingdom totaled 5510 in 2018, which is the sixth highest total number of requests in the EU plus Switzerland for transfers outside of the EU to another EU country. This data suggests that *non-refoulement* is still a concern, as all outgoing requests (5510) should require a *non-refoulement* assessment prior to transfer while all implemented transfers (209) should require a post-transfer monitoring mechanism to prevent further onward *refoulement*.[8]

The purpose of this chapter is therefore to explain the UK's domestic asylum system, particularly how it addresses *non-refoulement* of individuals. This chapter evaluates the UK's interpretation of *non-refoulement* in light of its obligations under EU law, ECHR law, and international law.[9] It demonstrates that the UK's domestic application of the principle of *non-refoulement* evidences a concerning trend: that policies of containment are at work within the UK and, by extension, the CEAS. This chapter begins by explaining the UK's domestic asylum laws, including the status of *non-refoulement* in the UK and the UK's obligations under EU law and ECHR law. This is done in order to provide the context for the UK's asylum system, which is examined in next section. Finally, this chapter considers how the UK's interpretation of *non-refoulement* through its domestic practice is demonstrative of containment theory in action.

5.2 UK Refugee Law

As international and European law set the standards upon which UK domestic law interprets and applies its *non-refoulement* obligations, it is vital to consider the relationship between each type of law.[10] The interplay between international, EU, ECHR, and UK national law is complex, as they have a push and pull effect on each other. For example, international law standards inform the minimum standards for EU, ECHR, and UK national law standards: they are considered to exert a 'pull' factor, in that both the EU and Member States are pulled towards compliance with international law standards.[11] At the same time, international law is influenced by State practice and national consensus on issues of asylum: this is

[8] An example of assessment or evaluation required by EU law is under Dublin III Regulation at art 46, where periodic monitoring is required.

[9] ECHR; The term 'European law' refers to both EU and ECHR law.

[10] This has been recognized by the House of Lords in House of Lords, European Union Committee, "Brexit: Refugee Protection and Asylum Policy", 11 October 2019 at paras 12, 16, 54.

[11] See, generally: Sarah Toucas, "Push and Pull Factors Towards and Against a Common European Migration Policy: France, Britain, and Their Approach to Irregular Migration", December 2008, https://www.ifri.org/sites/default/files/atoms/files/cadbury1.pdf.

considered a 'push' factor, in that Member State practice and consensus in turn pushes reform of international standards.[12] While the UK has exited the EU, it is still currently bound to EU law on asylum through the Withdrawal Agreement until the end of 2020. The end of the UK's transition period will clearly affect the interaction between international, European and UK refugee law. However, its influence with respect to *non-refoulement* will still echo through the EU for some time, since it remains part of the ECHR and will likely continue to contribute jurisprudence on *non-refoulement* within the ECtHR.

It is important to begin by first considering the EU and ECHR law applicable to the UK, and then the UK's domestic law on *non-refoulement*, because both the EU and ECHR law have informed the UK's law in the past. EU law will continue inform the UK's understanding of the content of its own domestic law until its exit from the CEAS at the end of 2020, and ECHR law will continue to bind the UK past that time.

As described in Chap. 3, the starting point for EU law on *non-refoulement* is Article 78(1) of the *Treaty on the Functioning of the EU*, which imposes legally binding obligations upon EU Member States to comply with international standards set by the Refugee Convention, including the *non-refoulement* obligation found under Article 33(1). Since the international law standard established by the Refugee Convention and other international human rights instruments provides the bare minimum standard with which States must comply, if EU law and ECHR law provide broader protection than the international standard, that is relevant to UK national law.[13]

EU asylum law holds primacy under UK national asylum law when the UK judicial system is applying EU asylum law provisions.[14] The 'principle of primacy' states that UK national law is secondary to EU law when UK national law is applying EU law provisions, which is also known as 'direct effect' under EU law.[15] However, when the protection standard granted by UK national law is broader than that granted under EU law, the UK can apply the broader standard pursuant to its national law (rather than the narrower EU law standard).[16]

---

[12] *Ibid.*

[13] See, for example, a discussion on the interplay between interpretation of EU and ECHR, and international and national law in European Asylum Support Office, "An Introduction to the Common European Asylum System for Courts and Tribunals: A Judicial Analysis", August 2016 at 70 [EASO Handbook]; For *non-refoulement* as a norm in international law, see Chap. 2; For *non-refoulement* as a norm in European law, see Chap. 3.

[14] See, for example, the determination of the CJEU in holding that EU Member States, when applying national law, must conform with EU law standards in *Stefano Melloni v Ministrio Fiscal,* CJEU Case C-399/11, Judgment of 26 February 2013 at para 63.

[15] *Jeremy F v Premier Ministre,* CJEU Case C-168/13 PPU, Judgment of 20 May 2013: 'It is settled case-law that, by virtue of the principle of primacy of EU law, which is an essential feature of the EU legal order [. . .] rules of national law, even of a constitutional order, cannot be allowed to undermine the effectiveness of EU law on the territory of that State'; For more, see EASO Handbook at 77.

[16] EU Charter at art 53.

While the 'principle of primacy' governs the EU–UK law relationship at the moment, the 'principle of subsidiarity' governs the relationship between ECHR law and UK national law.[17] Even though the UK will exit the CEAS at the end of 2020, it remains a State Party to the ECHR. Therefore, it is bound to this principle, which states that '[the] machinery of protection established by the [ECHR] is subsidiary to the national systems safeguarding human rights [. . .] [The EU institutions] become involved only through contentious proceedings and once all domestic remedies have been exhausted'.[18] This means that the UK is expected to implement and respect ECHR law, including the provisions of the ECHR applicable to *non-refoulement*.[19] If it does not, however, then affected parties may pursue domestic remedies, failing which a complaint can be laid before the ECtHR. That said, ECtHR Judge Villiger, in his concurring opinion in *M.S.S. v. Belgium and Greece*, held that, despite the 'principle of subsidiarity', the ECtHR should play a more restrictive role 'in light of the cardinal provision such as Article 3 [of the ECHR] in view of the central importance of the applicant's *refoulement* for this case'.[20] In other words, cardinal principles such as *non-refoulement* should be respected and protected at the international level, and are not to be undermined by domestic judicial interpretations of UK national courts where such interpretation may limit the scope of protection available to individuals the principle aims to protect.

The UK's *non-refoulement* obligations under EU law are affected by the EU law instruments that the UK has ratified, including the Qualification Directive of 2004/83 and Protocol 21, until the UK's exit from the CEAS. The UK has opted-out of the Qualification Directive (recast) of 13 December 2011, but currently remains bound by the Qualification Directive of 2004/83 of 29 April 2004, and Protocol 21 annexed to the *Treaty on European Union* and the TFEU.[21] The UK did not accept the Qualification Directive (recast) and therefore is not bound by it or subject to its application.[22] On *non-refoulement*, although not bound by Article 21 of the Qualification Directive (recast) on 'protection from *refoulement*' under EU law, the UK is bound by the same Article under the Qualification Directive of 2004/83 containing the exact same text.[23]

---

[17] ECHR at art 1.

[18] *Ibid.*

[19] As described in Chap. 3, these provisions include Article 3 of the ECHR formulated as the prohibition against torture.

[20] MSS.

[21] Qualification Directive at recital 50; See also: *Protocol on the Position of the United Kingdom and Ireland in Respect of the Area of Freedom, Security and Justice* annexed to the *Treaty on the Functioning of the European Union (Consolidated Version),* 26 October 2012, OJ L326/47-326/390, http://www.refworld.org/docid/52303e8d4.html [Protocol 21]; TEU.

[22] Qualification Directive recast at recital 50.

[23] *Ibid* at art 21; For a description of the United Kingdom's duties under international law and customary international law norm of *non-refoulement*, please see Chap. 2; See also: Qualification

The UK is also currently bound by the *non-refoulement* requirements of the post-*Treaty of Amsterdam* asylum directives (known as Phase I of the CEAS).[24] Phase I of the CEAS includes several key directives, namely the: Eurodac Regulation (2000); Temporary Protection Directive (2001); Dublin II Regulation (2003); Reception Conditions Directive (2003); Qualification Directive (2004); and Asylum Procedures Directive (2005).[25] The UK is also currently bound by *non-refoulement* obligations found (or inherent) in certain of the Phase II CEAS instruments, namely the Dublin III Regulation and the Eurodac Regulation (recast).[26] The UK has additionally opted into the Dublin III Regulation, which governs Dublin transfers.[27]

The UK's obligations under EU law to prohibit *refoulement* are complemented by its obligations under ECHR law. As a Member State of the Council of Europe, the UK is automatically a States Party to the ECHR, meaning that it is bound by ECHR provisions.[28] The UK's *non-refoulement* obligations under ECHR law are articulated through Article 3 of the ECHR on the prohibition against torture, which prohibits torture, including returning an individual to a situation in which he or she is at risk of torture or cruel treatment.[29]

The ECtHR has interpreted the Article 3 prohibition against torture in various cases, including in cases in which the UK was implicated. For instance, in the case of *Chahal v. the United Kingdom,* the ECtHR held that the UK violated Article 3 of the ECHR in that there were substantial grounds for believing that there was a real risk that the return of the claimant would have exposed him to torture, inhuman or degrading treatment.[30] Therefore, the court held that the UK violated the principle of *non-refoulement* as defined under international human rights law, despite

---

Directive recast at art 21: '1. Member States shall respect the principle of *non-refoulement* in accordance with their international obligations. 2. Where not prohibited by the international obligations mentioned in paragraph 1, Member States may *refoule* a refugee, whether formally recognised or not, when: (a) there are reasonable grounds for considering him or her as a danger to the security of the Member State in which he or she is present; or (b) he or she, having been convicted by a final judgment of a particularly serious crime, constitutes a danger to the community of that Member State. 3. Member States may revoke, end or refuse to renew or to grant the residence permit of (or to) a refugee to whom paragraph 2 applies'.

[24] *Treaty of Amsterdam Amending the Treaty on European Union, The Treaties Establishing the European Communities and Related Acts* OJ C340/1, 10 November 1997, http://www.refworld.org/docid/51c009ec4.html.

[25] European Asylum Support Office, "An Introduction to the Common European Asylum System for Courts and Tribunals: A Judicial Analysis", August 2016 https://www.easo.europa.eu/sites/default/files/public/BZ0216138ENN.PDF at 15.

[26] *Ibid* at 19; See also: Dublin III Regulation at arts 8, 9, 10; For a discussion of the implications of first and second phase instruments on Member States' compliance with *non-refoulement,* see Chap. 3.

[27] Costello Policy Primer at 5.

[28] *Ibid.*

[29] ECHR at art 3.

[30] Chahal.

arguing that the claimant posed a national security threat to the country if he remained.[31] Similarly, in UK cases the ECtHR confirmed the absolute nature of the Article 3 right, indicated that the harm can be inflicted by the State or non-State actors, and outlined the meaning of terms such as 'inhuman' or 'degrading' treatment or punishment.[32] On the question of the risk to the claimant, the ECtHR stressed in UK cases that a 'mere possibility' of ill-treatment in another country does not meet the threshold of 'real risk', and that the risk is future-oriented.[33] The Court has also specified in UK-related cases *Soering v. the United Kingdom*, *Vilvarajah and Others v. The United Kingdom* and *Babar Ahmed and Others v. The United Kingdom* that the *non-refoulement* norm applies to all forms of removal of an individual to another state: it does not matter whether the removal is done by deportation, expulsion or extradition.[34] Sometimes, the Court found, the UK might not be able to remove *any* person to a particular state without risking *refoulement* due to the general situation of violence in that country.[35] Additionally, UK-related jurisprudence has found that indirect *refoulement* is not permitted, and that the UK could be held responsible for the subsequent treatment of the claimant after that person is sent to a third state.[36] This is true even if the third state is a fellow EU Member State.[37]

Having described the EU and ECtHR legislation and jurisprudence which inform the UK's domestic interpretation of *non-refoulement*, it is important to examine how the principle is understood in UK domestic legislation and case law, as it is this law which is applied on a day-to-day basis within the UK's asylum system. The UK is a dualist legal system, meaning that international treaties must be transformed into domestic law in order to have domestic legal effect. The UK ratified the Refugee Convention in 1954 and acceded to the Protocol in 1968.[38] The UK transformed the obligation on *non-refoulement* under Article 33(1) of the

---

[31] *Ibid* at para 161(1); For more discussion on *non-refoulement* as defined under international human rights law, see Chap. 2.

[32] *Ibid* at paras. 80–81; Soering at para 88; Ahmed at paras 167–175; *A and Others v The United Kingdom* at para 127; *D v The United Kingdom*, No. 30240/96, Judgment of 2 May 1997, at para 49; *Sufi and Elmi v The United Kingdom*, Nos. 8319/07 and 11449/07, Judgment of 28 June 2011 at paras 282, 291.

[33] Vilvarajah at para 111; Chahal at para 86.

[34] Soering at para 91, Vilvarajah at para 103, and Ahmed at para 168.

[35] *NA v The United Kingdom*, No. 25904/07, Judgment of 17 July 2008 at para 115; *Sufi and Elmi v The United Kingdom*, Nos. 8319/07 and 11449/07, Judgment of 28 June 2011 at paras 241 (listing criteria such as whether the parties to the conflict were either employing methods and tactics of warfare targeting civilians, whether these tactics were widespread, whether the fighting was widespread, and the number of civilians killed, injured and displaced by the fighting) and 293.

[36] TI at 15; The ECtHR confirmed this approach in KRS.

[37] TI at 15.

[38] United Nations High Commissioner for Refugees, "States Parties to the 1951 Convention Relating to the Status of Refugees and the 1967 Protocol" at 4, http://www.unhcr.org/uk/protection/basic/3b73b0d63/states-parties-1951-convention-its-1967-protocol.html.

Refugee Convention into domestic law through paragraph 334 of the *Immigration Rules*.[39]

Apart from the *Immigration Rules*, here are several key pieces of legislation governing UK immigration and asylum processes and soft law instruments that provide guidance to asylum officials.[40] These are: the *Nationality, Immigration and Asylum Act* (2002); the *Asylum and Immigration (Treatment of Claimants, etc.) Act* (2004); and guidance instruments—Revocation of Refugee Status (2016); Exclusion Article 1F and Article 33 of the Refugee Convention (2016); Restricted Leave and Discretionary Leave (2015 & 2016), and Humanitarian Protection (2017).

The purpose of the *Nationality, Immigration and Asylum Act* is to 'make provision about nationality, immigration and asylum; to create offences in connection with international traffic in prostitution; to make provision about international projects connected with migration; and for connected purposes'.[41] For the purpose of the *Nationality, Immigration and Asylum Act,* an 'asylum seeker' means 'a person a) who is at least 18 years old, b) who is in the United Kingdom, c) who has made a claim for asylum at a place designated by the Secretary of State, d) whose claim has been recorded by the Secretary of State, and e) whose claim has not been determined'.[42] According to this definition, therefore, an individual claiming asylum outside of the territory of the UK or someone who has not yet reached the territory of the UK is not deemed an 'asylum seeker' for the purpose of the *Nationality, Immigration and Asylum Act.* However, Section 8(3) of the same Act is a saving provision.

Section 8(3) of the *Nationality, Immigration and Asylum Act* states that:

> (3) A claim for asylum is a claim by a person that to remove him from or require him to leave the United Kingdom would be contrary to the United Kingdom's obligations under (a) the Convention relating to the Status of Refugees done at Geneva on 28th July 1951 and its Protocol, or (b) Article 3 of the Convention for the Protection of Human Rights and Fundamental Freedoms agreed by the Council of Europe at Rome on 4th November 1950.[43]

In other words, even where an individual claiming asylum does not fall under the definition provided by Section 8(1), such as an individual who has not yet entered the territory of UK or such claim has not yet formally commenced, where that individual's return may constitute *refoulement* as per Article 33(1) of the Refugee Convention or Article 3 of the ECHR, then such a claim will constitute a claim for

---

[39] United Kingdom Home Office, "Immigration Rules Part 11: Asylum", https://www.gov.uk/guidance/immigration-rules/immigration-rules-part-11-asylum at para 334 [Immigration Rules].

[40] These include asylum policy guidance (instructions) found on the UK Visas and Immigration office website (which is part of the UK Home Office): United Kingdom, Visas and Immigration Office, www.gov.uk/government/collections/asylum-decision-making-guidance-asylum-instructions.

[41] *Nationality, Immigration and Asylum Act* [2002] c 41 at preamble, http://www.legislation.gov.uk/ukpga/2002/41/introduction [NIAA].

[42] *Ibid* at s 18(1).

[43] *Ibid* at s 18(3).

asylum for the purpose of the *Nationality, Immigration and Asylum Act.*[44] Section 8(3) is also important because it indicates the UK's intention to be bound by the Refugee Convention and the ECHR as per the words 'would be contrary to the United Kingdom's obligations under [. . .]'.[45]

Curiously, the *Nationality, Immigration and Asylum Act* does not have a provision which deals with the situation of unaccompanied minors seeking asylum, despite this scenario becoming increasingly common. Instead, the term 'dependent child' is used, and the provisions which concern the 'dependent child' are used not as the primary rights holder, but as a dependent of an asylum seeker, i.e. 'failed asylum-seeker with dependent child'.[46]

Other important provisions of the *Nationality, Immigration and Asylum Act* are Sections 72 to 80, regarding removal. The most important of these is Section 72. It should be noted at the outset that not all removals amount to *refoulement*. It is only when removals are to persecution, death, torture or other cruel, inhuman, degrading treatment or punishment, or other massive violations of human rights, that a violation of *refoulement* will take place.[47] Section 72, relating to 'serious criminals', provides for the construction and application of Article 33(2) of the Refugee Convention where the refugee is excluded from *non-refoulement* protection. It should be noted that Section 72 must be read in conjunction with Section 8(3) above. Section 72 permits the return of a refugee to *refoulement* where he or she is deemed to be a danger to the UK community or a national security threat to UK but only where that return does not breach the Section 8(3) prohibition of return to torture or cruel, inhuman or degrading treatment or punishment or gross, flagrant or mass violations of human rights.[48]

The purpose of the *Asylum and Immigration (Treatment of Claimants, etc.) Act* is to 'make provision about asylum and immigration.[49] Sections 33 to 35 are important to a consideration of *non-refoulement* because they focus on the 'removal and detention' of asylum claimants. In particular, Section 33 concerns removal of asylum claimants to 'safe third countries' and therefore invokes the 'safe third country' concept as it is currently understood in EU law. The 'safe third country' concept creates a duty on the sending State: the duty to ensure that the recipient State has adequate asylum procedures—including procedures prohibiting onward *refoulement* to other countries—for claimants to initiate their asylum applications. It is debatable whether the safe third country concept has any

[44] Refugee Convention at art 33(1); ECHR at art 3.

[45] NIAA at s 8(3).

[46] See, for example: NIAA at s 7A(1)(a)(i); *Immigration and Asylum Act* [1999] c 33 s 95(1)(b), http://www.legislation.gov.uk/ukpga/1999/33/section/95.

[47] For *non-refoulement* obligations under international law, see Chap. 2; For *non-refoulement* obligations under European law, see Chap. 3.

[48] CAT at art 3.

[49] *Asylum and immigration (Treatment of Claimants, etc.) Act* [2004] c 19 at preamble, http://www.legislation.gov.uk/ukpga/2004/19/introduction [Treatment of Claimants Act].

foundation in international law.[50] Schedule 3 of the *Asylum and Immigration (Treatment of Claimants, etc.) Act* lists 'safe third countries' to which asylum claimants are permitted under UK national law to be sent where it is considered 'safe' for these claimants to commence formal asylum procedures.[51] The list of countries designated as 'safe' under this Schedule are:

> Austria, Belgium, Republic of Cyprus, Czech Republic, Denmark, Estonia, Finland, France, Germany, Greece, Hungary, Iceland, Ireland, Italy, Latvia, Lithuania, Luxembourg, Malta, Netherlands, Norway, Poland, Portugal, Slovak Republic, Slovenia, Spain, and Sweden.[52]

This list contains countries—such as Greece—with inadequate asylum procedures as deemed by ECHR case law—and they remain on the list despite the ECtHR's rulings.[53] Part 2 of Schedule 3 also specifies that any person who has made an asylum claim or human rights claim may be removed from the UK 'to a State of which he is not a national or citizen'.[54] Under the Act, that State (the 'safe third country') shall be treated as a place 'from which a person will not be sent to another State in contravention of his Convention rights' (i.e. *refoulement*).[55]

Part 11 of the *Immigration Rules* concerns asylum and also contains relevant provisions which implicates the UK's obligation of *non-refoulement*.[56] For instance, paragraph 334 outlines the requirements for an individual to be granted refugee status in the UK, including that 'they are in the United Kingdom or have arrived at a port of entry in the United Kingdom'.[57] According to nongovernmental organizations, this is concerning: it seems to require presence in the UK, even though *non-refoulement* can potentially occur where the individual can be shown to be under the 'effective authority and control' of the UK, but nonetheless outside of the *physical* territory of the UK, such as in transit zones.[58] This interpretation of the UK's international law obligations is *narrower* than what is provided for under international law, as international law prohibits the *refoulement* of any individual to territories where they may face ill-treatment or threats of life regardless of whether the person has access to the territory of a State.[59]

---

[50] For a more detailed discussion, see Chap. 3, section on safe third countries.

[51] Treatment of Claimants Act at schedule 3 part 2.

[52] *Ibid* at schedule 3 part 2(2).

[53] It has been held, for example, by the ECtHR that Greece does not have adequate asylum procedures in place to facilitate proper examination of asylum claims, so that States such as the UK, may be held in violation of indirect *refoulement* when asylum claimants are nonetheless sent to Greece to have their claims processed in *MSS v Belgium and Greece*. For an in-depth discussion of the implications of indirect *refoulement,* see Chap. 3.

[54] Treatment of Claimants Act at schedule 3 part 2(3)(1)(b).

[55] *Ibid* at schedule 3 part 2(3)(2)(b).

[56] Immigration Rules.

[57] *Ibid* at para 334(i).

[58] *Ibid.*

[59] For the extraterritorial application of *non-refoulement*, see: Paulina Tandiono, "The Extraterritoriality of the Principle of Non-Refoulement: A Critique of the Sale case and Roma

Additionally, paragraph 345A to 345D of the *Immigration Rules* allows asylum claims to be declared inadmissible as a result of the claimant having made an earlier asylum claim in another country (a first country of asylum) or a 'safe' third country.[60] If these circumstances apply, the stories of asylum claimants themselves will not be substantively considered.[61] Although there are specific provisions precluding the asylum claimant's removal to his or her first country of asylum or 'safe' third country where *non-refoulement* obligations are not followed by those countries, permitting caseworkers to dismiss an application without having first substantively considered the application itself is already a breach of UK's international and European law obligations.[62] The *Immigration Rules* also permit caseworkers to 'decline to substantively consider an asylum claim if the applicant is transferable to another country in accordance with the Dublin Regulation'.[63] Preventing caseworkers from considering the merits of a claim by dismissing the application where Dublin Transfers may take place increases the risk of rejecting an asylum application at face value, without seriously considering the potential *refoulement* consequences if an asylum claimant is sent back.[64]

Although UK legislation does not have specific protection or provisions for unaccompanied minors seeking asylum, the *Immigration Rules* clearly address this group and obliges caseworkers to give 'particular priority and care [...] to the handling of their cases'.[65] It is useful to note, however, that the international and European standard of using the 'best interests of the child' test is not used in UK

case", https://blogs.lse.ac.uk/humanrights/2016/02/09/the-extraterritoriality-of-the-principle-of-non-refoulement-a-critique-of-the-sale-case-and-roma-case; See, also: Hirsi at 231.

[60] *Ibid* at paras 345A to 345E.

[61] *Ibid* at paras 345B and 345C.

[62] The asylum claimant cannot be removed to his or her first country of asylum or 'safe' third country where *non-refoulement* obligations are not followed by those countries, see, for instance, CAT at art 3; ICCPR at arts 6 and 7; Refugee Convention at art 33(1); An example of the breach of the UK's obligation is: not properly considering the claims on their merits, especially when much is at stake for the asylum claimant who may be removed to a first country of asylum or a 'safe' third country where the asylum system may be deficient. The European Court of Human Rights has held this to be in violation of *non-refoulement* obligations indirectly, in MSS; For more on how the principle of *non-refoulement* may be violated indirectly under European law, see Chap. 3. Further, permitting the transfer of asylum claimants to their first country of asylum or a 'safe' third country is a way for the UK to evade its responsibility for processing the asylum applicant. This method of responsibility shifting within the EU is inherently dangerous because it encourages asylum claimants who are otherwise not able to have their applications processed through legal channels to attempt illegal methods of getting to safety, including attempting perilous journeys across the Mediterranean Sea.

[63] Immigration Rules at para 345E.

[64] For a more in-depth discussion on Dublin Regulations and Dublin Transfers and how they are problematic, see Chap. 3.

[65] Immigration Rules at para 350.

domestic legislation.[66] Further, there is no mention of using the 'best interests of the child' test to assess the asylum application of an unaccompanied child in the *Immigration Rules*.[67]

The *Immigration Rules'* prohibition on *refoulement* is supposed to be applied at the various stages of the asylum process outlined below.[68] However, this does not always occur. For example, when an asylum claimant is rejected at first instance, there is a potential for *refoulement* to occur and therefore this potential should be assessed.[69] The guidance provided to asylum officers, or 'caseworkers', by the Home Office, reinforces this as an overarching approach, stating that 'the consideration of asylum claims deserves the greatest care—'anxious scrutiny' as the UK courts express it—so that just and fair decisions are made and protection granted to those who need it'.[70] In other words, the Home Office recognizes that the core principal obligation for signatory States of the Refugee Convention is not to return ('*refoule*') refugees. Even so, the UK has repeatedly been found to be in violation of the *non-refoulement* prohibition.[71]

There is a possibility that *non-refoulement* may be breached at each stage of the five different asylum procedures detailed below, which evidences containment practices of the UK. For example, during the accelerated procedure, the applicant's claim may be deemed by the asylum officer as either unfounded or manifestly unfounded. Where the claimant's application is deemed to be inadmissible as a result of being either unfounded or manifestly unfounded, *non-refoulement* considerations may arise. The Home Office's guidance towards deportation considers *refoulement* risks.[72] Another procedure where *non-refoulement* is implicated is the admissibility procedure. As guaranteed by Rule 345A(i) of the *Immigration*

---

[66] United Kingdom Home Office, "Asylum Policy Instruction: Revocation of Refugee Status: Version 4.0" at 1.4, https://www.gov.uk/government/uploads/system/uploads/attachment_data/file/493,918/revocation_of_refugee_status_v4_0_EXT.pdf [Revocation of Refugee Status].

[67] Immigration Rules at paras 350 to 352ZF.

[68] See, for example: Home Office, "Inadmissibility: EU grants of asylum, first country of asylum and safe third country concepts: Version 4.0", 1 October 2019 at 21.

[69] *Immigration Rules*.

[70] Home Office, "Asylum Policy Instruction: Assessing Credibility and Refugee Status: Version 9.0", 6 January 2015, https://assets.publishing.service.gov.uk/government/uploads/system/uploads/attachment_data/file/397,778/ASSESSING_CREDIBILITY_AND_REFUGEE_STATUS_V9_0.pdf at 4.

[71] See, for example: TI, which recognized that, in cases where the UK sends the asylum claimant back to Germany, where there is a high likelihood that the asylum claimant would be sent back to Sri Lanka to face torture contrary to Art 3 ECHR, the UK would be in violation of indirect *refoulement;* See, also: NS/ME, which recognized that, where the UK sends the asylum claimant back to Greece, where claimant's application would not be properly processed, it would contribute to the claimant's risk of *refoulement* from Greece.

[72] Home Office, "Inadmissibility: EU grants of asylum, first country of asylum and safe third country concepts: Version 4.0", 1 October 2019, https://assets.publishing.service.gov.uk/government/uploads/system/uploads/attachment_data/file/835,342/Inadmissibility-guidance-v4.0ext.pdf at 23 [Home Office Inadmissibility].

Rules, 'asylum inadmissibility decisions already made or being made in respect of removal to the EU, Iceland, Norway or Switzerland' must be certified against 'any human rights claim that relates to the risk of *refoulement* from the proposed country of removal under Part 2 Schedule 3 (paragraph 5(1) and 5(3))'.[73] Rules 345B and 345C, on the other hand, concern decisions 'already made or being made in respect of removal to any other country'.[74] In order to be removed, the case-worker must consider 'the human rights claim, including any protection issues regarding the country of removal and the risk of *refoulement* with specific reference to objective information regarding the conditions of removal'.[75] While these explicit protections against *refoulement* at these stages of the asylum process are positive, the actual application of the principle has been mixed and, at times, restrictive.

The case law of the UK interprets the principle of *non-refoulement* in a manner that is illustrative of a concerning trend: the narrowing of the norm to indicate that the room for protecting vulnerable asylum claimants is shrinking. This trend of a narrow interpretation of *non-refoulement* suggests that containment policies are at work in the UK. It has been held by the UK courts that the focus on determining whether there is a chance of the claimant being *refouled* should be based on 'systemic risks' rather than examining the individual's actual circumstances. For example, in the case of *Pour et al.*, the High Court of Justice, Queen's Bench Division (Administrative Court) held that there is no real risk that the applicants, if returned to Iran from Cyprus, would be *refouled* by the UK.[76] The Court found that the inclusion of Cyprus on the list of 'safe' third countries involved no incompatibility with the ECHR and, unlike the ECtHR, the Court sided with the CJEU in holding that *non-refoulement* claims should be evaluated based wholly on systemic risks, rather than particular individual circumstances.[77] Another case, *Medhanye R*, considered the proposed removal of an applicant from the UK to Italy under the Dublin II Regulation.[78] The UK High Court applied the judgments of both *M.S.S.* and *K.R.S.* and held that the evidence used by the claimant to rebut the presumption of mutual trust when contemplating removal must reveal a 'systemic failure on a significant scale' for that presumption to be rebutted.[79] The High Court held that particular weight will be given to the UNHCR and other intergovernmental bodies with appropriate mandates, while little or no weight would usually be given to expert reports in such cases.[80] As explained in Chap. 3, this focus on systemic

[73] *Ibid;* See, also: *Immigration Rules* at Part 2, Schedule 3 at para 5(1) and 5(3).

[74] Home Office Inadmissibility at 23.

[75] *Ibid;* See, also: *Immigration Rule* at Rules 345B and 345C.

[76] *Ibid.*

[77] *Esmaiel Mohammed Pour (1), Seid Jafar Hasini Hersari (2), Majid Ghulami (3) v The Secretary of State for the Home Department* [2016] EWHC 401 (Admin).

[78] *Medhanye, R (on the application of) v Secretary of State for the Home Department*, [2011] EWHC 3012 (Admin) [Medhanye].

[79] *Ibid.*

[80] *Ibid.*

issues in the transfer country raises serious concerns as to whether claimants' individual circumstances will be adequately evaluated against the potential for *refoulement* (as opposed to a blanket evaluation of general risk of *refoulement* of everyone sent to that country). As described in Chap. 2, under international law, an evaluation of the risk for *refoulement* is meant to be individualized.

Another example of a constricted understanding of the principle of *non-refoulement* can be seen in generous considerations of the presumption of mutual trust. This practice of restrictive interpretation of *non-refoulement* again demonstrates that containment policies are at work in the UK. In the case of *Tabrizagh et al.*, the claimant was being contemplated for removal from the UK to Italy. The UK High Court of Queen's Bench (Administrative Court) considered the Secretary of State's denial of the claimants' right of appeal against removal to Italy under the Dublin II Regulation.[81] The claimants argued that removal to Italy would expose them to real risk of a breach of Article 3 of the ECHR on the prohibition against torture.[82] The Court held that there was no evidence to rebut the presumption that Italy would comply with its obligations under EU laws or of special vulnerability in personal circumstances of any of the claimants.[83] This was despite the widespread breach by Italy of its obligations under EU laws at that time. In the case of *MS, NA, SG*, the High Court of Justice, Queen's Bench Division (Administrative Court) ruled that the presumption that Italy remains in compliance with its EU and international law obligations related to reception and integration of the asylum claimant and beneficiaries of international protection had not been rebutted.[84] Thus, the Court found, the asylum claimant and beneficiaries of international protection suffering from severe psychological trauma could be returned to Italy with no real risk of breaching Article 3 of the ECHR or Article 4 of the EU Charter, due to the presumption that Italy's reception capabilities has not been exceeded, and that while effective medical treatment is available under the same terms as Italian nationals.[85] Again, this ruling, which was also in 2015—the height of the influx of migrants into Italy—was contrary to the actual conditions on the ground in Italy, where refugee systems were virtually inoperative.[86]

The UK courts' interpretation of *non-refoulement* also considered the usage of 'safe' third country concepts by the Home Office as well as the UK's interpretation of EU secondary law provisions such as the Qualification Directive. The case of *Ex Parte Adan R* considered the case of asylum

[81] *The Queen on the Application of Mr Mohsen Pourali Tabrizagh, Mr Tahir Syed, Mr Saeed Ali, Mr Ali Omar Mohammed, Mr Edmond Karaj, AB (Sunda) v Secretary of State for the Home Department* [2015] EWHC 1095.

[82] *Ibid.*

[83] *Ibid.*

[84] *The Queen on the Application of MS, NA, SG and the Secretary of State for the Home Department,* [2015] EWHC 1095.

[85] *Ibid.*

[86] Asylum Information Database, "Country Report: Italy", December 2015, http://www.asylumineurope.org/reports/country/italy.

claimants originally from Somalia and Algeria who were concerned that, if they were transferred to another EU country, they would be *refouled* to their originating state: the UK argued that, in assessing whether a State is a 'safe' third country, it may determine whether the foreign State's interpretation of the Refugee Convention is reasonable.[87] It was held by the UK Court of Appeal that the Secretary of State for the Home Department had to be satisfied that the foreign State applied the 'one true interpretation' of the Refugee Convention decided by UK Courts rather than a narrower interpretation which could lead to *refoulement*.[88] This understanding of the principle of *non-refoulement* as having a fixed international meaning that cannot be undermined by other states' restrictive interpretations seems positive on its face. However, the approach of 'one true interpretation' of the Refugee Convention makes UK courts more likely to find a violation of *non-refoulement* can take place only within specific parameters that are predefined by the court, rather than allowing for potential new cases such as those related to health, which can also potentially violate the norm.

In another case, *EN (Serbia)*, the UK Court of Appeal considered the exception to *non-refoulement* under Article 33(2) of the Refugee Convention, where 'there are reasonable grounds for regarding [the claimant] as a danger to the security of the country in which he is, or who, having been convicted by a final judgment of a particularly serious crime, constitutes a danger to the community of that country', as implemented in the Qualification Directive Article 14.4(a).[89] The Court rejected the view that Article 33(2) must be interpreted narrowly and restrictively so as to give maximum effect to *non-refoulement*: such an interpretation adds an 'unjustified gloss' to Article 33(2), and the imposition of a rebuttable presumption that the claimant is a danger to the community is acceptable,[90] Similarly, the case of *Dudaev et al.* concerned the removal of a Chechnyan claimants from the UK to Sweden under the Dublin II Regulation, where the claimants argued that there was a real risk that they would be *refouled* to Russia if returned to Sweden.[91] The UK High Court of Queen's Bench Division found that the presumption of mutual trust in Sweden—the presumption that Sweden would comply with its international legal obligations (including not to *refoule*)—was not rebutted and that 'judicial comity between the courts of two democratic states' supported this, even though it recognized a lack of legal assistance for the claimants in Sweden.[92] In other words, in cases involving

---

[87] *Secretary of State for the Home Department, Ex Parte Adan R v Secretary of State for the Home Department Ex Parte Aitseguer, R v.* [2000] UKHL 67.

[88] *Ibid.*

[89] *EN (Serbia) v Secretary of State for the Home Department & Anor* [2009] EWCA Civ 630.

[90] *Ibid* at paras 40–43, 80.

[91] *Musud Dudaev, Kamila Dudaev and Denil Dudaev v Secretary of State for the Home Department*, [2015] EWHC 1641.

[92] *Ibid.*

claims of risk of *refoulement*, the presumption of mutual trust is wide, involving judicial deference to the courts of another democratic EU State.

As considered above, certain case law of the UK suggests a concerning narrowing of the interpretation of the UK's *non-refoulement* obligations, thus evidencing containment policies. First, the cases of *Pour et al.* and *Medhanye R* (citing *MSS* and *KRS*) examined how UK courts' interpretation of the presumption of mutual trust focused on 'systemic risks' rather than 'individual assessments'. This suggests that UK courts are predominately concerned with whether a given Member State has adequate procedures rather than considering the individual's circumstances to see if they may be more prone to *non-refoulement* risks. This is concerning because refugee status involves an individualized assessment of subjective fear of risk and therefore any assessment involving *non-refoulement* risks *should* include an assessment of the individual circumstances experienced by the claimant. The cases of *EN (Serbia), MS, NA & SG, Tabrizagh,* and *Dudaev* also indicate a restrictive interpretation of *non-refoulement.* For example, the case of *MS, NA & SG* reveals that Dublin transfers *can* occur even where the individual claimant is exposed to severe psychological trauma if transferred to a Member State. According to the UK court, such a transfer would *not* be considered a breach of Article 3 of the ECHR. This reasoning is problematic as it strengthens the European concept of the presumption of mutual trust among Member States without due regard to the individual's exposure to risk that can rise to the level of ill-treatment or torture, constituting a violation of *non-refoulement* in human rights law. As a result, these cases have demonstrated the UK courts' concerning trend towards a more restrictive interpretation of *non-refoulement.*

Finally, the case of *Ex Parte Adan R* suggests that UK courts are accustomed to a 'one true interpretation' of the Refugee Convention, including restrictive interpretations of what fits within that interpretation. By restricting *non-refoulement* to a specific 'true' interpretation, the UK courts may be less likely to recognize novel breaches of *non-refoulement* where these violations have not been previously recognized by UK case law.

5.3 The UK Domestic Asylum System: Institutional Structure

International and European law both set the standards upon which the UK's domestic asylum system is based. Those standards are applied through asylum procedures: these procedures are essentially the manner in which the law becomes operationalized. This section therefore examines the different roles played by various actors—namely the government, courts, tribunals, and immigration officers—and the interaction of these roles within the UK domestic asylum system.

The UK Visas and Immigration division is part of the Home Office and is responsible for 'making millions of decisions each year about who has the right to visit or stay in the country, with a firm emphasis on national security and a culture of customer satisfaction for people who come here legally'.[93] The UK Visas and Immigration division prioritizes securing borders and reducing immigration, cutting crime and protecting citizens from terrorism.[94] The division is also responsible for issuing 'soft law' guidance instruments, such as instructions for asylum officials in their day-to-day decision-making.[95] The immigration officers responsible for examining asylum claims are termed 'caseworkers' by the UK Visas and Immigration division.[96] The Asylum Intake and Casework unit is housed under a department of the UK Visas and Immigration division and is responsible for 'all aspects of immigration and asylum: entry, in-country applications for leave to remain, monitoring compliance with immigration conditions, and enforcement including detention and removal'.[97]

The administrative and judicial system addressing asylum issues is multifaceted. The First-Tier Tribunal (Immigration and Asylum) is responsible for handling appeals made by the Home Office in relation to permission to stay in the UK, deportation from the UK, and entry clearance to the UK, as well as immigration bail from individuals held in custody by the Home Office relating to immigration matters.[98] The Upper Tribunal (Immigration and Asylum Chamber) handles appeals by the First-Tier Tribunal (Immigration and Asylum) which relate to visa applications, asylum applications, and the right to enter or stay in the UK.[99] The Upper Tribunal also hears judicial review cases referred by the Home Office relevant to immigration, asylum and human rights claims.[100] Decisions of the Upper Tribunal may be appealed to the relevant higher court: the Court of Appeal in England and Wales, the Court of Appeal in Northern Ireland or the Court of Session in Scotland.[101] Decisions of the Court of Appeal may be appealed to the UK Supreme Court with leave from the lower court

[93] United Kingdom Office of Visas and Immigration, "What We Do", https://www.gov.uk/government/organisations/uk-visas-and-immigration.

[94] United Kingdom Office of Visas and Immigration, "Our Priorities", https://www.gov.uk/government/organisations/uk-visas-and-immigration/about#our-priorities.

[95] United Kingdom Office of Visas and Immigration, "Asylum Policy", https://www.gov.uk/topic/immigration-operational-guidance/asylum-policy.

[96] *Ibid.*

[97] Asylum Information Database, "Short Overview of the Asylum Procedure: UK", https://www.asylumineurope.org/reports/country/united-kingdom/asylum-procedure/general/short-overview-asylum-procedure [UK Overview].

[98] United Kingdom Office of Visas and Immigration, "First-Tier Tribunal (Immigration and Asylum)", https://www.gov.uk/courts-tribunals/first-tier-tribunal-immigration-and-asylum.

[99] United Kingdom Office of Visas and Immigration, "Upper Tribunal (Immigration and Asylum Chamber)", https://www.gov.uk/courts-tribunals/upper-tribunal-immigration-and-asylum-chamber.

[100] *Ibid.*

[101] United Kingdom Office of Visas and Immigration, "Appeal a Decision by the Immigration and Asylum Tribunal", https://www.gov.uk/upper-tribunal-immigration-asylum/the-tribunals-decision.

which handed down the judgment.[102] The UK Supreme Court hears appeals against certain decisions by the Court of Appeal where it concerns the greatest public and constitutional importance.[103]

As the above has shown, the asylum procedure in the UK involves multiple actors, including the UK Visas and Immigration division, various levels of courts and tribunals, and immigration officers. The importance of interpreting and applying international and European law accurately therefore is clear from the top of the hierarchy to the bottom; from the decision-making of the UK Visas and Immigration division offering directions through guidance instruments for immigration officers adjudicating individual asylum cases, to the interpretation of the actions taken by the State by the relevant courts and tribunals.

5.4 Claiming Asylum in the UK

The UK's asylum system is under constant strain ever since the onset of the Syrian civil war in 2011. Between 2018 and 2019, UK has, on average, 7860 asylum applications per quarter, which is over 30,000 asylum applications per year.[104] This picture suggests that examining the asylum procedure as well as safeguards within the UK is important, given the large number of asylum claimants affected.

This section therefore details the procedures involved in claiming asylum in the UK. It explains the UK's *Immigration Rules*, followed by the administrative process for numerous stages of the asylum determination process. The process itself is multi-layered and complex, which is why this section also includes a flowchart providing a visual representation of the system.

The UK's *Immigration Rules* create the foundation of the UK asylum system. They represent directions issued by the UK Home Office for immigration officers to follow when adjudicating asylum applications.[105] These Rules specify the criteria to determine whether an asylum claimant may be granted refugee status in the UK.[106] Mirroring the provisions under international and European law, paragraph 334 of the *Immigration Rules* provides the criteria for determining the

[102] UK Supreme Court, "How to Appeal", https://www.supremecourt.uk/procedures/how-to-appeal.html.

[103] UK Supreme Court, "Role of the Supreme Court", https://www.supremecourt.uk/about/role-of-the-supreme-court.html.

[104] UK Refugee Council, "Quarterly Asylum Statistics", August 2019, https://www.refugeecouncil.org.uk/wp-content/uploads/2019/09/Asylum-Statistics-Aug-2019.pdf at 1.

[105] United Kingdom, Home Office, "Immigration Rules", https://www.gov.uk/guidance/immigration-rules.

[106] *Ibid* at para 334.

grant of refugee status in the UK.[107] This paragraph in the *Immigration Rules* incorporates the definition of refugee from the Refugee Convention as incorporated into the Qualification regulations, as well as other aspects of the Refugee Convention, such as the 'danger to security' issue, and, most importantly for the purposes of this chapter, the prohibition on *non-refoulement* in (v).[108]

Most of the rules within the *Immigration Rules* concern procedure rather than substance of the asylum determination decision process,[109] but they do provide some guidance to decision-makers. For example, the *Rules* include factors immigration officers should consider when determining the credibility of the claimant, such as age, gender, and variations in the capacity of human memory.[110] Also, the claimant is expected to 'demonstrate a reasonable depth of personal experience and knowledge, allowing for any underlying factors'.[111] As well, the *Rules* indicate the timeline required for the Secretary of State for the Home Department to make a decision on a claimant's application for international protection for refugee status: the decision must be issued within six months from the date it was recorded.[112]

---

[107] *Ibid*, which states: 'i) they are in the United Kingdom or have arrived at a port of entry in the United Kingdom; (ii) they are a refugee, as defined in regulation 2 of *The Refugee or Person in Need of International Protection (Qualification) Regulations 2006*; (iii) there are no reasonable grounds for regarding them as a danger to the security of the United Kingdom; (iv) having been convicted by a final judgment of a particularly serious crime, they do not constitute a danger to the community of the United Kingdom; and (v) refusing their application would result in them being required to go (whether immediately or after the time limited by any existing leave to enter or remain) in breach of the Refugee Convention, to a country in which their life or freedom would be threatened on account of their race, religion, nationality, political opinion or membership of a particular social group'.

[108] *Ibid* at para 334(v).

[109] Part 11 of the *Immigration Rules* deals with the consideration of admissible applications for asylum and humanitarian protection: *Immigration Rules, Part 11* at para 326A. In particular, paragraphs 328 to 333 within the *Immigration Rules* specify that all asylum applications are determined by the Secretary of State for the Home Department in accordance with the Refugee Convention: *Ibid* at para 328. Paragraph 331 of the *Immigration Rules* describes the procedures for the immigration officer in the situation where a claimant is refused asylum: *Ibid* at para 331. In this case, the immigration officer will consider whether to grant or refuse permission to enter UK territory without interviewing the claimant further: *Ibid.* Where the immigration officer decides that a further interview is required, the examination of the application for asylum will be resumed pursuant to the *Immigration Rules*: *Ibid.*

[110] UK Overview; See, also: Home Office, "Asylum Policy Instruction: Assessing Credibility and Refugee Status: Version 9.0", 6 January 2015, which states: 'age; gender; variations in the capacity of human memory; physical and mental health; emotional trauma; lack of education; social status and cultural traditions; feelings of shame; painful memories; particularly those of a sexual nature',
https://assets.publishing.service.gov.uk/government/uploads/system/uploads/attachment_data/file/397,778/ASSESSING_CREDIBILITY_AND_REFUGEE_STATUS_V9_0.pdf at 14 [Assessing Credibility Guidance].

[111] Assessing Credibility Guidance at 14.

[112] Immigration Rules at para 333A.

The asylum procedures in the UK determine the methods for granting and withdrawing of international protection for refugee status.[113] Responsibility for the asylum process in the UK rests with the Secretary of State for the Home Department, who allocates asylum decision-making to the UK Visas and Immigration division and the Asylum Intake and Casework Directorate.[114]

At first instance, an interview takes place where biometric data is collected, and information regarding health and family, details of the travel route, as well as a broad outline of the reasons for claiming asylum are collected from the claimant.[115] After the initial screening stage where the claimant's fingerprint and health information is gathered by the Home Office, the claimant is then directed into one of five different possible procedures: the regular procedure, accelerated procedure, admissibility procedure, Dublin procedure, or border procedure.[116]

In general, an individual's asylum application will go through the regular procedure. This involves prioritizing the asylum claimant if he or she belongs to a vulnerable group of individuals such as unaccompanied minors, pregnant women, or individuals who are disabled.[117] The regular procedure involves 'straightforward' and 'non-straightforward' cases where the former would have a time-sensitive deadline of six months, or 182 days, while the latter is designated as 'non-straightforward' by the Home Office simply on the basis that the 182-day deadline was not met.[118] Vulnerable groups such as unaccompanied minors are referred to a specialized group of decision-makers.[119] Where the asylum claimant does not belong to a vulnerable group, the asylum officer considers—based on the information collected at this stage—whether to apply the

---

[113] Asylum Procedures Directive.

[114] Asylum Information Database, "Country Report: United Kingdom", 2017 at 15 [AIDA UK Report].

[115] *Ibid.*

[116] *Ibid* at 19.

[117] Asylum Information Database, "Country Report: United Kingdom", 2019 Update, https://www.asylumineurope.org/sites/default/files/report-download/aida_uk_2019update.pdf [AIDA UK Report 2019].

[118] *Ibid* at 22–23; See, also: The Parliament of the United Kingdom, "Asylum: Applications: Written Question—220305", 18 February 2019, which states: 'Until recently, our aim was to decide 98% of straight forward asylum claims within six months of the date of claim. However, many asylum claims are not straight-forward, which meant it was not always possible to make an initial decision within six months of the date of claim. Many of these cases had a barrier that needed to be overcome to make the asylum decision and many of these barriers were outside of the Home Office's control. To promote a greater understanding and transparency of the asylum system, we have prioritised deciding older claims and those made by more vulnerable individuals, whose claims are more complex. This has resulted in a reduction in the proportion of claims decided within 6 months', https://www.parliament.uk/business/publications/written-questions-answers-statements/written-question/Commons/2019-02-12/220,305.

[119] *Ibid;* For instance, s 55 of the *Borders Citizenship and Immigration Act* 2009 requires that the 'voice of the child is heard in the proceedings, and this was reiterated by the Supreme Court, affirming that the wishes and feelings of the child must be taken properly in to account by decision makers' in AIDA UK Report at 49; *ZH (Tanzania) v Secretary of State for the Home Department* [2011] UKSC 4, 1 February 2011.

accelerated procedure, under which where the application may be deemed to be unfounded or manifestly unfounded.[120]

During the admissibility procedure, the claimant will be sent to the Third Country Unit if he or she has passed through a 'safe' third country on the way to claiming asylum in the UK.[121] The asylum application will be declared inadmissible where:

> the applicant has been granted a refugee status from another EU Member State, comes from a first country of asylum, comes from a 'safe' third country, has been granted a status equivalent to refugee status in the UK; or is allowed to remain in the UK and is protected from *refoulement* pending the outcome of a safe third country procedure.[122]

There are two procedures related to transfers during the admissibility procedure: Dublin transfers and 'safe' third country transfers. The Dublin procedure initiates where the Member State responsible for examining the asylum application is not ascertained.[123] The Home Office then applies the Dublin criteria to determine the EU Member State responsible for processing the asylum application.[124] Based on the hierarchy of responsibility criteria laid down in Article 7 of the Dublin III

---

[120] *Ibid* at 42–43; Where 'unfounded' means 'a caseworker must be satisfied that the claim cannot, on any legitimate view, succeed'; The term 'manifestly unfounded' means 'a claim which is so clearly without substance that it is bound to fail' and 'it is possible for a claim to be manifestly unfounded even if it takes more than a cursory look at the evidence to come to a view that there is nothing of substance in it'; Factors for asylum officers to consider when determining whether a case is 'manifestly unfounded' include: 'the factual substance and detail of the claim', 'how it stands with the known background data', 'in the round whether it is capable of belief', 'whether some part is capable of belief', 'whether, if eventually believed in whole or part, it is capable of meeting the requirements of the Refugee Convention', see: Home Office, "Certification of protection and human rights claim under section 94 of the Nationality, Immigration and Asylum Act 2002 (clearly unfounded claims)", Version 4.0, 12 February 2019, https://assets.publishing.service.gov.uk/government/uploads/system/uploads/attachment_data/file/778,221/certification-s94-guidance-0219.pdf at 11; Asylum Procedures Directive at art 31(8).

[121] *Ibid* at 39.

[122] *Ibid;* See, also: Greater Manchester Immigration Aid Unit, "Briefing paper on the experiences of children from the Calais camp in the north west of England", March 2017, https://gmiau.org/briefing-paper-experiences-children-calais-camp-north-west-england.

[123] Dublin III Regulation at art 3(2).

[124] *Ibid;* The Dublin criteria is as follows: 'For example, if an asylum claimant arrives in a member state, the asylum official first determines the category under which the applicant for international protection falls, such as, whether he or she is a minor and/or has family member(s) in another member state, in order to determine the member state responsible for processing the asylum application. Next, the asylum official considers whether the applicant is in possession of a visa or residence permit in a member state, and whether the applicant has entered the EU irregularly or regularly. In processing the asylum application, in certain countries, the asylum official would consider whether the criteria for transferring the applicant to a safe third country apply pursuant to the Asylum Procedures Directive (2013/32/EU). If the criteria for safe third country do not apply, and the applicant for international protection does not qualify for refugee status, then the asylum official will consider granting subsidiary protection pursuant to the Qualification Directive (2011/95/EU). The asylum official will also consider whether humanitarian and compassionate grounds apply, for example, in order to bring together family members, relatives or any other family relations', see: Jenny Poon, "ESIL Reflections: The EU Commission

Regulation, the UK may deem itself as the responsible Member State, in which case no transfer takes place.[125] The Dublin III Regulation specifies that the Dublin State where the claim for asylum is first lodged will send a request to the Dublin State it deems responsible according to certain criteria.[126] Thus, the UK will send a request to the country it identifies as responsible and, upon acceptance (provided actively or by default), the Home Office will initiate a 'take back' request, wherein the Member State responsible for processing the asylum application will be requested to 'take charge' of the claimant pursuant to the Dublin III Regulation.[127]

Individuals being contemplated for return to a 'safe' third country will undergo the 'safe' third country procedure under UK domestic law and their files will be assigned to the Third Country Unit within the UK Visas and Immigration division.[128] Where the Third Country Unit has certified that the individual claiming asylum came from a 'safe' third country on the way to claiming asylum in the UK, his or her asylum application will not be decided in the UK.[129] Instead, the individual will be returned to the 'safe' third country that he or she has passed through, where a connection may be established between the applicant and the third country deemed 'safe'.[130] The *Immigration Rules* specify the connection criteria necessary in order to remove an individual back to the 'safe' third country through which he or she has passed.[131] The *Immigration Rules* set out a list of non-exhaustive criteria for establishing such a connection, these include:

> a. Time spent in the country; b. Relations with persons in that country, who may be nationals of that country, habitually resident non-nationals, or family members seeking protection there; c. Family lineage, regardless of whether family is present in that country; and d. Any cultural or ethnic connections.[132]

If an individual has made an asylum claim upon arriving at the UK border, as opposed to within the UK, the substance of the claim is not examined—this is because, in the UK, 'there is no provision for asylum decisions to be taken at the border'.[133] During the border procedure, immigration officers may carry out the screening interview, but

on 'Dublin IV': Sufficient Safeguards for Asylum Claimants?" (2016) 5(9) *European Society of International Law Reflection Series* 1–10 at 2.

[125] United Kingdom, Home Office, "Dublin III Regulation, Version 1.0", 2 November 2017 at 22 [UK DRIII].

[126] *Ibid;* See, also: Dublin III Regulation at art 3(2).

[127] UK DRIII at 22; Dublin III Regulation at arts 18 and 20; See, also: Asylum Information Database, "The Implementation of the Dublin III Regulation in 2018", March 2019, http://www.asylumineurope.org/sites/default/files/aida_2018update_dublin.pdf at 11–13.

[128] AIDA UK Report at 15.

[129] *Ibid* at 54–55.

[130] *Ibid;* Immigration Rules Part 11 at para 345D.

[131] AIDA UK Report.

[132] *Ibid* at 55.

[133] *Ibid* at 41.

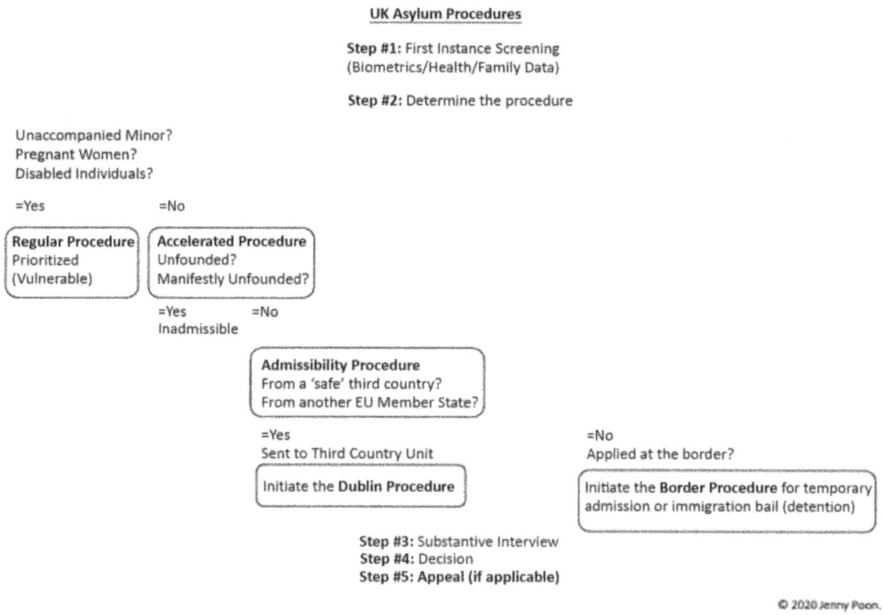

Fig. 5.1 UK asylum procedures

then refer the claim to the regular procedure; the officers have the power to grant temporary admission to territory or immigration bail to permit the claim to be made.[134]

Figure 5.1 reproduces the asylum procedure that takes place in the UK from registration to appeal.[135]

As the above description and Figure shows, the asylum procedure within the UK is a complex one which involves different stages and procedures depending on the situation of the claimant. The principle of *non-refoulement* is to be applied at each of these stages.

5.5 Containment by the UK Through Procedural Methods and Evidentiary Thresholds

Apart from the restricted understanding of *non-refoulement* in UK case law discussed above, *non-refoulement* protection is also constricted through procedural and evidentiary means. For example, although there are provisions within the

[134] *Ibid;* See, also: Home Office, "Immigration Bail: Version 5.0", 28 February 2020, https://assets.publishing.service.gov.uk/government/uploads/system/uploads/attachment_data/file/869,352/Immigration-bail-v5.0ext.pdf.

[135] AIDA UK Report at 13; Where UASC stands for Unaccompanied Asylum-Seeking Child.

Dublin III Regulation which require asylum claimants to be interviewed so they can tell their stories to decision-makers, in practice, the merits of the applications of claimants being contemplated for transfer are often not examined.[136] Steps where interviews are not permitted in the UK's asylum procedure were outlined above. These practices not only raise the risk that a claimant will be *refouled* without being able to raise the argument of fear of persecution on return, they also run counter to the case of *M.S.S.* In that case, the ECtHR noted that Belgium did not give M.S.S. the chance to say why he should not be sent to Greece (due to no personal interview), and this was a contributing factor in finding that Belgium did not fulfill its responsibilities to M.S.S. under the ECHR.[137]

The gap between the *non-refoulement* principle and practice in UK asylum practice is also evident in the requirement that asylum claimants who wish to challenge transfer cases must present an 'arguable case' in which they must meet a high burden of proof. This is an issue, first, when asylum claimants are being contemplated for a Dublin transfer to another EU Member State, and second, when an asylum claimant is being contemplated for transfer under a 'safe' third country agreement. The UK requires asylum claimants to satisfy a higher evidentiary threshold than is expected under international law.[138] As a consequence, the high evidentiary threshold acts as a form of control under the containment theory described in Chap. 4.

If asylum claimants are being considered for Dublin transfers to other EU Member States, these claimants can only challenge the transfer if they successfully rebut the presumption of mutual trust.[139] As described in Chap. 3, this presumption assumes that all EU Member States comply with their international and European law obligations. Case law from both the ECtHR and the CJEU—particularly a trilogy of cases from 2009 to 2013—establishes the requisite threshold necessary to determine whether the asylum claimant has satisfactorily rebutted the

[136] Dublin III Regulation at art 5.

[137] *MSS.*

[138] Hemme Battjes and Evelien Brouwer, "The Dublin Regulation and Mutual Trust: Judicial Coherence in EU Asylum Law" (2015) 8(2) *Review of European Administrative Law* 182–214 at 191, which states: 'the 'systemic breaches' requirement, developed by the CJEU in the *NS v. SSHD* judgement and incorporated into the Dublin III Regulation, has been criticized by several authors not only as being too high a threshold for rebutting trust, but also because of the lack of precise standards on the basis of which national courts must consider trust as rebutted' [Battjes]; See, also: Evelien Brouwer, "Mutual Trust and the Dublin Regulation: Protection of Fundamental Rights in the EU and the Burden of Proof" (2013) 9(1) *Utrecht Law Review* 135–147; For critiques on the high threshold of proof by other scholars, see: Elspeth Guild, Cathryn Costello, Madeline Garlick and Violeta Moreno-Lax, "Enhancing the Common European Asylum System and Alternatives to Dublin", CEPS Paper No 83, September 2015, http://www.epgencms.europarl.europa.eu/cmsdata/upload/983a50a5-69d6-48b1-a0bd-2b34cced9e36/Sessions_1_and_2_-_Study_European_Asylum_System_and_Alternatives_to_Dublin.pdf.

[139] *YB (Eritrea) v Secretary of State for the Home Department* [2008] EWCA Civ 360 at para 27 [Eritrea].

presumption of mutual trust, so that they are not subjected to Dublin transfers.[140] This case law was described in detail in Chap. 3 discussion of the presumption of mutual trust, and will be briefly reviewed here in order to provide context for the discussion of the UK. These cases indicated that the initial onus, or burden of proof, is placed upon the claimant to satisfy the Member State that the presumption of mutual trust permitting a Dublin transfer has been rebutted by presenting an 'arguable case' that his or her return to a country deemed 'safe' will place the claimant at risk of threats to life or liberty on any ECHR ground.[141] Where the claimant is unable to discharge the burden of proof on a standard of an 'arguable case', then paragraph 6, Schedule 3 of the UK's 2004 *Treatment of Claimants Act* will apply, without qualification.[142] Paragraph 6 states:

> A person who is outside the United Kingdom *may not bring an immigration appeal* on any ground that is inconsistent with treating a State to which this Part applies as a place - (a) where a person's life and liberty are not threatened by reason of his race, religion, nationality, membership of a particular social group or political opinion, (b) from which a person will not be sent to another State in contravention of his Convention rights, and (c) from which a person will not be sent to another State otherwise than in accordance with the Refugee Convention (emphasis added).

Where the claimant is unable to discharge his or her burden of proof, he or she will be ordered returned to the country without the possibility of appeal, thereby potentially raising the same *refoulement* risks enumerated under this provision.[143] If the claimant presents an 'arguable case', then the burden of proof is then reversed to the Member State applying the Dublin transfer procedure to 'dispel any doubts'.[144]

The first case in the trilogy was the 2008 ECtHR judgment in *K.R.S. v. United Kingdom.*[145] In that case, the asylum claimant from Iran had travelled through Greece before making an asylum claim in the UK.[146] The UK made a request for Greece to accept responsibility for considering the applicant's asylum claim under the Dublin II Regulation, which Greece accepted.[147] The UK declared the asylum claim inadmissible and directed his transfer to Greece.[148] The claimant challenged his Dublin transfer back to Greece before the ECtHR on the

---

[140] MSS; KRS; NS/ME.

[141] *Saadi v Italy,* App no 37201/06 (ECHR, 28 February 2008) at para 129; *VT (Dublin Regulation: Post-Removal Appeal) Sri Lanka* [2012] UKUT 00308 (IAC) at 1–2 [VT]; This is pursuant to the relevant provision listed under paragraph 6, Schedule 3 of 2004 Act. See also Treatment of Claimants Act at para 6, schedule 3, and Battjes at 16.

[142] *Ibid* at 2 para 4.

[143] Treatment of Claimants Act at para 6(a), schedule 3.

[144] Saadi at para 129.

[145] KRS; Eritrea at para 28.

[146] KRS at 2.

[147] *Ibid* at 3.

[148] *Ibid* at 2.

basis that he would likely be *refouled* to Iran from there.[149] The claimant relied upon several reports that had raised serious concerns with the situation of asylum seekers in Greece, including documents from Amnesty International, the Norwegian Organisation for Asylum Seekers, the Norwegian Helsinki Committee, Greek Helsinki Monitor and notably, the UNHCR.[150] The UNHCR had issued a position paper advising EU Member States to refrain from returning asylum seekers to Greece under the Dublin Regulation until further notice.[151] The ECtHR found that, while the UNHCR's 'reliability and objectivity are [...] beyond doubt', the reports of all of the organizations listed did not help the claimant to satisfy his burden of proof.[152] This is because Greece was not sending individuals back to Iran and therefore the claimant could not be *refouled* to Iran, and, in the absence of any proof to the contrary, it was to be presumed that Greece would comply with its other EU obligations to asylum seekers on its territory (including not to mistreat such individuals).[153] Thus, the claimant did not have an 'arguable claim' that he would be subjected to torture or inhuman or degrading treatment or punishment.[154] Many commentators, including the UNHCR, have critiqued the presumption made in this case that Greece would not mistreat the claimant (in other words that *refoulement* could not happen from the UK to Greece).[155] As well, many expressed concerns at the high bar the claimant must meet in order to make an 'arguable claim' that an EU Member State could subject an asylum claimant to the sort of treatment prohibited by the principle of *non-refoulement*.[156]

The second case was the 2011 judgment of the ECtHR in *M.S.S. v. Belgium and Greece*.[157] In that case, an Afghan asylum seeker entered the EU through Greece and continued on to Belgium, where he applied for asylum.[158] Belgium undertook

[149] *Ibid* at 3.

[150] *Ibid* at 12–14.

[151] *Ibid* at 11.

[152] *Ibid* at 16.

[153] *Ibid* at 18.

[154] *Ibid*.

[155] See, for example: Alexander Orakhelashvili, "N.S. v. Secretary of State for the Home Department" (2012) 106(3) *American Journal of International Law* 616–624 at 621 [Orakhelashvili], which states: 'Even though significant problems in the situation of asylum seekers in Greece and the risk of *refoulement* had been pointed out by the United Nations High Commissioner for Refugees (UNHCR), the Court was confident that, as an EU member state, Greece would respect all relevant rules, including those pursuant to the ECHR. The Human Rights Court declared the application inadmissible, finding that were any claim to arise under the Convention, it should be pursued first with the Greek domestic authorities and thereafter in an application to the Court'; See, also: KRS.

[156] *Ibid*.

[157] MSS at paras 9–11; Eritrea at para 29.

[158] MSS at para 9.

a Dublin transfer to send the asylum claimant back to Greece.[159] The claimant was detained in Greece.[160] He put forward reports by international organizations, including the UNHCR, and numerous nongovernmental organizations to support his claim that the detention was in degrading conditions, and that there was a real risk of him being *refouled* to Afghanistan.[161] In this case, the ECtHR accepted that the claimant had made an 'arguable claim' on both counts.[162] Additionally, Belgium could not rely on Greece's diplomatic assurances, which did not relate to this specific claimant.[163] The ECtHR held that:

> *seeking assurances from the Greek government* that the applicant faced no risk of treatment contrary to ECHR was not sufficient to ensure adequate protection against the risk where reliable sources had reported practices that were tolerated by the authorities and which were manifestly contrary to the principles of the Convention (emphasis added).[164]

The ECtHR therefore considered that the diplomatic assurances did not displace the evidence put forward by the claimant. In particular, the ECtHR found that the Belgian authorities knew or ought to have known that the claimant had no guarantee that the Greek authorities would seriously examine his asylum application, and therefore could not presume that the applicant would be treated in conformity with ECHR obligations, including the prohibition on *refoulement*.[165] This judgment is positive for claimants: the ECtHR decided that 'reliable sources' could include, for example, UNHCR reports, and that the presumption of mutual trust in Greece was not automatic in the face of the transferring state being aware of serious violations of the rights of asylum claimants in Greece. This approach is consistent with the views of the Committee Against Torture, expressed in a complaint against the UK, in which the Committee expressed concern about the UK's reliance on diplomatic assurances in cases involving transfers of claimants to third countries.[166]

---

[159] *Ibid* at para 17.

[160] *Ibid* at paras 44–45.

[161] *Ibid* at para 27.

[162] *Ibid* at para 297.

[163] *Ibid* at para 354.

[164] *Ibid* at para 353; See, also: Saadi at para 147.

[165] MSS at para 358.

[166] *Ibid* at paras 18–20; The Committee Against Torture has warned States Parties against the misuse of diplomatic assurances. In its 2013 country report on the UK, the Committee stated that it: '[. . .] notes with concern the [UK's] reliance on diplomatic assurances to justify the deportation of foreign nationals suspected of terrorism related offences to countries in which the widespread practice of torture is alleged', see: Committee Against Torture, 'Concluding observations on the fifth periodic report of the United Kingdom, adopted by the Committee at its fiftieth session (6–31 May 2013): Advanced Unedited Version" at para 18; The Committee urged the UK to 'refrain from seeking and relying on diplomatic assurances 'where there are substantial grounds [to believe] that [the person] would be in danger of being subjected to torture'', see: CAT at art 3; In the situation of transfers of detainees to another country, the Committee recommended that the UK 'ensure [that] in practice[,] the transfer [. . .] is clearly prohibited when there are substantial

M.S.S. is a significant judgment of the ECtHR. The Court clearly affirms that EU Member States, in undertaking Dublin transfers, cannot simply presume that the claimant will be treated in line with ECHR obligations.[167]. Rather, 'States must make sure that the intermediary country's asylum procedure affords sufficient guarantees to avoid an asylum seeker being removed, directly or indirectly, to his country of origin' in a manner risking *refoulement*.[168] In other words, the sending Member State must ensure an individual assessment of the claimant's situation if the claimant is subjected to the Dublin transfer.[169] This judgment assisted in countering the negative implications of *K.R.S.* on the burden of proof in Dublin transfer cases by requiring an individualized evaluation of each Dublin transfer.[170] The *M.S.S.* case was also relied upon by the CJEU in the next case of concern, *N.S.*

grounds for believing that [the detainee] would be in danger of being subjected to torture', see: *Ibid* at para 19; The Committee further recommended that the UK 'recognize that diplomatic assurances and monitoring arrangements will not be relied upon to justify transfers when such substantial risk of torture exists'. Moreover, the Committee was of the view that the UK should 'observe safeguards ensuring respect for the principle of *non-refoulement* [. . .] indicating that the asylum-seeker might be in danger of torture or ill-treatment upon deportation', see: *Ibid* at para 20; The Committee called upon the UK to 'submit situations covered by article 3 of the [CAT] to a thorough risk assessment, notably by taking into consideration evidence from [the country of destination] whose post removal torture claim were found credible, and revise its country guidance accordingly', see: *Ibid;* Therefore, the Committee was of the view that the UK should not rely upon diplomatic assurances when contemplating returns of claimants to third countries.

[167] MSS; See, also: European Database of Asylum Law, "ECtHR—M.S.S. v Belgium and Greece [GC], Application No. 30696/09", 21 January 2011, https://www.asylumlawdatabase.eu/en/content/ecthr-mss-v-belgium-and-greece-gc-application-no-3069609

[168] *Ibid* at para 342.

[169] *Ibid* at 91 (Concurring Opinion of Judge Rozakis), which states: 'The existence of those international obligations of Greece—and notably, vis-à-vis the European Union—to treat asylum seekers in conformity with these requirements weighed heavily in the Court's decision to find a violation of Article 3. The Court has held on numerous occasions that to fall within the scope of Article 3 ill-treatment must attain a minimum level of severity. The assessment of this minimum is relative and it depends on all the circumstances of the case (such as the duration of the treatment, its physical and mental effects and, in some instances, the sex, age and state of health of the victim). In the circumstances of the present case the combination of the long duration of the applicant's treatment, coupled with Greece's international obligation to treat asylum seekers in accordance with what the judgment calls current positive law, justifies the distinction the Court makes between treatment endured by other categories of people—where Article 3 has not been found to be transgressed—and the treatment of an asylum seeker, who clearly enjoys a particularly advanced level of protection'.

[170] See, for example: *Tarakhel v Switzerland,* Application No 29,217/12 (ECHR, 4 November 2014), which states: 'The source of the risk does nothing to alter the level of protection guaranteed by the Convention or the Convention obligations of the State ordering the person's removal. It does not exempt that State from carrying out a thorough and individualised examination of the situation of the person concerned and from suspending enforcement of the removal order should the risk of inhuman or degrading treatment be established' at para 104; The case of E-6629 of the Swiss Federal Administrative Court also cites *Tarakhel* in seeking assurances prior to the transfer decision, see: Maria Hennessy, "Vulnerability, the Right to

The third case in the trilogy is the joint case of *N.S. & M.E.*, which involved an Afghan asylum claimant seeking to resist his removal from the UK to Greece under the Dublin II Regulation.[171] Under Article 17 of the Dublin II Regulation, UK authorities informed Greece to 'take charge' of the applicant, N.S., as the responsible Member State.[172] N.S. challenged the decision by the UK to have him sent back to Greece before the UK courts by arguing that the return to Greece would expose him to risks that infringe his fundamental rights.[173] The applicants in *M.E.* were five asylum claimants from Afghanistan, Iran and Algeria, and involved the examination of the legal responsibilities of the transferring Member States under the Dublin II Regulation, EU Charter, and the Asylum Procedures Directive.[174] The five asylum claimants entered the EU through Greece and traveled to Ireland, where they claimed asylum.[175] Both the UK courts and the High Court of Ireland separately referred the case to the CJEU, which heard the case jointly.[176]

The legal issues examined by the CJEU for the joint case of *N.S. & M.E.* were: a) whether the exercise of the 'sovereignty clause' falls within the scope of EU law and b) whether the transfer under the Dublin II Regulation was prohibited.[177] The CJEU stated that:

> Member states may not transfer an asylum seeker to the responsible member state where they 'cannot be unaware' that systemic deficiencies in that country's asylum procedure provide substantial grounds for believing that the asylum seeker would face a real risk of being subjected to inhuman or degrading treatment within the meaning of Charter Article 4.[178]

The CJEU also found that that 'systemic flaws' in the asylum procedure and reception conditions for asylum applicants in the Member State responsible resulted in inhuman or degrading treatment and raised the risk of *refoulement*, and therefore a Dublin transfer should not occur.[179] This confirmed the approach in *M.S.S.* and indicated that the claimant can bring evidence of the 'systemic flaws' in order to rebut the presumption of mutual trust between EU Member States. The CJEU's judgment has significance for the interpretation of fundamental rights for EU Member States as well as the threshold to rebut the presumption of mutual

---

Asylum and the Dublin System", 14 April 2015, http://www.reflaw.org/vulnerability-the-right-to-asylum-and-the-dublin-system; See, also: European Database of Asylum Law, "ECtHR—Tarakhel v. Switzerland, Application No. 29217/12", https://www.asylumlawdatabase.eu/en/content/ecthr-tarakhel-v-switzerland-application-no-2921712.

171 NS/ME at para 47; See, also: Cathryn Costello, "Dublin-case NS/ME: Finally, an end to blind trust across the EU?" (2012) 2 *A&MR* 83–92 at 86 [Costello NS/ME].

172 Orakhelashvili at 617.

173 *Ibid.*

174 Costello NS/ME at 86.

175 Orakhelashvili at 618.

176 *Ibid.*

177 *Ibid* at 87.

178 NS/ME at para 106; See, also: Orakhelashvili at 619.

179 NS/ME at para 86.

trust. For example, in considering the threshold to rebut the presumption of mutual trust, the CJEU placed heavy emphasis on *M.S.S.*[180] Furthermore, as stated in *M.S. S.*, the ECtHR asserted the importance of human rights protection for asylum claimants the need for EU Member States to safeguard the fundamental principle of *non-refoulement*.[181] Scholars have argued that the test created by *N.S.* on the threshold for rebutting the presumption of mutual trust is a more difficult threshold for the asylum claimant to meet if it is an additional requirement for the claimant to be met.[182] Further, there is reason to suggest that the *N.S.* judgment 'only deals with treatment contrary to Article 4 EUCFR [on the prohibition of torture]. The extent to which breaches of other EU fundamental rights should prevent removal remains to be seen'.[183]

According to the UK Court of Appeal in *Eritrea* in 2008, it was the *N.S.* case which set the test for establishing the necessary threshold for claimants to rebut the presumption of mutual trust, 'which exists nowhere else in refugee law'.[184] On appeal, the Supreme Court was of the view that Member States should be presumed to be complying with their international and EU law obligations, but that presumption may be rebutted in one of two ways.[185] One way is if the claimant presents 'sufficient evidence of substantial operational difficulties' in the receiving State. Another way is where 'on the individual facts of the case viewed against the overall situation [. . .] there were substantial grounds for believing that there would be a real risk [to the claimant of *refoulement*] on

[180] Orakhelashvili at 620, which states: 'The ECJ placed considerable reliance on *M.S.S.*, which concerned an Afghan national who had illegally entered he Union from Turkey via Greece and had then been detained in Greece'.

[181] MSS at para 216, which states: 'the confinement of aliens, accompanied by suitable safeguards for the persons concerned, is acceptable only in order to enable States to prevent unlawful immigration while complying with their international obligations, in particular under the Refugee Convention and the European Convention for the Protection of Human Rights and Fundamental Freedoms (ECHR). States' legitimate concern to foil the increasingly frequent attempts to circumvent immigration restrictions must not deprive asylum seekers of the protection afforded by these conventions'.

[182] Costello NS/ME at 89.

[183] *Ibid* at 90.

[184] *Ibid* at para 39; Eritrea at para 61, the case concerns the difference that exists between *sur place* activities pursued by political dissident against his or her government in the country where he or she is seeking asylum which may expose him or her to risk of ill-treatment or persecution versus activities that were pursued solely with motive of creating such a risk; The Court of Appeal held that it requires an assessment of whether authorities in the country of origin are likely to observe the claimant's activities and the fear of consequent ill-treatment not well-founded.

[185] Eritrea at para 67; See, also: *R (on the application of Ibrahimi) Abasi v Secretary of State for the Home Department* [2016] EWHC 2049 at para 71 [Ibrahimi], which concerns an application against the decision of the Secretary of State refusing to consider merits of claimants' contentions on the basis that Hungary was a 'safe' third country that would presumably comply with its EU and international law obligations; The High Court was of the opinion that the risk of *refoulement*

return'.[186] At the same time, the Court reaffirmed the ECtHR's position that the UK, like all EU Member States, must make an individualized assessment of a claimant's situation prior to being subjected to a Dublin transfer, rather than relying on a blanket assessment.[187]

In 2013, the UK Court of Appeal reconsidered the issue of the burden of proof on asylum claimants wishing to argue against Dublin transfers, in the case of *E.M. & MA*.[188] In that case, the Court of Appeal considered the question of whether it is arguable that the return of any claimants to Italy would entail a real risk of inhuman or degrading treatment in violation of Article 3 of the ECHR.[189] The Court of Appeal held that: 'the assessment of risk on return is seen by the Strasbourg court as depending on a combination of personal experience and systemic shortcomings which in total may suffice to rebut the presumption of compliance'.[190] It then formulated a new test. This new test seems to be a compromise between the approaches of the ECtHR and the CJEU. Unfortunately, a mixed approach combining both the ECtHR's 'individual assessments' test in *M.S.S.* and the CJEU's 'systemic deficiencies' test in *N.S.* does not reconcile the inherent differences between the two thresholds and may, in fact, be more difficult for UK adjudicators to implement.

The *N.S.* case demonstrated that, of the interveners to the case before the CJEU, the views regarding the burden of proof to rebut the presumption of mutual trust are divergent: on the one hand, the applicants, Amnesty International, and the AIRE Centre argued that 'the transferring state was obliged to assess compliance with Article 18 EUCFR [European Union Charter of Fundamental Rights], the Asylum Directives, and DR and indeed, all the EUCFR provisions', on the other hand, Member States including Belgium, Germany, France, the European Commission, and the UNHCR all argued that 'there was a presumption of compliance with EU law, although it was rebuttable'.[191] This divergence in views show that there is a lack of consensus among EU Member States themselves as to how high or low the threshold to rebut the presumption of mutual trust should be, and the case law provided by the ECtHR and the CJEU on this point is unclear.[192] The Advocate General of the CJEU was of the view that there is a 'wide gulf' between the legal

to Iran if removed to Hungary would breach Article 3 of the ECHR; It was held that if removed, claimants would have a real risk of chain *refoulement* to Iran.

186 *Ibid.*

187 *Ibid.*

188 EM/MA.

189 *Ibid* at para 1.

190 *Ibid* at para 39.

191 NS/ME at paras 41–42; The divergence extends beyond the mentioned parties, namely: 'The Irish, Italian, Netherlands, Czech, Polish and Finnish governments all argued against a duty to examine compliance with the named sources, with Greece and Portugal going so far as to contend that it would be contrary to EU law for one Member State to review the conformity of the actions of another with EU law', see: Costello NS/ME at 91.

192 Costello NS/ME at 84; See, also: Court of Justice of the EU, "Opinion of Advocate General Trstenjak delivered on 22 September 2011", Case C-493/10, *M.E., A.S.M., M.T., K.P., E.*

standards of EU law on the one hand, and the *actual practice* of EU law, on the other hand.[193] Another important impact of *N.S.* on asylum law in Europe is that it reveals what the ECtHR and the CJEU both agreed upon: 'Blind trust between governments is incompatible with fundamental rights'.[194] In other words, to protect asylum claimants and their fundamental rights, EU Member States cannot rely on blind trust in the transfer of applicants from Member State to Member State through Dublin transfers.[195] Despite the potential significance of *N.S.* to EU refugee law, the CJEU failed to resolve the most important issue at bar, namely that the standard for rebutting the presumption of compliance or mutual trust is not ascertained.[196] Scholars have rightly pointed out that the premise of the Dublin system should *not* be based on the presumption of blind trust between Member States, but that the 'trust between Member States would be better sustained by ensuring checks for fundamental rights protection, rather than permitting governments to turn a blind eye to the others' shortcomings'.[197]

The UK High Court suggested in a subsequent judgment, *Tabrizagh,* that the UK Supreme Court's decision was consistent with *N.S.*[198] In the relevant paragraph, and citing reasons of judicial dialogue between the CJEU and ECtHR, the UK High Court proceeded to 'assume that the decision of the Supreme Court is consistent with the decision of CJEU in *NS*'.[199] The case concerns the decision of the Secretary of State

H. v Refugee Applications Commissioner, Minister for Justice, Equality and Law Reform, http://www.statewatch.org/news/2011/sep/ecj-m-e-case-493-advocate-general-opinion.pdf at para 51, which states: 'The referring court asks these questions because it has clear evidence that *there is a wide gulf between the European Union rules applicable to Greece as regards the organisation of its asylum system and its asylum procedure, on the one hand, and the actual treatment of asylum seekers in Greece, on the other*, such that there may even be a risk that asylum seekers' fundamental rights will be violated if they are transferred to Greece' (emphasis added).

[193] *Ibid.*

[194] Costello NS/ME at 92.

[195] *Ibid,* Costello is also of the view that: 'NS/ME is an important legal vindication of the rights of asylum seekers, with Luxembourg bolstering the Strasbourg ruling'.

[196] Costello NS/ME at 92; Further, the CJEU 'explicitly left it up to the national systems to establish the rules on the burden and standard of proof' in establishing a rebuttal against the presumption of mutual trust for asylum claimants.

[197] *Ibid* at 90; See, also: Olivier de Schutter, "The Promotion of Fundamental Rights by the Union as a contribution to the European Legal Space (I): Mutual Recognition and Mutual Trust in the Establishment of the Area of Freedom, Security and Justice", *RefGov Working Paper,* 2006.

[198] *Tabrizagh et al. v Secretary of State for the Home Department* [2014] EWHC 1914 (Admin) at para 152 [Tabrizagh], which states: 'For its part, the Supreme Court has interpreted the decision in *NS*, for the benefit of litigants and courts in the United Kingdom. The Supreme Court cannot depart from the decision in *NS*, or encourage the courts here to do so. For present purposes I must assume that the decision of the Supreme Court is consistent with the decision of the CJEU in *NS*. The approach of the ECtHR in the admissibility decisions is also to follow NS. I must, and the FTT [First-Tier Tribunal of the Asylum and Immigration Chamber] would be bound to, assume that, all three courts, have adopted the same approach; and that is, the approach in *NS* as interpreted by the Supreme Court in *EM* (*Eritrea*)'.

[199] *Ibid.*

for the Home Department in refusing the asylum claimant's appeal against being removed to Italy under the Dublin Regulation.[200] Tabrizagh is an Iranian national who fled Iran and entered the UK through Italy.[201] He was fingerprinted in Italy through the Eurodac system but did not claim asylum there.[202] The issue before the UK High Court of Justice, Queen's Bench Division (Administrative) Court was whether: a) the claimants have an arguable claim pursuant to Article 3 of the ECHR as a result of the Secretary of State's intention to return them to Italy; and b) whether the evidence which the claimants have relied upon satisfy the test envisioned by Article 3 of the ECHR.[203] The UK court noted that there is a presumption of mutual trust in favour of Italy, wherein claimants who have passed through there who could have claimed asylum but did not can be returned to Italy through the procedure enumerated by the Dublin II Regulation.[204] In referencing the ECtHR in *M.S.S.,* the court held that Article 3 of the ECHR does not entail a corresponding right to grant asylum claimants with accommodation or a particular standard of living.[205] Therefore, a failure to provide an adequate standard of living would not reach the level of severity required to breach Article 3 of the ECHR.[206] The court also examined the case of *EM (Eritrea)* and noted that the removal decision through a Dublin transfer would depend on the circumstances of the country of removal and, in order to establish an Article 3 breach, the systemic shortcomings must be a 'widespread problem' known to exist in the country of removal.[207]

The challenge for claimants is that lower courts have interpreted these attempts to either marry the *M.S.S.* and *N.S.* approaches or to choose to interpret *N.S.* in a restrictive manner. This was evident in the *Ibrahimi* decision of the UK High Court, Queen's Bench, which articulated a three-prong test for claimants to meet in order to overcome the presumption of mutual trust in a Dublin transfer.[208] The first step is that the claimant must establish that the flaws or weaknesses will lead to n ECHR human rights violation which would entail examining any potential *refoulement* chain reaction.[209] The second step is that the claimant must

---

[200] European Database of Asylum Law, "UK—The Queen on the application of Mr Mohsen Pourali Tabrizagh, Mr Tahir Syed, Mr Saeed Ali, Mr Ali Omar Mohammed, Mr Edmond Karaj, AB (Sudan) v Secretary of State for the Home Department", https://www.asylumlawdatabase.eu/en/case-law/uk-queen-application-mr-mohsen-pourali-tabrizagh-mr-tahir-syed-mr-saeed-ali-mr-ali-omar at 1 [EDAL Tabrizagh].

[201] *Ibid;* See, also: Tabrizagh at para 1.

[202] *Ibid.*

[203] Tabrizagh at para 3.

[204] EDAL Tabrizagh at 2.

[205] *Ibid* at 3; Tabrizagh at paras 173–175.

[206] *Ibid.*

[207] Tabrizagh at para 87, which states: 'It would not be open to the FTT to find that they show either, that there are systemic deficiencies in Italy's asylum system (as explained in *EM (Eritrea)*, that is, omissions on a widespread or substantial scale, or substantial operational problems)'.

[208] *Ibrahimi* at para 50.

[209] *Ibid.*

demonstrate that there is a risk of prospective *refoulement* to a third State.[210] Third, the claimant must show 'substantial' grounds for believing that the risk will eventuate, where 'substantial' means 'real'—not fanciful or *de minimis*—and it requires an overall and thorough review of the facts and evidence.[211]

Similarly, the lower courts have created certain barriers to the type of evidence claimants can rely upon when attempting to rebut the presumption of mutual trust. In particular, the UNHCR,[212] International Organization for Migration, Amnesty International and Human Rights Watchare considered to be 'reliable sources'.[213] However, the UK High Court of Justice, Queen's Bench, Administrative Court has indicated that independent expert reports are not.[214] As well, as was found in *Medhanye*, reports from reputable nongovernmental organizations may not be sufficient for a claimant to meet the burden of proof.[215] Further, it is up to the national adjudicators to determine whether the test of 'reliable sources' has been met by the claimant.[216] Thus, for cases involving assessment of a future risk of *refoulement* to ill-treatment, the threshold of 'reliable sources' precludes the application of independent expert reports but relies heavily upon published reports from highly-regarded bodies, though nongovernmental reports might not be sufficient.[217]

As the above has shown, the UK jurisprudence surrounding the claimant's burden in rebutting the presumption of mutual trust leaves the claimant with a significant burden, one which, in practice, is exceedingly hard to meet.[218] For instance, as compared with the ECtHR on the test of rebutting the presumption of mutual trust, the CJEU's test involves the specific wording of 'cannot be unaware' that 'systemic deficiencies' exist in the asylum procedures and reception

---

[210] *Ibid.*

[211] *Ibid.*

[212] The opinions of the UNHCR have been regarded by the ECtHR in *M.S.S.* as 'pre-eminent and possibly decisive', and have been cited by the UK Court of Appeal in *Eritrea* as having 'unique and unrivalled expertise [. . .] in the field of asylum and refugee law': MSS at para 41; Eritrea at paras 71 and 73. Further, the unique position of the UNHCR, as compared to courts, permits the UNHCR to 'assemble and monitor information from year to year and to apply to it standards of knowledge and judgment which are ordinarily beyond the reach of a court': MSS at para 41. The expertise of UNHCR in this context has also been affirmed in the decision of the UK Supreme Court in *I.A. (Iran): IA (Iran) v Secretary of State for the Home Department* [2014] UKSC 6 at para 44.

[213] *R (on the application of Elayathamby) v Secretary of State for the Home Department* [2011] EWHC 2182 (Admin) at para 42(i) [Elayathamby].

[214] *Ibid* at para 59.

[215] Medhanye at para 40.

[216] NS/ME at para 135.

[217] Elayathamby at para 59; Medhanye at paras 35 and 40.

[218] Costello NS/ME at 89.

conditions of the Member State to which the applicant would be transferred *but for* rebuttals that justify his or her non-removal.[219] Another foreseeable issue with the requirement for the claimant to rebut the presumption of mutual trust between EU Member States is the Advocate General's opinion that 'the precise working of the procedure for rebutting the presumption 'were a matter for the legal orders of the individual Member States'.[220] These create additional procedural barriers for claimants to access international protection for refugee status in the UK and accordingly increase the probability that the UK will shift its responsibility for processing asylum applications to another Member State in situations which create risk for mistreatment or onward *refoulement*, thus reinforcing the EU's containment policies.

In sum, the UK's threshold for rebutting the presumption of mutual trust is a high one. A high threshold for rebutting the presumption means that the UK uses a blanket assumption and applies it broadly across all Member States—without procedural safeguards to ensure the country is, in fact, in compliance with international and European law. A containment policy is therefore demonstrated in the UK's practice of returning asylum claimants to another Member State deemed to be in compliance with its international and European law obligations. First, this containment policy shows the UK's attempts at shifting its responsibility for processing asylum applications to another Member State. Second, this same policy demonstrates that the UK is evading international law by placing the burden of proving an 'arguable case' upon the claimant to discharge. Third, the UK's efforts at containing asylum claimants to other Member States means that, where the claimant is unable to rebut the presumption, his or her return to the country will be without qualification.[221] Finally, an inability to rebut the presumption by a claimant may result in severe consequences for him or her, including an increased risk of being returned to face persecution in violation of *non-refoulement*. This inability to rebut the

---

[219] The wording of the CJEU judgment is tantamount to this analysis: 'Member States, including national courts, *may not transfer asylum seekers to the responsible State where they* 'cannot be unaware that systemic deficiencies in the asylum procedure and in the reception conditions of asylum seekers in that Member State amount to substantial grounds for believing that the asylum seeker would face a real risk of being subjected to inhuman and degrading treatment within the meaning of Article 4 of the Charter', see: NS/ME at paras 86, 94, and 106.

[220] Costello NS/ME at 88; See, also: Court of Justice of the EU, "Opinion of Advocate General Trstenjak delivered on 22 September 2011", Case C-411/10, *N.S. v Secretary of State for the Home Department*, http://www.statewatch.org/news/2011/sep/ecj-n-s-case-opinion-advocate-general.pdf at para 135, which states: 'f the Member States thus decide to introduce the rebuttable presumption that the asylum seeker's human rights and fundamental rights will be observed in the Member State which is primarily responsible, the asylum seekers must be given the possibility, procedurally, actually to rebut that presumption. Having regard to the principle of effectiveness, the specific form of the available evidence and *the definition of the rules and principles governing the assessment of evidence are, in turn, a matter for the national legal orders of the individual Member States*' (emphasis added).

[221] *VT* at 2 para 4; See, also: Treatment of Claimants Act at schedule 3, para 6.

presumption of mutual trust by the claimant may violate international law and European law when it prevents the claimant from accessing international protection as a result of lacking procedural safeguards against removal to *refoulement*—i.e. by not permitting the claimant an opportunity to rebut the case against him or her.

5.6 Concluding Remarks

Despite the departure of UK from the EU, the legacy of the EU will continue in UK asylum law for some time, given its transformation of EU law into its system and case law and its continued obligations under the ECHR. On the other hand, UK law has diverged from EU law to adopt a narrower approach which benefits the State in either Dublin or 'safe' third country transfers, and in certain procedures which do not allow the claimant to be heard about risks of *refoulemen*t.

In a world where there is an increasing number of those forcibly displaced as a result of conflicts occurring elsewhere, the need for a coordinated response from the international community is necessary.[222] This is also true from the standpoint of international organizations such as the UNHCR, which has called for solidarity and cooperation among States in order to tackle mass influx situations as well as to 'reinforce support for the institution of asylum and international refugee protection'.[223] However, despite these attempts and calls for coordinated response from the international community, responsibility-sharing has become increasingly difficult especially in the CEAS when both the deficiencies of the system itself and the inconsistent interpretation and implementation of the system among Member States contribute towards further instability.[224] Most notably, inconsistencies in the interpretation and application of the Dublin System by the UK are revealed in its domestic jurisprudence, which incorporates references to both ECtHR and CJEU decisions. There are several inconsistencies which are transposed from regional European frameworks to the UK's domestic jurisprudence, including the threshold for rebutting the presumption of mutual trust and the source of evidence that may be relied upon by Member States in rebutting the presumption of mutual trust.

This chapter explored the principle of *non-refoulement* in the UK. It demonstrated that the UK is showing a concerning trend: that the interpretation of the norm in UK domestic law has become narrower and more restrictive. For instance, on the threshold to establish a rebuttal to the

[222] Eritrea at para 40.

[223] Vulker Turk and Madeline Garlick, "From Burdens and Responsibilities to Opportunities: The Comprehensive Refugee Response Framework and a Global Compact on Refugees" (2016) 28:4 *International Journal of Refugee Law* 656–678 at 673 [Turk and Garlick].

[224] For more on the deficiencies of the Dublin System, as well as inconsistent interpretation and implementation by Member States, see Chap. 3.

presumption of mutual trust to prevent Dublin transfers, UK has not shown consistency with the approach taken towards the standard of proof for the asylum claimant. In referring to ECtHR and CJEU case law, UK has not been able to ascertain its own interpretation of the presumption of mutual trust threshold. Rather, UK is prone to compromise between the two supranational courts' approaches, leading to more inconsistency and difficulty in implementation for national adjudicators.

This chapter also examined the procedures for claiming asylum in the UK, including how applicants for international protection for refugee status qualify for international protection, how their international protection is granted or withdrawn, and the points in the system during which the possibilities of *refoulement* are considered.

The final part of this chapter outlined the UK's domestic jurisprudence and how it demonstrates that the country is actually following a policy of containment in three key respects. A trilogy of cases established the threshold to determine the standard by which claimants can rebut the presumption of mutual trust in the UK. The threshold on 'reliable sources' which claimants must prove to establish an 'arguable case' requires the use of reports or observations from reputable international organizations such as the UNHCR and the International Organization for Migration and well-respected human rights monitoring bodies such as Amnesty International and Human Rights Watch—but sometimes even that is not enough. Finally, the problem with the rebuttable presumption is that the onus is placed upon the claimant and is detrimental to the claimant where he or she is unable to discharge such a heavy burden, potentially being returned to face risks of persecution, violating *non-refoulement*. The Committee Against Torture has recognized the risks in the UK's approach—for example, cautioning the UK against the use of diplomatic assurances (as part of mutual trust) when contemplating the deportation of claimants to third countries.[225] The Committee recommends that the UK adopt a clear policy and to ensure that the transfer of claimants, including detainees, to another country is strongly prohibited in situations where there are substantial grounds for believing that their transfer would expose them to a real risk of torture.[226]

The next chapter examines the gaps between the law and practice on *non-refoulement* in Germany, which makes for an interesting comparison with the UK approach, as another important refugee-receiving country in Europe.

[225] See above section of the presumption of mutual trust for explanation.

[226] *Ibid.*

References

Asylum Information Database (2015) Country report: Italy, http://www.asylumineurope.org/reports/country/italy.

Asylum Information Database (2019a) Country report: United Kingdom, https://www.asylumineurope.org/sites/default/files/report-download/aida_uk_2019update.pdf

Asylum Information Database (2019b) The implementation of the Dublin III regulation in 2018, http://www.asylumineurope.org/sites/default/files/aida_2018update_dublin.pdf

Asylum Information Database, Short Overview of the Asylum Procedure: UK, https://www.asylumineurope.org/reports/country/united-kingdom/asylum-procedure/general/short-overview-asylum-procedure

Brouwer E (2013) Mutual trust and the Dublin regulation: protection of fundamental rights in the EU and the burden of proof. Utrecht Law Review 9(1):135–147

Battjes H, Brouwer E (2015) The Dublin regulation and mutual trust: judicial coherence in EU Asylum Law. Rev Euro Admin Law 8(2):182–214

Costello C (2012) Dublin-case NS/ME: finally, an end to blind trust across the EU? A&MR 2:83–92

de Schutter O (2006) The promotion of fundamental rights by the union as a contribution to the European legal space (I): mutual recognition and mutual trust in the establishment of the area of freedom, security and justice, *RefGov Working Paper*

European Database of Asylum Law (2011) ECtHR–M.S.S. v Belgium and Greece [GC], Application No. 30696/09, https://www.asylumlawdatabase.eu/en/content/ecthr-mss-v-belgium-and-greece-gc-application-no-3069609

European Database of Asylum Law, ECtHR—tarakhel v. Switzerland, Application No. 29217/12, https://www.asylumlawdatabase.eu/en/content/ecthr-tarakhel-v-switzerland-application-no-2921712

European Database of Asylum Law, UK—The Queen on the application of Mr Mohsen Pourali Tabrizagh, Mr Tahir Syed, Mr Saeed Ali, Mr Ali Omar Mohammed, Mr Edmond Karaj, AB (Sudan) v Secretary of State for the Home Department", https://www.asylumlawdatabase.eu/en/case-law/uk-queen-application-mr-mohsen-pourali-tabrizagh-mr-tahir-syed-mr-saeed-ali-mr-ali-omar.

European Asylum Support Office (2016a) An introduction to the common European Asylum system for courts and tribunals: a judicial analysis, https://www.easo.europa.eu/sites/default/files/public/BZ0216138ENN.PDF

European Asylum Support Office (2016b) An Introduction to the common European Asylum system for courts and tribunals: a judicial analysis

EuroStat (2018) Dublin III Transfers 2018 by Country

European Union Committee (2019) Brexit: refugee Protection and Asylum Policy

Guild E, Costello C, Garlick M, Moreno-Lax V (2015) Enhancing the common european asylum system and alternatives to Dublin, CEPS Paper No 83, http://www.epgencms.europarl.europa.eu/cmsdata/upload/983a50a5-69d6-48b1-a0bd-2b34cced9e36/Sessions_1_and_2_-_Study_European_Asylum_System_and_Alternatives_to_Dublin.pdf

Greater Manchester Immigration Aid Unit (2017) Briefing paper on the experiences of children from the Calais camp in the north west of England, https://gmiau.org/briefing-paper-experiences-children-calais-camp-north-west-england

Hennessy M (2015) Vulnerability, the right to asylum and the Dublin system, http://www.reflaw.org/vulnerability-the-right-to-asylum-and-the-dublin-system

Home Office (2015a) "Asylum policy instruction: assessing credibility and refugee status: version 9.0, https://assets.publishing.service.gov.uk/government/uploads/system/uploads/attachment_data/file/397778/ASSESSING_CREDIBILITY_AND_REFUGEE_STATUS_V9_0.pdf

Home Office (2015b) Asylum Policy Instruction: assessing Credibility and Refugee Status: version 9.0, https://assets.publishing.service.gov.uk/government/uploads/system/uploads/attachment_data/file/397778/ASSESSING_CREDIBILITY_AND_REFUGEE_STATUS_V9_0.pdf

Home Office (2017) Dublin III Regulation, Version 1.0, 2 November 2017

House of Commons Library (2018) What is Dublin III regulation? will it be affected by Brexit?, https://commonslibrary.parliament.uk/home-affairs/immigration/what-is-the-dublin-iii-regulation-will-it-be-affected-by-brexit

Home Office (2019a) Inadmissibility: EU grants of asylum, first country of asylum and safe third country concepts: version 4.0, https://assets.publishing.service.gov.uk/government/uploads/system/uploads/attachment_data/file/835342/Inadmissibility-guidance-v4.0ext.pdf

Home Office (2019b) Certification of protection and human rights claim under section 94 of the Nationality, Immigration and Asylum Act 2002 (clearly unfounded claims), https://assets.publishing.service.gov.uk/government/uploads/system/uploads/attachment_data/file/778221/certification-s94-guidance-0219.pdf

Home Office (2020) Immigration Bail: version 5.0, https://assets.publishing.service.gov.uk/government/uploads/system/uploads/attachment_data/file/869352/Immigration-bail-v5.0ext.pdf

Orakhelashvili A (2012) N.S. V. Secretary of state for the home department. Am J Int Law 106(3):616–624

Poon J (2016) ESIL reflections: the EU commission on 'Dublin IV': sufficient safeguards for Asylum Claimants? Euro Soc Int Law Reflect Ser 5(9):1–10. at 2

Tandiono P, The extraterritoriality of the principle of non-refoulement: a critique of the sale case and Roma case, https://blogs.lse.ac.uk/humanrights/2016/02/09/the-extraterritoriality-of-the-principle-of-non-refoulement-a-critique-of-the-sale-case-and-roma-case

Toucas S (2008) Push and pull factors towards and against a common European migration policy: France, Britain, and their approach to irregular migration, https://www.ifri.org/sites/default/files/atoms/files/cadbury1.pdf

Turk V, Garlick M (2016) From burdens and responsibilities to opportunities: the comprehensive refugee response framework and a global compact on refugees. Int J Refugee Law 28(4):656–678

The Parliament of the United Kingdom (2019) Asylum: applications: written Question – 220305, https://www.parliament.uk/business/publications/written-questions-answers-statements/written-question/Commons/2019-02-12/220305

UNHCR, States Parties to the 1951 Convention Relating to the Status of Refugees and the 1967 Protocol, http://www.unhcr.org/uk/protection/basic/3b73b0d63/states-parties-1951-convention-its-1967-protocol.html

United Kingdom, Home Office, Immigration rules part 11: Asylum, https://www.gov.uk/guidance/immigration-rules/immigration-rules-part-11-asylum.

United Kingdom, Visas and Immigration Office, www.gov.uk/government/collections/asylum-decision-making-guidance-asylum-instructions.

United Kingdom, Home Office, Asylum Policy Instruction: revocation of Refugee Status: version 4.0, https://www.gov.uk/government/uploads/system/uploads/attachment_data/file/493918/revocation_of_refugee_status_v4_0_EXT.pdf.

United Kingdom Office of Visas and Immigration, What We Do, https://www.gov.uk/government/organisations/uk-visas-and-immigration

United Kingdom Office of Visas and Immigration, Our Priorities, https://www.gov.uk/government/organisations/uk-visas-and-immigration/about#our-priorities

United Kingdom Office of Visas and Immigration, Asylum Policy, https://www.gov.uk/topic/immigration-operational-guidance/asylum-policy

United Kingdom Office of Visas and Immigration, First-Tier Tribunal (Immigration and Asylum), https://www.gov.uk/courts-tribunals/first-tier-tribunal-immigration-and-asylum

United Kingdom Office of Visas and Immigration, Upper Tribunal (Immigration and Asylum Chamber), https://www.gov.uk/courts-tribunals/upper-tribunal-immigration-and-asylum-chamber

United Kingdom Office of Visas and Immigration, Appeal a Decision by the Immigration and Asylum Tribunal, https://www.gov.uk/upper-tribunal-immigration-asylum/the-tribunals-decision

United Kingdom Supreme Court, How to Appeal, https://www.supremecourt.uk/procedures/how-to-appeal.html

United Kingdom Supreme Court, Role of the Supreme Court, https://www.supremecourt.uk/about/role-of-the-supreme-court.html

United Kingdom, Home Office, Immigration Rules, https://www.gov.uk/guidance/immigration-rules

United Kingdom Refugee Council (2019) Quarterly Asylum Statistics, https://www.refugeecouncil.org.uk/wp-content/uploads/2019/09/Asylum-Statistics-Aug-2019.pdf

Chapter 6
Germany and *Non-Refoulement*

6.1 Introduction

In 2019, Germany received 165,615 asylum applications for international protection, down from a high of 745,160 in 2016, and 222,565 and 184,180 in 2017 and 2018 respectively.[1] Year over year since significant refugee influxes began in 2012, Germany has received the highest number of asylum applications within the EU.[2] 'Germany's desirability as a destination for asylum seekers is long standing: over the past 30 years it received a reported 30% of all asylum applications in Europe—a greater share than any other country.'[3] As a result of the high number of asylum claimants, Germany has increased its efforts to transfer asylum claimants from Germany to other EU Member States, particularly the Member State deemed responsible for processing the asylum application pursuant to the Dublin III Regulation (known as 'Dublin transfers').[4] While Dublin transfers have been temporary halted due to COVID-19-related travel restrictions, Germany transferred 8423 asylum applicants under this system in 2019, particularly to Italy and France.[5]

---

[1] EuroStat: Asylum and first time asylum applicants—annual aggregated data (rounded), https://ec.europa.eu/eurostat/tgm/table.do?tab = table&init = 1&language = en&pcode = tps00191&plugin = 1.

[2] As compared to Germany, France received 128,940 claims, Spain received 117,800 claims, while Italy received 43,770 claims in 2019, see, *ibid.*

[3] Stefan Trines, "Lessons From Germany's Refugee Crisis: Integration, Costs, and Benefits", https://wenr.wes.org/2017/05/lessons-germanys-refugee-crisis-integration-costs-benefits.

[4] European Council on Refugees and Exiles, "Germany Steps Up Dublin Transfers Putting Asylum Seekers at Risk", 21 March 2019, https://www.ecre.org/germany-steps-up-dublin-transfers-putting-asylum-seekers-at-risk. [ECRE News].

[5] European Council on Refugees and Exiles News, "Germany: Temporary Suspension of Dublin Returns Due to COVID-19", https://www.ecre.org/germany-temporary-suspension-of-dublin-returns-due-to-covid-10/.

J. Poon, *Counteracting Containment Policies in the EU*, European Union and its Neighbours in a Globalized World 31,
https://doi.org/10.1007/978-3-032-08351-7_6

Similarly, in 2018, Germany returned the highest number of asylum claimants through Dublin transfers to Italy, raising concerns about their treatment in Italy and fears of onward *refoulement* to countries of origin.[6] As part of this trend, Germany has also reversed policy on 'church asylum', under which asylum claimants subject to Dublin transfers who sought shelter in German churches for fear of onward *refoulement* are removed and forcibly transferred.[7] These increased efforts of Germany to use Dublin transfers has led to criticism. According to the European Council on Refugees and Exiles, this practice puts asylum claimants at risk of human rights violations and exacerbates deficiencies in the domestic German asylum procedures by creating an additional heavier burden upon claimants to disprove the presumption of mutual trust.[8] Members of Parliament from the German parliamentary faction Die Linke have commented that this practice, which is permitted within the Dublin System, is 'unjust in principle as it tends to shift the responsibility for processing asylum claims to countries that have suffered from EU austerity measures and treated asylum seekers like tradeable goods'.[9] Ultimately, Germany's approach raises similar concerns with respect to *refoulement* as highlighted in the previous chapter's case study of the United Kingdom.

The purpose of this chapter is to examine how Germany's domestic asylum system addresses the principle of *non-refoulement.* This chapter therefore analyzes and evaluates Germany's domestic asylum system as well as Germany's interpretation and implementation of the principle of *non-refoulement*. This chapter also situates Germany's interpretation and implementation of *non-refoulement* within the European legal framework on asylum issues and within the CEAS. First, the chapter begins by explaining the German refugee law system. Next, it explains the German domestic asylum system. This is done in order to provide the legal and procedural context within which German refugee law, including on *non-refoulement*, is applied. The chapter then outlines Germany's interpretation and implementation of *non-refoulement.* The chapter ends by discussing responsibility-sharing and examples of containment policies in Germany. This chapter concludes that, first, Germany's interpretation of the principle of *non-refoulement* is mixed and, in some cases, becoming narrower. Second, Germany's reliance on the presumption of mutual trust in Dublin transfers furthers the EU's containment policies by shifting the responsibility to process asylum applications elsewhere—outside of Germany to another EU Member State deemed responsible or to a third country deemed 'safe' under the Asylum Procedures Directive (recast).

---

[6] ECRE News; See, also: European Council on Refugees and Exiles, "Italy: Vulnerable Dublin Returnees at Risk of Destitution", 14 December 2018, https://www.ecre.org/italy-vulnerable-dublin-returnees-at-risk-of-destitution.

[7] European Council on Refugees and Exiles, Germany: Dublin Transfer to Denmark despite Church Asylum, https://www.ecre.org/germany-dublin-transfer-to-denmark-despite-church-asylum/. Previously, German authorities did not forcibly remove individuals subject to Dublin transfers from the churches in which they sought 'Church asylum'.

[8] *Ibid.*

[9] ECRE News.

6.2 German Refugee Law

German refugee law is informed by three types of law: international treaty law, EU and ECHR law, and domestic law. This section will explore each of these types of law in turn.

Germany acceded to the Refugee Convention on November 5, 1969 and ratified it on December 1, 1953.[10] Germany also acceded to, and ratified, the 1967 Protocol on September 4, 1990, with the geographical and temporal limitations imposed by the Refugee Convention in Article 1A removed.[11] Germany has not made any reservations to the Refugee Convention.[12] Germany is a monist country which implements international treaties directly within domestic law, particularly through Article 25 of the *Basic Law*; therefore, the content of the Refugee Convention forms part of German domestic law.[13] That said, the *Bundesverfassungsgerricht* (BverG)—the German Federal Constitutional Court—has shown tendencies towards the dualist model.[14] In particular, the *Basic Law* states:

> *Treaties that regulate the political relations of the Federation* or relate to subjects of federal legislation *shall require the consent or participation, in the form of a federal law, of the bodies responsible in such a case for the enactment of federal law.* In the case of executive agreements the provisions concerning the federal administration shall apply, *mutatis mutandis* (emphasis added).[15]

The German approach means that, in theory, asylum claimants are able to rely directly upon the Refugee Convention in domestic courts. However, in reality, such direct application may not be determinative.

Germany, as a Member State of the Council of Europe, has also ratified the ECHR and is legally bound by it.[16] This means, for example, that the *non-refoulement*

---

[10] United Nations High Commissioner for Refugees, "States Parties to the 1951 Convention relating to the Status of Refugees and the 1967 Protocol", http://www.unhcr.org/protection/basic/3b73b0d63/states-parties-1951-convention-its-1967-protocol.html.

[11] United Nations, "Depositary: Status of Treaties—5. Protocol Relating to the Status of Refugees", https://treaties.un.org/pages/ViewDetails.aspx?src=TREATY&mtdsg_no=V-5&chapter=5&lang=en.

[12] United Nations High Commissioner for Refugees, "2. Convention Relating to the Status of Refugees: Geneva, 28 July 1951", http://www.unhcr.org/protection/convention/3d9abe177/reservations-declarations-1951-refugee-convention.html.

[13] However, some scholars contend that 'the provisions of the *Basic Law* neither conforms nor deny the proposition that Germany is a monist system', see: Daniel Lovric, "A Constitution Friendly to International Law: Germany and its Volkerrectsfreundlichkeit" (2006) 25 *Australian Yearbook of International Law* 75–104 at 81–82.

[14] *Ibid* at 82; Furthermore, the BverG was of the view that, in accordance with Article 59(2) of the *Basic Law,* it serves as a bridge between international treaty law and German domestic law, and also adopts a 'dualist approach to international treaty law', see: Frank Hoffmeister, "Germany: Status of European Convention on Human Rights in Domestic Law" (2006) 4(4) *I-CON,* 722–731 at 726–727 [Hoffmeister].

[15] Deutscher Bundestag, *Basic Law for the Federal Republic of Germany,* last amended 28 March 2019, https://www.btg-bestellservice.de/pdf/80,201,000.pdf at art 59(2) [Basic Law].

[16] ECHR at 5.

provisions of the ECHR are directly incorporated into Germany's domestic law since Article 3 of the ECHR prohibits torture.[17] Since the ECHR has been implemented domestically by Germany into its domestic legislation, the ECtHR's jurisprudence therefore serves as 'interpretative tools of German norms of a constitutional nature'.[18] Also, while the ECHR has been implemented domestically in Germany, the principle of subsidiarity of the ECtHR jurisprudence suggests that the ECtHR is a court of last resort and that domestic remedies must have been exhausted before national courts may refer a case to the ECtHR.[19] In particular, the principle of subsidiarity requires national courts to 'have the opportunity to consider and redress the alleged violation-(s)'.[20] In the *Case No. 2 BvR 1481.04* before the BverG, the court held that 'the responsible authorities or courts must discernibly consider the decision and, if necessary, justify understandably why they nevertheless do not follow the international-law interpretation of the law'.[21] This judgment signals to the national courts that the BverG's view of ECtHR judgments—including those on refugee law—do not oblige German national courts to follow the ECtHR's judgments in all circumstances, where they can put forward reasons for deviating from the ECtHR's jurisprudence.[22] However, it was subsequently held by the BverG that the ECtHR's jurisprudence must be considered by German national courts in a 'methodologically sound manner, but only as long as this did not lead to a weakening of the *Basic Law*'s standard of constitutional protection'.[23]

As a Member State of the EU, Germany is bound by EU law, especially when implementing EU law in its domestic legislation.[24] The regulations and directives are automatically binding upon Germany on the date they enter into force and directives must be incorporated by EU countries into their domestic legislations.[25]

[17] *Convention for the Protection of Human Rights and Basic Liberties,* 7 August 1952, BGBl.II at 685; See, also: Hoffmeister at 724, which states: 'the ECHR enjoys the status of a federal statute in Germany since the German parliament (the Bundestag) adopted it in 1952 by law, according to article 59(2) of the *Basic Law*. Having become part of German domestic law, the Convention had to be applied by German courts, like other federal statutes, "in the framework of accepted methods of interpretation"'.

[18] *Ibid* at 724; See, also: *Case No. 2 BvR 1481/04, October 14, 2004.*

[19] Council of Bars and Law Societies of Europe, "The European Court of Human Rights: Questions & Answers for Lawyers", 2014, https://www.echr.coe.int/Documents/Guide_ECHR_lawyers_ENG.pdf at 4.

[20] *Ibid.*

[21] BverG, Judgment of 14 October 2004—BverG 2 BvR 1481/04 at para 50.

[22] Birgit Peters, "Germany's Dialogue with Strasbourg: Extrapolating the *Bundesverfassungsgericht's* Relationship with the European Court of Human Rights in the Preventive Detention Decision" (2012) 13:6 *German Law Journal* 758–722 at 760.

[23] *Ibid* at 763; BverG, Judgment of 4 February 2010—BverG 2 BvR 2307/06 at para 21.

[24] European Union, "Countries", https://europa.eu/european-union/about-eu/countries_en#the-28-member-countries-of-the-eu. As an EU Member State, Germany is bound by the EU Charter pursuant to Article 6 of the TEU and relevant EU directives and regulations: European Union, *Consolidated Version of the Treaty on European Union*, OJ C-326/13, 26 October 2012 at art 6.

[25] *Ibid.*

Germany did not opt out of any of the relevant EU directives and regulations on asylum.[26] Germany has transposed key CEAS instruments into its domestic legislation. For instance, Qualification Directive (recast) has been transposed as the *Act for the Transposition of the Directive 2011/95/EU,* the Asylum Procedures Directive (recast) as the *Asylum Procedures Acceleration Act,* the Reception Conditions Directive (recast) as the *Act on classification of further states as safe countries of origin and on the facilitation of access to the labour market for asylum seekers and tolerated foreigners,* and the Dublin III Regulation as the *Act on the redefinition of the right to stay and on the termination of stay.*[27]

In terms of Germany's responsibilities under EU law for responsibility-sharing, the Dublin III Regulation applies to determine the Member State responsible for processing asylum applications.[28] The relevant sections in the Dublin III Regulation have been transposed in German law under Section 71a(1) of the *Asylum Act* (described further below) and Sections 51(1) to 51(3) of the *Administrative Procedure Act.*[29] The *Asylum Act* specifies additional asylum procedures to be carried out if Germany is deemed to be the responsible Member State to process the claimant's application for asylum and the *Administrative Procedure Act* sets out the conditions upon which these asylum procedures are to take place.[30]

Turning now to domestic German law, there are two sources of German law: statute law (*Gesetz*) and customary law (*Gewohnheitsrecht*).[31] The Constitution of Germany, the *Basic Law*, is the highest law of Germany.[32] Next in the hierarchy of the *Gesetz* are regulations (*Rechtsverordnungen*) and bylaws (*Satzungen*).[33] German refugee law is generally found in the *Gesetz*, particularly in its regulations. The courts function to interpret law but the judicial decisions are not binding upon lower courts.[34] This means that, although a certain case may be helpful to protect claimants from *refoulement* in Germany, it does not create binding precedent and therefore lower courts may decide differently, even against the claimant's protection.

---

[26] See, for example, where the UK and Ireland has opted-out of the Qualification Directive of 2011/95/EU pursuant to Protocol 21 annexed to the Lisbon Treaty in European Union, *Protocol No. 21*, OJ C-202/295.

[27] Asylum Information Database, "Annex I—Transposition of the CEAS in National Legislation: Germany", http://www.asylumineurope.org/reports/country/germany/annex-i-%E2%80%93-transposition-ceas-national-legislation.

[28] Dublin III Regulation at art 3(2); See also: BVerWG, Judgment of 16 November 2015—BVerWG 1 C 4.15 at para 2.3.

[29] Asylum Act at s 71a(1); *Baden-Württemberg State Administrative Procedure Act* (Verwaltungsverfahrensgesetz, VwVfG), 25 May 1976, Federal Law Gazette I, 102, as amended at s 51(1), 51(2) and 51(3) [Administrative Procedure Act].

[30] *Ibid.*

[31] Raymond Youngs, *Sourcebook on German Law* (London: Cavendish Publishing Limited, 2002) at 4 [Youngs].

[32] *Ibid.*

[33] *Ibid.*

[34] *Ibid* at 5.

The *Basic Law* applies to 'the entire German people'.[35] However, the language of the *Basic Law* uses repeatedly the terms 'every person', 'all persons', and 'persons',[36] whereas other parts of the *Basic Law* refer to 'all Germans'.[37] This distinction is important for asylum claimants, who have certain rights under certain parts of the *Basic Law* as a result.

Most relevant to the interpretation of international law is Article 25 of the *Basic Law*, which provides for the 'primacy of international law'.[38] It states: 'the general rules of international law *shall be* an integral part of federal law.[39] They *shall take precedence over the laws and directly create rights and duties for the inhabitants of the federal territory*' (emphasis added).[40] This provision signifies that the *Basic Law*, as the constitution and the highest law of the land, deems Germany as a monist system, under which general principles of international law directly become national law, without the need for separate domestic implementation, as dualist systems require.[41]

The 'right of asylum' is guaranteed to 'persons persecuted on political grounds' pursuant to Article 16(a)(1) of the *Basic Law*.[42] However, this 'right of asylum' is not invoked where, pursuant to Article 16(a)(2), the person 'enters the federal territory from a member state of the European Communities or from another third state in which application of the Convention Relating to the Status of Refugees and of the Convention for the Protection of Human Rights and Fundamental Freedoms is assured'.[43] In other words, asylum claimants who pass through an EU Member State on their way to Germany or who pass through a third country where the Refugee Convention and ECHR are enforced, cannot invoke the 'right of asylum'. On this basis, Germany draws on the presumption of mutual trust which assumes the safety of the third country for the specific asylum claimant being contemplated for return.

The *Basic Law* is interpreted by the BverG, the Federal Constitutional Court of Germany.[44] The main duty of the court is to interpret the Constitution of the Federal Republic of Germany (the *Grundgesetz* or the *Basic Law*), and to ensure

---

[35] Basic Law at 13.

[36] See, for example: *Ibid* at arts 2, 3(1), and 12(a)(3).

[37] *Ibid* at art 8(1).

[38] *Ibid* at art 25.

[39] *Ibid.*

[40] *Ibid.*

[41] *Ibid;* See a brief discussion above regarding the dualist model employed by the BverG in its case law interpretation of international law.

[42] *Ibid* at art 16(a)(1); This 'right of asylum' is fundamental to, and reflects the importance of, Germany's view on political asylum as reflected in the UDHR, where many of the provisions are considered customary international law, see: UDHR at art 14.

[43] Basic Law at art 16(a)(2).

[44] Bundesverfassungsgericht, "Court and Constitutional Organ", https://www.bundesverfassungsgericht.de/EN/Das-Gericht/Gericht-und-Verfassungsorgan/gericht-und-verfassungsorgan_node.html.

that it is obeyed.[45] The *Basic Law* is the most relevant law when it comes to refugee law, given its emphasis on fundamental rights.[46] The decisions of the BverG are final and all other German government institutions are bound by its case law.[47] The BverG's jurisdiction extends to any conflicts which arise in the interpretation of the *Basic Law*.[48] The BverG has the power to declare a law unconstitutional based on its interpretation of the *Basic Law*.[49] Unlike ordinary courts in Germany, the BverG is vested with the power to declare German laws and statutes unconstitutional, void, or reverse a decision to remand the matter to a competent court, including the competence to enforce fundamental rights as provided for under the *Basic Law*.[50] The BverG cannot, however, issue awards in damages or initiate criminal proceedings.[51]

As a constitutional court, the BverG sees itself as part of the international legal order, where it maintains judicial dialogue with other national and international courts.[52] Any person may lodge a complaint alleging that their fundamental rights as provided for under the *Basic Law* has been violated by a public authority.[53] The BverG is a court of last resort, meaning that all other legal remedies must have been exhausted before the BverG will consider a complaint.[54]

There are two methods of application used by the BverG in its interpretation of international law norms—including refugee law norms—in domestic German case law. The first involves a 'static interpretation' of international law norms, namely through determining Article 16(2) of the *Basic Law* according to the contents of international law.[55] Another method involves a 'dynamic interpretation' of international law norms through the consideration of the content of such an international law norm as it is applied by German organs.[56] The German legislature has made clear that it would not follow the dynamic interpretation of international law

---

[45] *Ibid.*

[46] Bundesverfassungsgericht, "The Court's Duties", https://www.bundesverfassungsgericht.de/EN/Das-Gericht/Aufgaben/aufgaben_node.html.

[47] *Ibid.*

[48] *Ibid.*

[49] *Ibid.*

[50] *Ibid.*

[51] *Ibid.*

[52] Bundesverfassungsgericht, "International Perspectives", https://www.bundesverfassungsgericht.de/EN/Das-Gericht/Internationale-Perspektiven/internationale-perspektiven_node.html.

[53] Bundesverfassungsgericht, "How to Lodge a Constitutional Complaint", https://www.bundesverfassungsgericht.de/EN/Homepage/_zielgruppeneinstieg/Merkblatt/Merkblatt.html.

[54] *Ibid.*

[55] Rainer Hofmann, "Recent Jurisprudence of the German Federal Constitutional Court on Asylum Law" in Gudmundur Alfredsson and Peter Macalister-Smith (eds) *The Living Law of Nations: Essays on refugees, minorities, indigenous peoples and the human rights of other vulnerable groups in memory of Atle Grahl-Madsen* (Germany: NP Engel Publisher, 1996) at 101.

[56] *Ibid.*

norms, meaning that international law norms should be interpreted only according to the content of international law rather than how they have been applied by German organs.[57] German case law is also not binding upon lower courts and previous decisions of a court are not binding upon the same court.[58]

Apart from the *Basic Law*, the *Asylgesetz* or, the *Asylum Act of Germany* (Asylum Act) is a key aspect of German refugee law. The Asylum Act contains 90 chapters and two annexes which apply to foreigners. The *Asylum Act* defines a 'refugee' in the same way as the Refugee Convention.[59] The *Asylum Act* allows for three outcomes: a grant of refugee status, a grant of subsidiary protection as defined under the Qualification Directive, or denial of the claim.[60]

With regards to the 'safe' third country concept, the *Asylum Act* provides under Article 26 that:

> any foreigner who has entered the federal territory from a third country within the meaning of Article 16(2), first sentence of the Basic Law (safe third country) [. . .] shall not be granted asylum.[61]

However, the provision on 'safe' third country does not apply where: 'the Federal Republic of Germany is responsible for processing an asylum application based on European Community law or an international treaty with the safe third country' and '[i]n addition to the Member States of the European Union, safe third countries are those listed in Annex I'.[62] The 'safe' third countries listed in Annex I are Norway and Switzerland.[63] This means that Germany unequivocally accepts and applies the concept of 'safe' third countries in its refugee law.[64]

The principle of proportionality guides judicial decision-making in Germany, including decisions involving asylum claims. The principle is primarily derived from Articles 2(1) and 14 of the *Basic Law*, and this principle was also later incorporated into EU law.[65] The principle of proportionality places fundamental rights as set out under the *Basic Law* at the centre of German law, including the

---

[57] Jasper Finke, "Granting Asylum and Protection from Deportation to Civil War Refugees under German Constitutional Law and the German Aliens Act: The Judgment of the German Federal Constitutional Court of 10 August 2000" (2000) 43 *German Yearbook of International Law* 283–297 at 292.

[58] See, for example: Administrative Court of Potsdam, 4 September 2015, Case No. 4 L 810/15.A.

[59] *Ibid* at s 3.

[60] *Asylum Act of Germany*, 2 September 2008 (Federal Law Gazette I, p 1798), last amended by art 2 of Act 11 March 2016 (Federal Law Gazette I, p 394) at s 1(1) [Asylum Act].

[61] *Ibid* at s 26(a)(1).

[62] *Ibid* at s 26(a)(1)(2) and 26(a)(2).

[63] *Ibid* at Annex I.

[64] See, for example: Kathleen Marie Whitney, "Does the European Convention on Human Rights Protect Refugees from "Safe" Countries" (1997) 26 *Georgia Journal of International & Comparative Law* 375–407 at 386, which states: 'Germany is an example of a Contracting State that has adopted use of the "safe" country concept to create a *cordon sanitaire* around its borders".

[65] *Internationale Handelsgesellschaft GmbH v EV St*, C-11/70, 17 December 1970 at 1128.

right of asylum, with other laws carefully balanced so as to protect those rights.[66] The principle of proportionality states that: 'the law must be appropriate for attaining its objectives, it must be necessary in the attainment of its objectives, and its purpose and method should be weighed against each other in a proportionate manner so that there is minimal interference in the fundamental rights guaranteed in the Basic Law'.[67]

In the context of asylum decision-making, German courts have held that the principle of proportionality is violated when a 'blanket approach in the absence of a case by case examination' is used, in particular to justify detention of asylum claimants deemed to be flight risks.[68] The BverG has also held that the principle of proportionality requires that limitations of fundamental rights as guaranteed under the EU Charter are permitted only if these limitations are 'necessary and genuinely meet objectives of general interest recognised by the Union'.[69] The principle of proportionality is transposed into Section 34a of the *Asylum Procedure Act*, which also requires that transfers of asylum claimants under the Dublin procedures be in compliance with the Dublin III Regulation, and in accordance with the functions of the CEAS.[70] The *Baden-Württemberg State Administrative Procedure Act* also stated that, in instances of decision-making (including on asylum matters), the executive authority must apply a method that is least likely to interfere with the individual concerned and the general public.[71]

In the context of allocating responsibility for determining an asylum application, the *Bundesverwaltungsgericht* (BverWG), or the Federal Administrative Court of Germany, held in *Case No. 1 C 26.14* that, where an asylum claimant has decided to apply for asylum in Germany and the decision on the Member State responsible for the processing of the asylum application is against him or her, the claimant must first lodge an appeal to the *Bundesamt für Migration und Flüchtlinge* (BAMF), or the Federal Office for Migration and Refugees of Germany, before he or she may initiate a second action in court against the responsible authority issuing the rejection.[72]

The BAMF is a federal authority within the Federal Ministry of the Interior which makes decisions on asylum applications.[73] The BAMF works on the basis of

---

[66] Youngs at Chap. 3.

[67] *Ibid.*

[68] European Asylum Law Database, "Germany—Administrative Court of Oldenburg, 12th Chamber, 2 October 2015, 12 A 2572/15", http://www.asylumlawdatabase.eu/en/case-law/germany-administrative-court-oldenburg-12th-chamber-2-october-2015-12-257,215. [EDAL Oldenburg].

[69] BVerWG, Judgment of 17 September 2015—BverWG 1 C 26.14 at para 3(a) [Case No. 1 C 26.14]; See, also: EU Charter at art 52(1).

[70] *Asylum Procedure Act* (Asylverfahrensgesetz, AsylVfG), 2 September 2008, Federal Law Gazette I, 1798, as amended at s 34a.

[71] Administrative Procedure Act at s 19(2).

[72] Case No. 1 C 26.14 at para 3b.

[73] Federal Office for Migration and Refugees, "The Authority", http://www.bamf.de/EN/DasBAMF/Aufgaben/Beh%C3%B6rde/die-behoerde-node.html.

interpreting the *Asylum Act*, as well as relevant EU directives and regulations such as the Dublin III Regulation.[74] The decisions of the BAMF can be appealed to the courts. The BAMF produces various 'soft law' guidance instruments, including official instructions and working guidelines for decision-makers.[75] These guides aim to ensure uniform assessment of asylum applications but do not replace individual examinations and assessments of asylum applications by adjudicators.[76] The guides reflect the current policy of the BAMF and there is an ongoing dialogue between the BAMF and courts in the practice of asylum decision-making.[77] These 'soft law' guidance instruments are not available to the public and are considered internal documents.[78]

Having considered the sources of German refugee law and methods of interpreting German law that are relevant to asylum cases, the next section turns to the structure of the German domestic asylum system.

6.3 The German Domestic Asylum System

Germany's domestic asylum system is structured quite differently from that of the United Kingdom. Asylum cases are handled by regular administrative courts, rather than specialized tribunals similar to the ones in the UK.[79] Decisions of the regular administrative courts may be appealed to the High Administrative Court of the relevant state in Germany, such as Bavaria and North Rhine-Westphalia, which deal with questions of both fact and law.[80] At the top of the appeals hierarchy is the BverWG, the Federal Administrative Court of Germany, which is responsible for the administrative claims of refugee claimants and only decides on questions of law and not of fact.[81] On the other hand, the BverG, the Federal Constitutional Court of Germany, can also rule on issues of asylum because the 'right of asylum' is guaranteed in the *Basic Law*.[82] The BverWG may deviate from the BverG's ruling on asylum issues only where the BverWG's ruling concerns EU law, which prevails over German national law.[83] The BverWG can also refer cases to the

[74] Asylum Act.

[75] Federal Office for Migration and Refugees, "Procedure Management and Quality Assurance", http://www.bamf.de/EN/Fluechtlingsschutz/VerfahrenssteuerungQualitaetssicherung/verfahrenssteuerung-node.html.

[76] *Ibid.*

[77] *Ibid.*

[78] *Ibid.*

[79] Justice Harald Dörig, "Germany: The Handling of Leading Asylum Cases by National Courts" (2013) 25:2 *International Journal of Refugee Law* 373–376 at 373.

[80] *Ibid* at 373.

[81] *Ibid.*

[82] *Ibid* at 374.

[83] *Ibid.*

CJEU on questions related to interpretation of EU law and has done so on previous occasions pursuant to Article 267 of the TFEU.[84]

There are five main steps in the German asylum process: first instance screening; determination of the applicable procedure (accelerated, regular or Dublin); substantive interview for refugee determination; decision on refugee determination; and appeal (if applicable).[85] Each of these steps will be described in turn. The authority responsible for the domestic processing of asylum applications in Germany is the BAMF, unless the application for asylum took place at the border, in which case the German border police will be the competent authority to handle the application.[86]

The first step in the Germany asylum process is first instance screening, which can take place at the border, at the airport or within German territory. Individuals begin this process by indicating that they wish to apply for international protection for refugee status. They are then briefly questioned to determine certain facts, such as where they are from and how they got to Germany from their country of origin, including the countries they have passed through to arrive at Germany. For asylum claimants who arrive at the border trying to enter Germany without the requisite landing documents such as passports, their entry to German territory will be denied by the border police on the grounds that they have traveled to Germany through a 'safe' third country to which they should return and from where they should have applied for asylum.[87] Thus, these individuals are immediately diverted outside of the system by being considered 'inadmissible' on the basis of having passed through a 'safe' third country.[88] If, however, they have documentation, then they are instead permitted to continue to the second step of the asylum process. If an individual applies for asylum either at the border or at an international airport in Germany, the applicant will be accommodated in an 'initial reception centre' (*Aufnahmeeinrichtung*) for up to 6 months during the first stage of his or her asylum procedures.[89] These 'initial reception centres' are located on the premises of the BAMF, but subsequent to the initial reception period of 6 months, for the

[84] *Ibid;* See, also: TFEU at art 267: 'The Court of Justice of the European Union shall have jurisdiction to give preliminary rulings concerning: (a) the interpretation of the Treaties; (b) the validity and interpretation of acts of the institutions, bodies, offices or agencies of the Union'.

[85] Asylum Information Database, "Country Report: Germany", 2017 at 14 [AIDA Country Report Germany]. See also the chart below.

[86] AIDA Country Report Germany at 18–42.

[87] *Ibid* at 15.

[88] *Ibid* at 60, which states: 'Asylum seekers can be sent back to safe third countries with neither an asylum application, nor an application for international or national protection being considered [. . .] Furthermore, Federal Police shall immediately initiate removal to a safe third country if an asylum seeker is apprehended at the border without the necessary documents'.

[89] *Ibid.*

remainder of their time, claimants will be sent to decentralized reception centres for appeal procedures, if applicable.[90] If a person makes an asylum claim while they are already within Germany territory, then he or she will be sent to the responsible authority (such as the BAMF) to determine his or her asylum application.[91]

The second step in the asylum process involves determining the correct procedure to follow. At this stage, claimants are briefly interviewed in order to be evaluated against a series of considerations: is the claimant from a 'safe' country of origin? Has the claimant misled German authorities? Did the claimant act in bad faith in making the application, including attempting to deceive the asylum official or trying to conceal the truth? Has the claimant filed a subsequent application for asylum in another country after leaving Germany? Has the claimant applied for asylum to frustrate the process, such as applying for the purpose of causing procedural delays? Did the claimant refuse to be fingerprinted as required under the Eurodac Regulation at the point of arrival in the EU or in Germany? Has this claimant ever been expelled from Germany on national security grounds? If the answer to any of these questions is 'yes' at this preliminary stage, then the claimant is subjected to the accelerated procedure. If the answer is 'no' to all of these questions, then the individuals is processed through the regular procedure.

The accelerated procedure is a procedure which takes place in an abbreviated period of time, in comparison to the regular procedure. Under the accelerated procedure, the BAMF, which is the office that carries out the procedure, has seven calendar days to decide on a claimant's application.[92] During the accelerated procedure, claimants are detained at 'special reception centres'.[93] As mentioned, asylum claimants may undertake the accelerated procedure if they are deemed to be from a 'safe country of origin', which is defined as:

> a country where, on the basis of the legal situation, the application of the law within a democratic system, and the general political circumstances, it can be shown that there is generally and consistently no persecution as defined in Art. 9 of Directive 2011/95/EU (Recast Qualification Directive), no inhuman or degrading treatment or punishment and no threat by reason of indiscriminate violence in situations of international or internal armed conflict.[94]

Asylum claimants may also be required to undertake the accelerated procedure where they were found to have deliberately misled the German authorities about their identity.[95] The accelerated procedure is also used where applicants have acted in bad faith, filed a subsequent application after they left Germany and their initial asylum application had concluded, made an application for the purpose of causing

---

[90] *Ibid.*

[91] *Ibid.*

[92] *Ibid* at 48.

[93] *Ibid.*

[94] European Commission, Migration and Home Affairs, "Safe Country of Origin", https://ec.europa.eu/home-affairs/content/safe-country-origin-0_en.

[95] AIDA Country Report Germany at 15.

procedural delay, refused to provide their fingerprints, or were expelled from Germany due to serious reasons of public security or for constituting a danger to the community of Germany.[96] These claimants are accommodated in 'special reception centres' (*besondere Aufnahmeeinrichtung*) where they stay for the duration of the accelerated procedure.[97]

The regular procedure differs from the accelerated procedure in that there is not a set time limit for the BAMF, the responsible authority, to decide on an application.[98] Claimants who are directed into the regular procedure are evaluated to see if they travelled through a 'safe' third country prior to arriving in Germany. If the answer is that the claimant travelled through a 'safe' third country which is *not* an EU country, then Germany's stance is that the individual should have applied for asylum in that country. Germany will not consider that person for the granting of asylum and instead will initiate the 'safe' third country transfer process.[99] This is the case even where it is impossible to return the individual to the 'safe' third country (i.e. where there is lack of information provided by the applicant).[100] Germany uses 'safe' third country lists, which include non-EU countries such as Norway and Switzerland.[101]

If, during the personal interview at the competent branch office of the BAMF, the claimant is determined to have travelled through an EU Member State before filing the asylum claim in Germany, then that individual will be considered for a potential Dublin transfer.[102] During this preliminary interview, the applicant is 'informed [. . .] about the procedure and asked to state any reasons why he or she should not be transferred to another Member State'.[103] The content of this interview is to determine the competent Member State responsible for examining the application for the claimant and to examine any procedural barriers to deporting the claimant under the Dublin III Regulation.[104] Germany then evaluates whether it is the responsible Member State or not. If it determines that it is not the responsible Member State, then German authorities do not conduct a substantive interview of the claimant, raising the risk of *refoulement* as the individual is not provided with a chance to address the situation regarding the State determined to be responsible

---

[96] *Ibid* at 47–48.

[97] *Ibid.*

[98] *Ibid* at 20, which states: 'If no decision has been taken within 6 months, the BAMF has to notify asylum seekers upon request about when the decision is likely to be taken'.

[99] United Nations High Commissioner for Refugees, "Asylum Seeking Process", https://help.unhcr.org/germany/asylum-in-germany/asylum-seeking-process [UNHCR Asylum Process].

[100] *Ibid.*

[101] *Ibid.*

[102] Federal Office for Migration and Refugees, "The stages of the German asylum procedure", 2/2019, https://www.bamf.de/SharedDocs/Anlagen/EN/AsylFluechtlingsschutz/Asylverfahren/das-deutsche-asylverfahren.pdf?__blob = publicationFile&v = 12 at 16 [BAMF Asylum Procedures].

[103] *Ibid.*

[104] *Ibid.*

for processing his or her claim.[105] Where another Member State is determined, under the Dublin III Regulation, to be the responsible Member State, Germany will submit a 'take charge' request to the responsible Member State to undertake responsibility for the claimant.[106] Where the responsible Member State approves the 'take charge' request from Germany, the BAMF will find the application inadmissible in Germany and order the deportation of the claimant to the responsible Member State.[107] Under the Dublin procedure, Germany is not permitted to transfer the applicant to another EU Member State where the applicant's spouse or minor children are already recognized as a refugee or are entitled to subsidiary protection in Germany; the applicant's spouse or minor children have applied for asylum and the responsible Member State is Germany; the applicant is an unaccompanied minor and does not have parents or siblings in the Dublin responsible State; the applicant is seriously ill and the illness can be worsened with the transfer; or Germany decides to invoke the 'sovereignty clause' under Article 3(2) of the Dublin III Regulation to 'take charge' of the applicant.[108] Germany is required to transfer the applicant to the responsible Member State within six months of the agreement of the Member State under the Dublin III Regulation.[109]

If the applicant is not subject to a 'safe' third country or Dublin transfer, then that individual will be sent to the third step in Germany's asylum process: the substantive interview, in which case their refugee status will be determined in Germany.[110] At this step, the substantive interview is conducted in order to consider whether the claimant fits within the required definition of 'refugee'. Under domestic German law, persons who are subjected to serious human rights violations when they are returned to their country of origin are entitled to asylum where they are able to demonstrate that they have been persecuted on a number of grounds consisting of: race, nationality, political opinion, fundamental religious conviction, or membership of a particular social group, without having access to protection against persecution or an alternative form of refuge in the country of origin.[111] Examples of acts which may be regarded as persecution under domestic German law include:

> [The] use of physical or psychological violence, including sexual coercion; legal, administrative, police and/or judicial measures which as such are discriminatory, or are applied in a discriminatory manner; disproportionate or discriminatory prosecution or punishment;

---

[105] UNHCR Asylum Process.

[106] BAMF Asylum Procedures at 17.

[107] *Ibid.*

[108] Handbook Germany, "Dublin Procedure", https://handbookgermany.de/en/rights-laws/asylum/dublin-procedure.html.

[109] BAMF Asylum Procedures at 17.

[110] *Ibid* at 18–19.

[111] Federal Office for Migration and Refugees, "Entitlement to Asylum", 1 October 2016, http://www.bamf.de/EN/Fluechtlingsschutz/AblaufAsylv/Schutzformen/Asylberechtigung/asylberechtigung-node.html;jsessionid = B5FDF16C53BC807E0861D803C0F4BCED.2_cid368 [BAMF Asylum Entitlement]; See, also: *Basic Law* at art 16a.

> refusal to provide judicial legal protection, leading to disproportionate or discriminatory punishment [and] acts linked to sexuality or which target children.[112]

Under German law, only persecution from the State is considered for asylum applications.[113] In cases where the persecution was carried out by a non-State actor, Germany will only—in exceptional circumstances—consider granting asylum when the non-State persecution is attributable to the State.[114]

If the determination of refugee status is negative, then claimants may enter the appeal procedure and submit their appeal to a regular administrative court (*Verwaltungsgericht*).[115] Appeals that take place have 'suspensive effect' or 'suspensive recourse', meaning that for the duration of the appeal procedure, applicants are entitled to stay on German territory until the outcome of their appeal decision is made known.[116] However, in cases where it has been deemed that the asylum application is rejected as 'manifestly unfounded' or 'inadmissible', applicants will have one week to seek leave from the court to restore the suspensive effect so that they may remain on German territory for a determined period of time.[117]

There are certain procedural guarantees for those exercising their right to suspensive recourse in Germany.[118] For example, the asylum claimant seeking to exercise his or her suspensive recourse must be given the benefit of the doubt and this must be balanced against the public interest to deport the applicant.[119] The factors upon which to assess whether the applicant's interest in remaining in the present Member State pending a decision on appeal are whether there is a lack of knowledge about the actual living conditions of refugees in the third country to which the applicant is being sent, and whether there are any negative public reports regarding such living conditions in the country of destination.[120] In the case where there is such a lack of knowledge of the living conditions and the presence of negative public reports regarding those living conditions, the applicant's right to remain in the Member State where the asylum is sought will prevail.[121]

---

[112] Federal Office for Migration and Refugees, "Refugee Protection", 1 October 2016, http://www.bamf.de/EN/Fluechtlingsschutz/AblaufAsylv/Schutzformen/Fluechtlingsschutz/fluechtlingsschutz-node.html.

[113] BAMF Asylum Entitlement.

[114] *Ibid.*

[115] *Ibid* at 16.

[116] *Ibid.*

[117] *Ibid.*

[118] For cases involving suspensive recourse in Germany, see: Administrative court of Potsdam, *C 6 L 87/16.A,* 4 February 2016; High Administrative Court, *C Az.1A 11,020/14,* 5 August 2015; Administrative Court of Luneburg, *C 6B 64/13,* 16 December 2013.

[119] *Ibid.*

[120] *Ibid.*

[121] *Ibid.*

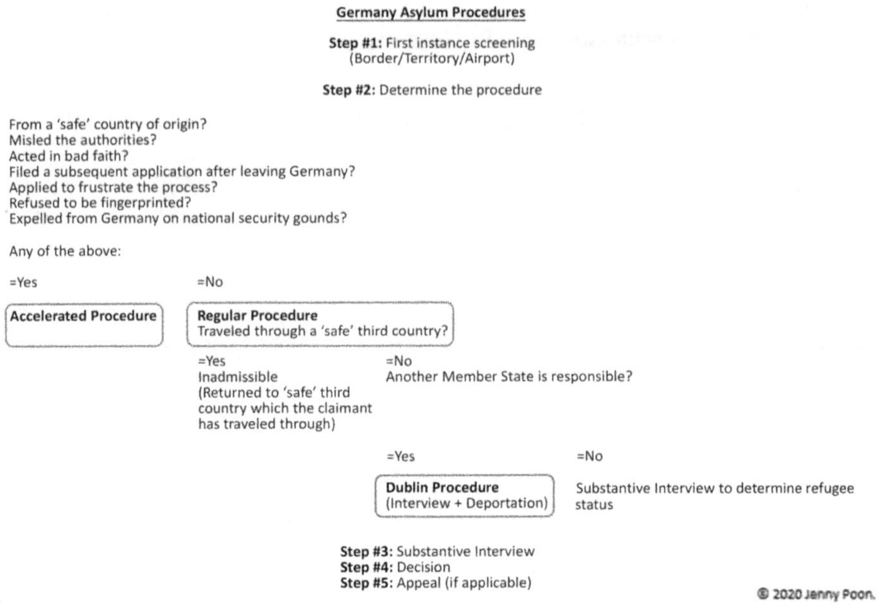

Fig. 6.1 Germany asylum procedures

Figure 6.1 Depicts the process of claiming asylum in Germany from registration to appeal:[122]

The next subsection discusses the current practice of *non-refoulement* in Germany. It demonstrates that Germany's interpretation and application of *non-refoulement* reveals and reinforces the EU's containment policies.

6.4 Non-Refoulement in Germany

As one of the more powerful and well-resourced Member States in the EU, and as a significant refugee-receiving country, Germany's interpretation and application of the fundamental principle of *non-refoulement* sets a pattern for other EU Member States. The purpose of this section is to describe how Germany has interpreted the *non-refoulement* obligation.

Under German law, the principle of *non-refoulement* is formulated as the prohibition against torture, which is also found under Article 3 of the ECHR.[123]

---

[122] Adapted from: Asylum Information Database, "National Country Report: Germany", May 2014 at 11.

[123] *Act Concerning the Entry and Residence of Aliens in the Territory of the Federal Republic* (English Translation), 1 January 1991, as amended, at s 53.

Article 3 of the ECHR is implemented in German law in Section 53 of the *Act Concerning the Entry and Residence of Aliens in the Territory of the Federal Republic* (Aliens Act).[124] Section 53(1) of the *Aliens Act* prohibits return to torture, which is a direct implementation of Article 3 of the *Convention Against Torture*.[125] Section 53(2) prohibits expulsion to a State where the alien is sought for a crime in which the death penalty applies, while Section 53(4) forbids expulsion if it would be contrary to the ECHR.[126] Obligations within the ECHR have been interpreted by various levels of court within Germany, including local administrative courts, the BverWG, the Federal Court of Justice, and the BverG.[127]

The EU laws on *non-refoulement* are implemented in Germany through several domestic laws. The principle of *non-refoulement* is codified in Section 51 of the 1990 *Aliens Act* (now Section 53(6)) which 'forbids deportation to states where asylum-seekers' lives or freedom would be threatened on account of their race, religion, nationality, political opinion, or membership in a particular social group'.[128] However, the provision has been critiqued by scholars as 'lesser asylum', wherein the letter of the law protects asylum claimants from *refoulement*, but does not provide corresponding protection to asylum claimants with refugee status. *Non-refoulement* obligations found under the CEAS' key instruments therefore bind Germany and the relevant provisions which protect asylum claimants from torture and cruel treatment also apply to Germany.[129]

It should be noted, however, that Germany has a 'margin of discretion' in its interpretation of the EU laws on *non-refoulement*.[130] The CJEU has recognized this discretion in the case of *Germany v. Leifer*, where it held that 'Member States have discretion in invoking the security exception to Community legislation which

[124] *Ibid;* (1) An alien may not be expelled to a State in which there is actual danger of his being subjected to torture. (2) An alien may not be expelled to a State in which he is being sought for a criminal act and there is a risk of capital punishment. In such cases, the provisions on extradition will apply. (3) Where another State has made a formal request for extradition, or for arrest in connection with notification of a request for extradition, the alien may not be expelled to that State until a decision has been made on the extradition. (4) An alien may not be expelled if the expulsion is inadmissible under the Convention on the Protection of Human Rights and Fundamental Freedoms, of 4 November 1950 (BGBl. 1952 II, p. 686).

[125] *Ibid*; See, also: Bertold Huber, "The Application of Human Rights Standards by German Courts to Asylum-Seekers, Refugees and Other Migrants", (2001) 3 *European Journal of Migration and Law* 171–184 at 176 [Huber].

[126] *Ibid* at s 53(2) and 53(4); Huber at 176.

[127] See, for example: Administrative Court of Oldenburg, Case No. 12A 2572/15, 2 October 2015.

[128] *Ausltindergesetz* § 51, v. 9.7.1990 (BGB1. I S.1354, 1356), *zuletzt geandert durch Art. 3 Geetz,* v,15.07.93 (BGB1. H S.1010) [Aliens Law of July 9, 1990 as amended]; See, also: Maryellen Fullerton, "Failing the Test: Germany Leads Europe in Dismantling Refugee Protection" (2001) 36 *Texas International Law Journal* 231–275 at 266.

[129] See, for example: Qualification Directive at art 15(b); See, also: EU Charter at art 4.

[130] *Germany v Leifer,* C-83/94 [1995] ECR I-3231 [Leifer].

generally bars the introduction of unilateral sanctions on third states'.[131] This means that, where there is a threat to public security, national authorities enjoy a 'scope of discretion' adjudicating matters of EU law.[132] Other CJEU cases involving Germany have also recognized the 'margin of discretion' doctrine, as well as its limitations, including with respect to *non-refoulement*.[133] In the *Case No. 21 K 3263/07.A*, the Administrative Court of Düsseldorf, North Rhine-Westphalia, the court rejected the deportation of an asylum claimant back to Jordan because of the risk of *refoulement* in that country.[134] Although Germany sought and received diplomatic assurances from Jordan, the court held in the case that the assurances were inadequate to prevent *refoulement*.[135] In another case regarding diplomatic assurances, the Administrative Court in Düsseldorf held that an asylum claimant cannot be *refouled* back to Tunisia because of the risks of torture and other ill-treatment upon return.[136] The court held that the diplomatic assurances guaranteed by Tunisia were 'not legally binding [...] and by nature hardly trustworthy or verifiable'.[137] Again, the courts recognized that Germany's discretion does not extend to receiving assurances from third States that are not reliable interlocutors in terms of *non-refoulement*. Similarly, German national courts such as the Administrative Court of Hannover in *Case No. 1 B 5946/15* held that, for cases involving humanitarian considerations, there may be no room for discretion by the BAMF.[138] As in the previous cases of diplomatic assurances, where the court has held that returning the claimant would be too risky and could potentially expose him or her to risks of *refoulement*, the court in *Case No. 1 B 5946/15* took a cautious approach towards interpreting humanitarian cases. Humanitarian cases include cases where the individual is being contemplated for protection other than refugee status but on humanitarian and compassionate grounds. This could include, for instance, situations where the claimant may be

---

[131] Yuval Shany, "Toward a General Margin of Appreciation Doctrine in International Law?" (2006) 16:5 *European Journal of International Law* 907–940 at 927.

[132] Leifer at summary.

[133] See, for example: *Vereinigte Familiapress Zeitungsverlags und vertriebs GmbH v Heinrich Bauer Verlag*, C-368/95 [1997] ECR I-3689 at 3716; *Elliniki Radiophonia Tileorassi AE (ERT) v Dimotiki Etairia Pliroforissis* (DEP), C-260/89 [1991] ECR I-2925 at 2960; *Dory v Bundesrepublik Deutschland*, C-186/01 [2003] ECR I-2479 at para 36; *Kreil v Bundesrepublik Deutschland*, C-285/98 [2000] ECR I-69 at 105; *R v Secretary of State for Home Affairs, ex parte Santillo*, C-131/79 [1980] ECR 1585 at 1600–1611; *R v Henn*, C-34/79 [1979] ECR 3795 at 3818–3814.

[134] Administrative court Düsseldorf, *21 K 3263/07.A*, 16 January 2009; See, also: Amnesty International, "Germany: Briefing to Committee Against Torture, October 2011", Index EUR 23/002/2011 at 26.

[135] *Ibid.*

[136] Administrative Court Düsseldorf, *11 K 4716/07.A*, 4 March 2009.

[137] *Ibid;* This judgment was affirmed in Higher Administrative Court North Rhine-Westphalia, 17 May 2010, *11 A 960/09 A*.

[138] European Database of Asylum Law, "Germany—Administrative Court (of) Hannover, Case No. 1 B 5946/15, 7 March 2016", http://www.asylumlawdatabase.eu/en/case-law/germany-administrative-court-hannover-case-no-1-b-594,615-7-march-2016.

at risk of facing serious harm below the threshold of *non-refoulement* but nonetheless requiring protection.[139] This is despite the BAMF's enjoyment of discretionary powers when applying Article 17(1) of the Dublin III Regulation.[140] Article 17(1) of the Dublin III Regulation provides that a Member State of the EU may elect to examine the application of the claimant without being deemed, under the Dublin rules, to be the responsible Member State.[141] This provision is known as the 'sovereignty clause'.[142] The potential for risks of *refoulement* can occur over the use of the 'sovereignty clause' due to the discretion granted to Member States to elect themselves as the responsible Member State. German courts have taken a broadly protective approach in such cases.

Germany's domestic law, therefore, reflects the broad nature of the principle of *non-refoulement* as expressed in European law. German law indicates it applies at all times to all people under a country's control, as is the case under international and ECHR human rights law.[143] It also specifically protects asylum claimants as a group under the *Aliens Act*.[144] The prohibition against *refoulement* in the *Aliens Act* is enumerated under Section 53 on the 'grounds for refusing to expel'.[145] More specifically, *refoulement* is prohibited unless the asylum claimant is 'threatened with criminal prosecution and punishment in another State', which 'will not constitute a bar to expulsion'.[146]

This fulsome approach within the letter of the law is not, however, always reflected in the interpretation of the principle by German courts, which have a mixed record in this respect. This is the case in two main ways: first, with respect to the question of the future-looking nature of the threat to life and well-being, and second, with respect to the question of undertaking Dublin transfers.

As was discussed in Chap. 2, *non-refoulement* is understood as future-oriented in terms of the assessment made of the risk to harm. For instance, *non-refoulement*

[139] Migration and Home Affairs, "Subsidiary Protection", https://ec.europa.eu/home-affairs/what-we-do/networks/european_migration_network/glossary_search/subsidiary-protection_en.

[140] Administrative Court of Hannover, Case No. 1 B 5946/15, 7 March 2016.

[141] Dublin III Regulation at art 17(1), the relevant paragraph states: 'By way of derogation from Article 3(1), each Member State may decide to examine an application for international protection lodged with it by a third-country national or a stateless person, even if such examination is not its responsibility under the criteria laid down in this Regulation'.

[142] European Council on Refugees and Exiles, "The Dublin System in the First Half of 2019", https://www.asylumineurope.org/news/27-08-2019/dublin-system-first-half-2019.

[143] The exception that exists in German law prohibiting the application of the rights enshrined in the *Aliens Act* must be in accordance with established German law, see: Refworld, "Germany: Act Concerning the Entry and Residence of Aliens in the Territory of the Federal Republic (Aliens Act)", 1 January 1991, https://www.refworld.org/docid/3ae6b55a0.html [Aliens Act].

[144] *Ibid.*

[145] *Ibid* at s 53.

[146] *Ibid* at s 53(5), which states: 'A general risk that an alien may be threatened with criminal prosecution and punishment in another State and, unless otherwise determined by paragraphs 1 to 4, a specific risk of a statutory penalty pursuant to the laws of another State, will not constitute a bar to expulsion'.

forbids the return of asylum claimants to territories where they may face a future risk of torture, ill-treatment or mass violations of human rights.[147] That said, Germany courts have narrowed the application of the future-oriented approach. In *Case No. 10 C 27.07,* which concerns the interpretation of Article 28(2) of the *Asylum Procedure Act* regarding post-flight decisions which the claimant has deliberately made after fleeing persecution, the BverWG held that the prohibition against *refoulement* 'does not confer any particular status on a foreigner threatened with political persecution elsewhere, *but merely guarantees protection against deportment for the duration of the threat*' (emphasis added).[148] This interpretation of *non-refoulement* by the BverWG is a narrow one because it places a time limit on protecting the claimant from deportation towards a threat, whether perceived or real. This is contrary to international law, which considers the application of *non-refoulement* protection to be a future-oriented one, including protection from future threats that need not have actually occurred.[149]

On the other hand, the idea that *non-refoulement* protection must be guaranteed *after* the granting of international protection was affirmed in *Case No. A 11 S 2151/16* of the Administrative Court of Justice Baden-Württemberg.[150] In that case, the Administrative Court of Justice held, regarding the transfer of a beneficiary of international protection to the responsible Member State, that effective and humane refugee protection must be guaranteed not only during the period of applying for international protection but also *after* such period.[151] This interpretation of *non-refoulement* protection is in line with relevant international refugee law.[152]

Another example of the mixed record of German courts on *non-refoulement* can be seen in cases addressing Dublin transfers. This is evident in a case involving an unaccompanied minor who applied for asylum in Belgium and then travelled to Germany to do the same. Germany deported the minor back to Belgium as the responsible State under the Dublin transfer system. The minor appealed in the case

---

[147] CAT at art 3; ICCPR at arts 6 and 7; Refugee Convention at art 33(1).

[148] BVerWG, Judgment of 18 December 2008—BVerWG 10 C 27.07 at para 2c [Case No. 10 C 27.07].

[149] For instance, the prohibition against torture as considered by the CAT Committee does not consider whether the 'the applicant would *be tortured if* returned, but rather whether there are substantial grounds for believing that he or she would *be in danger of being tortured*' in Weissbrodt and Hörtreiter at 14; The duty of States to evaluate future-oriented risk includes 'not whether a given event happened but the extent of future risk. This depends upon an evaluation of the evidence of the appellant's conduct against a broad range of facts which they may interact', see: *Secretary of State for the Home Department v Rehman* [2003] 1 AC 153, [2001] UKHL 47 at para 56.

[150] European Database of Asylum Law, "Germany—Administrative Court of Justice Baden-Württemberg, 15 March 2017, A 11 S 2151/16", http://www.asylumlawdatabase.eu/en/case-law/germany-%E2%80%93-administrative-court-justice-baden-w%C3%BCrttemberg-15-march-2017-11-s-215,116; Administrative Court of Justice Baden-Württemberg, 15 March 2017, A 11 S 2151/16.

[151] *Ibid.*

[152] Refugee Convention at preamble.

of *Case No. 1 C 4.15*. The BVerWG held that Germany was the Member State responsible for the processing of the asylum application and not Belgium.[153] This is based on three reasons. First, Germany cannot evade its responsibilities for the processing of the asylum application through the use of the 'safe' third country concept by requesting that Belgium 'take back' the applicant for processing.[154] Second, Germany *is* the responsible Member State for the processing of asylum applications in this case because Germany is the last country of presence of the minor applicant where he filed his asylum application.[155] Third, although Belgium is the Member State where the minor applicant had first filed his asylum application, Belgium cannot be the responsible Member State to process his claim because the minor applicant falls under special considerations pursuant to Article 6(2) of the (then) Dublin II Regulation.[156] In the event that there are competing asylum applications being made by the individual who falls under special considerations, for unaccompanied minors, the responsible Member State is *not* the Member State of first application, but rather, the Member State where the minor was last present where the application was filed.[157] In sum, the court indicated that a Member State cannot evade its responsibility for processing asylum applications and shift that responsibility to another Member State because special considerations must be in place for vulnerable persons such as unaccompanied minors. This is particularly the case when considerations given to unaccompanied minors would involve the 'best interests of the child' test, which precludes returns to situations where the child is not able to access 'suitable care, housing, education, language support and health care'.[158]

---

[153] Case No. 1 C 4.15 at paras 4 and 7.

[154] *Ibid* at paras 4 and 22; The CJEU has also held that mere acceptance of a request to take charge or take back of an applicant does not in itself result in a transfer of responsibility for the processing of an asylum application, see: CJEU, *R, on the application of MA, BT, DA v Secretary of State for the Home Department,* C-648/11, 6 June 2013 [MA et al]; See, also: Council Regulation (EC) No. 343/2003 of 18 February 2003 establishing the criteria and mechanisms for determining the Member State responsible for examining an asylum application lodged in one of the Member States by a third-country national, OJ L50/1, 25 February 2003 at arts 18(7) and 20(1)(d) [Dublin II Regulation].

[155] *Ibid.*

[156] Dublin II Regulation at art 6(2); See also Dublin III Regulation at art 3(1).

[157] Dublin II Regulation at art 8.

[158] EMN Focussed Study 2017, "(Member) States' Approaches to Unaccompanied Minors Following Status Determination: Common Template for EMN Focussed Study 2017: Final Version", https://ec.europa.eu/home-affairs/sites/homeaffairs/files/29a_norway_unaccompanied_minors_2017_en_0.pdf at 27; See, also: United Nations High Commissioner for Refugees, "UNHCR Guidelines on Determining the Best Interests of the Child", https://www.unhcr.org/4566b16b2.pdf at 70, which states: 'voluntary repatriation cannot be considered to be in the child's best interests "if it would lead to a "reasonable risk" that such return would result in the violation of fundamental human rights of the child" (General Comment No. 6 by the Committee on the Rights of the Child, paragraph 84). Similarly, return would not be in the child's best interests if adequate care arrangements are not available upon return'.

A second case echoes the concerns raised by the applicant in the first case. In *Case No. 1 C 4.16,* the BverWG held that the Dublin III Regulation governs the responsibility for the processing of asylum applications lodged in an EU Member State, and Member States may only refuse an application as inadmissible on the grounds listed in German domestic law: Section 29(1)(5) of the *Asylum Act.* Section 29(1)(5) of the *Asylum Act* states:

> An application for asylum shall be inadmissible if [. . .] in the case of follow-up applications pursuant to Section 71 or secondary applications pursuant to Section 71a, another asylum application is not to be conducted.[159]

The BverWG held in the case that, pursuant to Section 71a(1) of the *Asylum Act,* where an applicant of international protection for refugee status applied unsuccessfully in a 'safe' third country before applying for asylum in Germany, Germany is deemed not responsible (through its domestic law) for the processing of that individual's application.[160] Under domestic German law, Germany will not be responsible for a further asylum procedure involving examination of admissibility and a subsequent procedure of substantive examination of the merits of the application unless Germany is deemed the responsible Member State to process the asylum application pursuant to the Dublin III Regulation.[161] In this case, the applicant was an Afghan national who entered German territory in 2012 and applied for asylum.[162] Upon his arrival, his fingerprint showed up as a 'positive hit' in the Eurodac system, indicating that he traveled through Hungary before arriving to claim asylum in Germany.[163] Germany determined that he should have applied for asylum in Hungary but did not and requested Hungary to 'take charge' of the applicant.[164] Hungary consented to 'take back' the applicant. In this case, the claimant was concerned that he would be exposed to a real risk of *refoulement* if returned to Hungary because of the deficient asylum system there.[165] However, the transfer was still deemed acceptable.

Two recent cases heard by the BverG also illustrate the mixed record of German courts with respect to Dublin transfers and *non-refoulement.* In a case involving the transfer of a female asylum claimant from Somalia and her infant, the BverG stopped the Dublin transfer of the claimants to Italy.[166] Even though Italy had

[159] *Asylum Act* at s 29(1)(5).

[160] *Ibid* at s 71a(1).

[161] *Ibid;* See, also: Case No. 1 C 4.16 at para 24.

[162] BverWG *1 C 4.16,* 14 December 2016 [English-Translated Version] at para 1.

[163] *Ibid* at para 2.

[164] *Ibid.*

[165] See, for example: European Council on Refugees and Exiles, "Hungary: Dublin Transfers Suspended by Germany", https://www.asylumineurope.org/news/29-08-2017/hungary-dublin-transfers-suspended-germany.

[166] European Council on Refugees and Exiles, "Germany: Constitutional Court Strengthens Rights of Asylum Seekers Subject to Dublin", https://www.ecre.org/germany-constitutional-court-strengthens-rights-of-asylum-seekers-subject-to-dublin; *BVerfG 2 BvR 1380/19; BVerG 2 BvR 721/19.*

provided a blanket assurance in January 2019 that asylum seekers returned to Italy would be provided with due process and adequate living conditions, the court found that this was not enough in cases of very vulnerable claimants.[167] The BverG had evidence indicating that the mother and baby would likely be rendered homeless for a period of time on arrival in Italy, and without access to health care for the baby.[168] This creates peril for the baby in particular and amounts to a prospective violation of the baby's fundamental rights and therefore the transfer must be halted.[169] The second case involved an asylum seeker from Afghanistan ordered to be sent by Dublin transfer back to Greece. He had registered as an asylum seeker in Greece before travelling on to Germany and making another asylum claim.[170] The BverG ruled that the transfer must be paused because of the risk of inhuman and degrading treatment in Greece.[171] The lower court decisions denying both requests to freeze the Dublin transfers can be contrasted with Germany's highest court's recognition of the dangers inherent in these transfers.

A legal loophole exists in the Dublin III Regulation which could permit Member States to evade their responsibility for processing asylum applications during the use of Dublin transfers.[172] The legal loophole works by requiring that only one Member State be the responsible Member State to process asylum applications, granting Member States the option of requesting a 'take charge' or 'take back' of an applicant, and not requiring a substantive review of an asylum application before making the decision to send that individual back to a third country he or she passed through which is deemed 'safe'. It raises three concerns.

First, the Dublin III Regulation requires that only one EU Member State is responsible for the processing of asylum applications.[173] This Member State is, pursuant to the regular Dublin procedure (where not falling under the special considerations criteria), the Member State where the applicant first lodges his or her asylum application.[174] This may make sense in terms of the situation of some applications, but for other applicants this may create difficulties and dangers.

Second, under the Dublin procedures, Member States have the option of requesting a 'take charge' or 'take back' of an applicant where they deem another Member State to be responsible for processing the asylum application.[175] The rules for 'take charge' apply when the requirements of Articles 16(1)(c), (d), or (e) of the (then) Dublin II Regulation are not met, for example when a person has stayed in another Member State before entering the Member State in which he first applied

[167] BverfG *2 BvR 1380/19* at paras 5 and 21.

[168] *Ibid* at para 18.

[169] *Ibid* at para 27.

[170] *BVerG 2 BvR 721/19* at para 1.

[171] *Ibid* at paras 22 and 24.

[172] See above cases: 1C 4.15 and 1C 4.16.

[173] Dublin III Regulation at art 3(1).

[174] *Ibid.*

[175] *Ibid* at Chp V.

for asylum.[176] In contrast, the rules for 'take back' apply if one of the conditions under Article 16(1)(c), (d), or (e) of the (then) Dublin II Regulation is met, such as when the asylum applicant has already applied for asylum in another Member State.[177] Although the CJEU has held that the mere request of a 'take charge' or 'take back' request of a Member State is not a transfer of responsibility, in practice, as seen through *Cases No. 1 C 4.15 and 1 C 4.16* above, the Member State that made such a request (including Germany) often *presumes* that responsibility has been transferred and deportations of that applicant will follow.[178]

German case law consistently holds that an applicant subjected to a Dublin transfer must have, and be seen to have, a right to a personal interview.[179] This interview must take into account the subjective circumstances of the applicant and the authorities must conclude that there are no obstacles to the transfer decision.[180] However, in reality, there is no consistent practice for interviews in Dublin procedures in Germany.[181] Compounding this is the fact that, in Germany, the Dublin procedures are part of admissibility assessment—meaning that, once another Member State is deemed responsible for the processing of the claimant's application, the application in Germany will immediately be deemed 'inadmissible', and the claimant transferred to the responsible Member State without the chance of a substantive interview.[182] This deportation will take place 'as soon as it has been ascertained that the deportation can be carried out'.[183]

Third, where the asylum applicant has passed through a 'safe' third country, the Asylum Procedures Directive permits the Member State to send the applicant back to that country deemed 'safe' without requiring that the sending Member State

[176] Dublin II Regulation at art 16(1)(c), (d) and (e); BverWG, *1 C 26.14,* 17 September 2015 at para 32; For more cases on 'take back' and 'take charge' requests in Germany, see: BverG, *1 C 22.15,* 27 April 2016; Higher Administrative Court of Saxony, *C 5 B 259/15.A,* 5 October 2015; BverWG, *1 C 32.14, 1 C 33.14, 1 C 34.14,* 27 October 2015; BverWG, *1C 24.15,* 27 April 2016: 'Where a Member State responsible for carrying out the asylum procedure pursuant to the Dublin III Regulation, an applicant may invoke that Member State's responsibility for processing his or her asylum application if it has not been positively established that another Member State is willing to take charge of him or her. In this case, the object and purpose of the Dublin System would require that the individual applicant is entitled to have his/her asylum application reviewed by the responsible Member State'.

[177] *Ibid.*

[178] MA et al.

[179] Administrative Court of Düsseldorf, *C 12L 4591/17.A,* 26 October 2017; BverG, *C 2 BvR 1795/14,* 17 September 2014; Administrative Court of Wiesbaden, *C 6L 4438/17.WI,* 15 September 2017; Administrative Court of Minden, *C 10L 314/16.A,* 29 March 2016; BverG, *1 C 26.14,* 17 September 2015; BverWG, *C 2 BvR 746/15,* 30 April 2015; Administrative Court of Freiburg, *C A 1K 3128/14,* 14 January 2015.

[180] *Ibid;* Dublin III Regulation at art 5.

[181] AIDA Country Report Germany at 31–32.

[182] *Asylum Act* at s 29; AIDA Country Report Germany at 32.

[183] *Ibid.*

undertake an examination of admissibility or substantive examination.[184] Indeed, this is exactly how the German asylum process is structured. This creates the possibility that the applicant may be sent back to a country that is deemed 'safe' pursuant to the domestic law of the Member State, but that country may in fact be unsafe based on the individual circumstances of the applicant.[185]

The principle of *non-refoulement* is at risk of being violated in instances such as these—when responsibility for the processing of the asylum application is shifted elsewhere—where a proper examination of either the admissibility or the substance of the asylum application does not take place, before a decision to send the claimant back is made.

Having indicated the law and judicial practice with respect to *non-refoulement* in Germany, the next section argues that Germany's interpretation and application of its *non-refoulement* obligations in conjunction with the threshold on the presumption of mutual trust during Dublin transfers is problematic and demonstrates that the EU's containment policies are at work in Germany.

6.5 Containment in Germany as Illustrated by the Presumption of Mutual Trust

The presumption of mutual trust is the key to permitting Dublin transfers between Member States as it is the basis upon which Member States may transfer claimants from one Member State to the Member State deemed responsible for processing the asylum application. The presumption of mutual trust is an assumption that all Member States of the EU are compliant with relevant international and European law and this is the basis upon which claimants may be transferred from one Member State to another Member State without the substance of their claims examined.[186]

This section therefore details Germany's interpretation of the presumption of mutual trust during Dublin transfers. It begins by comparing the interpretation by domestic German courts of the presumption of mutual trust against the CJEU and the ECtHR's interpretations. It then connects the presumption of mutual trust as interpreted by German courts with the principle of *non-refoulement.* Next, it discusses some examples of containment policies at work within the German domestic asylum system and ends by drawing conclusions on Germany's interpretations of the principle of *non-refoulement* in domestic law.

---

[184] Asylum Procedures Directive at art 38.

[185] For an illustrative example, see: Gloria Fernández Arribas, "The EU-Turkey Agreement: A Controversial Attempt at Patching up a Major Problem" (2016) 1:3 *European Papers* 1097–1104; Recall that international law requires that individual circumstances be considered in establishing a 'well-founded fear of persecution' and that an individual interview must be granted pursuant to Article 33(2) of the Refugee Convention in expulsion situations.

[186] Battjes at 10.

The Administrative Court of Oldenburg, 12th Chamber, discussed the presumption of mutual trust in *Case No. 12 A 2672/15.*[187] The case concerned an Iraqi national who appealed the decision of the BAMF to transfer him from Germany to Hungary through the Dublin transfer procedures.[188] The Administrative Court of Oldenburg found that the transfer of the applicant from Germany to Hungary is contrary to Article 4 of the EU Charter as a result of there being a real risk of exposing the applicant to treatment substantially likely to be inhuman or degrading.[189] The applicant's exposure to ill-treatment is also a result of 'systemic flaws' in the Hungarian asylum system and reception conditions.[190] Most notably, the Administrative Court of Oldenburg cited the ECtHR's decision in *M.S.S.*, where the ECtHR held that:

> The Court considers treatment to be "inhuman" when it was "premeditated, was applied for hours at a stretch and caused either actual bodily injury or intense physical or mental suffering". Treatment is considered to be "degrading" when it humiliates or debases an individual, showing a lack of respect for, or diminishing, his or her human dignity, or arouses feelings of fear, anguish or inferiority capable of breaking an individual's moral and physical resistance.[191]

The Administrative Court of Oldenburg referred to the ECtHR's decision in *M.S.S.*, and in particular, the definitions of 'inhuman' and 'degrading' to find that the applicant would be at risk of inhuman or degrading treatment contrary to Article 4 of the EU Charter.[192] In its decision, the Administrative Court of Oldenburg also referred to the CJEU's decision in *Puid* and *N.S.*, where the CJEU held:

> Member States may not transfer an asylum seeker to the Member State which the criteria set out in Chapter III of the Regulation indicate is responsible, *where they cannot be unaware that systemic deficiencies in the asylum procedure and in the conditions for the reception of asylum seekers in that Member State* provide substantial grounds for believing that the asylum seeker would face a real risk of being subjected to inhuman or degrading treatment within the meaning of Article 4 of the Charter of Fundamental Rights of the European Union (emphasis added).[193]

In addition to the relevant paragraphs cited in *M.S.S.* and *Puid* above, the Administrative Court of Oldenburg held that 'systemic flaws':

> can be rooted in the national asylum system itself which affects asylum seekers in a manner that is neither accidental nor isolated and is objectively predictable or may arise due to an implementation of the system which in practice renders partially or wholly inoperable.[194]

---

[187] Administrative Court of Oldenburg, 12th Chamber, 2 October 2015, 12 A 2572/15.

[188] EDAL Oldenburg at 696.

[189] *Ibid.*

[190] *Ibid.*

[191] MSS at para 220.

[192] EDAL Oldenburg.

[193] *Bundesrepublik Deutschland v Kaveh Puid*, C-4/11, Judgment of 14 November 2013 at para 30 [Puid]; See also, corresponding paragraphs in NS/ME at paras 94 and 106.

[194] EDAL Oldenburg.

It has also been held by the Administrative Court of Minden that 'systemic flaws' are:

> structural, significant malfunctions that may be rooted in any stage of the asylum procedure. *According to the court, the personal experiences of the Applicant are irrelevant to assessing systemic flaws*, however, they must be taken into account in the context of the overall assessment (emphasis added).[195]

The Administrative Court of Minden's interpretation of 'systemic flaws' seems to contradict the ECtHR's 'individual assessment' criterion. The Administrative Court of Magdeburg, Chamber, regarded 'systemic deficiencies' to require that:

> the asylum procedure or the terms of reception conditions in the member state concerned are regularly so deficient that it may be presumed that there is a considerable likelihood that the person seeking asylum is at risk of suffering from inhuman or degrading treatment.[196]

The Administrative Court of Magdeburg deviated from the well-cited threshold established by the Committee Against Torture in deciding whether the claimant would be at risk of being subjected to torture as defined in Article 1 of the CAT, by using the threshold of 'considerable likelihood', rather than 'substantial grounds for believing'.[197] While there may not be a universal understanding or definition of 'considerable likelihood', the Committee Against Torture has proposed a number of non-exhaustive questions as relevant for determining what constitutes 'substantial grounds for believing'.[198] This is important because the threshold for the asylum claimant to establish 'substantial grounds for believing' is essential for determining whether the claimant is at risk of being exposed to torture upon return.

---

[195] European Database of Asylum Law, "Germany—Administrative Court of Minden, 2 October 2015, Case No. 10 L 923/15.A", http://www.asylumlawdatabase.eu/en/case-law/germany-administrative-court-minden-2-october-2015-case-no-10-l-92315a.

[196] European Database of Asylum Law, "Germany—Administrative Court of Magdeburg, Chamber, 26 January 2016, Case No. 8 A 108/16", http://www.asylumlawdatabase.eu/en/case-law/germany-%E2%80%93-administrative-court-magdeburg-chamber-8-26-january-2016-8a-108-16.

[197] CAT Committee, "General Comment No. 1: Communications concerning the return of a person to a State where there may be grounds he would be subjected to torture (article 3 in the context of article 22)", UN Doc A/53/44, annex IX at 52 (1998) at para 1.

[198] *Ibid* at para 8: '(a) Is the State concerned one in which there is evidence of a consistent pattern of gross, flagrant or mass violations of human rights (see article 3, pare. 2)? (b) Has the author been tortured or maltreated by or at the instigation of or with the consent or acquiescence of a public official or other person acting in an official capacity in the past? If so, was this the recent past? (c) Is there medical or other independent evidence to support a claim by the author that he/she has been tortured or maltreated in the past? Has the torture had aftereffects? (d) Has the situation referred to in (a) above changed? Has the internal situation in respect of human rights altered? (e) Has the author engaged in political or other activity within or outside the State concerned which would appear to make him/her particularly vulnerable to the risk of being placed in danger of torture were he/she to be expelled, returned or extradited to the State in question? (f) Is there any evidence as to the credibility of the author? (g) Are there factual inconsistencies in the claim of the author? If so, are they relevant?'.

The presumption of mutual trust is connected with responsibility-sharing in the CEAS. The presumption is the basis upon which Dublin transfers are premised: responsibility-sharing in the EU is based on the reciprocal concept that, in order to share responsibility, there must be mutual trust among the Member States.[199] In fact, the entire Dublin System is based on the presumption that all Member States in the EU are safe countries which '[respect] the principle of non-refoulement [and] are considered safe countries for third country nationals'.[200]

Responsibility-sharing in the context of Germany's *non-refoulement* obligations also entails following one of the core aims of the Dublin System, which is to 'set up clear, workable and fair criteria for responsibility so as to guarantee that the persons concerned have rapid and effective access to a substantive review'.[201] The intent and purpose of the Dublin System also call for 'a general effect protecting the individual' and to prevent 'the situation of [a] 'refugee in orbit''.[202]

Other cases in German domestic jurisprudence also demonstrate the tensions between the CJEU and ECtHR's tests on assessing whether an applicant may be able to rebut a decision to have him or her transferred to the Member State responsible for processing the asylum application.[203] These series of cases illustrate that Germany follows the CJEU approach in determining whether an applicant's transfer decision should be rebutted. For example, the German domestic case law suggests that there is a pattern for determining whether a Dublin transfer of the applicant may be permissible is whether there are 'systemic deficiencies' or 'systemic flaws' in the asylum procedure and reception conditions, which would put the applicant at a serious risk of suffering inhuman or degrading treatment within the meaning of Article 4 of the EU Charter and Article 3 of the ECHR.[204] The standard upon which to evaluate whether a Dublin transfer would result in 'systemic flaws' is based on a standard of 'substantive grounds for believing' whether the transfer would result in a real risk of treatment contrary to Article 4 of the EU Charter or Article 3 of the ECHR.[205] The assessment involves asking whether the 'systemic flaws' within the asylum system of the Member State in question would pose a real risk of infringement of Article 4 of the EU Charter.[206]

---

199 Battjes at 2.2.

200 *Ibid.*

201 Dublin III Regulation at recitals 4 and 5.

202 BVerWG, Judgment of 27 April 2016—BVerWG 1 C 24.15 at para 2.3 [Case No. 1 C 24.15]; The term 'refugee in orbit' means the situation where a refugee is in legal limbo—turned away from his or her country of origin yet at the same time not received in the country of asylum.

203 Administrative Court of Hannover, *C 10A 5157/15,* 5 November 2015; Administrative Court of Oldenburg, *C 12A 2572/15,* 2 October 2015; Administrative Court of Düsseldorf, *C 22L 2944/ 15A,* 3 September 2015; Administrative Court of Düsseldorf, *C 12L 4591/17.A,* 26 October 2017; Administrative Court of Aachen, *C Az. 8 K 658/15.A,* 17 November 2015.

204 *Ibid.*

205 *Ibid.*

206 *Ibid.*

By analogy, the Committee Against Torture jurisprudence also sheds light on the tensions between 'systemic deficiencies' and 'individual assessments' tests when deciding on Article 3 of the CAT. Recall from the Committee Against Torture jurisprudence that the risk of ill-treatment or prohibition against torture is a personal one, meaning that the test for determining whether an individual would be at risk of being subjected to torture is an assessment about whether the complainant would be 'personally at risk'.[207] This means that, for the complainant to defend the allegation against the State that he or she would be subjected to torture if returned, the threshold is on 'a foreseeable, real and personal risk' standard.[208] At the same time, where 'a consistent pattern of gross, flagrant or mass violations of human rights' exists in the destination country, such a pattern is indicative of the possibility or even probability of torture.[209] However, it has also been held by the Committee Against Torture that even the existence of such a pattern of gross, flagrant or mass violations of human rights may not, in the specific case of the complainant, amount to torture for *that particular complainant*.[210] Therefore, taking into account the Committee Against Torture's assessment of the application of Article 3 of the CAT by States Parties, the Committee seems to side in favour of an 'individual assessments' test rather than a 'systemic deficiencies' test. In other words, when assessing whether Article 3 of the CAT is engaged, whether the risk of torture is particularized for the individual is of more concern to the Committee than whether the risk of torture is a systemic one in the destination country.

This section discussed Germany's approach when interpreting the threshold to rebut the presumption of mutual trust to prevent a Dublin transfer. It also demonstrated that the presumption of mutual trust is linked with responsibility-sharing within the CEAS, as the Dublin System is premised upon mutual trust among Member States in the allocation of responsibility for processing asylum applications. However, the tensions between the CJEU and the ECtHR's interpretations of the threshold to rebut the presumption of mutual trust are not resolved by Germany's domestic jurisprudence. Unlike the UK, Germany does not have a new approach to interpreting the threshold to rebut the presumption; instead, Germany seems to agree with the CJEU's test of 'systemic deficiencies'. Lastly, the Committee Against Torture's observations were also drawn upon to compare and contrast the international standard with the CJEU and Germany's domestic approach to the threshold to rebut the presumption of mutual trust. In sum, German jurisprudence is mixed on *non-refoulement* protections. The fact that there is no clear baseline protection *in practice* in all circumstances—including, and perhaps especially, with respect to Dublin transfers—is concerning.

---

[207] Committee Against Torture, *MAK*, 5 May 2004, UN Doc CAT/C32/D/214/2002 [MAK].

[208] *Ibid.*

[209] *Ibid.*

[210] *Ibid.*

6.6 Concluding Remarks

As demonstrated in this chapter, Germany's *non-refoulement* obligations entail an understanding of Germany's asylum system as it is situated in the CEAS. Regular administrative courts of Germany, through their cases, have interpreted and applied EU law and ECHR law relevant to assessing the scope of *non-refoulement.*[211] Case law of Germany's administrative courts have shown the tendency to sometimes interpret *non-refoulement* obligations narrowly, including deciding that *non-refoulement* obligations would apply only during the 'duration of a threat'.[212] Based on all of the positive case law that is covered above, a pattern emerges indicating that many German courts adopt a broad interpretation of *non-refoulement*. The mixed nature of the cases with negative decisions at the administrative and lower court levels did not adopt as wide a view of *non-refoulement* as do other courts. Intrinsically linked to this evaluation of *non-refoulement* obligations is the presumption of mutual trust and Germany's interpretation of this presumption. Unlike the UK courts, the administrative courts of Germany consistently agree with the CJEU's approach of 'systemic deficiencies' in assessing whether the presumption of mutual trust is rebuttable.[213] Responsibility-sharing in Germany, therefore, reveals a narrower interpretation of *non-refoulement* obligations as well as a discrepancy with UK and ECHR jurisprudence in the interpretation of the threshold for rebutting the presumption of mutual trust.[214]

The first part of this chapter examined German refugee law, including its relation to international and European law. The *Basic Law* is the supreme law of the land in Germany and provides for the 'primacy of international law', which integrates international law as an integral part of federal German law. The *Asylum Act* is the main legislation that codified the 'right of asylum' for foreigners. It provides for the definition of a 'refugee', the 'safe' third country concept, and the possible outcomes in a refugee status determination procedure. The BAMF is responsible for making decisions on asylum applications. These decisions may be appealed to the regular administrative courts and the BverWG or the BverG depending on whether the question is an administrative or constitutional one.

The second part of this chapter examined the procedures for claiming asylum in Germany. First, it explained the procedures for applicants to qualify for international protection. Next, it discussed the procedures for applicants to be granted or have their international protection withdrawn. Finally, it ended with outlining the reception conditions for applicants of international protection.

---

[211] See, for example: Case No. 10 C 27.07.

[212] *Ibid;* As *non-refoulement* is customary international law, it binds all States and is applicable wherever a State exercises jurisdiction.

[213] See, for example: Administrative Court of Minden, 2 October 2015, Case No. 10 L 923/15.A.

[214] For a deeper analysis, see the UK Chapter.

The third part of this chapter examined Germany's *non-refoulement* obligations. It was demonstrated through case law that many German courts' interpretation of its *non-refoulement* obligations is twofold. First, these courts seem to have a more liberal reading of *non-refoulement* law than UK; Second, the case law on the interpretation of the principle suggests that the mixed jurisprudence requires fine-tuning for a more streamlined, consistent approach to interpreting the norm.

The final part of this chapter reviewed evidence of containment theory at work in Germany. It detailed Germany's interpretation of the presumption of mutual trust in Dublin transfers. It ended with examples of containment policies in the German domestic asylum system and explained how a legal loophole within the Dublin III Regulation permits Member States such as Germany to evade their responsibility to process asylum applications and shift that responsibility elsewhere, which further reinforced the idea that the CEAS is premised upon the EU's containment policies.

This chapter provides important context for the final chapter of this book, which compares the national cases between the UK and Germany as well as provides an analysis on the future direction of *non-refoulement* within the EU. That chapter proposes adopting a new framework that would enhance interpretations of *non-refoulement* protection and ends with an analysis of the implications of this finding, including predictions for the future direction of *non-refoulement* in the international refugee law regime.

References

Asylum Information Database (2014) National country report: Germany

Asylum Information Database (2017) Country report: Germany

Asylum Information Database, Annex I – Transposition of the CEAS in National Legislation: Germany, http://www.asylumineurope.org/reports/country/germany/annex-i-%E2%80%93-transposition-ceas-national-legislation

Bertold Huber (2001) The application of human rights standards by German courts to Asylum-Seekers, refugees and other migrants. Euro J Migration Law 3:171–184

Bundestag D, Basic law for the Federal Republic of Germany, last amended 28 March 2019, https://www.btg-bestellservice.de/pdf/80201000.pdf at Art 59(2) [Basic Law]

Bundesverfassungsgericht, Court and constitutional organ, https://www.bundesverfassungsgericht.de/EN/Das-Gericht/Gericht-und-Verfassungsorgan/gericht-und-verfassungsorgan_node.html

Bundesverfassungsgericht, How to lodge a constitutional complaint,

Bundesverfassungsgericht, International perspectives, https://www.bundesverfassungsgericht.de/EN/Das-Gericht/Internationale-Perspektiven/internationale-perspektiven_node.html

Bundesverfassungsgericht, The court's duties, https://www.bundesverfassungsgericht.de/EN/Das-Gericht/Aufgaben/aufgaben_node.html

Committee CAT (1998) General comment no. 1: communications concerning the return of a person to a state where there may be grounds he would be subjected to torture (article 3 in the context of article 22), UN Doc A/53/44, annex IX at 52

Council of Bars and Law Societies of Europe (2014) The European court of human rights: questions and answers for lawyers. https://www.echr.coe.int/Documents/Guide_ECHR_lawyers_ENG.pdf at 4

Database EAL, Germany – administrative court of Oldenburg, 12th Chamber, 2 October 2015, 12 A 257215, http://www.asylumlawdatabase.eu/en/case-law/germany-administrative-court-oldenburg-12th-chamber-2-october-2015-12-257215

ECRE News ; See, also: European council on refugees and exiles, Italy: vulnerable dublin returnees at risk of destitution, 14 December 2018, https://www.ecre.org/italy-vulnerable-dublin-returnees-at-risk-of-destitution

EMN Focussed Study 2017, (Member) states' approaches to unaccompanied minors following status determination: common template for EMN focussed study 2017: final version, https://ec.europa.eu/home-affairs/sites/homeaffairs/files/29a_norway_unaccompanied_minors_2017_en_0.pdf

European Commission, Migration and Home Affairs, safe country of origin, https://ec.europa.eu/home-affairs/content/safe-country-origin-0_en

European Council on Refugees and Exiles, Germany steps up dublin transfers putting asylum seekers at risk, 21 March 2019, https://www.ecre.org/germany-steps-up-dublin-transfers-putting-asylum-seekers-at-risk. [ECRE News]

European Council on Refugees and Exiles, Germany: Dublin Transfer to Denmark despite Church Asylum, https://www.ecre.org/germany-dublin-transfer-to-denmark-despite-church-asylum

European Council on Refugees and Exiles News, Germany: temporary suspension of dublin returns due to COVID-19, https://www.ecre.org/germany-temporary-suspension-of-dublin-returns-due-to-covid-10

European Council on Refugees and Exiles, Germany: constitutional court strengthens rights of asylum seekers subject to Dublin, https://www.ecre.org/germany-constitutional-court-strengthens-rights-of-asylum-seekers-subject-to-dublin

European Council on Refugees and Exiles, Hungary: dublin transfers suspended by Germany, https://www.asylumineurope.org/news/29-08-2017/hungary-dublin-transfers-suspended-germany

European Council on Refugees and Exiles, The Dublin system in the first half of 2019, https://www.asylumineurope.org/news/27-08-2019/dublin-system-first-half-2019

European Database of Asylum Law, Germany—administrative court of justice Baden-Württemberg, 15 March 2017, A 11 S 2151/16, http://www.asylumlawdatabase.eu/en/case-law/germany-%E2%80%93-administrative-court-justice-baden-w%C3%BCrttemberg-15-march-2017-11-s-215116

European Database of Asylum Law, Germany—administrative court of magdeburg, Chamber, 26 January 2016, Case No. 8 A 108/16, http://www.asylumlawdatabase.eu/en/case-law/germany-%E2%80%93-administrative-court-magdeburg-chamber-8-26-january-2016-8a-108-16

European Database of Asylum Law, Germany—administrative court of minden, 2 October 2015, Case No. 10 L 923/15.A, http://www.asylumlawdatabase.eu/en/case-law/germany-administrative-court-minden-2-october-2015-case-no-10-l-92315a

European Database of Asylum Law, Germany—administrative court (of) Hannover, Case No. 1 B 5946/15, 7 March 2016, http://www.asylumlawdatabase.eu/en/case-law/germany-administrative-court-hannover-case-no-1-b-594615-7-march-2016

European Union, Countries, https://europa.eu/european-union/about-eu/countries_en#the-28-member-countries-of-the-eu

EuroStat: Asylum and first time asylum applicants—annual aggregated data (rounded), https://ec.europa.eu/eurostat/tgm/table.do?tab=table&init=1&language=en&pcode=tps00191&plugin=1

Federal Office for Migration and Refugees, The stages of the German asylum procedure, 2/2019, https://www.bamf.de/SharedDocs/Anlagen/EN/AsylFluechtlingsschutz/Asylverfahren/das-deutsche-asylverfahren.pdf?__blob=publicationFile&v=12

Federal Office for Migration and Refugees, Entitlement to Asylum, 1 October 2016, http://www.bamf.de/EN/Fluechtlingsschutz/AblaufAsylv/Schutzformen/Asylberechtigung/asylberechtigung-node.html;jsessionid=B5FDF16C53BC807E0861D803C0F4BCED.2_cid368

Federal Office for Migration and Refugees, Procedure management and quality assurance, http://www.bamf.de/EN/Fluechtlingsschutz/VerfahrenssteuerungQualitaetssicherung/verfahrenssteuerung-node.html.

Federal Office for Migration and Refugees, Refugee protection, 1 October 2016, http://www.bamf.de/EN/Fluechtlingsschutz/AblaufAsylv/Schutzformen/Fluechtlingsschutz/fluechtlingsschutz-node.html

Federal Office for Migration and Refugees, The authority, http://www.bamf.de/EN/DasBAMF/Aufgaben/Beh%C3%B6rde/die-behoerde-node.html

Fernández Arribas G (2016) The EU-Turkey agreement: a controversial attempt at patching up a major Prob. Euro Pap 1(3):1097-1104

Finke J (2000) Granting Asylum and protection from deportation to civil war refugees under German constitutional law and the German aliens act: the judgment of the German federal constitutional court of 10 August 2000. German Yearbook Int Law 43:283–297

Fullerton M (2001) Failing the test: Germany leads Europe in dismantling refugee protection. Texas Int Law J 36:231–275 at 266

Germany H, Dublin procedure, https://handbookgermany.de/en/rights-laws/asylum/dublin-procedure.html, https://ec.europa.eu/eurostat/tgm/table.do?tab=table&init=1&language=en&pcode=tps00191&plugin=1, https://www.bundesverfassungsgericht.de/EN/Homepage/_zielgruppeneinstieg/Merkblatt/Merkblatt.html

Hoffmeister F (2006) Germany: status of European convention on human rights in domestic law. 4(4):I–CON, 722–731 at 726–727 [Hoffmeister]

Hofmann R (1996) Recent Jurisprudence of the German federal constitutional court on Asylum law, in Alfredsson G, Macalister-Smith P (eds), The living law of nations: essays on refugees, minorities, indigenous peoples and the human rights of other vulnerable groups in memory of Atle Grahl-Madsen (Germany: NP Engel Publisher)

Justice Harald Dörig (2013) Germany: the handling of leading Asylum cases by national courts. Int J Refugee Law 25(2):373–376

Lovric D (2006) A constitution friendly to international law: Germany and its Volkerrectsfreundlichkeit. Australian Yearbook Int Law 25:75–104, at 81–82

Migration and Home Affairs, Subsidiary protection, https://ec.europa.eu/home-affairs/what-we-do/networks/european_migration_network/glossary_search/subsidiary-protection_en

Peters B (2012) Germany's dialogue with Strasbourg: extrapolating the Bundesverfassungsgericht's relationship with the European court of human rights in the preventive detention decision. German Law J 13(6):758–722

Refworld (1991) Germany: act concerning the entry and residence of aliens in the territory of the federal republic (Aliens Act). https://www.refworld.org/docid/3ae6b55a0.html

Shany Y (2006) Toward a general margin of appreciation doctrine in international law? Euro J Int Law 16(5):907–940 at 927

Trines S, Lessons from Germany's refugee crisis: integration, costs, and benefits. https://wenr.wes.org/2017/05/lessons-germanys-refugee-crisis-integration-costs-benefits

UNHCR, Asylum seeking process. https://help.unhcr.org/germany/asylum-in-germany/asylum-seeking-process [UNHCR Asylum Process]

UNHCR, UNHCR guidelines on determining the best interests of the child. https://www.unhcr.org/4566b16b2.pdf

United Nations, Depositary: status of treaties – 5. protocol relating to the status of refugees. https://treaties.un.org/pages/ViewDetails.aspx?src=TREATY&mtdsg_no=V-5&chapter=5&lang=en

United Nations High Commissioner for Refugees. Convention relating to the status of refugees: Geneva, Vol. 2, 28 July 1951. http://www.unhcr.org/protection/convention/3d9abe177/reservations-declarations-1951-refugee-convention.html

United Nations High Commissioner for Refugees, States parties to the 1951 convention relating to the status of refugees and the 1967 protocol. http://www.unhcr.org/protection/basic/3b73b0d63/states-parties-1951-convention-its-1967-protocol.html

Whitney KM (1997) Does the European convention on human rights protect refugees from "safe" countries. Georgia J Int Compar Law 26:375–407

Youngs R (2002) Sourcebook on German law. Cavendish Publishing Limited, London

Chapter 7
Conclusion: Protecting *Non-Refoulement*

7.1 Introduction

This book has focused on what has been described as the 'paradox' at the heart of refugee law and policy: the disjuncture between the commitments made by EU Member States to a robust understanding of asylum rights, including *non-refoulement*, and the actual implementation of these commitments as narrowed and constrained through containment efforts.[1] This book has intentionally taken a wide lens—from the international to the domestic, from legal conceptualization to actual practice—in examining the norm of *non-refoulement*. Each chapter provided elucidation on an aspect of the understanding of *non-refoulement*.

Chapter 2 explained the origins and sources of international refugee law, including a brief history of the treaty negotiations which took place in the drafting of the 1951 Refugee Convention, resulting in the present-day Article 33(1) on *non-refoulement* protection. It explained the subsequent dual life of the *non-refoulement* norm, existing simultaneously in international refugee law and international human rights law. In refugee law, *non-refoulement* protection benefits both asylum claimants and refugees, while in human rights law, its scope is widened to include protection from torture for everyone. Under refugee law, the principle of *non-refoulement* is not guaranteed to everyone without limits. For instance, those who have been deemed to be a danger to the community of the country of refuge do not benefit from *non-refoulement* protection. However, this exception does not exist in international human rights law as the prohibition against torture protects everyone regardless of their legal or political status.

[1] Dallal Stevens and Maria O'Sullivan, 'States, the Law and Access to Refugee Protection: Concluding Reflections', in Maria O'Sullivan and Dallal Stevens (eds) *States, the Law and Access to Refugee Protection: Fortresses and Fairness* (Portland, Oregon: Hart Publishing, 2017) at 297 [Stevens].

J. Poon, *Counteracting Containment Policies in the EU*, European Union and its Neighbours in a Globalized World 31,
https://doi.org/10.1007/978-3-032-08351-7_7

Within both international refugee and human rights law, the principle applies both territorially as well as outside of the territories of a State, including over persons or areas where the State can exercise its 'effective authority and control'.

Under EU law, the principle of *non-refoulement* is found under the EU Charter, the Dublin III Regulation, as well as key directives, and largely reflects international refugee law's approach. However, with the application of ECHR law, the principle is codified under Article 3 as the prohibition against torture. This means that the law on *non-refoulement* within Europe is quite robust, reflecting the simultaneous application of both international refugee law and international human rights law approaches. That said, the actual practice with respect to this norm has been the opposite: constrained and contained. This is explored further in Chaps. 3 and 4.

Chapter 3 explained the EU law applicable to the principle of *non-refoulement*, including its multi-layered aspects. It also examined how two European courts—the ECtHR and the CJEU—have interpreted and applied the prohibition against *refoulement.* The legislative and jurisprudential picture that emerged confirmed what had been indicated in Chapter 2: that *non-refoulement* is a relatively robust norm under European law. However, this chapter also indicated that the actual practice of some EU Member States has been to adopt a narrower understanding of *non-refoulement*, one that is limited through domestic interpretation as a result of the 'margin of discretion' allowed to Member States when transposing directives, and limited through the presumption of mutual trust when transferring asylum claimants to other ('responsible') States.

Chapter 4 described the theory of containment, derived from the fields of human and spatial geography and migration studies. Containment through migration control seeks to control, divide, and discipline 'unruly' migration (as perceived by states)—that is, migration in which migrants try to manage where they seek asylum. Techniques to identify and select migrants by categorizing, partitioning, and channeling them serve as methods to dominate and constrain the 'disobedience' of migrants. While rarely applied within public international law and specifically international refugee law, the theory of containment holds particular significance as an explanatory theory for these fields. The theory suggests that policies of containment are methods used by EU Member States to circumvent their international refugee law and human rights law obligations. It also provides the underlying rationale for violations of *non-refoulement* by EU Member States. In other words, containment theory provides a rationale for the gaps between the fulsome statements of *non-refoulement* law in, for example, treaties and the actual interpretation and application of that law through policies within the EU. These gaps were illustrated through explanations of Dublin transfers, 'safe' third country agreements, the interception of asylum seekers prior to reaching Europe, migrant tracking, narrow interpretations of the Refugee Convention, and deterrence policies. The chapter concluded that, while containment may be facilitated by law, containment occurs not because of the law itself, but because of the policies and practices around the application of that law.

Chapter 5 on the United Kingdom examined the domestic law and procedures for claiming asylum in the UK, including how applicants for international protection for refugee status qualify for international protection, how their international protection is granted or withdrawn, and the points in the system during which the possibilities of *refoulement* are considered. It also explored how the principle of *non-refoulement* has been interpreted in the UK in a narrow, restrictive manner, particularly with respect to the presumption of mutual trust and the burden placed on the claimant to rebut that presumption.

Chapter 6 on Germany examined domestic German refugee law, including on non-refoulement, and the procedures for claiming asylum in Germany. German legislation appears to have a more liberal reading of *non-refoulement* than the UK, but the mixed jurisprudence suggests that the application of *non-refoulement* requires fine-tuning for a more streamlined, consistent approach to interpreting the norm. The final part of this chapter reviewed evidence of containment theory at work in Germany, including Germany's interpretation of the presumption of mutual trust in Dublin transfers.

The purpose of this chapter is to reiterate the centrality of *non-refoulement* as a cardinal principle of refugee protection, and to analyze changes that should be made within the CEAS to better conform to that principle. In other words, this chapter aims to reduce the disjuncture between the law of *non-refoulement* and the practice of that law. This discussion begins with a focus on the domestic level, comparing the UK and Germany's practices on *non-refoulement*, particularly 'safe' third country concepts and Dublin transfers. It then considers recommended changes at the regional level that would help to align the expansive norm on *non-refoulement* with the actual application of the principle at the domestic and regional levels.

7.1.1 Situating Non-Refoulement *Within the Domestic: Comparing UK and German Practices*

In order to consider improvements to the system that would better protect against *refoulement*, this section compares and contrasts the practices of the UK and Germany on the 'safe' third country concept and Dublin transfers. These practices are the focal point of this chapter because they evidence containment policies in both countries which have the potential to undermine *non-refoulement* protection when misused—and, as shown in Chaps. 5 and 6, case law has demonstrated that this has, in fact, occurred in the past. In particular, the misuse of these concepts can occur when the substance of the claimant's application is not examined prior to returning him or her back to a third country deemed 'safe'. Another way that these concepts can be misused is when an EU Member State relies upon a blanket declaration that the responsible Member State is in compliance with relevant international and European law obligations, or blanket assurances to this effect, in order to return a claimant via a Dublin transfer without an individualized assessment of whether this is correct *vis-à-vis* the claimant.

This section therefore begins by explaining how the UK and German practices on 'safe' third country concepts are similar and different. Then, it explores and compares the UK and German practices on Dublin transfers. This method of comparison between the UK and Germany on the 'safe' third country concept and Dublin transfers reveals implications for the future of *non-refoulement* in the region.

Both the UK and Germany have different domestic asylum procedures for determining whether an asylum claimant may be removed to a third country deemed 'safe' based on their legislation. For the UK, in order to initiate the 'safe' third country procedure, first the Third Country Unit of the UK Visas and Immigration division must certify that the asylum claimant came from a 'safe' third country.[2] A 'safe' third country is a country which the UK has deemed to be safe and is listed in the *Asylum and Immigration (Treatment of Claimants etc.) Act* 2004.[3] This Act lists all EU Member States (except Croatia), Norway, Iceland and Switzerland.[4] Additionally, other countries can be designated as 'safe' on a case-by-case basis, such as Canada and the United States.[5] Once the Secretary of State for the Home Department has certified that the asylum claimant has come from a 'safe' third country and that the claimant's application is therefore 'clearly unfounded',[6] the applicant may be removed to the third country deemed 'safe' unless, 'on a legitimate view of the facts, a tribunal properly directing itself could

---

[2] See, for example: *Esmaiel Mohammed Pour et al v Secretary of State for the Home Department* [2016] EWHC 401 (Admin) [Pour]; Asylum Information Database, "Safe Third Country: UK", http://www.asylumineurope.org/reports/country/united-kingdom/asylum-procedure/safe-country-concepts/safe-third-country.

[3] *Asylum and Immigration (Treatment of Claimants, etc.) Act,* 2004 c 19.

[4] *Ibid* at Schedule 3 Part 2.

[5] Asylum Information Database, "Safe Third Country: United Kingdom", https://www.asylumineurope.org/reports/country/united-kingdom/asylum-procedure/safe-country-concepts/safe-third-country.

[6] Under the procedure to determine whether an individual asylum claimant may be removed to a 'safe' country of which he or she is not a national, the Secretary of State for the Home Department must certify that such a claim is 'clearly unfounded' under paragraph 5(4) of Part 2 of Schedule 3 of the *Asylum and Immigration (Treatment of Claimants etc.) Act 2004 c 19;* In order to prove that an asylum application is 'clearly unfounded', the caseworker must be satisfied that the claim cannot, on any legitimate view, succeed: United Kingdom, Home Office, "Certification of Protection and Human Rights Claims under Section 94 of Nationality, Immigration and Asylum Act 2002 (clearly unfounded claims): Version 4.0", 12 February 2019 at 11. Under the guidance notes issued by the Secretary of State for the Home Department, caseworkers may consider that an asylum application is 'manifestly unfounded' where: the claim is so clearly without substance that it is bound to fail, and it is possible to declare an asylum application to be 'manifestly unfounded' even where 'it takes more than a cursory look at the evidence to come to a view that there is nothing of substance in it': *Ibid;* See, also: *Ex Parte Thangarasa and Ex Parte Yogathas* [2002] UKHL 36 [Ex P Thangarasa]; *ZL and VL v Secretary of State for the Home Department* [2003] EWCA Civ 25.

conclude that there were substantial grounds for believing that the return of [the claimant] to [the third country] would involve a real risk of a flagrant breach of [Article 3 of the ECHR] or a flagrant breach of other relevant rights applying [the ECtHR] jurisprudence'.[7] Where a tribunal finds that there are substantial grounds for believing that removing the claimant to a third country deemed 'safe' would expose him or her to treatment contrary to Article 3 of the ECHR, such a removal is not permitted as being contrary to the ECHR.[8] In other words, the UK's certification system acts as a double-check that claimants will be able to properly access the asylum system in the 'safe' third State.

For Germany, once an asylum claimant has applied for asylum at the border or at an international airport and it has been established that the claimant has passed through a 'safe' third country on his or her way to Germany, the claimant will be removed without any further assessment.[9] The individual's asylum application will not be considered and that individual will not be granted asylum.[10] However, exceptions to this general rule may be permitted where the claimant fits within one of three grounds: first, when the claimant has a residency permit in Germany at the time he or she entered the 'safe' third country; second, when Germany is deemed to be the responsible Member State pursuant to the Dublin III Regulation or an international treaty with the 'safe' third country; and third, when the claimant has not been refused entry or removed pursuant to a Section 18(4) No. (2) order by the Federal Ministry of the Interior on humanitarian grounds, for reasons of international law, or in the political interests of Germany.[11]

Germany's *Asylum Act* defines all EU Member States as well as non-EU countries such as Norway and Switzerland as 'safe' third countries.[12] This blanket designation means that there is no individualized evaluation to determine whether that individual will be safe upon return to those countries. This raises the risk that onward *refoulement* may occur when the individual is returned to one of these countries deemed 'safe'.[13] In this respect, the UK provides a stronger safeguard against *refoulement* through its certification process, which Germany lacks.

---

[7] *Esmaiel Mohammed Pour* at paras 26 and 169.

[8] *Ibid* at para 9.

[9] See, for example: Federal Office for Migration and Refugees, "Entitlement to Asylum", 1 October 2016, http://www.bamf.de/EN/Fluechtlingsschutz/AblaufAsylv/Schutzformen/Asylberechtigung/asylberechtigung-node.html [Entitlement to Asylum]. The 'safe' third country concept is applicable where the asylum claimant has passed through a 'safe' third country on the way to Germany, has arrived at Germany, and makes an asylum request at the border: Asylum Information Database, "Safe Third Country: Germany", http://www.asylumineurope.org/reports/country/germany/asylum-procedure/safe-country-concepts/safe-third-country.

[10] Asylum Information Database, "Safe Third Country: Germany", http://www.asylumineurope.org/reports/country/germany/asylum-procedure/safe-country-concepts/safe-third-country; *See also: Asylum Act (Federal Law Gazette, p 1798),* 2 September 2008, last amended by Article 2 of the Act of 11 March 2016 (Federal Law Gazette I, p 394) at s 26a.

[11] *Ibid* at s 26a(1).

[12] *Ibid;* Asylum Act at Annex I.

[13] *Ibid.*

Germany does have some protections, however: German law indicates that asylum claimants cannot receive protection from a third country when that country is either not listed as 'safe' third country or there is not sufficient information to determine whether it is 'safe'.[14] This means that Germany will not return claimants to third countries where there is insufficient information about the third country.

Both the UK and Germany incorporate 'safe' third country lists into their domestic legislation. These 'safe' third country lists are lists of countries which are deemed to be 'safe' under the domestic law of both the UK and Germany and, as such, are destinations predetermined to be 'safe' to which claimants may be sent to on arrival in the UK or Germany. For the UK, the determination of whether a third country is deemed to be 'safe' is based on a determination of whether that countries' domestic asylum procedures comply with the UK's criteria under Rule 345C of the *Immigration Rules*.[15] The text of Rule 345C states:

> A country is a safe third country for a particular applicant if: (i) the applicant's life and liberty will not be threatened on account of race, religion, nationality, membership of a particular social group or political opinion in that country; (ii) the principle of *non-refoulement* will be respected in that country in accordance with the Refugee Convention; (iii) the prohibition of removal, in violation of the right to freedom from torture and cruel, inhuman or degrading treatment as laid down in international law, is respected in that country; (iv) the possibility exists to request refugee status and, if found to be a refugee, to receive protection in accordance with the Refugee Convention in that country; (v) there is a sufficient degree of connection between the person seeking asylum and that country on the basis of which it would be reasonable for them to go there; and (vi) the applicant will be admitted to that country.[16]

Criterion (v) on 'sufficient degree of connection' is further defined under the *Immigration Rules*[17]: to determine whether an applicant has the requisite 'sufficient degree of connection' with the third country deemed 'safe' for removal, the Secretary of State for the Home Department must be satisfied that he or she has spent time in the third country, has relationships with citizens or habitually resident non-citizens of the third country, or has other close family ties or cultural or ethnic connections with the third country.[18] The significance of the 'sufficient degree of connection' rule cannot be understated, as, although not required under international law, without such a connection, it would become unreasonable and

---

[14] Entitlement to Asylum.

[15] United Kingdom, Home Office, "Inadmissibility: EU Grants of Asylum, First Country of Asylum and Safe Third Country Concepts: Version 2.0", 15 October 2018 at 12.

[16] *Ibid.*

[17] *Ibid* at 345D: 'In order to determine whether it is reasonable for an individual to be removed to a safe third country in accordance with paragraph 345C(v), the Secretary of State may have regard to, but is not limited to: (i) any time the applicant has spent in the third country; (ii) any relationship with persons in the third country which may include: a. nationals of the third country; b. non-citizens who are habitually resident in the third country; c. family members seeking status in the third country; (iii) family lineage, regardless of whether close family are present in the third country; or (iv) any cultural or ethnic connections'.

[18] *Ibid.*

unsustainable for a person to claim asylum in the third country.[19] The UNHCR is of the view that having a 'sufficient degree of connection' with the third country increases:

> the viability of the return or transfer from the viewpoint of both the individual and the state. As such, it reduces the risk of irregular onward movement, prevents the creation of 'orbit' situations and advances international cooperation and responsibility-sharing.[20]

The UNHCR cautions, however, that transfers to third countries should be 'aimed at enhancing burden- and responsibility-sharing and international/regional cooperation, and not be burden shifting'.[21]

For Germany, the determination of whether a third country is deemed 'safe' is based on a set of criteria established by the BverG in a 1996 landmark decision.[22] In the decision in *Case No. 2 BvR 1938/93,* the BverG held that the 'safe' third country rule in the *Basic Law* and the German domestic *Asylverfahrensgesetz* (Asylum Procedure Act) is compatible with the *Basic Law*.[23] The BverG relied upon a newly-created concept of 'normative establishment of certainty' (*normative Vergewisserung*), according to which whether a third country is deemed 'safe' is based on criteria set by legislators.[24] This presumption of 'safety' in third countries does not need to be individually rebuttable nor is it possible for claimants to challenge it.[25] This judgment is problematic: it essentially permits the return of asylum claimants to third countries even though there is no opportunity to rebut the presumption of safety or to review the grounds which determine whether a third country is 'safe'.[26] Additionally, access to asylum procedures within Germany is denied to these claimants.[27]

The practice of the UK with respect to 'safe' third countries clearly reveals two key points of divergence from the practice of Germany. First, the UK has a

[19] United Nations High Commissioner for Refugees, "Legal considerations regarding access to protection and a connection between the refugee and the third country in the context of return or transfer to safe third countries", April 2018 at para 6 [STC Legal Considerations].

[20] *Ibid;* See, also: United Nations High Commissioner for Refugees, EXCOM Conclusion No 87 (L), 1999 at para I: 'asylum seekers and refugees must be [treated] in accordance with the highest possible standards of protection'.

[21] STC Legal Considerations at para 6.

[22] 2 BvR 1938/93.

[23] "Five Case Abstracts" (1997) 9:2 *International Journal of Refugee Law* 292–307 at 293 [Five Cases].

[24] *Ibid* at 294.

[25] *Ibid;* Note that the a non-rebuttable presumption of safety for 'safe' third countries may mean that the constitutional 'right to asylum' in German law does not extend to an asylum claimant who comes to Germany through a 'safe' third country and that such a person therefore does not have access to an asylum procedure in Germany. However, after BverG's 1996 decision, the APD including its recast has come into place, meaning that Germany must aim to achieve the goals set out in the APD.

[26] 2 BvR 1938/93.

[27] Five Cases at 293–294.

certification system in place that acts as a double-check that claimants will be able to access the asylum system in the 'safe' third state, and Germany does not. Second, the UK has a cumulative list that is considered when designating countries as 'safe', which includes consideration of whether the claimant has a 'sufficient degree of connection' with the third country. Germany's blanket approach to designation precludes this consideration.[28]

While the UK's certification process provides an additional safeguard that Germany does not possess, it should be pointed out that it does not necessarily provide complete protection against *refoulement*. As noted by Foster in a compelling analysis, an evaluation of whether or not a third country is 'safe' must—under international refugee law—consider three factors. First, 'the sending state must be satisfied that the third (receiving) State has an adjudication procedure in place to assess refugee status' and that this procedure is 'adequate'.[29] The UK certification procedure considers this through application of Rule 345C(iv), set out above. Second, 'the third (receiving) state must guarantee access to that system for refugees in question: thus, for example, the sending state must ensure that refugees are not barred from the system by procedural rules or other impediments'.[30] It is not *prima facie* obvious from legislation or practice that this evaluation forms a standard part of the UK's certification process, though UK case law has considered the actual ability of claimants to access the third country's asylum system.[31] Third, 'the sending state must be satisfied that the receiving state interprets the Refugee Convention in a manner that respects the "true and autonomous meaning" of the definition in Article 1 of the Convention'.[32] This means that, if a person is likely to be recognized as a refugee in the UK but, due to significant differences in interpretation, is unlikely to be recognized as such in the third state, then 'the sending state is prohibited from transferring the applicant to the third state'.[33] This require-

[28] European Commission, "The Law and Practice on Safe Country Principles Against the Background of the Common European Asylum System and the Goal of a Common Asylum Procedure: Final Report", DG JAI-A2/2002/04 at 97, which states: 'In Germany, the criteria for a 'sufficient link' are to be found in case law: It is not necessary to prove from which particular country the applicant came from, as long as the third country is a listed country. The main criterion in this respect seems to be whether there is a reasonable opportunity to submit the case to the third country' [Law and Practice].

[29] Michelle Foster, "Responsibility Sharing or Shifting? "Safe" Third Countries and International Law" (2008) 25:2 *Refuge*, 64–78 at 70 [Foster]; Michelle Foster is a well-known refugee law scholar.

[30] *Ibid.*

[31] See, for example: *EM (Eritrea),* where the Court of Appeal stated that 'the situation in Italy is in no way comparable to that of Greece and that a general ban on returns to Italy cannot be justified'; With regards to returns to Greece and Hungary, returns under the Dublin III Regulation has been suspended as a result of the 'systemic deficiencies' in those countries, see, for example: AIDA UK Report 2019 at 34.

[32] Foster at 71.

[33] *Ibid* at 71.

ment has been recognized by UK courts as serving as part of the UK's analysis.[34] While this analysis indicates that the UK's process reflects best practices, as identified by Foster, there is an area of concern related to the UK's method of assessment. An individualized assessment of the risk of *refoulement* is required[35]—something more than an 'initial assessment'[36]—but, as described in Chap. 5, the UK asylum procedures preclude a truly individualized assessment because the 'safe' third country determination occurs *prior* to the substantive interview phase. Therefore, the UK's certification process is not based on a substantive understanding of the claimant's case.[37] As the individualized assessment does not consider enough facts, the full story has not been gathered yet from the claimant during this stage in the procedure.

There is another concern with the UK's practice: the lack of monitoring of an individual's outcome after transfer to the third state. The lack of proper post-transfer monitoring in the UK is evident in the judgment of *Ex Parte Thangarasa.* In the case, Lord Bingham of Cornhill was of the opinion that:

> the Home Secretary and the courts should not readily infer that a friendly sovereign state which is party to the Geneva Convention will not perform the obligations it has solemnly undertaken. This consideration *does not absolve the Home Secretary from his duty to inform himself of the facts and monitor the decisions made by a third country* in order to satisfy himself that the third country will not send the applicant to another country otherwise than in accordance with the convention (emphasis added).[38]

Furthermore, in *Adan and Aitsegur,* the UK Court of Appeal held that, unless the Secretary of State for the Home Department can be satisfied that 'the third country would apply the Refugee Convention's "international meaning" or "core values"

---

[34] *R. (Yogathas) v. Secretary of State for the Home Department* [2003] 1 A.C. 920 at para 9; See also: *R. (ex parte Adan) v. Secretary of State for the Home Department* [2001] 2 A.C. 477; (2001) 2 W.L.R. 143.

[35] Foster at 71–72.

[36] *Ibid* at 72.

[37] See, for example: AIDA UK Report 2019 at 17, which states: 'Potential safe third country cases are referred to the third country unit of the Home Office, which decides whether to issue a certificate initiating a return to a safe third country, including to another EU Member State in the context of the Dublin Regulation. In this case the claim is not substantively considered in the UK. This decision can only be challenged by judicial review, an application made to the Upper Tribunal, which can only be made with permission of that tribunal.10 Judicial review proceedings do not consider the merits of a decision, but only whether the decision maker has approached the matter in the correct way'.

[38] Ex P Thangarasa at para 9; Lord Bingham goes on to state that: 'the [Geneva] convention is directed to a very important but very simple and very practical end, preventing the return of applicants to places where they will or may suffer persecution. Legal niceties and refinements should not be allowed to obstruct that purpose. It can never, save in extreme circumstances, be appropriate to compare an applicant's living conditions in different countries if, in each of them, he will be safe from persecution or the risk of it'.

then he could not return asylum seekers to that country as a safe country'.[39] In contrast with the UK, in order to be eligible to be considered as a safe country on Germany's 'safe' third country list, German law requires that the country be a signatory to and have ratified the Refugee Convention and the ECHR.[40] However, it is unclear how Germany ensures that these countries considered 'safe' are in fact observing their international law obligations as required under these international instruments.[41]

The practice of the UK and Germany with respect to Dublin transfers also differs. For the UK, the procedure involves a separate consideration by the Third Country Unit, which is a unit housed within the UK Visas and Immigration division that also considers 'safe' third country procedures for claimants who have passed through a third country deemed 'safe' before entering the UK to claim asylum.[42] For Germany, the Dublin procedure is part of the admissibility assessment conducted in the regular procedure.[43]

For the UK, once the Dublin transfer case has been transferred from the National Asylum Allocation Unit to the Third Country Unit for determination, the Third Country Unit will consider whether the Secretary of State for the Home Department should decline to examine the asylum claim substantively before issuing a 'safe third country' or 'asylum' certificate under Schedule 3 of the *Asylum and Immigration (Treatment of Claimants, etc.) Act* 2004.[44] In considering whether there are any family members present in a Dublin State, the caseworkers rely on the asylum claimant to show that they have family connections in those Member States.[45]

For Germany, the Dublin procedure is part of the admissibility assessment as part of the regular procedure.[46] When an asylum claimant is apprehended at the

---

[39] *Adan and Aitsegur* [1999] 3 WLR 1569; Law and Practice, which states: 'the Secretary of State owed a duty under the then section 2(2)(c) of the AIA to examine the practice in the third country to ensure that it was consistent with the Convention's true interpretation. There was a margin of discretion by the signatory States in their application of the Refugee Convention, but a signatory had to apply the Refugee Convention, whose very purpose was to offer international protection to people falling within objectively defined classes'.

[40] Law and Practice at 99.

[41] *Ibid.*

[42] AIDA UK Report at 26; United Kingdom, Home Office, "Dublin III Regulation: Version 1.0", 2 November 2017 at 22.

[43] AIDA Country Report Germany at 29.

[44] *Asylum and Immigration (Treatment of Claimants, etc.) Act* [2004] Ch 19 at Schedule 3.

[45] The Dublin States cover 32 countries—The 'Dublin countries' are: Austria, Belgium, Bulgaria, Croatia, Cyprus, Czech Republic, Denmark, Estonia, Finland, France, Germany, Greece, Hungary, Ireland, Italy, Latvia, Lithuania, Luxembourg, Malta, Netherlands, Poland, Portugal, Romania, Slovakia, Solvenia, Spain, Sweden, UK and 4 countries 'associated' with the Dublin system: Norway, Iceland, Switzerland, and Liechtenstein in UK Visas and Immigration, "Asylum Claims and the Dublin Regulations", 29 December 2014, https://www.gov.uk/government/collections/asylum-claims-and-the-dublin-regulations.

[46] AIDA Country Report Germany at 29.

border by the border police, and where there is an indication that another Member State may be responsible for carrying out the examination of the asylum application, the border police will inform the Federal Office for Migration and Refugees (BAMF).[47] The Dublin procedure is then carried out by the BAMF, which has the power to issue a deportation order as a result of the Dublin procedure.[48] The border police is then tasked with the forcible return of the asylum claimant or have the option of requesting a detention order from a court if it is deemed that the asylum applicant is a flight risk.[49]

In comparing how Member States designate a third country as 'safe', under German law, the designation of a third country as 'safe' is done by way of a predetermined list.[50] The claimant may challenge the designation of the third country as 'safe' by taking the matter to the BverG through a constitutional challenge.[51] The designation itself is made through an Act of Parliament in accordance with Article 16a(1) of the *Basic Law*.[52] In the UK, the designation of a third country as 'safe' is only challengeable by way of judicial review under Section 80 of the *Nationality, Immigration and Asylum Act (2002)*.[53] In the UK, 'safe' third countries are designated as 'safe' countries to which asylum claimants can be returned to through the Dublin III Regulation which provides a mechanism for determining which Member State is responsible for determining the asylum application.[54] Further, a claimant can challenge the legality of the 'safe' third country transfer on the grounds of his or her individual circumstances.[55]

Table 7.1 Summarizes the similarities and differences between the 'safe' third country and Dublin transfer procedures in the UK and Germany outlined above.

The two examples above illustrate that different states—in this case, the UK and Germany—take different approaches to implementing the 'safe' third country concept and Dublin transfers, therefore creating gaps at different points of the process which raise the risk of *refoulement*, such as the lack of substantive personal

[47] *Ibid.*

[48] *Ibid.*

[49] *Ibid.*

[50] Law and Practice at 40, which states: 'EU member states are qualified by the Basic Law itself, art. 16a (2) GG. Additional safe countries are specified by an Act of Parliament in accordance with art. 16a (1) of the Basic Law (§ 26a (2) Annex I AsylVfG). These provisions aim at giving effect to standards laid down in the Geneva Convention and the ECHR'.

[51] *Basic Law* at art 93.

[52] *Ibid* at art 16a(1), which states: 'Persons persecuted on political grounds shall have the right of asylum'.

[53] Law and Practice at 76; This section of the Act has been repealed by section 33(3)(a) of the *Asylum and Immigration (Treatment of Claimant, etc.) Act 2004* where Schedule 3 maintains a list of countries known to protect refugees and to respect human rights ('safe' third country list).

[54] Law and Practice at 76.

[55] *Ibid* at 77; See, also: *Adan and Aitsegur* (i.e. 'Country X is not a safe third country because it does not interpret the 1951 Convention in an acceptable manner').

Table 7.1 Comparing United Kingdom and German Practices

	UNITED KINGDOM	GERMANY
	'Safe' Third Country Concept	
1. Competent Authority	• Third Country Unit	• BAMF
2. Certification Procedure	• 'A tribunal directing itself properly could conclude that there were substantial grounds for believing that the return of the claimant to Cyprus would involve a real risk of a breach of Article 3, or a flagrant breach of other relevant rights applying [ECtHR] jurisprudence' (*Esmaiel Mohammed Pour* et al. *v. SSHD* [2016] EWHC 401 (Admin), para 26)	• Claimants can be sent back to 'safe' third countries with neither an asylum application, nor an application for international or national protection being considered
3. 'Safe' Third Country List	• All EU Member States (except Croatia) as well as Norway, Iceland and Switzerland	• All EU Member States as well as Norway and Switzerland
	Dublin Transfer	
1. Legal Basis	• *Asylum and Immigration (Treatment of Claimants) Act* 2004	• *Asylum Act (Asylgesetz)*
2. Interview	• Yes (Art 5 Dublin III Regulation)	• Yes, but no consistent practice (Art 5 Dublin III Regulation)
3. Interview Factors	• Family details in the UK and other Dublin States • Travel routes taken on the way to UK • Previous asylum claims	• Travel routes of the claimant on the way to Germany • Existence of relatives in Germany
4. Competent Authority	• Third Country Unit	• 'Dublin division' of the BAMF
5. Certification Procedure	• 'Safe' Third Country or Asylum certificate (Schedule 3 *Asylum and Immigration (Treatment of Claimants) Act 2004)*	• Border police may initiate removal procedure immediately to a 'safe' third country if an asylum claimant is apprehended at the border without necessary documents
6. Unaccompanied Minors	• Best interests of the child considerations	• Conducted by special officers • No specific training for special officers dealing with vulnerable groups
7. Take Charge Requests	• As quickly as possible and within 3 months from the date which the application for asylum was lodged in UK	• Starts from the moment that a Member State becomes aware of an asylum claimant's intention to apply for asylum • Where the Member State fails to submit a request within the time limits defined in DRIII, this Member State becomes responsible for carrying out the procedure (CJEU, Case C-670/16, *Mengesteab*, 26 July 2017)
8. Take Back Requests	• As quickly as possible and within 2 months of receiving a fingerprint 'hit' on the Eurodac • As quickly as possible and within 3 months of the date which asylum claim was lodged in the UK	

interviews prior to the decision on transfer. As raised in previous chapters, this is an example of the exercise of the 'margin of discretion', but also of the lack of a cohesive and comprehensive approach to the practice within the EU to protecting against *refoulement*. The section considers how these gaps and differences might be remedied within countries throughout the EU (and the UK, despite its impending separation from the European asylum system).

7.1.2 The Future of Non-Refoulement *Protection in International Refugee Law*

EU Member states have codified a fulsome understanding of the principle of *non-refoulement* in regional treaty and domestic laws. At the same time, the EU is following a policy of 'extraterritorialization' as a form of containment, in its 'attempts to regulate migration flows'.[56] El-Anany has characterized EU practices in reinforcing external border controls to counteract migrant movement as 'one of the greatest exclusionary projects of today'.[57] The reliance of EU countries on migration control methods such as 'safe' third country or Dublin transfers demonstrate attempts by Member States to shift their responsibility for processing asylum applications elsewhere—outside of the EU (to, for example, Turkey), and within the EU (particularly to countries on the Mediterranean Sea boundary of the EU, such as Greece and Italy).[58] While the transfer of applicants within or outside of the EU is not in itself a violation of international law, it is a violation of international law when a Member State evades its responsibility to process asylum applications without any or with few procedural safeguards to ensure that claimants are not at risk of onward *refoulement*. These ongoing patterns of evading responsibility for processing asylum applications through reliance on 'safe' third country concepts are not only found within the EU: they can also be seen internationally, including in offshore processing practices in Australia, and in the Safe Third Country Agreement signed between Canada and the United States.[59] This is incredibly

[56] Tom de Boer and Marjoleine Zieck, "The Legal Abyss of Discretion in the Resettlement of Refugees: Cherry-Picking and the Lack of Due Process in the EU" (2020) 32:1 *International Journal of Refugee Law* 54–85 at 56 [Boer].

[57] Nadine El-Enany, 'Asylum in the Context of Immigration Control: Exclusion by Default or Design?' in Maria O'Sullivan and Dallal Stevens (eds), *States, the Law and Access to Refugee Protection: Fortresses and Fairness* (Hart Publishing, Oxford: 2017) 29 at 34.

[58] See, for example: European Council, "Statement of the EU Heads of State or Government, 07/03/2016", 8 March 2016, https://www.consilium.europa.eu/en/press/press-releases/2016/03/08/eu-turkey-meeting-statement.

[59] See, generally: Daniel Ghezelbash, *Refuge Lost: Asylum Law in an Interdependent World* (Cambridge: Cambridge University Press, 2018); Offshore processing and *non-refoulement* obligations was further explored in: Jenny Poon, "Non-Refoulement Obligations in Offshore Detention Facilities", *E-International Relations Blog,* 16 October 2018, https://www.e-ir.info/2018/10/16/non-refoulement-obligations-in-offshore-detention-facilities.

concerning: it means that there are likely asylum claimants being sent back from EU countries to persecution and torture.

This book therefore proposes four main ways to address and to counteract containment policies in order to strengthen the implementation of the *non-refoulement* norm: strengthening procedural guarantees in order to ensure access to asylum justice; reshaping the determination of mutual trust; re-evaluating the use of diplomatic assurances in transfer cases; and the implementation of periodic review coupled with a judicial review mechanism. Each proposal is explained and evaluated in turn.

7.1.2.1 Strengthening Procedural Guarantees

The first recommendation for strengthening implementation of the fulsome legal understanding of *non-refoulement* is the addition or reinforcement of procedural safeguards where they are currently limited or do not exist. The question of access to due process in this manner has 'not been sufficiently discussed in the literature', but yet is fundamental to increasing 'access to asylum justice'.[60] The procedural safeguards that require fortification are those aimed at ensuring that claimants received *individualized* attention to their specific situations and concerns at key junctures. Individualization is built into refugee status determination, which is based on assessing the *individual's* circumstance and the subjective fear faced *by the person fleeing persecution*.[61] In the *Hirsi* ECtHR judgment, Judge Albuquerque clearly and cogently articulated basic requirements of individualization in a fair asylum process:

> (1) a reasonable time-limit in which to submit the asylum application, (2) a personal interview with the asylum applicant before the decision on the application is taken, (3) the opportunity to submit evidence in support of the application and dispute evidence submitted against the application, (4) a fully reasoned written decision by an independent first-instance body, based on the asylum seeker's individual situation and not solely on a general evaluation of his or her country of origin, the asylum seeker having the right to rebut the presumption of safety of any country in his or her regard, (5) a reasonable time-limit in which to appeal against the decision and automatic suspensive effect of an appeal against the first-instance decision, (6) full and speedy judicial review of both the factual and legal grounds of the first instance decision, and (7) free legal advice and representation

---

[60] The term 'access to asylum justice' was introduced by O'Sullivan and Stephens: Maria O'Sullivan and Dallal Stevens, 'Access to Refugee Protection: Key Concepts and Contemporary Challenges' in Maria O'Sullivan and Dallal Stevens (eds), *States, the Law and Access to Refugee Protection: Fortresses and Fairness* (Hart Publishing, Oxford: 2017) 3 at 20 [O'Sullivan and Stevens, 'Access']. The lack of scholarly focus on access to due process is discussed by Dallal Stevens and Maria O'Sullivan, 'States, the Law and Access to Refugee Protection: Concluding Reflections' in Maria O'Sullivan and Dallal Stevens (eds), *States, the Law and Access to Refugee Protection: Fortresses and Fairness* (Hart Publishing, Oxford: 2017) 297 at 298 [Stevens and O'Sullivan, 'Concluding Observations'].

[61] UNHCR Handbook at para 11.

> and, if necessary, free linguistic assistance at both first and second instance, and unrestricted access to the UNCHR or any other organisation working on behalf of the UNHCR.[62]

Under Judge Albuquerque's approach, implementing individualization at various points in the asylum system—through a personal interview, the opportunity to personally respond to evidence, the receipt of a decision taking into account the claimant's personal situation, and assistance by experts—assists in preventing *refoulement*. Individualization requires States to evaluate the individual situation of the claimant at various stages in enough depth to understand the nature of the claimant's fear of return to his or her original state or to a third State. This includes informing the claimant of any adverse information.[63]

These individualized procedural safeguards must be implemented from the earliest point at which a state becomes liable for *non-refoulement*. While this would usually be at the border or when an individual applies for asylum in-country, this could be as early as at the point of interdiction of a boatload of presumptive asylum seekers at sea (before these individuals explicitly make an application for international protection).[64] At any of these points of contact, under EU law individuals must be proactively informed of the ability to submit reasons as to why they fear *refoulement* if transferred to a third country or their country of origin.[65] The problem is not the law, which *requires* an individualized procedural safeguard at the point of first contact to protect against *refoulement*. Rather, as been argued throughout this book, the problem is in the gap between the law and its implementation: as Pollet observes, 'the gap between legal safeguards in the law and the actual practice at the borders could not be greater'.[66]

---

[62] Judge Albuquerque in Hirsi ECtHR, separate opinion, at 75.

[63] O'Sullivan and Stephens, 'Access', at 25. This is part of 'procedural fairness': *ibid.*

[64] Hirsi; also Regulation (EU) No 656/2014 of the European Parliament and of the Council of 15 May 2014 establishing rules for the surveillance of the external sea borders in the context of operational cooperation coordinated by the European Agency for the Management of Operational Cooperation at the External Borders of the Member States of the European Union, at Article 4: https://eur-lex.europa.eu/legal-content/en/ALL/?uri=celex:32014R0656; and, Kris Pollet, 'Accessing Fair and Efficient Asylum Procedures in the EU: Legal Safeguards and Loopholes in the Common European Asylum System' in Maria O'Sullivan and Dallal Stevens (eds), *States, the Law and Access to Refugee Protection: Fortresses and Fairness* (Hart Publishing, Oxford: 2017) 137 at 141 [Pollet].

[65] As Pollet notes, this obligation stems from a number of sources, including Articles 3 and 13 of the ECHR, under which, 'as soon as a person comes within the jurisdiction and effective control of an EU Member State, authorities are bound by their obligation to 'proactively' ensure compliance with the principle of *non-refoulement*', Pollet at 143–144; See also *Hirsi Jamaa*: there must be a procedure made available to persons intercepted at sea under which they 'obtain sufficient information to enable them to gain effective access to the relevant procedures and to substantiate their complaints': Hirsi at para 204.

[66] Pollet, at 144.

The procedural safeguards can and should take several forms: for example, requiring that claimants have access to information on how and where to apply for international protection, including protection against *refoulement*[67]; requiring that claimants have access to information about the Member State deemed responsible in Dublin transfer cases or the third state in 'safe' third country transfers, and the ability to submit *refoulement* concerns prior to decisions on transfers[68]; and access to a quality personal interview and an accurate record of that interview.[69]

Of these procedural safeguards, access to a quality personal interview is absolutely central to an individualized process, as such an interview provides the information necessary for countries to make an informed evaluation on the risk of *refoulement*. The centrality of personal interviews to a fair asylum process is already recognized in Article 14(1) of the EU's Asylum Procedures Directive (recast): 'Before a decision is taken by the determining authority, the applicant shall be given the opportunity of a personal interview on his or her application for international protection with a person competent under national law to conduct such an interview'.[70] This requirement applies both with respect to decisions on admissibility and decisions on the substance of the claimant's application.[71] The individuals conducting the personal interviews must be properly trained and competent.[72] The interviews must be conducted by a same-sex interviewers and interpreter where possible, in a child-friendly manner, and taking into account the

[67] *Ibid* at 147–148.

[68] As Pollet notes, this means that anyone who is likely to register an asylum claim (police authorities, border guards and immigration authorities) must receive the necessary training and instructions to inform applicants of the procedural safeguards: *Pollet* at 151.

[69] Pollet at 154–158. Another procedural safeguard is access to well-researched and supported country of origin and third country information. Access to current and reliable country of origin information is important because it is used by claimants to support their individual claim of a well-founded fear of persecution under the definition of 'refugee' and any fears of *refoulement* if returned. It is also used by decision-makers to assess the credibility of the claimant's application: Pollet at 152–153. Country of origin and third country information comes from sources such as the European Asylum Support Office, UNHCR and 'relevant international human rights organizations': Asylum Procedures Directive (recast) at art 10(3)(b). Decision-makers must protect the fact that the claimant has made an asylum application, so as to ensure that agents of persecution in the country of origin do not take actions that 'would endanger the applicants' or his or her dependents' or family members' safety and physical integrity': Asylum Procedures Directive (recast) at art 30.

[70] Asylum Procedures Directive (recast) at art 14(1).

[71] Asylum Procedures Directive (recast) at arts 14(1) and 34(1), which states: 'Member States shall allow applicants to present their views with regard to the application of the grounds referred to in Article 33 in their particular circumstances before the determining authority decides on the admissibility of an application for international protection. To that end, Member States shall conduct a personal interview on the admissibility of the application'.

[72] *Ibid* at arts 4(1) and 4(3).

claimant's cultural origin, gender, sexual orientation, gender identity or vulnerabilities.[73] During the interview, the claimant must be able to clarify his or her statements, to ensure that the record is as accurate as possible, and either a transcript or a 'thorough and factual report containing all substantive elements' must be made of the personal interview.[74]

Personal interviews are clearly vitally necessary in order to properly assess a claimant's admissibility and the substance of his or her application to determine if there are *refoulement* concerns, but the Asylum Procedures Directive 2005—the version prior to the current recast version—permitted Member States to avoid personal interviews in a wide range of circumstances (including that the person was from a 'safe' country of origin or a 'safe' third country).[75] There are Member States not currently bound by the recast Asylum Procedures Directive, and there are Member States not conducting personal interviews at the admissibility or substantive decision stages, raising serious concerns about how such states could make informed decisions on the risk of *refoulement* to that individual.[76]

An example of a State not fulfilling the personal interview requirement is Germany, which lacks a consistent practice of requiring an interview with claimants identified for Dublin transfers before a removal decision is made.[77] This is despite the requirement under EU law and specifically under the Dublin III Regulation that an interview must take place prior to an applicant being subjected to a Dublin transfer.[78] As EU law provides the common minimum standards with which all EU Member States are to comply, and a 'regulation' under EU law is binding in its entirety on Member States, Germany's inconsistent practice in interviewing Dublin returnees is problematic.[79] Inconsistency in interviewing

---

[73] Asylum Procedures Directive (recast) at art 15(3)(c), which states: 'select an interpreter who is able to ensure appropriate communication between the applicant and the person who conducts the interview. The communication shall take place in the language preferred by the applicant unless there is another language which he or she understands and in which he or she is able to communicate clearly. Wherever possible, Member States shall provide an interpreter of the same sex if the applicant so requests, unless the determining authority has reasons to believe that such a request is based on grounds which are not related to difficulties on the part of the applicant to present the grounds of his or her application in a comprehensive manner'.

[74] Asylum Procedures Directive (recast) at art 17. This is important, as a number of EU Member States use small inconsistencies in these statements as a reason to deny asylum: UNHCR, 'Beyond Proof—Credibility Assessment in EU Asylum Systems (May 2013) at 164, https://www.unhcr.org/51a8a08a9.pdf.

[75] Asylum Procedures Directive 2005 at art 12(2)(c).

[76] One of the concerns expressed by the ECtHR in the *MSS* case is that Belgium did not provide any chance for claimants to explain why they should not be transferred to another EU country (where they fear *refoulement*): MSS at para 351; Asylum Information Database, 'Not There Yet: An NGO Perspective on Challenges to a Fair and Effective Common European Asylum System' (Annual Report 2012–2013) at 57–58.

[77] AIDA Country Report Germany at 31–32.

[78] Dublin III Regulation at art 5.

[79] European Union, "Regulations, Directives and other acts", 7 March 2019, https://europa.eu/european-union/eu-law/legal-acts_en.

Dublin returnees makes access to asylum justice for those who are being contemplated for return inequitable: there is individualization for some, and not for others.[80] As well, inconsistency in interviewing Dublin returnees means that some applicants are able to exercise their right to be heard while others are not, which is contrary to Article 32(2) of the Refugee Convention, regulating expulsion of claimants:

> except where compelling reasons of national security otherwise require, the refugee shall be allowed to submit evidence to clear himself, and to appeal to and be represented for the purpose before competent authority or a person or persons specially designated by the competent authority.[81]

Similarly, in making a 'take back' or 'take charge' request[82] to another EU Member State for a Dublin transfer, Germany presumes that responsibility for the applicant has already transferred and that deportation of the applicant will then occur without providing the applicant with a substantive review.[83] The lack of substantive review means that the claimant has no chance to rebut any allegations against him or her.[84] Germany is therefore an example of a state where procedural guarantees should be strengthened in order to permit greater individualization of the Dublin transfer process, so individuals identified for transfer can express any fears of either direct or indirect *refoulement* and therefore take steps to appeal the transfer.

Stevens and O'Sullivan identify two branches of access to asylum justice. The first branch is the one just discussed: providing claimants with access to quality asylum procedures,[85] including access to quality personal interviews. The second branch is providing claimants with access to territory, whether by removing unnecessary physical impediments (such as fences and interdiction at sea) or by removing unnecessary legal roadblocks.[86] The fact that the CEAS provides for certain legal impediments to access to territory has been discussed throughout this book, particularly with respect to Dublin transfers and 'safe' third country

---

[80] Access to justice means 'having a case heard in a court of law' in European Agency for Fundamental Rights, "Access to Justice", https://fra.europa.eu/en/theme/access-justice; EU Charter at art 47.

[81] Refugee Convention at art 32(2); Note that this provision is applicable in cases of expulsion of a refugee lawfully in the territory of the country of asylum.

[82] A 'take back' request refers to a request by the sending Member State to the Member State responsible to 'take back' the applicant who has withdrawn the application under examination or whose application has been rejected and who has made an application in another Member State. A 'take charge' request refers to a request by the sending Member State to the Member State responsible to 'take charge' of the applicant who has lodged an application in a different Member State, see: Dublin III Regulation at chp V.

[83] MA et al.

[84] The Refugee Convention provides that refugees must be guaranteed a right to be heard in the case of expulsions and to answer the case against him or her, see: Refugee Convention at art 32 (2).

[85] Stevens and O'Sullivan, 'Concluding Observations', at 297.

[86] *Ibid* at 297–298.

transfers. These impediments include the threshold for claimants to rebut a Dublin transfer, and the use of diplomatic assurances to facilitate 'safe' third country transfers, explored in more detail in the next subsection.

7.1.2.2 Reshaping the Presumption of Mutual Trust

Within the CEAS, the presumption of mutual trust is the presumption that EU Member States are 'safe' destinations to which claimants can return, as explained in Chap. 3. The premise underlying the presumption of mutual trust is that EU Member States all have asylum systems that are compliant with EU fundamental rights. However, as discussed in previous chapters, not all EU Member States are, in fact, compliant with EU refugee law.[87] Despite this, the courts of Member States place the onus on claimants, rather than the EU Member State wishing to transfer the claimant, to rebut the presumption of mutual trust in order to successfully challenge a Dublin transfer. This subsection discusses ways in which the presumption of mutual trust can be reshaped[88] in order to promote access to asylum justice for claimants and increased compliance with the principle of *non-refoulement* by EU Member States.

As outlined in Chap. 3, two European courts have diverged on the threshold to rebut the presumption of mutual trust. First, in 2011, the CJEU in *N.S.* held that the test for determining whether an asylum claimant has met the threshold for rebutting the presumption of mutual trust to prevent removal via Dublin transfers is demonstration of 'systemic deficiencies' in the receiving country's asylum system.[89] In the same year, the ECtHR in *M.S.S.* referred to the CJEU's judgment in *N.S.,* but instead of following the CJEU's 'systemic deficiencies' test, it established its own test of 'individual assessments'.[90] For the first test of 'systemic deficiencies', the onus is upon the asylum claimant to prove that the presumption of mutual trust can be rebutted where there are 'systemic deficiencies' in the asylum procedures and reception conditions of the Member State receiving the claimant.[91] For the second test of 'individual assessments', the ECtHR instead took the view that the particular circumstance and situation faced by the individual claimant at the moment in time when he or she is being contemplated for transfer back to the responsible Member State should be the proper test.[92] The CJEU and ECtHR have therefore established

[87] Juss has critiqued this assumption, arguing that the Dublin system is 'still anchored in the mindset of colonial Europe. It assumes that every area in Europe—from Sicily in the south to Scandinavia in the north—is a safe territory for a refugee to access protection once he or she gets there': Satvinder S. Juss, 'The Post-Colonial Refugee, Dublin II, and the end of non-refoulement' (2013) 20 *International Journal on Minority and Group Rights* at 310.

[88] Vicini argues for reshaping the presumption of mutual trust, albeit in a different way than proposed here: Vicini.

[89] NS/ME at para 86.

[90] MSS.

[91] *Ibid.*

[92] *Ibid.*

different approaches in interpreting the threshold to rebut the presumption of mutual trust in the cases of *M.S.S.* and *N.S.* The 'systemic deficiencies' test, in fact, creates a higher, more 'restrictive' threshold for a claimant to meet in order to rebut the presumption of mutual trust.[93] This is because only the 'presence of major operational problems', as opposed to individual human rights violations, can serve to rebut the presumption of mutual trust.[94] This approach was further entrenched within the CJEU in subsequent case law.[95] In contrast, the ECtHR has reconfirmed its 'individual assessments' approach in *Tarakhel.*[96]

The UN Committee Against Torture has also entered the debate, indicating that the threshold to rebut the presumption of mutual trust should be based on an individual's real risk of facing torture upon return, which aligns with the ECtHR's approach of the 'individual assessments' test.[97] The standard of protection envisioned by both the Committee Against Torture and the ECtHR entails the examination of an applicant's individual and subjective risk to torture.[98] When the applicant is able to prove, on an 'arguable case', that he or she may be subjected to a real risk of torture upon return based on 'individual risk' or 'individual assessments', the presumption that the EU Member State is in compliance with relevant international and European law is rebutted.[99]

Clearly, the test of 'systemic deficiencies' is not individualized, unlike the 'individual assessments' threshold, and has been critiqued for this reason as violating fundamental human rights and the individualization approach of the Refugee Convention. Vicini has argued that the 'individual assessments' approach is more widely protective of the principle of *non-refoulement* because the application of Article 3 of the ECHR (under which *non-refoulement* falls) is triggered in the presence of an individual risk, while the 'systemic deficiencies' approach does not automatically trigger Article 4 of the European Charter (under which *non-refoulement* also falls).[100] In other words, the ECtHR's approach to the threshold to rebut the presumption against mutual trust creates a lower test for *non-refoulement* protection, and less of a barrier for the claimant.[101] Under the 'systemic deficiencies' approach, *non-refoulement* prohibits any removal from an EU Member State to another EU Member State where there are 'systemic deficiencies' that make it

---

[93] Vicini at 57.

[94] *Ibid* at 60, interpreting para 85 of NS/ME.

[95] *Abdullahi v Bundesasylamt* [2013] CJEU at para 62, confirming that the assessment of the claimant's individual situation is not necessary or sufficient to rebut the presumption of mutual trust; and Puid [2013].

[96] Tarakhel at para 59.

[97] Administrative Court of Magdeburg, *Case No. 8 A 108/16,* 26 January 2016.

[98] *Ibid;* MSS.

[99] *Ibid.*

[100] Vicini at 65.

[101] *Ibid* at 66.

highly likely that the claimant may be exposed to inhuman or degrading treatment upon return.[102] This interpretation of the *non-refoulement* principle for claimants is narrower in scope than returns to *any territory* where 'substantial grounds for believing' that a real risk of torture would occur.[103]

Some scholars also argue that 'by requiring the standard of a "systemic deficiency" to be met, individual suffering, or local, non-institutionalized abuse of power loses its relevance'.[104] Further to the lack of clarity and consistency of the legal threshold of 'systemic deficiency', scholars have contended that, by creating a legal standard of 'systemic deficiency', 'a hierarchy of suffering [is created and only the] suffering of some asylum seekers and refugees is recognised as grievable'.[105]

This lack of consistency between the interpretations of the two regional European courts essentially forces Member States to exercise their 'margin of discretion' at the domestic level.[106] Some have selected between the two approaches, choosing the higher-threshold approach as Germany did,[107] or adopting a compromise approach, as was done in the UK.[108] Given that this margin is wide, Member States have adopted inconsistent approaches, some with weaker procedural protections, thereby increasing the possibility of *refoulement*.

---

[102] *Ibid.*

[103] This test as created by the CJEU in *Abdullahi* referring to Article 4 of the EU Charter is narrower in scope than the ECHR's Article 3 because the former refers only to removal which does not require the presence of an individual risk, see: Vicini at 64–65.

[104] Eliana Barrera and Friederike Vetter, "'Systemic Deficiency': Legal Standard Setting, Human Rights, and Its Effect on the Individual in the Common European Asylum System" *SPECTRA Journal*, https://spectrajournal.org/articles/10.21061/spectra.v2i2.210.

[105] *Ibid*; The authors go on to discuss the *E.M.* case, in which the appellants would be exposed again to their previous suffering if their grievances are not seen to be caused by 'systemic deficiencies'.

[106] For a discussion of the 'margin of discretion' or 'margin of appreciation' in international law, see generally: Yuval Shany, "Toward a General Margin of Appreciation Doctrine in International Law?" (2006) *European Journal of International Law* 907–940.

[107] The Administrative Court of Minden in Germany ruled against the test of 'individual assessments' established by the ECtHR and instead agreed with the CJEU's test of 'systemic deficiencies': Administrative Court of Minden, *Case No. 10 L 923/15.A,* 2 October 2015. Adopting the approach of the CJEU rather than the approach of the ECtHR means that the individual circumstances of the applicant is not the focal point of the requirement to rebut the presumption of mutual trust. Instead, the CJEU approach focuses on determining whether there are deficiencies, of a systemic kind, in the asylum procedures and reception conditions of the destination Member State for the applicant.

[108] The UK has combined the approach of both the CJEU and the ECtHR in the judgment of *E.M. and M.A.*: EM/MA at para 39. In that case, the UK Court of Appeal held that rebutting the presumption of mutual trust requires both an assessment of 'systemic deficiencies' and 'individual assessments': *Ibid.* While the UK approach to the threshold for rebutting the presumption of mutual trust incorporates both 'systemic deficiencies' and 'individual assessments', it is not yet a best practice as a result of the requirement to prioritize individual circumstances in refugee status decision-making: *Ibid;* See, also: UNHCR Handbook.

What is the solution for the lack of consistency regarding the threshold the claimant must meet to rebut the presumption of mutual trust? The solution is threefold. First, there should be a uniform assessment within the EU for the presumption of mutual trust—a standard which either adopts the individualized ECtHR test as more consistent with the individualized nature of refugee determination, or that harmonizes the tests established by the ECtHR and CJEU jurisprudence in a manner providing some individualization.[109] Second, the presumption of mutual trust should be reversed so that the presumption is one that is *against* its use rather than *for* its use.[110] The presumption against its use means that the Member State deemed not responsible for the processing of the asylum application will be required to actively evaluate, in its decision to send the claimant to the responsible Member State, whether that Member State is in fact in compliance with its international and European law obligations.[111] Third, the presumption of mutual trust should be a rebuttable presumption where the burden of proof must be upon the sending Member State, rather than the claimant, to discharge.[112] A corollary of this is that the sending state would have the obligation to evaluate future risks to the claimant when deciding upon transfer.[113]

While this threefold approach would radically change the current application of the presumption of mutual trust, 'shifting the burden of proof onto the national authorities [...] seems fair especially where it concerns the implementation of the Dublin system, as a decision to transfer an asylum seeker to another Member State falls completely outside the control or influence of the asylum seeker'.[114] As Brouwer argues, this approach 'seems justified to require the transferring state to substantiate that this transfer does not violate the fundamental rights of the asylum seeker' when the state, but not the claimant, may be aware of the systemic and rights-depriving problems in the asylum procedure and reception conditions in the

[109] Koen Bovend'Eerdt, "The Joined Cases *Aranyosi* and *Caldararu:* A New Limit to the Mutual Trust Presumption in the Area of Freedom, Security, and Justice?" (2016) 32:83 *Utrecht Journal of International and European Law*, 112–121 at 118.

[110] See Stefano Montaldo, "On a Collision Course! Mutual Recognition, Mutual Trust and the Protection of Fundamental Rights in the Recent Case-Law of the Court of Justice" (2016) 1 *European Papers* 3, 965–996 at 978–980.

[111] MSS at paras 352 and 358.

[112] *Ibid;* See, also: Brouwer at 142: 'As the general situation was known, the ECtHR held that 'the applicant should not be expected to bear the entire burden of proof' and a more active role of the transferring state was required: '[I]t was in fact up to the Belgian authorities (...) not merely to assume that the applicant would be treated in conformity with the Convention standards but, on the contrary, to first verify how the Greek authorities applied their legislation on asylum in practice'. Of course, the swapping of the burden of proof goes against the 'general principle underlying asylum law procedures that the primary responsibility lies with the asylum seeker to submit grounds to the effect that his or her transfer to another Member State would result in a violation of his or her rights under Article 4 of the EU Charter on Fundamental Rights': Brouwer at 143.

[113] *Ibid.*

[114] Brouwer at 143.

receiving State.[115] An alternate expression of this is that there is no 'equality of arms' between claimants and the sending state: shifting the onus to the sending state simply helps to equalize the information available, assisting in the evaluation of the *non-refoulement* concerns of the claimant and the opposing arguments of the State.

The UNHCR comes at the issue of Dublin transfers and the problems with the presumption of mutual trust in a completely different manner: it recommends that EU Member States afford asylum claimants an opportunity to choose the option of voluntary transfer to another Member State under the Dublin procedures.[116] The emphasis under this recommendation is the word 'voluntary', so that claimants would have the option of choosing whether to undertake the Dublin transfer procedures, rather than, as is currently the case under EU law, that such transfers take place involuntarily.[117] Barring this approach, however, the UNHCR recommends that the EU Member State undertaking the Dublin transfer ensure that claimants are able to contest the decision[118] and that the claimant be provided with proper legal representation pursuant to Article 13 of the ECHR on the right to effective remedy.[119] The UNHCR also recommends that EU Member States suspend transfers to other Member States which do not have proper asylum procedures in place.[120] This last recommendation has been followed in certain cases—for example, Dublin transfers to Hungary have been suspended by Member States due to worsening conditions for asylum claimants in the country and a high risk of onward *refoulement* to claimants being sent from Hungary to another country.[121]

While there are different options for reshaping the presumption of mutual trust, this book recommends the approach that best balances the human rights of asylum seekers and the duties of EU Member States (and therefore provides access to asylum justice): articulation of a uniform threshold assessing in some manner the individual situation of the claimant, a reversal of the presumption *against* its use rather than *for* its use, and placement of the burden of proof for the use of the presumption on the sending state, and not on the claimant.

---

[115] *Ibid* at 143–144.

[116] United Nations High Commissioner for Refugees, "Left in Limbo: UNHCR Study on the Implementation of the Dublin III Regulation: Recommendations", August 2017 at 9 [UNHCR Recommendations].

[117] Dublin III Regulation at chp 5.

[118] UNHCR Recommendations.

[119] *Ibid* at 9; See, also: ECHR at art 13.

[120] United Nations High Commissioner for Refugees, "The Dublin Regulation: Asylum in Europe", https://www.unhcr.org/4a9d13d59.pdf.

[121] European Council on Refugees & Exiles, "Germany follows UNHCR call for suspension of Dublin transfers to Hungary", 14 April 2017, https://www.ecre.org/germany-follows-unhcr-call-for-suspension-of-dublin-transfers-to-hungary; See, also: European Council on Refugees & Exiles, "Case Law Fact Sheet: Prevention of Dublin Transfers to Hungary", January 2016, http://statewatch.org/news/2016/jan/eu-ecre-factsheet-dublin-transfers-to-hungary-1-16.pdf.

7.1.2.3 Re-Evaluating the Use of Diplomatic Assurances to Facilitate 'Safe' Third Country and Dublin Transfers

As explained in Chap. 4, another containment method used by EU Member States to control the movement of asylum seekers is to send them back to third countries deemed 'safe' or to transfer them internally. Since the principle of *non-refoulement* does not permit individuals to be sent to countries where they are at risk of serious human right violations, EU Member States—including Germany and the UK (while it was within the EU)—have adopted the practice of relying on diplomatic assurances from third or EU countries as proof that they properly evaluated the *refoulement* risk prior to transfer. These assurances have been used to presume that the receiving country's human rights record and access to asylum procedures both comply with relevant international and European law standards. Seeking these assurances is permitted within the EU, as is using them as one mode of evaluation.[122] As explained in previous chapters, however, this presumption of compliance based on a diplomatic assertion is problematic when it does not correspond to reality and when courts take these presumptions at face value without delving deeper. According to the ECtHR jurisprudence and, in particular, in *Tarakhel,* the ECtHR's practice has been that diplomatic assurances should be obtained *before* a transfer decision is taken under the Dublin III Regulation.[123] This is so that 'the individuals concerned have the opportunity to ask for a comprehensive risk assessment, including of the assurances, by the domestic Courts under Article 3 ECHR'.[124]

International organizations and nongovernmental organizations have pressed EU Member States (and all States) to restrict their reliance on diplomatic assurances. They urge sending states to carry out a multi-faceted evaluation by taking positive steps to evaluate any potential future risks to the claimant of serious human rights violations and examining the human rights record of the receiving State before the transfer takes place.[125] When diplomatic assurances are used, these

[122] Diplomatic assurances are permitted in the CEAS and can be one piece of evidence of the situation in the third country but should not be the entirety of the evidence. However, as stated in *MSS* at para 354, diplomatic assurances are not a sufficient guarantee; See, also: European Commission, "Presentation of ECtHR case Tarakehel vs. Switzerland and the relevant legal and jurisprudential context" at slide 13, https://ec.europa.eu/transparency/regexpert/index.cfm?do=groupDetail.groupMeetingDoc&docid=13083.

[123] Tarakhel; See, also: *Abu Qatada v UK,* Application No 8139/09 (ECHR, 17 January 2012) at para 189.

[124] Fanny De Weck, *Non-Refoulement under the European Convention on Human Rights and the UN Convention Against Torture* (Leiden: Brill Nijhoff, 2017) at 183.

[125] It has been suggested that *de jure* compliance with the Refugee Convention, including being a signatory to the Refugee Convention does not in itself indicate that the third country is 'safe' for the claimant to be sent to. Further, the question of whether the same third country has ratified the Refugee Convention is an irrelevant consideration, as it is not in itself indicative of whether the provisions within the Refugee Convention have been complied with domestically, see: Michelle Foster, "Protection Elsewhere: The Legal Implications of Requiring Refugees to Seek Protection

organizations recommend that there should be a presumption *against* reliance upon these assurances.[126] The concern here is that requiring claimants to rebut a presumption *in favour of* mutual trust of those assurances would put an unnecessary (and additional) evidentiary burden on the claimants.[127] Similarly, these commentators argue that diplomatic assurances should only be used in favour of the asylum claimant so that the burden to discharge the presumption against the use of diplomatic assurances should be a burden for the receiving Member State to discharge, rather than an onus for the claimant to prove.[128] The UNHCR has reiterated that diplomatic assurances, when used:

> should not result in the denial of access to asylum procedures [. . .] Diplomatic assurances are concerned with treatment of the individual concerned in the receiving State, and thus affect the substance of the person's asylum application. They could not, therefore, give rise to a declaration of inadmissibility.[129]

Additionally, they propose that, when diplomatic assurances are relied upon, post-transfer monitoring should be in place to ensure that the receiving Member State has, in fact, complied with its relevant international and European law obligations.[130] It has been suggested that post-transfer monitoring can 'help [to] improve refugee policy in at least three ways: firstly, by enabling the provision of support to asylum seekers who are deported; secondly, by helping to identify and document where the fears of forcibly returned asylum seekers are well-founded; and thirdly,

---

in Another State" (2007) 28 *Michigan Journal of International Law* 2, 223–286 at 239 [Protection Elsewhere].

[126] See, for example: Columbia Law School Human Rights Initiative, "Promises to Keep: Diplomatic Assurances Against Torture in US Terrorism Transfers", December 2010 at 23: 'For immigration cases, establish a presumption against the resort to assurances unless there are compelling reasons for removal, e.g. the deportee poses a danger to the community'.

[127] *Ibid.*

[128] United Nations High Commissioner for Refugees, "UNHCR Note on Diplomatic Assurances and International Protection", August 2006 at para 19: 'Under the above-mentioned obligations, *the sending State has a duty to establish*, prior to implementing any removal measure, that the person whom it intends to remove from its territory or jurisdiction would not be exposed to a danger of serious human rights violations such as those mentioned above. Where the receiving State has given diplomatic assurances with regard to a particular individual, or where there are assurances in the form of clauses concerning the treatment of persons transferred under a general agreement on deportations or other forms of removal, these form part of the elements to be assessed in making this determination. Such assurances do not, however, affect the sending State's obligations under customary international law as well as international and regional human rights treaties to which it is party' (emphasis added) [Note on Diplomatic Assurances].

[129] *Ibid* at para 42.

[130] Foster at 72: 'The final point to note is that it is not sufficient for a state to rely on a written agreement, written assurances, or an initial assessment that transfer to a third country complies with the Refugee Convention. Rather the state must monitor the treatment of refugees in the receiving state to assess on an ongoing basis whether transfers can continue to be undertaken in accordance with international law'.

by providing valuable insights for Country of Origin Information reports'.[131] Further, the Human Rights Committee is of the view that: 'When a State party expels a person to another State on the basis of assurances as to that person's treatment by the receiving State, it must institute credible mechanisms for ensuring compliance by the receiving State with these assurances from the moment of expulsion'.[132]

As is evident, these organizations strongly argue that reliance upon diplomatic assurances must only be used with great caution.[133] The UNHCR has issued a note on the use of diplomatic assurances and the importance of observing the principle of *non-refoulement* during their use.[134] In that note, the UNHCR warns that the assessment in determining the weight attached to diplomatic assurances 'must be made in light of the general human rights situation in the receiving State at the relevant time'.[135] Further, the Committee Against Torture has reiterated the need to prohibit the use of diplomatic assurances 'as a loophole to undermine the principle of *non-refoulement* as set out in Article 3 of the [*Convention Against Torture*], where there are substantial grounds for believing that he/she would be in danger of being subjected to torture in that State'.[136] The Committee Against Torture has also stressed that the 'procurement of diplomatic assurances cannot be used by States to escape their absolute obligation to refrain from *non-refoulement* (*Agiza v. Sweden*)'.[137] The UN Secretary-General has also affirmed that diplomatic assurances are ''unreliable and ineffective' in the protection against torture and other ill-treatment, with post-return monitoring mechanisms doing little to mitigate the risk of torture'.[138] Further, the UN General Assembly stated that:

> States cannot resort to diplomatic assurances as a safeguard against torture and ill-treatment where there are substantial grounds for believing that a person would be in danger of being subjected to such treatment.[139]

Based on these warnings from the UNHCR, the Committee Against Torture, the UN Secretary-General and the UN General Assembly, the presumption in favour of diplomatic assurances should be removed, so that diplomatic assurances cannot be

[131] Jill Alpes, Charlotte Blondel, Nausicaa Preiss and Meritxell Sayos Monras, "Post-Deportation Risks for Failed Asylum Seekers' (2017) *Forced Migration Review* 1–3.

[132] Protection Elsewhere at 284.

[133] Note on Diplomatic Assurances.

[134] *Ibid* at 4–11.

[135] *Ibid* at para 21.

[136] CAT NR Comment at para 20.

[137] United Nations General Assembly, "Torture and other cruel, inhuman or degrading treatment or punishment: Note by the Secretary-General", 7 August 2015, UN Doc A/70/303 at para 40; Committee Against Torture, *Agiza v Sweden,* 24 May 2005, UN Doc CAT/C/34/D/233/2003.

[138] United Nations General Assembly, "Torture and other cruel, inhuman or degrading treatment or punishment: Note by the Secretary-General", 30 August 2005, UN Doc A/60/316 at para 51.

[139] United Nations General Assembly, "Resolution 60/148", 21 February 2006, UN Doc A/RES/ 60/148 at para 8.

relied upon by States Parties to the Refugee Convention as a method to approve transfers to receiving countries deemed 'safe'.

It has also been suggested by the Supreme Court of Canada in *Suresh v. Canada (Minister of Citizenship and Immigration)*, and affirmed in *India v. Badesha*, that the weight to be given to diplomatic assurances involves considering multiple factors.[140] These factors include:

> the human rights record of the government giving the assurances, the government's record in complying with its assurances, and the capacity of the government to fulfill the assurances, particularly where there is doubt about the government's ability to control its security forces.[141]

Further, the ECtHR in *Othman (Abu Qatada) v. the United Kingdom* has created a non-exhaustive list of factors for courts in different jurisdictions to consider:

> Whether the assurances are specific or are general and vague; Who has given the assurances and whether that person can bind the receiving state; If the assurances have been issued by the central government of the receiving state, whether local authorities can be expected to abide by them; Whether the assurances concern treatment which is legal or illegal in the receiving state; The length and strength of bilateral relations between the sending and receiving states, including the receiving state's record in abiding by similar assurances; Whether compliance with the assurances can be objectively verified through diplomatic or other monitoring mechanisms, including providing unfettered access to the individual's lawyers; Whether there is an effective system of protection against torture in the receiving state, including whether it is willing to cooperate with international monitoring mechanisms (including international human rights NGOs) and whether it is willing to investigate allegations of torture and to punish those responsible; and whether the individual has previously been ill-treated in the receiving state.[142]

As State practice from other countries outside of the EU has shown, diplomatic assurances should be used with caution and must involve the assessment of the situation in the receiving country.[143] This assessment requires the consideration of multiple factors—including those set out by the ECtHR and courts in Canada and India—and should be assessed on a case-by-case basis.[144] Under this approach, countries such as

---

[140] *India v Badesha* [2017] 2 SCR 127 at para 48 [Badesha].

[141] *Suresh v Canada (Minister of Citizenship and Immigration)* [2002] 1 SCR 3 at para 125 [Suresh]; It has also been argued by the Human Rights Watch that 'Diplomatic assurances, however, do nothing to mitigate that risk. As a result, relying on diplomatic assurances, an ineffective safeguard against torture, to effect such deportations in fact would place the Canadian government within the terms of the *Suresh* "exception" and would violate the absolute prohibition against torture and *refoulement*', see: Human Rights Watch, "Still at Risk: Diplomatic Assurances No Safeguard Against Torture", 15 April 2005, https://www.refworld.org/docid/42c3bd400.html.

[142] *Ibid.*

[143] See: Suresh and Badesha at footnotes 1285 and 1284 respectively.

[144] See: Suresh; Badesha at para 48: 'The reliability of diplomatic assurances depends crucially on the circumstances of the particular case'; Suresh at para 45: 'Deportation to torture, for example, requires us to consider a variety of factors, including the circumstances or conditions of the potential deportee, the danger that the deportee presents to Canadians or the country's security, and the threat of terrorism to Canada. In contexts in which the most significant considerations are

the UK and Germany should both amend their approaches to diplomatic assurances, to ensure that such assurances are not taken at face value; rather, any diplomatic assurances given by the receiving country should be thoroughly investigated and not be used as a loophole to circumvent *non-refoulement* obligations.[145]

7.1.2.4 Periodic Monitoring and Judicial Review of Transfers

The Dublin III Regulation has a built-in monitoring and evaluating mechanism. This mechanism requires the 'effective monitoring of the application of [the] Regulation [. . .] at regular intervals'.[146] What the provision does not specify is how often that monitoring and evaluation occurs, as well as what type of evaluation takes place by the European Commission.[147] Another similar provision is found under Article 46 of the Dublin III Regulation, which requires Member States to 'forward to the Commission all information appropriate for the preparation of that report'.[148] In practice, the European Commission publishes a report detailing an evaluation of the implementation of the Dublin III Regulation.[149] In these reports, the European Commission highlighted the low percentage rate (8%) of the total number of 'take back' and 'take charge' requests in physical transfers under the Dublin III Regulation.[150] That means, according to European Commission statistics, the final stage of the actual physical transfer of the individual *after* a Member State requests a 'take charge' request from the Member State responsible often does not occur as a result of non-acceptance by the Member State responsible. Other potential explanations can be partly due to delays caused by Dublin transfers or the suspensive effect of the Dublin transfer pending results of appeal.[151]

The reports were published in December 2015 and March 2016 and they reiterated the law governing EU Member States in their domestic implementation of the Dublin III Regulation rather than providing a critical evaluation of the application of

---

general ones, it is likely that the balance will be struck the same way in most cases. It would be impossible to say in advance, however, that the balance will necessarily be struck the same way in every case'.

[145] Committee Against Torture, "General Comment No. 4 (2017) on the implementation of article 3 of the Convention in the context of article 22", 9 February 2018 at para 19.

[146] Dublin III Regulation at recital para 38.

[147] *Ibid* at art 46.

[148] *Ibid.*

[149] European Commission, "Evaluation of the Dublin III Regulation: Final Report", 4 December 2015, https://ec.europa.eu/home-affairs/sites/homeaffairs/files/what-we-do/policies/asylum/examination-of-applicants/docs/evaluation_of_the_dublin_iii_regulation_en.pdf [DRIII 2015 Report]; European Commission, "Evaluation of the Implementation of the Dublin III Regulation: Final Report", 18 March 2016, https://ec.europa.eu/home-affairs/sites/homeaffairs/files/what-we-do/policies/asylum/examination-of-applicants/docs/evaluation_of_the_implementation_of_the_dublin_iii_regulation_en.pdf [DRIII 2016 Report].

[150] DRIII 2015 Report at 6.

[151] *Ibid.*

that law.[152] Thus, they do not, in actuality, provide monitoring or evaluation of how well Member States' transfers comply with CEAS law. There was also a report by the European Parliament on the "Dublin Regulation on International Protection Applications: European Implementation Assessment", which highlighted the structural deficiencies of the Dublin III Regulation.[153] These highlights were no more than a repeat of the Dublin IV Proposal language calling for stronger coherence in the implementation of the Dublin III Regulation on transfers among Member States and did not amount to monitoring or evaluation of EU countries' laws and practices, nor did they discuss potential solutions or policy recommendations. Instead, a form of monitoring and evaluation of transfers was done in reports by international organizations and nongovernmental organizations including the UNHCR.[154]

The proposal to reform the Dublin III Regulation, termed the Dublin IV Proposal, has also specified a monitoring requirement which states: 'on an annual basis Member States will report on the implementation of the multiannual programme' and they must 'set up a Monitoring Committee to which the Commission may participate in advisory capacity'.[155] This monitoring requirement pertains to the implementation of the Dublin Regulation as a whole in the Member State rather than a monitoring and evaluation tool to specifically observe the conduct of Member States during transfer or post-transfer of claimants. Thus, it is unclear how much attention this monitoring mechanism, once implemented, will pay to Dublin and 'safe' third country transfers.

The UNHCR has recommended that States adopt a 'variety of measures which have proven effective in preventing unlawful or irregular removal of refugees and asylum-seekers'.[156] These measures include: 'establishing a monitoring and

[152] *Ibid;* According to the Europe External Policy Advisors, the European Commission highlighted the shortcomings of the Dublin Regulation through three studies—2015, 2016, and a 2018 study that has yet to be produced: 'The European Commission published one study on the evaluation of the Regulation in 2015 and another on its implementation by member states in 2016. The next evaluation of the Dublin Regulation was planned in 2018 but has not yet been produced. In addition to the official Commission evaluations, a number of other actors, such as the European Parliament, have published studies about the Regulation. The European Implementation Assessment is the most recent of such studies. Since the evaluation in 2015 until now, weaknesses were described within the Dublin Regulation; recent evaluations show that rather than improving, these weaknesses have increased'.

[153] European Parliament, "Dublin Regulation on International Protection Applications: European Implementation Assessment", February 2020, https://www.europarl.europa.eu/RegData/etudes/STUD/2020/642813/EPRS_STU(2020)642813_EN.pdf.

[154] United Nations High Commissioner for Refugees, "Left In Limbo: UNHCR Study on the Implementation of The Dublin III Regulation: Executive Summary", https://www.refworld.org/docid/59d5dd1a4.html; Asylum Information Database, "The Implementation of the Dublin III Regulation 2018", March 2019, http://www.asylumineurope.org/sites/default/files/aida_2018update_dublin.pdf.

[155] Dublin IV Proposal at 101.

[156] United Nations High Commissioner for Refugees, "Guidance Note on Safeguards Against Unlawful or Irregular Removal of Refugees and Asylum-Seekers", https://www.refworld.org/pdfid/530afbd84.pdf at para 6.

reporting mechanism, and conducting regular checks [. . .] to monitor the safety and well-being of the individuals concerned, and responding to any threats identified'.[157] These monitoring mechanisms can include the involvement of independent and impartial international and nongovernmental organizations to periodically evaluate the relevant Member States' removal record—to ensure that *non-refoulement* obligations are complied with in each case.[158] Further, monitoring mechanisms can include not only a stronger role from both international organizations and civil society to participate in Member State monitoring but also the involvement of governments from each Member State in consultation with each other on best practices.[159]

Problematic application of Dublin transfers and 'safe' third country agreements as containment policies can be counteracted by coupling the existing law (the Dublin III Regulation and its domestic implementation) with regular and focused review that goes beyond the Commission's reporting. In particular, the creation of a periodic monitoring mechanism for the CEAS focused specifically on Dublin and 'safe' third country transfers would permit rights-violating patterns and practices within EU Member States to be highlighted and corrected, thereby leading to more consistency within CEAS processes. Such monitoring reports could also be valuable to those carrying out the certification process within the UK 'safe' third country evaluations.

A domestic judicial review mechanism focused directly on Dublin and 'safe' third country transfers could serve as an important second and complementary form of monitoring, providing individual asylum seekers the chance to challenge these transfers, including the chance to raise arguments regarding the implementation of *non-refoulement* protections. This would help to correct the problems that exist in a number of domestic EU systems, such as in Germany, in which truly individualized assessments in the form set out above are not currently available. The subject-matter expertise that is available at a specialized tribunal may offer insights and critiques that a general court does not and cannot provide. This can potentially lead to faster and more informed decisions for procedures related to asylum claims and related adjudication. The establishment of an office or an appeals tribunal similar to the International Protection Appeals Tribunal in Ireland, which reviews Ireland's decisions on the Dublin System, might provide a good exemplar for such a domestic mechanism.[160] This Tribunal can serve as a role model for other Member States because, similar to the Immigration and Refugee Board of Canada, the International Protection Appeals Tribunal in

---

157 *Ibid* at para 6(vi).

158 See, for example: Michelle Foster, "Responsibility Sharing of Shifting? "Safe" Third Countries and International Law", 25(2) *Refuge* 64–78 at 70.

159 See, for example: *R (Yogathas) v Secretary of State for the Home Department* [2003] 1 AC 920 at para 9.

160 International Protection Appeals Tribunal, Ireland, "About Us", http://www.protectionappeals.ie/website/rat/ratweb.nsf/page/about_the_tribunal-en.

Ireland issues Chairperson's guidelines to assist members in interpreting asylum law, including with respect to issues of relevance to *non-refoulement* and transfers.[161] For example, the guidance on taking evidence indicates practices to ensure the fulsome capturing of an individual's information, which assists in individualization, discussed above.[162] These guidelines can serve to enhance procedural safeguards for claimants as they provide much needed direction for asylum officers.

As considered by the European Policy Centre, the lack of monitoring mechanisms in place is detrimental to claimants who are being contemplated for return either through a 'safe' third country agreement or through Dublin transfers. Potential benefits of monitoring mechanisms for returnees include providing information for Member States to correct any action or inaction leading to a heightened risk of *refoulement*, the possibility of incorporating *non-refoulement* safeguards in current or future third country partnership agreements, and future evaluation of return procedures for claimants.[163]

A supranational judicial review mechanism within one of the regional European courts might be a viable addition or alternative to the domestic mechanism proposed immediately above. It could allow asylum claimants who have been ordered to be removed to be able to seek judicial review of the transfer decision of the government. While currently the ECtHR does offer an avenue for asylum claimants to bring their cases forward, a sub-committee or a tribunal with specialization on removal orders and expertise in *non-refoulement* protection could significantly add to the strength of the process and counteract containment policies.

In sum, the four proposals for strengthening access to justice set out in this section aim to address and counteract containment policies in order to strengthen the implementation of the *non-refoulement* norm. The proposals are mutually reinforcing, in that strengthened procedural guarantees (through individualization) to ensure access to asylum justice can also be backstopped by the implementation of periodic review and judicial review on Dublin and 'safe' third country transfers. Similarly, reshaping the determination of mutual trust involves a re-evaluation of the use of diplomatic assurances in transfer cases.

---

[161] International Protection Appeals Tribunal, Ireland, "Publications", http://www.protectionappeals.ie/website/rat/ratweb.nsf/page/Publications-en.

[162] See, for example: The International Protection Appeals Tribunal, "Chairperson's Guideline No. 2019/1 on Taking Evidence from Appellants and Other Witnesses", http://www.protectionappeals.ie/website/rat/ratweb.nsf/page/MXKY-B9KK4514334220-en/$File/Guideline%202019-1%20on%20Taking%20Evidence%20from%20Appellants%20and%20Other%20Witnesses.pdf and "Chairperson's Guideline No: 2018/1: Application of 'Compelling Reasons' in the consideration of refugee status appeals originally submitted to the Tribunal pursuant to s.16(1) of the Refugee Act 1996, prior to the commencement of the International Protection Act 2015", http://www.protectionappeals.ie/website/rat/ratweb.nsf/page/MJOF-AXAA8J7595728-en/$File/IP%20Guideline%202018-1%20on%20Compelling%20Grounds.pdf.

[163] Olivia Sundberg Diez, "Diminishing safeguards, increasing returns: Non-refoulement gaps in the EU return and readmission system", 4 October 2019 at 14.

7.1.3 *Conclusion: Future Directions for* Non-Refoulement

'The drive for detailed common standards of the CEAS has not prevented the simultaneous drive by states to restrict asylum' through legal, administrative and political measures.[164] in fact, these methods to contain the 'unwanted' have become a globalized trend.[165] The EU's containment policies as demonstrated in the CEAS and State practices of both the UK and Germany show that the principle of *non-refoulement* is at risk of—and is—being eroded. When the cornerstone of refugee protection is no longer safeguarded, the human rights of those who benefit from this principle—asylum claimants and refugees under refugee law, and everyone under human rights law—are jeopardized.

As international law sets the standard upon which regional asylum systems, including the CEAS, carry out important safeguards for asylum claimants and refugees, these standards must be complied with and interpreted in a manner that continues to protect the integrity of the institution of asylum, particularly the cardinal principle of *non-refoulement*. To counteract measures of containment, the incorporation of additional procedural safeguards, a reshaped approach to the presumption of mutual trust, a re-evaluated approach to diplomatic assurances and periodic monitoring plus judicial review mechanisms will enhance *non-refoulement* protection for claimants. These recommendations require Member States to take active steps to provide access to individualized asylum justice and to seriously consider multiple factors before issuing transfer decisions.

Much more work needs to be done in order to improve the CEAS, including harmonizing common European standards on asylum procedures and enhancing efficiency in the processing of asylum applications. While there is no overnight solution to ongoing problems of the CEAS, the human rights of asylum claimants and refugees need to be at the forefront of the agenda for each EU Member State. The work that must be done requires the cooperation of all countries including Member States, governments, civil society, international organizations, as well as

---

[164] Stevens and O'Sullivan at 302.

[165] See, for example: "EU laws designed to deter refugees", *The New Humanitarian,* 27 January 2016, http://www.thenewhumanitarian.org/news/2016/01/27/eu-laws-designed-deter-refugees; On the Canada-United States Safe Third Country Agreement, see: The Washington Post, "Canadian court says sending asylum seekers back to U.S. violates their rights", 22 July 2020, https://www.washingtonpost.com/world/the_americas/canadian-court-says-border-agreement-with-us-violates-asylum-seekers-rights/2020/07/22/a8b3e908-cc3a-11ea-91f1-28aca4d833a0_story.html; The Conversation, "Canadian court correctly finds the U.S. is unsafe for refugees", 24 July 2020, https://theconversation.com/canadian-court-correctly-finds-the-u-s-is-unsafe-for-refugees-143239; Global News, "Federal Court rules Canada-U.S. Safe Third Country Agreement unconstitutional", 22 July 2020, https://globalnews.ca/news/7205230/federal-court-rules-canada-u-s-safe-third-country-agreement-unconstitutional; On Australia's offshore processing practices, see: Camilia Ioli, "Australia's Offshore Processing System: An Exemplar for the EU?", January 2018, https://www.asyluminsight.com/c-camilla-ioli#.XyQiGzV7mUk; Madeline Gleeson, *Offshore: Behind the wire on Manus and Nauru* (Australia: NewSouth Publishing, 2016).

private actors. Now more than ever, the principle of *non-refoulement* must be safeguarded against erosion and the rights of asylum claimants and refugees championed above State interests.

References

Alpes J, Blondel C, Preiss N, Monras MS (2017) Post-deportation risks for failed asylum seekers. Forced Migration Rev 1–3

Asylum Information Database (2019) The Implementation of the Dublin III Regulation 2018. http://www.asylumineurope.org/sites/default/files/aida_2018update_dublin.pdf

Asylum Information Database, Not there yet: an NGO perspective on challenges to a fair and effective common European asylum system. (Annual Report 2012–2013) at 57–58

Asylum Information Database, Safe third country: Germany. http://www.asylumineurope.org/reports/country/germany/asylum-procedure/safe-country-concepts/safe-third-country

Asylum Information Database, Safe third country: United Kingdom. https://www.asylumineurope.org/reports/country/united-kingdom/asylum-procedure/safe-country-concepts/safe-third-country

Barrera E, Vetter F 'Systemic deficiency': legal standard setting, human rights, and its effect on the individual in the common European asylum system. SPECTRA J https://spectrajournal.org/articles/10.21061/spectra.v2i2.210

Bovend'Eerdt K (2016) The joined cases aranyosi and caldararu: a new limit to the mutual trust presumption in the area of freedom, security, and justice? Utrecht J Int Eur Law 32(83): 112–121

Committee Against Torture (2005) Agiza v Sweden. UN Doc CAT/C/34/D/233/2003

Camilia Ioli (2018) Australia's offshore processing system: an exemplar for the EU? https://www.asyluminsight.com/c-camilla-ioli#.XyQiGzV7mUk

Columbia Law School Human Rights Initiative (2010) Promises to keep: diplomatic assurances against torture in US terrorism transfers

Committee Against Torture (2018) General Comment No. 4 (2017) on the implementation of article 3 of the Convention in the context of article 22

de Boer T, Zieck M (2020) The legal abyss of discretion in the resettlement of Refugees: cherry-picking and the lack of due process in the EU. Int J Refug Law 32(1):54–85

De Weck F (2017) Non-refoulement under the European Convention on Human Rights and the UN Convention Against Torture. Brill Nijhoff, Leiden

Diez OS, (2019) Diminishing safeguards, increasing returns: non-refoulement gaps in the EU return and readmission system

El-Enany N (2017) Asylum in the context of immigration control: exclusion by default or design? In: O'Sullivan M, Stevens D (eds) States, the law and access to refugee protection: fortresses and fairness. Hart Publishing, Oxford, p 29

EU laws designed to deter refugees (2016) The new humanitarian. http://www.thenewhumanitarian.org/news/2016/01/27/eu-laws-designed-deter-refugees

European Agency for Fundamental Rights, Access to justice. https://fra.europa.eu/en/theme/access-justice

European Commission (2015) Evaluation of the Dublin III Regulation: final report. https://ec.europa.eu/home-affairs/sites/homeaffairs/files/what-we-do/policies/asylum/examination-of-applicants/docs/evaluation_of_the_dublin_iii_regulation_en.pdf

European Commission (2016) Evaluation of the Implementation of the Dublin III Regulation: final report. https://ec.europa.eu/home-affairs/sites/homeaffairs/files/what-we-do/policies/asylum/examination-of-applicants/docs/evaluation_of_the_implementation_of_the_dublin_iii_regulation_en.pdf

European Commission, Presentation of ECtHR case Tarakehel vs. Switzerland and the relevant legal and jurisprudential context at slide 13. https://ec.europa.eu/transparency/regexpert/index.cfm?do=groupDetail.groupMeetingDoc&docid=13083
European Commission, The law and practice on safe country principles against the background of the common European asylum system and the goal of a common asylum procedure: final report. DG JAI-A2/2002/04
European Council (2016) Statement of the EU heads of state or government, 07/03/2016. https://www.consilium.europa.eu/en/press/press-releases/2016/03/08/eu-turkey-meeting-statement
European Council on Refugees & Exiles (2016) Case law fact sheet: prevention of Dublin transfers to Hungary. http://statewatch.org/news/2016/jan/eu-ecre-factsheet-dublin-transfers-to-hungary-1-16.pdf
European Council on Refugees & Exiles (2017) Germany follows UNHCR call for suspension of Dublin transfers to Hungary. https://www.ecre.org/germany-follows-unhcr-call-for-suspension-of-dublin-transfers-to-hungary
European Parliament (2020) Dublin Regulation on international protection applications: European implementation assessment. https://www.europarl.europa.eu/RegData/etudes/STUD/2020/642813/EPRS_STU(2020)642813_EN.pdf
European Union (2019) Regulations, directives and other acts. https://europa.eu/european-union/eu-law/legal-acts_en
Federal Office for Migration and Refugees (2016) Entitlement to asylum. http://www.bamf.de/EN/Fluechtlingsschutz/AblaufAsylv/Schutzformen/Asylberechtigung/asylberechtigung-node.html
Foster M (2007) Protection elsewhere: the legal implications of requiring refugees to seek protection in another state. Mich J Int Law 28(2):223–286
Foster M (2008) Responsibility sharing or shifting? "Safe" third countries and international law. Refuge 25(2):64–78
Foster M, Responsibility sharing of shifting? "Safe" third countries and international law. Refuge 25(2) 64–78
Ghezelbash D (2018) Refuge lost: asylum law in an interdependent world. Cambridge University Press, Cambridge
Gleeson M (2016) Offshore: behind the wire on Manus and Nauru. NewSouth Publishing, Australia
Global News (2020) Federal Court rules Canada-U.S. Safe Third Country Agreement unconstitutional. https://globalnews.ca/news/7205230/federal-court-rules-canada-u-s-safe-third-country-agreement-unconstitutional
Human Rights Watch (2005) Still at risk: diplomatic assurances no safeguard against torture. https://www.refworld.org/docid/42c3bd400.html
International protection appeals tribunal, Ireland, About us. http://www.protectionappeals.ie/website/rat/ratweb.nsf/page/about_the_tribunal-en
International protection appeals tribunal, Ireland, Publications. http://www.protectionappeals.ie/website/rat/ratweb.nsf/page/Publications-en
Juss SS, (2013) The post-colonial refugee, Dublin II, and the end of non-refoulement. 20 International Journal on Minority and Group Rights at 310
Montaldo S (2016) On a collision course! mutual recognition, mutual trust and the protection of fundamental rights in the recent case-law of the court of justice. Eur Papers 1(3):965–996. at 978–980
O'Sullivan M, Stevens D (2017) Access to refugee protection: key concepts and contemporary challenges. In: O'Sullivan M, Stevens D (eds) States, the law and access to refugee protection: fortresses and fairness. Hart Publishing, Oxford, p 3
Pollet K (2017) Accessing fair and efficient asylum procedures in the EU: legal safeguards and loopholes in the common european asylum system. In: O'Sullivan M, Stevens D (eds) States, the law and access to refugee protection: fortresses and fairness Hart Publishing. Oxford, p 137

Poon J (2018) Non-refoulement obligations in offshore detention facilities, E-International Relations Blog. https://www.e-ir.info/2018/10/16/non-refoulement-obligations-in-offshore-detention-facilities
Shany Y (2006) Toward a general margin of appreciation doctrine in international law? Eur J Int Law 907–940
Stevens D, O'Sullivan M (2017) States, the law and access to refugee protection: concluding reflections. In: O'Sullivan M, Stevens D (eds) States, the law and access to refugee protection: fortresses and fairness. Hart Publishing, 297 Portland, Oregon Stevens
Stevens D, O'Sullivan M (2017) States, the law and access to refugee protection: concluding reflections. In: O'Sullivan M, Stevens D (eds) States, the law and access to refugee protection: fortresses and fairness. Hart Publishing. Oxford, p 297
The Conversation (2020) Canadian court correctly finds the U.S. is unsafe for refugees. https://theconversation.com/canadian-court-correctly-finds-the-u-s-is-unsafe-for-refugees-143239
The International Protection Appeals Tribunal, Chairperson's guideline no: 2018/1: application of 'compelling reasons' in the consideration of refugee status appeals originally submitted to the Tribunal pursuant to s.16(1) of the Refugee Act 1996, prior to the commencement of the International Protection Act 2015. http://www.protectionappeals.ie/website/rat/ratweb.nsf/page/MJOF-AXAA8J7595728-en/$File/IP%20Guideline%202018-1%20on%20Compelling%20Grounds.pdf
The International Protection Appeals Tribunal, Chairperson's guideline no. 2019/1 on taking evidence from appellants and other witnesses. http://www.protectionappeals.ie/website/rat/ratweb.nsf/page/MXKY-B9KK4514334220-en/$File/Guideline%202019-1%20on%20Taking%20Evidence%20from%20Appellants%20and%20Other%20Witnesses.pdf
The Washington Post (2020) Canadian court says sending asylum seekers back to U.S. violates their rights. https://www.washingtonpost.com/world/the_americas/canadian-court-says-border-agreement-with-us-violates-asylum-seekers-rights/2020/07/22/a8b3e908-cc3a-11ea-91f1-28aca4d833a0_story.html
UK Visas and Immigration (2014) Asylum claims and the Dublin Regulations. https://www.gov.uk/government/collections/asylum-claims-and-the-dublin-regulations
UNHCR (1999) EXCOM conclusion No 87 (L)
UNHCR (2006) UNHCR note on diplomatic assurances and international protection
UNHCR (2017) Left in limbo: UNHCR study on the implementation of the Dublin III Regulation: recommendations
UNHCR (2018) Legal considerations regarding access to protection and a connection between the refugee and the third country in the context of return or transfer to safe third countries
UNHCR, 'Beyond proof – credibility assessment in eu asylum systems (May 2013) at 164 https://www.unhcr.org/51a8a08a9.pdf
UNHCR, Guidance note on safeguards against unlawful or irregular removal of refugees and asylum-seekers. https://www.refworld.org/pdfid/530afbd84.pdf
UNHCR, Left in limbo: UNHCR study on the implementation of The Dublin III Regulation: executive Summary. https://www.refworld.org/docid/59d5dd1a4.html
UNHCR, The Dublin Regulation: asylum in Europe, https://www.unhcr.org/4a9d13d59.pdf
United Kingdom, Home Office (2017) Dublin III Regulation: version 1.0
United Kingdom, Home Office (2018) Inadmissibility: EU grants of asylum, first country of asylum and safe third country concepts: version 2.0
United Nations General Assembly (2005) Torture and other cruel, inhuman or degrading treatment or punishment: note by the Secretary-General. UN Doc A/60/316
United Nations General Assembly (2006) Resolution 60/148. UN Doc A/RES/60/148
United Nations General Assembly (2015) Torture and other cruel, inhuman or degrading treatment or punishment: note by the Secretary-General. UN Doc A/70/303

Appendix: Bibliography

A.1 Treaties and International Conventions

A.1.1 UN Treaties

Convention Against Torture and Other Cruel, Inhuman or Degrading Treatment or Punishment 1465 UNTS 85 (adopted 10 December 1984, entered into force 26 June 1987).

Convention on the Rights of the Child 1577 UNTS 3 (adopted 20 November 1989, entered into force 2 September 1990).

Charter of the United Nations 1 UNTS XVI, 24 October 1945.

Convention Relating to the International Status of Refugees, CLIX LNTS 3663, 28 October 1933.

Convention Relating to the Status of Refugees, 189 UNTS 137 (adopted 28 July 1951, entered into force 22 April 1954).

Geneva Convention Relative to the Protection of Civilian Persons in Time of War (Geneva Convention IV) 75 UNTS 287 (adopted 12 August 1949, entered into force 21 October 1950).

Inter-American Convention on Extradition (adopted 25 February 1981, entered into force 28 March 1992).

J. Poon, *Counteracting Containment Policies in the EU*, European Union and its Neighbours in a Globalized World 31,
https://doi.org/10.1007/978-3-032-08351-7

International Convention on the Elimination of All Forms of Racial Discrimination 660 UNTS 195 (adopted 21 December 1965, entered into force 4 January 1969).

International Covenant on Civil and Political Rights 999 UNTS 171 (adopted 16 December 1966, entered into force 23 March 1976).

Protocol Relating to the Status of Refugees, 606 UNTS 267 (adopted 31 January 1967, entered into force 4 October 1967).

Statue of the International Court of Justice, 18 April 1946.

United Nations Declaration on Principles of International Law concerning Friendly Relations and Cooperation among States in Accordance with the Charter of the United Nations, annexed to UNGA res 2625(XXV), 24 October 1970.

United Nations Declaration on Territorial Asylum UNTS 189, UN Doc A/RES/2312(XXII), 14 December 1967.

Universal Declaration of Human Rights, 10 December 1948, 217 A(III).

Vienna Convention on the Law of Treaties, 1155 UNTS 331 (adopted 23 May 1969, entered into force 27 January 1980).

A.1.2 European Primary Legislation

Charter of Fundamental Rights of the European Union, 26 October 2012, 2012/C326/02.

Convention implementing the Schengen Agreement of 14 June 1985 between the Governments of States of the Benelux Economic Union, the Federal Republic of Germany and the French Republic on the gradual abolition of checks at their common borders, OJ 2000 L249/19.

European Convention for the Protection of Human Rights and Fundamental Freedoms, as amended by Protocols 11 and 14 (adopted 4 November 1950, entered into force 3 September 1953), ETS 5.

European Convention on Extradition ETS 24 (adopted 13 December 1957, entered into force 18 April 1960).

Protocol on the Position of the United Kingdom and Ireland in Respect of the Area of Freedom, Security and Justice.

Treaty of Amsterdam Amending the Treaty on European Union, The Treaties Establishing the European Communities and Related Acts OJ C340/1, 10 November 1997.

Treaty of Lisbon Amending the Treaty on European Union and the Treaty Establishing the European Community, Treaty of Lisbon, 13 December 2007, 2007 C306/01.

Treaty on European Union (Consolidated Version), Treaty of Maastricht, 7 February 1992, OJ C325/5, 24 December 2002.

Treaty on European Union (Consolidated Version), Treaty of Amsterdam (adopted 2 October 1997, entered into force 1 May 1999).

Treaty on the Functioning of the European Union (Consolidated Version), 26 October 2012, OJ L326/47-326/390.

A.1.3 European Secondary Legislation

Convention determining the State responsible for examining applications for asylum lodged in one of the Member States of the European Communities, *Official Journal of the European Union,* 19 August 1997, No C254/1.

Convention implementing the Schengen Agreement of 14 June 1985 between the Governments of States of the Benelux Economic Union, the Federal Republic of Germany and the French Republic on the gradual abolition of checks at their common borders, OJ 2000 L249/19.

Council Directive 2001/55/EC of 20 July 2001 on minimum standards for giving temporary protection in the event of a mass influx of displaced persons and on measures promoting a balance of efforts between Member States in receiving such persons and bearing the consequences thereof, OJ L212/12, 7 August 2001.

Council Directive 2003/86/EC of 22 September 2003 on the right to family reunification, OJ L251/12, 3 October 2003.

Council Directive 2011/95/EU of the European Parliament and of the Council of 13 December 2011 on standards for the qualification of third-country nationals or stateless persons as beneficiaries of international protection, for a uniform status for refugees or for persons eligible for subsidiary protection, and for the content of the protection granted (recast) (2011) OJ L337/9.

Council Directive 2013/32/EU of the European Parliament and of the Council of 26 June 2013 on common procedures for granting and withdrawing international protection (recast), OJ L180/60, 29 June 2013.

Council Directive 2013/33/EU of the European Parliament and of the Council of 26 June 2013 laying down standards for the reception of applicants for international protection (recast), OJ L180/96, 29 June 2013.

Council Regulation (EC) No 343/2003 of 18 February 2003 establishing the criteria and mechanisms for determining the Member State responsible for examining an asylum application lodged in one of the Member States by a third-country national, *Official Journal of the European Union,* 25 February 2003, L50/1.

Council Regulation (EC) No 604/2013 of the European Parliament and of the Council of 26 June 2013 establishing the criteria and mechanisms for determining the Member State responsible for examining an application for international protection lodged in one of the Member States by a third-country national or a stateless person (recast).

Council Regulation (EU) No 656/2014 of the European Parliament and of the Council of 15 May 2014 establishing rules for the surveillance of the external sea borders in the context of operational cooperation coordinated by the European Agency for the Management of Operational Cooperation at the External Borders of the Member States of the European Union.

A.1.4 UK Legislation

Asylum and immigration (Treatment of Claimants, etc.) Act [2004] c. 19.

Immigration Act [1971] c. 77.

Immigration and Asylum Act [1999] c. 33.

Nationality, Immigration and Asylum Act [2002] c. 41.

Refugee or Person in Need of International Protection (Qualification) Regulations [2006].

A.1.5 German Legislation

Act Concerning the Entry and Residence of Aliens in the Territory of the Federal Republic (English Translation), 1 January 1991, as amended.

Asylum Act of Germany, 2 September 2008 (Federal Law Gazette I, p 1798), last amended by art 2 of Act 11 March 2016 (Federal Law Gazette I, p 394).

Asylum Procedure Act (Asylverfahrensgesetz, AsylVfG), 2 September 2008, Federal Law Gazette I, 1798, as amended.

Ausltindergesetz § 51, v. 9.7.1990 (BGB1. I S.1354, 1356), zuletzt geandert durch Art. 3 Geetz, v,15.07.93 (BGB1. H S.1010).

Baden-Württemberg State Administrative Procedure Act (Verwaltungsverfahrensgesetz, VwVfG), 25 May 1976, Federal Law Gazette I, 102, as amended.

Basic Law for the Federal Republic of Germany, last amended 23 December 2014.

Convention for the Protection of Human Rights and Basic Liberties, 7 August 1952, BGBl.II.

Convention on the Protection of Human Rights and Fundamental Freedoms, 4 November 1950 (BGBl. 1952 II, p. 686).

A.2 Jurisprudence

A.2.1 International Court of Justice

Advisory Opinion on the Legality of the Threat or Use of Nuclear Weapons, 8 July 1996.

Case Concerning Armed Activities on the Territory of the Congo (Democratic Republic of the Congo v. Uganda), Judgment of 19 December 2005.

Consequences of the Construction of a Wall in the Occupied Palestinian Territory, Advisory Opinion, ICJ Gen List No 131, 9 July 2004.

Legal Consequences of the Construction of a Wall in the Occupied Palestinian Territory, Advisory Opinion, ICJ Gen List No 131, 9 July 2004.

Legality of the Threat or Use of Nuclear Weapons (Advisory Opinion) [1996] ICJ Rep 226.

North Sea Continental Shelf Cases (Federal Republic of Germany v Denmark; Federal Republic of Germany v Netherlands), 20 February 1969, ICJ Rep 3.

A.2.2 European Court of Human Rights

A. and Others v. the United Kingdom, Application No 3455/05, (ECHR, 19 February 2009).

A.B. v. France, App No 11,593/12 (ECHR, 12 July 2016).

Abu Qatada v. the United Kingdom, Application No 8139/09 (ECHR, 17 January 2012).

Ahmed v. Austria, App No 25,964/94 (ECHR, 17 December 1996).

Al-Moayad v. Germany, App no 35,865/03 (ECHR, 20 February 2007).

Al-Nashri v. Poland, App No 28,761/11 (ECHR, 24 July 2014).

Al-Skeini and Others v. the United Kingdom, App No 55,721/07 (ECHR, 7 July 2011).

A.M.E. v. the Netherlands, App No 51,428/10 (ECHR, 5 February 2015).

Bankovic et. al. v. Belgium and 16 Other Contracting States, App No 52,207/99 (ECHR, 12 December 2001).

Brannigan and McBride v. the United Kingdom, App Nos 14,553/89, 14,554/89 (ECHR, 25 May 1993).

Chahal v. United Kingdom, App No 22,414/93 (ECHR, 5 November 1996).

Cruz Varaz and others v Sweden, Series A, No 201.

D. v. the United Kingdom, App No 30,240/96 (ECHR, 2 May 1997).

Einhorn v. France, App no 71,555/01 (ECHR, 16 October 2001).

El Haski v. Belgium, App No 649/08 (ECHR, 25 September 2012).

Fadele v the United Kingdom, App No 13,078/87 (ECHR, 12 February 1990).

Hirsi Jamaa and Others v. Italy, App No 27,765/09 (ECHR, 23 February 2012).

Ireland v. the United Kingdom, App No 5310/71 (ECHR, 18 January 1978).

Iskandarov v. Russia, App No 17,185/05 (ECHR, 23 September 2010).

Jabari v. Turkey, App No 40,035/98 (ECHR, 11 July 2000).

K.R.S. v. United Kingdom (2009) 48 EHRR SE8.

M.H. v. Serbia, App No 62,410/17, (ECHR, 4 March 2019).

M.N. and Others v. Belgium, App No 3599/18 (ECHR, 5 May 2020).

M.S.S. v. Belgium and Greece, App No 30,696/09 (ECHR, 21 January 2011).

N. v. Finland, App No 38,885/02 (ECHR, 26 July 2005).

N.S. (Afghanistan) v. Secretary of State for the Home Department (Amnesty International Ltd. and others intervening) [2013] QB 102.

Ocalan v. Turkey, App No 6221/99 (ECHR, 12 May 2005).

Othman (Abu Qatada) v. United Kingdom, App No 8139/09 (ECHR, 9 May 2012).

Saadi v. Italy, App No 37,201/06 (ECHR, 28 February 2008).

Salah Sheekh v the Netherlands, App No 1948/04 (ECHR, 11 January 2007).

S.H.H. v. United Kingdom, App no 60,367/10 (ECHR, 29 January 2013).

Soering v. the United Kingdom, App No 14,038/88 (ECHR, 7 July 1989).

Tarakhel v. Switzerland, App No 29,217/12 (ECHR, 4 November 2014).

T.I. v. The United Kingdom, App No 43,844/98 (ECHR, 7 March 2000).

V.O. v. France, App No 53,924/00 (ECHR, 8 July 2014).

Vilvarajah v. the United Kingdom, Series A, No 215.

W.M. v. Denmark, App No 17,392/90 (ECHR, 14 October 1992).

A.2.3 Court of Justice of the EU

Abdullahi v. Bundesasylamt C-394/12, 10 December 2013.

Bundesrepublik Deutschland v. B. and D., C-57/09 and C-101/09, 9 November 2010.

Bundesrepublik Deutschland v. Puid, C-411/13, 14 November 2013.

Dory v. Bundesrepublik Deutschland, C-186/01 [2003] ECR I-2479.

Elliniki Radiophonia Tileorassi AE (ERT) v. Dimotiki Etairia Pliroforissis (DEP), C-260/89 [1991] ECR I-2925.

Germany v Leifer, C-83/94 [1995] ECR I-3231.

H.T. v. Land Baden-Württemberg, C-373/13, 24 June 2015.

Jeremy F. v. Premier Ministre, C-168/13 PPU, 20 May 2013.

Kadi II, C-584/10 P, C-593/10 P and C-595/10 P, 18 July 2013.

Kreil v. Bundesrepublik Deutschland, C-285/98 [2000] ECR I-69.

Internationale Handelsgesellschaft GmbH v. EV St, C-11/70, 17 December 1970.

Mehrdad Ghezelbash v. Staatssecretaris van Veiligheid en Justitie, C-63/15, 7 June 2016.

Melloni v. Ministrio Fiscal, C-399/11, 26 February 2013.

N.S. v. Secretary of State for the Home Department and M.E. and others v. Refugee Applications Commissioner, Minister for Justice, Equality and Law Reform, C-411/10 and C-493/10, 21 December 2011.

Nilsson, C-162/97 [1998] ECR I-7477.

R. v. Henn, C-34/79 [1979] ECR 3795.

R., on the application of M.A., B.T., D.A. v. Secretary of State for the Home Department, C-648/11, 6 June 2013.

R. v. Secretary of State for Home Affairs, ex parte Santillo, C-131/79 [1980] ECR 1585.

Stefano Melloni v. Ministrio Fiscal, C-399/11, 26 February 2013.

T.B. v. Bevándorlási és Menekültügyi Hivatal, C-519/18, 5 September 2019.

Vereinigte Familiapress Zeitungsverlags und vertriebs GmbH v. Heinrich Bauer Verlag, C-368/95 [1997] ECR I-3689.

A.2.4 CAT Committee

Aemei v. Switzerland, Communication No 34/1995, 29 May 1997.

Agiza v. Sweden, UN Doc CAT/C/34/D/233/2003, 24 May 2005.

Gorki Ernesto Tapia Paez v. Sweden, Communication No 39/1996, 28 April 1997.

Khan v. Canada, Communication No 15/1994, 18 November 1994.

M.A.K., UN Doc CAT/C32/D/214/2002, 5 May 2004.

M.B.B. v. Sweden, Communication No 104/1998, 21 June 1999.

Paez v. Sweden, Communication No 39/1997, 28 April 1997.

S.V. et. al. v. Canada, Communication No 48/1996, 15 May 2001.

A.2.5 Human Rights Committee

Human Rights Committee, "Concluding Observations of the Human Rights Committee, United States of America", 3 October 1995, UN Doc CCPR/C/79/Add.50.

Human Rights Committee, "Concluding Observations of the Human Rights Committee, United States of America", 18 December 2006, UN Doc CCPR/C/USA/CO/3/Rev.1.

Human Rights Committee, "General Comment No 3: The Obligations of States Parties under the Optional Protocol to the International Covenant on Civil and Political Rights", 5 November 2008, UN Doc CCPR/C/GC/33.

Human Rights Committee, "General Comment No. 24 (52)" (1994), UN Doc CCPR/C/21/Rev.1/Add.6, 2 November 1994.

A.2.6 Domestic Jurisprudence (United Kingdom)

Adan and Aitsegur [1999] 3 WLR 1569.

Al-Sirri v. Secretary of State for the Home Department and D.D. (Afghanistan) v. Secretary of State for the Home Department [2012] UKSC 54.

E.M. and M.A. [2013] 1 WLR 576.

E.M. (Eritrea) & Others v. Secretary of State for the Home Department [2012] EWCA Civ 1336.

E.N. (Serbia) v. Secretary of State for the Home Department & Anor [2009] EWCA Civ 630.

Esmaiel Mohammed Pour (1), Seid Jafar Hasini Hersari (2), Majid Ghulami (3) v The Secretary of State for the Home Department [2016] EWHC 401 (Admin).

Ex Parte Thangarasa and Ex Parte Yogathas [2002] UKHL 36.

Germany v. Leifer, C-83/94 [1995] ECR I-3231.

I.A. (Iran) v. Secretary of State for the Home Department [2014] UKSC 6.

J.S. (Sri Lanka) v. Secretary of State for the Home Department [2010] UKSC 15.

M70/2011 and M106/2011 v. Minister of Immigration and Citizenship & Anor [2011] HCA 32.

Medhanye, R (on the application of) v. Secretary of State for the Home Department [2011] EWHC 3012 (Admin).

Musud Dudaev, Kamila Dudaev and Denil Dudaev v. Secretary of State for the Home Department, [2015] EWHC 1641.

R. (ex parte Adan) v. Secretary of State for the Home Department [2001] 2 A.C. 477; (2001) 2 W.L.R. 143.

R. (on the application of EM (Eritrea)) and Others (Appellants) v. Secretary of State for the Home Department (Respondent) [2014] UKSC 12.

R. (on the application of Elayathamby) v. Secretary of State for the Home Department [2011] EWHC 2182 (Admin).

R (on the application of Ibrahimi) Abasi v. Secretary of State for the Home Department [2016] EWHC 2049.

R. (Yogathas) v. Secretary of State for the Home Department [2003] 1 A.C. 920.

Secretary of State for the Home Department, Ex Parte Adan R v. Secretary of State for the Home Department Ex Parte Aitseguer, R v. [2000] UKHL 67.

Secretary of State for the Home Department v. Rehman [2003] 1 AC 153, [2001] UKHL 47.

Tabrizagh & Ors, R (On the Application Of) v. Secretary of State for the Home Department [2014] EWHC 1914 (Admin).

The Queen on the Application of Mr Mohsen Pourali Tabrizagh, Mr Tahir Syed, Mr Saeed Ali, Mr Ali Omar Mohammed, Mr Edmond Karaj, AB (Sunda) v. Secretary of State for the Home Department [2015] EWHC 1095.

The Queen on the Application of M.S., N.A., S.G. and the Secretary of State for the Home Department, [2015] EWHC 1095.

V.T. (Dublin Regulation: Post-Removal Appeal) Sri Lanka [2012] UKUT 00308 (IAC).

Y.B. (Eritrea) v. Secretary of State for the Home Department [2008] EWCA Civ 360.

Z.H. (Tanzania) v. Secretary of State for the Home Department [2011] UKSC 4.

Z.L. and V.L. v. Secretary of State for the Home Department [2003] EWCA Civ 25.

A.2.7 Domestic Jurisprudence (Germany)

Administrative Court of Aachen, 17 November 2015, Case No. C Az. 8 K 658/15.A.

Administrative Court of Düsseldorf, 16 January 2009, Case No. 21 K 3263/07.A.

Administrative Court of Düsseldorf, 4 March 2009, Case No. 11 K 4716/07.A.

Administrative Court of Düsseldorf, 3 September 2015, Case No. C 22 L 2944/ 15A.

Administrative Court of Düsseldorf, 26 October 2017, Case No. C 12 L 4591/ 17.A.

Administrative Court of Freiburg, 14 January 2015, Case No. C A 1 K 3128/14.

Administrative Court of Hannover, 7 March 2016, Case No. 1 B 5946/15.

Administrative Court of Hannover, 5 November 2015, Case No. C 10A 5157/ 15.

Administrative Court of Justice Baden-Württemberg, 15 March 2017, Case No. A 11 S 2151/16.

Administrative Court of Lueneburg, 16 December 2013, Case No. 6B 64/13.

Administrative Court of Magdeburg, Chamber, 26 January 2016, Case No 8 A 108/16.

Administrative Court of Minden, 2 October 2015, Case No. 10 L 923/15.A.

Administrative Court of Minden, 29 March 2016, Case No. 10 L 314/16.A.

Administrative Court of Oldenburg, 2 October 2015, Case No. 12A 2572/15.

Administrative Court of Potsdam, 4 September 2015, Case No. 4 L 810/15.A.

Administrative Court of Potsdam, 4 February 2016, Case No. 6 L 87/16.A.

Administrative Court of Wiesbaden, 15 September 2017, Case No. 6 L 4438/17. WI.

BverG, Judgment of 14 October 2004—BverG 2 BvR 1481/04.

BverG, Judgment of 4 February 2010—BverG 2 BvR 2307/06.

BverG, Judgment of 17 September 2014—BverG 2 BvR 1795/14.

BverG, Judgment of 17 September 2015—BverG 2 BvR1 C 26.14.

BVerfG, Judgment of 4 September 2019—BverG 2 BvR 1380/19.

BVerfG, Judgment of 7 October 2019—BverG 2 BvR 721/19.

BVerwG, Judgment of 18 December 2008—BVerwG 10 C 27.07.

BVerwG, Judgment of 17 September 2015—BverwG 1 C 26.14.

BVerwG, Judgment of 16 November 2015—BVerwG 1 C 4.15.

BVerwG, Judgment of 27 April 2016—BVerwG 1 C 24.15.

BverwG, Judgment of 30 April 2015—BVerwG C 2 BvR 746/15.

BVerwG Judgment of 14 December 2016—BVerwG 1 C 4.16.

BVerwG, Judgment of 27 October 2015—BVerwG 1 C 32.14, 1 C 33.14, 1 C 34.14.

High Administrative Court Nordrhein-Westfalen, 27 March 2007, Case No. 8 A 4728/05.A.

High Administrative Court North Rhine-Westphalia, 17 May 2010, Case No. 11 A 960/09.A.

High Administrative Court, 5 August 2015, Case No. C Az.1A 11,020/14.

Higher Administrative Court of Saxony, 5 October 2015, Case No. C 5 B 259/15.A.

A.2.8 Domestic Jurisprudence (Other)

Ezokola v. Canada (Citizenship and Immigration) [2013] 2 SCR 678.

India v. Badesha [2017] 2 SCR 127.

Institute for Human Rights and Development in Africa (on behalf of Sierra Leonean refugees in Guinea) v. Guinea, African Commission on Human and Peoples' Rights, Communication No. 240/02, December 2004.

Németh v. Canada [2010] 3 SCR 281.

Sale v. Haitian Ctr Council, Inc, 509 US 155 (1993).

Suresh v. Canada (Minister of Citizenship and Immigration) [2002] 1 SCR 3.

A.3 Secondary Material: Monographs and Edited Collections

Agnès Hurwitz, *The Collective Responsibility of States to Protect Refugees* (Oxford: Oxford University Press, 2009).

Bertold Huber, "The Application of Human Rights Standards by German Courts to Asylum-Seekers, Refugees and Other Migrants", (2001) 3 *European Journal of Migration and Law* 171–184.

Bimal Ghosh, *Elusive Protection, Uncertain Lands: Migrants' Access to Human Rights* (Geneva, International Organization for Migration, 2003).

Cathryn Costello, *The Human Rights of Migrants and Refugees in European Law* (Oxford: Oxford University Press, 2016).

Council of Europe, *Handbook on European Law relating to Asylum, Borders and Immigration* (Strasbourg: Council of Europe Publishing, 2014).

Daniel Ghezelbash, *Refuge Lost: Asylum Law in an Interdependent World* (Cambridge: Cambridge University Press, 2018).

David Weisbrot, *Australian Lawyers* (Longman Cheshire, 1999).

Elizabeth Collett and Camille Le Coz, *After the Storm: Learning from the EU Response to the Migration Crisis* (Brussels, Migration Policy Institute Europe, 2018).

Eman Hamdan, *The Principle of Non-Refoulement under the ECHR and the UN Convention Against Torture and Other Cruel, Inhuman or Degrading Treatment or Punishment* (Netherlands: Brill Nijhoff, 2016).

Fanny De Weck, *Non-Refoulement under the European Convention on Human Rights and the UN Convention Against Torture* (Leiden: Brill Nijhoff, 2017).

Guy S. Goodwin-Gill, *The Principle of Non-Refoulement: Its Standing and Scope in International Law: A Study* (Geneva: UNHCR, Division of International Protection, 1993).

Guy S. Goodwin-Gill and Jane McAdam, *The Refugee in International Law* (3rd ed) (New York: Oxford University Press Inc., 2007).

Hemme Battjes, *European Asylum Law and International Law* (Leiden/Boston: Martinus Nijhoff, 2006).

James C. Hathaway, *The Rights of Refugees under International Law* (Cambridge: Cambridge University Press 2005).

James C. Hathaway and Michelle Foster, *Law of Refugee Status* (2nd ed, Oxford University Press, 2014).

James Crawford, *Brownlie's Principles of Public International Law* (8th ed, Oxford University Press, 2012).

Jane McAdam, *Complementary Protection in International Refugee Law* (Oxford University Press, 2007).

John Rawls, *A Theory of Justice* (Boston: Harvard University Press, 1999).

John H. Currie, Joanna Harrington, Craig Forcese, Valerie Oosterveld (eds) *International Law: Doctrine, Practice, and Theory* (Irwin Law, 2014).

Karen Da Costa, *The Extraterritorial Application of Selected Human Rights Treaties* (Leiden: Martinus Nijhoff Publishers, 2013).

Karin Loevy, *Emergencies in Public Law: The Legal Politics of Containment* (Cambridge: Cambridge University Press, 2016).

Kees (Cornelis) Wouters, *International Legal Standards for the Protection from Refoulement: A Legal Analysis of the Prohibitions on Refoulement contained in the Refugee Convention, the European Convention on Human Rights, the International Covenant on Civil and Political Rights and the Convention against Torture* (Oxford: Intersentia, 2009).

Maarten den Heijer, *Europe and Extraterritorial Asylum* (Oxford and Portland: Hart Publishing, 2012).

Manfred Nowak, *UN Covenant on Civil and Political Rights: CCPR Commentary* (2nd edn) (NP Engel Publisher, 2005).

Marko Milanovic, *Extraterritorial Application of Human Rights Treaties: Law, Principles, and Policy* (Oxford: Oxford University Press, 2011) at 118–119.

Matthew Gibney, "Asylum and the Principle of Proximity" (2000) 3:3 *Ethics, Place & Environment*, 313–317.

Olga Ferguson Sidorenko, *The Common European Asylum System: Background, Current State of Affairs, Future Direction.* (The Hague: TMC Asser Press, 2007).

Philippe De Bruycker, Alice Bloomfield, Evangelia (Lilian) Tsourdi, Joanna Petin (eds) *Alternatives to Immigration and Asylum Detention in the EU: Time for Implementation* (Brussels: Odysseus Academic Network Publishing, 2015).

Raymond Youngs, *Sourcebook on German Law* (London: Cavendish Publishing Limited, 2002).

Richard Plender, *International Migration Law* (2nd ed) (Dordrecht, 1988).

Sandro Mezzadra and Brent Neilson, *Border as Method, or, the Multiplication of Labor*. (Durham: Duke University Press, 2013).

Steven Greer, *The Margin of Appreciation: Interpretation and Discretion under the European Convention on Human Rights* (Strasbourg: Council of Europe Publishing, 2000).

Thomas Gammeltoft-Hansen, *Access to Asylum: International Refugee Law and the Globalisation of Migration Control* (Cambridge: Cambridge University Press, 2011).

Valsamis Mitsilegas, *EU Criminal Law* (Oxford: Hart Publishing, 2009).

Vera Gowlland-Debbas (ed) *The Problem of Refugees in the Light of Contemporary International Law Issues* (Martinus Nijhoff Publishers, 1994).

Violeta Moreno-Lax, *Accessing Asylum in Europe: Extraterritorial Border Controls and Refugee Rights under EU Law* (Oxford: Oxford University Press, 2017).

Vincent Chetail, *International Migration Law* (Oxford: Oxford University Press, 2019).

A.4 Secondary Material: Chapters in Edited Collection

Anja Klug, "Regional Developments: Europe" in Andreas Zimmermann (ed) *The 1951 Convention Relating to the Status of Refugees and Its 1967 Protocol: A Commentary* (Oxford: Oxford University Press, 2011).

Cathryn Costello, "The Search for the Outer Edges of *Non-refoulement* in Europe: Exceptionality and Flagrant Breaches" in Bruce Burson and James Cantor (eds), *Human Rights and the Refugee Definition* (Netherlands: Brill, 2016).

Claudena M. Skran, "Background, Historical Development of International Refugee Law" in Andreas Zimmermann (ed) *1951 Convention Relating to the Status of Refugees and its 1967 Protocol: A Commentary* (Oxford: Oxford University Press, 2011).

Claudena M. Skran, "Part One: Background, Historical Development of International Refugee Law" in Andreas Zimmermann, Felix Machts and Jonas Dörschner (eds) *The 1951 Convention Relating to the Status of Refugees and its 1967 Protocol: A Commentary* (Oxford: Oxford University Press, 2011).

Dallal Stevens and Maria O'Sullivan, 'States, the Law and Access to Refugee Protection: Concluding Reflections', in Maria O'Sullivan and Dallal Stevens (eds) *States, the Law and Access to Refugee Protection: Fortresses and Fairness* (Portland, Oregon: Hart Publishing, 2017).

Guy S. Goodwin-Gill, "Article 31 of the 1951 Convention Relating to the Status of Refugees: Non-Penalization, Detention, and Protection" in Erika Feller, Volker Türk and Frances Nicholson (eds) *Refugee Protection in International Law: UNHCR's Global Consultations on International Protection* (Cambridge: Cambridge University Press, 2003).

Guy S. Goodwin-Gill, "The International Law of Refugee Protection" in Elena Fiddian-Qasmiyeh, Gil Loescher, Katy Long and Nando Sigona (eds) *The Oxford Handbook of Refugee and Forced Migration Studies* (Oxford: Oxford University Press, 2014).

Hemme Battjes, "Mutual Trust in Asylum Matters: The Dublin System" in Hemme Battjes, Evelien Brouwer, Paulien de Morree, and Jannemieke Ouwerkerk (eds), *Mutual Trust in European Asylum, Migration, and Criminal Law: Reconciling Trust and Fundamental Rights* (Netherlands: FORUM, 2011).

Jane Freedman, "A Gendered Analysis of the European Refugee "Crisis"" in Cecilia Menji var, Marie Ruiz, Immanuel Ness (eds) *The Oxford Handbook of Migration Crises* (Oxford: Oxford University Press, 2019).

Jane McAdam, "Interpretation of the 1951 Convention" in Andreas Zimmermann (ed) *The 1951 Convention Relating to the Status of Refugees and Its 1967 Protocol: A Commentary* (Oxford: Oxford University Press, 2011).

James C Hathaway, "Refugees and Asylum" in B. Opeskin, R. Perruchoud, and J. Redpath-Cross (eds) *Foundations of International Migration Law* (Cambridge: Cambridge University Press).

Jennifer Hyndman and Alison Mountz, "Refuge or Refusal: The Geography of Exclusion" in Derek Gregory and Allan Pred (eds) *Violent Geographies: Fear, Terror, and Political Violence* (New York: Routledge, 2007).

Kathleen Marie Whitney, "Does the European Convention on Human Rights Protect Refugees from "Safe" Countries" (1997) 26 *Georgia Journal of International & Comparative Law* 375–407.

Kay Hailbronner, "Comments On: The Right to Leave, the Right to Return and the Question of a Right to Remain" in Vera Gowlland-Debbas (ed) *The Problem of Refugees in The Light of Contemporary International Law Issues* (The Hague: Martinus Nijhoff Publishers, 1994).

Kris Pollet, "Accessing Fair and Efficient Asylum Procedures in the EU: Legal Safeguards and Loopholes in the Common European Asylum System" in Maria O'Sullivan and Dallal Stevens (eds), *States, the Law and Access to Refugee Protection: Fortresses and Fairness* (Hart Publishing, Oxford: 2017).

Martin Gottwald, "Burden Sharing and Refugee Protection" in Elena Fiddian-Qasmiyeh, Gil Loescher, Katy Long and Nando Sigona (eds) *The Oxford Handbook of Refugee and Forced Migration Studies* (Oxford: Oxford University Press, 2014).

Matthew Gibney, "Political Theory, Ethics, and Forced Migration" in Elena Fiddian-Qasmiyeh, Gil Loescher, Katy Long and Nando Sigona (eds) *Oxford Handbook of Refugee and Forced Migration Studies* (Oxford: Oxford University Press, 2014).

Nadine El-Enany, 'Asylum in the Context of Immigration Control: Exclusion by Default or Design?' in Maria O'Sullivan and Dallal Stevens (eds), *States, the Law and Access to Refugee Protection: Fortresses and Fairness* (Hart Publishing, Oxford: 2017).

Noel Castree, Rob Kitchin, Alisdair Rogers, "Migration" in *A Dictionary of Human Geography* (Oxford: Oxford University Press, 2013).

O'Sullivan and Stephens: Maria O'Sullivan and Dallal Stevens, "Access to Refugee Protection: Key Concepts and Contemporary Challenges" in Maria O'Sullivan and Dallal Stevens (eds), *States, the Law and Access to Refugee Protection: Fortresses and Fairness* (Hart Publishing, Oxford: 2017).

R. J. Beck, "Britain and the 1933 Refugee Convention: National or State Sovereignty?" in R. Beck and T. Ambrosio (eds) *International Law and the Rise of Nations: The State System and the Challenge of Ethnic Groups* (New York: Seven Bridges Press, 2002).

Ralph Wilde, "Compliance with Human Rights Norms Extraterritorially: 'Human Rights Imperialism'?" in L. Chazournes and M. Kohen (eds) *International Law and the Quest for its Implementation* (Boston: Brill, 2010).

Rainer Hofmann, "Recent Jurisprudence of the German Federal Constitutional Court on Asylum Law" in Gudmundur Alfredsson and Peter Macalister-Smith (eds) *The Living Law of Nations: Essays on refugees, minorities, indigenous peoples and the human rights of other vulnerable groups in memory of Atle Grahl-Madsen* (Germany: NP Engel Publisher, 1996).

Robert S Litwak, "Containment" in Joel Krieger (ed) *The Oxford Companion to Politics of the World* (Oxford: Oxford University Press, 2004).

S. Taekema and B. Van Klink, 'On the Border: Limits and Possibilities of Interdisciplinary Research' in B. Van Klink and S. Taekema (eds.) *Law and Method.*

Sir Elihu Lauterpacht and Daniel Bethlehem, "The Scope and Content of the Principle of Non-Refoulement: Opinion" in Erika Feller, Volker Türk and Frances Nicholson (eds) *UNHCR's Global Consultations on International Protection* (Cambridge: Cambridge University Press, 2003).

Terje Einarsen, "Background, Drafting History of the 1951 Convention and the 1967 Protocol" in Andreas Zimmermann (ed) *The 1951 Convention Relating to the Status of Refugees and its 1967 Protocol: A Commentary* (Oxford: Oxford University Press, 2011).

Valsamis Mitsilegas, "Solidarity Beyond the State in Europe's Common European Asylum System" in Marianna Karakoulaki, Laura Southgate, and Jakob Steiner (eds) *Critical Perspectives on Migration in the twenty-first Century* (Bristol: E-International Relations, 2018).

Vincent Chetail, "Are Refugee Rights Human Rights? An Unorthodox Questioning of the Relations between Refugee Law and Human Rights Law" in Ruth Rubio-Marín (eds) *Human Rights and Immigration* (Oxford: Oxford University Press, 2014).

Vincent Chetail, "Armed Conflict and Forced Migration: A Systematic Approach to International Humanitarian Law, Refugee Law, and International Human Rights Law" in Andrew Clapham and Paola Gaeta (eds) *The Oxford Handbook of International Law in Armed Conflict* (Oxford: Oxford University Press, 2014).

Violeta Moreno-Lax, "EU Non-Refoulement (The Irrelevance of) Territoriality and Pre-Border Controls" in *Accessing Asylum in Europe: Extraterritorial Border Controls and Refugee Rights under EU Law* (Oxford: Oxford University Press, 2017).

Violeta Moreno-Lax, "The Legality of the 'Safe Third Country' Notion Contested: Insights from the Law of Treaties" in Guy S. Goodwin-Gill and Phillippe Weckel (eds) *Migration & Refugee Protection in the twenty-first Century: Legal Aspects, The Hague Academy of International Law Centre for Research* (The Hague: Martinus Nijhoff, 2015), 665–721.

Violeta Moreno-Lax and Mariagiulia Giuffré, "The Raise of Consensual Containment: From 'Contactless Control' to 'Contactless Responsibility' for Forced Migration Flows" in Savinder Juss (ed) *Research Handbook on International Refugee Law* (Edward Elgar, 2016).

Walter Kälin, Martina Caroni and Lukas Heim, "Article 33, para. 1 (Prohibition of Expulsion or Return ('*Refoulement*')" in Andreas Zimmermann (ed) *The 1951 Convention Relating to the Status of Refugees and its 1967 Protocol: A Commentary* (Oxford: Oxford University Press, 2011).

Walter Kälin, Martina Caroni, and Lukas Heim, "Part Six: Administrative Measures, Article 33, para. 1" in Andreas Zimmermann, Felxi Machts and Jonas Dörschner (eds) *The 1951 Convention Relating to the Status of Refugees and its 1967 Protocol: A Commentary* (Oxford: Oxford University Press, 2011).

A.5 Secondary Material: Journal Articles

A. Duffy, "Expulsion to Face Torture? *Non-refoulement* in International Law", (2008) 20:3 *International Journal of Refugee Law* 373–390.

Alexander Orakhelashvili, "N.S. v. Secretary of State for the Home Department" (2012) 106(3) *American Journal of International Law* 616–624.

Alexander Betts, "International Cooperation in the Global Refugee Regime" (2008) *Global Economic Governance Programme, Oxford, Working Paper 2008/44.*

Alexander Sager, "The Implications of Migration Theory for Distributive Justice" (2012) 5 *Global Justice: Theory Practice Rhetoric,* 56–70.

Alison Mountz, "The enforcement archipelago: Detention, haunting, and asylum on islands" (2011) *Political Geography* 30(3): 118–128.

Alison Mountz, Kate Coddington, R Tina Catania, and Jenna M Loyd, "Conceptualizing Detention: Mobility, Containment, Bordering, and Exclusion" (2013) 37:4 *Progress in Human Geography* 522–541.

Andrew G. Pizor, "Sale v. Haitian Centres Council: The Return of Haitian Refugees" (1993) 17:4 *Fordham International Law Journal* 1062–1114.

Andrew Shacknove, "From Asylum to Containment" (1993) 5(4) *International Journal of Refugee Law,* 516–533.

Anna Lübbe, "'Systemic Flaws' and Dublin Transfers: Incompatible Tests before the CJEU and the ECtHR?" (2015) 27:1 *International Journal of Refugee Law* 135–140.

Annick Pijnenburg, "From Italian Pushbacks to Libyan Pullbacks: Is *Hirsi 2.0* in the Making in Strasbourg?" (2018) 20 *European Journal of Migration and Law* 396–426.

Atle Grahl-Madsen, *The Status of Refugees in International Law,* Vol 1 (Leyden, 1966).

Basak Cali, Cathryn Costello, and Stewart Cunningham, "Hard Protection through Soft Courts? Non-Refoulement before the United Nations Treaty Bodies" (2020) 21 *German Law Journal* 355–384.

Bertold Huber, "The Application of Human Rights Standards by German Courts to Asylum-Seekers, Refugees and Other Migrants", (2001) 3 *European Journal of Migration and Law* 171–184.

Bill Frelick, Ian M Kysel, and Jennifer Podkul, "The Impact of Externalization of Migration Controls on the Rights of Asylum Seekers and Other Migrants" (2016) 4:4 *Journal of Migration and Human Security*, 190–220.

Birgit Peters, "Germany's Dialogue with Strasbourg: Extrapolating the *Bundesverfassungsgericht's* Relationship with the European Court of Human Rights in the Preventive Detention Decision" (2012) 13:6 *German Law Journal* 758–722.

Cathryn Costello, "Dublin-case NS/ME: Finally, an end to blind trust across the EU?" (2012) 2 *A&MR* 83–92.

Cathryn Costello, "Overcoming Refugee Containment and Crisis" (2020) 21 *German Law Journal,* 17–22.

Cathryn Costello and Michelle Foster, "Non-Refoulement as Custom and Jus Cogens? Putting the Prohibition to the Test" (2016) *Netherlands Yearbook of International Law* 46, 273–327.

Channe Lindstrøm, "European Union Policy on Asylum and Immigration. Addressing the Root Causes of Forced Migration: A Justice and Home Affairs Policy of Freedom, Security and Justice?" (2005) 39(6) *Social Policy & Administration* 587–605.

Claudena M. Skran, "Profiles of the First Two High Commissioners" (1988) 1 (3–4) *Journal of Refugee Studies* at 277–296.

David Weissbrodt and Isabel Hortreiter, "The Principle of *Non-refoulement*: Article 3 of the Convention against Torture and Other Cruel, Inhuman or Degrading Treatment or Punishment in Comparison with the *Non-refoulement* Provisions of other International Human Rights Treaties" (1999) 5:1 *Buffalo Human Rights Law Review* 1–74.

David James Cantor, "The End of Refugee Law?" (2017) *Journal of Human Rights Practice* 9(2).

Daniel Lovric, "A Constitution Friendly to International Law: Germany and its Volkerrechtfreundlichkeit" (2006) 25 *Australian Yearbook of International Law* 75.

D.J. Miller, "Holding States to their Convention Obligations: The United Nations Convention against Torture and the Need for a Broad Interpretation of State Action" (2003) 17 *Georgetown Immigration Law Journal* 299–323.

Edward J. Eberle, "The Methodology of Comparative Law" (2011) 16:51 *Roger Williams University Law Review.*

Eliana Barrera and Friederike Vetter, "'Systemic Deficiency': Legal Standard Setting, Human Rights, and Its Effect on the Individual in the Common European Asylum System" (2013) 2:2 *Spectra Journal*.

Elspeth Guild, Cathryn Costello, Madeline Garlick and Violeta Moreno-Lax, "Enhancing the Common European Asylum System and Alternatives to Dublin" (2015) *CEPS Paper No. 83*, 8–89.

Emanuela-Chiara Gillard, "There's No Place Like Home: States' Obligations in Relation to Transfers of Persons" (2008) 90 *International Review of the Red Cross* 871.

Erika Feller, "Asylum, Migration and Refugee Protection: Realities, Myths and the Promise of Things to Come" (2006) 18(3) *International Journal of Refugee Law* 509–536.

European Commission of Human Rights, *The Greek Case*, Application No's 3321/67, 3322/67, 3323/67 and 3344/67 (1969) *Yearbook of European Convention on Human Rights*.

Evelien Brouwer, "Mutual Trust and the Dublin Regulation: Protection of Fundamental Rights in the EU and the Burden of Proof" (2013) 9:1 *Utrecht Law Review* 135–147.

Esin Küçük, "The Principle of Solidarity and Fairness in Sharing Responsibility: More than Window Dressing?" (2016) 22 *European Law Journal*, 448–469.

"Five Case Abstracts" (1997) 9:2 *International Journal of Refugee Law* 292–307.

Florian Trauner, "Asylum Policy: the EU's 'crises' and the looming policy regime failure" 38(3) *Journal of European Integration* 311–325.

Frank Hoffmeister, "Germany: Status of European Convention on Human Rights in Domestic Law" (2006) 4(4) *I-CON*, 722–731.

Geoff Gilbert, "Why Europe Does Not Have a Refugee Crisis" (2015) *International Journal of Refugee Law* 27(4), 531–535.

Gilbert Jaeger, "On the History of the International Protection of Refugees" (2001) 83:843 *International Review of the Red Cross* 727–736.

Giulia Vicini, "The Dublin Regulation between Strasbourg and Luxembourg: Reshaping Non-Refoulement in the Name of Mutual Trust?" (2015) *European Journal of Legal Studies* 8(2), 50–72.

Gloria Fernández Arribas, "The EU-Turkey Agreement: A Controversial Attempt at Patching up a Major Problem" (2016) 1:3 *European Papers* 1097–1104.

Guy S. Goodwin-Gill, "The Dynamic of International Refugee Law" (2014) 25:4 *International Journal of Refugee Law* 651–666.

Guy S. Goodwin-Gill, "Transnational Legal Problems of Refugees" (1982) *Michigan Yearbook of International Legal Studies.*

Hemme Battjes and Evelien Brouwer, "The Dublin Regulation and Mutual Trust: Judicial Coherence in EU Asylum Law" (2015) 8(2) *Review of European Administrative Law* 182–214.

Henk Van Houtum, "Human Blacklisting: The global apartheid of the EU's external border regime" (2010) 28(6) *Environment and Planning D: Society and Space*, 957–976.

Hiliary Charlesworth, "Universal Declaration of Human Rights (1948)" (2008) *Max Planck Encyclopedia of Public International Law.*

I. Ashutosh and A. Mountz, "Migration management for the benefit of whom? Interrogating the work of the International Organization for Migration" (2012) *Citizenship Studies* 15, 21–38.

J. Vranken, 'Exciting Times for Legal Scholarship', 2 *Recht en Methode in Onderzoek en Onderwijs* 42.

Jack I. Garvey, "The Future Legal Management of Mass Migration" (2018) 51:2 *The International Lawyer* 121–169.

James C. Hathaway, "Leveraging Asylum" (2009) *University of Melbourne Law School Research Series* 6.

James C. Hathaway, "Reconceiving Refugee Law as Human Rights Protection" (1991) 4 *Journal of Refugee Studies* 113.

James C. Hathaway, "The Emerging Politics of Non-Entree" 91 *Refugees* 40–41.

James C. Hathway and Thomas Gammeltoft-Hansen, "Non-Refoulement in a World of Cooperative Deterrence" (2014) *University of Michigan, Law & Economics Working Papers No 106,* 1–64.

Jane McAdam, "The Refugee Convention as a Rights Blueprint for Persons in Need of International Protection" (July 2006), *UNHCR Research Paper* No 125.

Jasper Finke, "Granting Asylum and Protection from Deportation to Civil War Refugees under German Constitutional Law and the German Aliens Act: The Judgment of the German Federal Constitutional Court of 10 August 2000" (2000) 43 *German Yearbook of International Law* 283–297.

Jenny Poon, "ESIL Reflections: The EU Commission on 'Dublin IV': Sufficient Safeguards for Asylum Claimants?" (2016) 5(9) *European Society of International Law Reflection Series* 1–10.

Jenny Poon, "Extraterritorial Application of *Non-Refoulement:* Triggering the Prohibition on the High Seas" (2020) 4 *Refugee Review,* 114–128.

Jenny Poon, "Non-Refoulement in the International Refugee law Regime: A Lex Specialis?" (2017) 3 *Cornell International Law Journal Online* 31–33.

Jenny Poon, "The Protection Nexus between Non-Penalisation and National Security Exception under the Refugee Convention" (2019) 3 *Philippe Kirsch Institute Global Justice Journal* 37.

Jill Alpes, Charlotte Blondel, Nausicaa Preiss and Meritxell Sayos Monras, "Post-Deportation Risks for Failed Asylum Seekers' (2017) *Forced Migration Review* 1–3.

Justice Harald Dörig, "Germany: The Handling of Leading Asylum Cases by National Courts" (2013) 25:2 *International Journal of Refugee Law* 373–376.

Kirsten McConnachie, "Camps of Containment: A Genealogy of the Refugee Camp" (2016) 7 (3) *Humanity: An International Journal of Human Rights, Humanitarianism, and Development,* 397–412.

Leslie Groves, "Strengthening the voices of refugees in UNHCR planning" (2006) *Forced Migration Review,* 64–66.

Luiza Bialasiewicz, "Off-shoring and out-sourcing the borders of Europe: Libya and EU border work in the Mediterranean" (2012) *Geopolitics* 17, 843–866.

M. Collyer and R. King, "Producing transnational space: International migration and the extra-territorial reach of state power" (2015) *Progress in Human Geography* 39, 185–204.

Markus Möstl, "Preconditions and Limits of Mutual Recognition" (2010) 47 *Common Market Law Review* 405.

Martina Tazzioli, "Containment through Mobility: Migrants' Spatial Disobediences and the Reshaping of Control through the Hotspot System" (2018) 44:16 *Journal of Ethnic and Migration Studies* 2764–2779.

Martina Tazzioli and Glenda Garelli, "Containment Beyond Detention: The Hotspot System and the Disrupted Migration Movements Across Europe" (2018) *Society and Space* 1–19.

Martti Koskenniemi, 'Methodology of International Law' in Rüdiger Wolfrum (ed), *Max Planck Encyclopedia of Public International Law.*

Maryellen Fullerton, "Failing the Test: Germany Leads Europe in Dismantling Refugee Protection" (2001) 36 *Texas International Law Journal* 231–275.

Merris Amos, "The Dialogue Between United Kingdom Courts and the European Court of Human Rights" (2012) 61:3 *International & Comparative Law Quarterly* 557–584.

Michelle Foster, "Protection Elsewhere: The Legal Implications of Requiring Refugees to Seek Protection in Another State" (2007) 28:2 *Michigan Journal of International Law* 223–286.

Michelle Foster, "Responsibility Sharing of Shifting? "Safe" Third Countries and International Law", 25(2) *Refuge* 64–78.

Moira Sy, "UNHCR and Preventing Indirect *Refoulement* in Europe" (2015) 27:3 *International Journal of Refugee Law* 457.

Nikolas Feith Tan and Thomas Gammeltoft-Hansen, "A Topographical Approach to Accountability for Human Rights Violations in Migration Control" (2020) 21(3) *German Law Journal,* 335–354.

Olivier de Schutter, "The Promotion of Fundamental Rights by the Union as a contribution to the European Legal Space (I): Mutual Recognition and Mutual Trust in the Establishment of the Area of Freedom, Security and Justice", *RefGov Working Paper,* 2006.

Patricia Mallia, "Case of MSS v Belgium and Greece: A Catalyst in the Re-Thinking of the Dublin II Regulation" (2011) 30 *Refugee Survey Quarterly* 107–128.

Paul Weis, "The Development of Refugee Law" (1982) 3:1 *Michigan Journal of International Law* 27–42.

Rebecca Dowd and Jane McAdam, "International Cooperation and Responsibility-Sharing to Protect Refugees: What, Why and How?" (2017) *International and Comparative Law Quarterly* 863–892.

Robert L. Newmark, "Non-Refoulement Run Afoul: The Questionable Legality of Exterritorial Repatriation Programs" (1993) 71:3 *Washington University Law Review* 833–870.

Sacha Prechal, "Mutual Trust before the Court of Justice of the European Union" (2017) *European Papers* 2(1), 75–92.

Satvinder S. Juss, "The Post-Colonial Refugee, Dublin II, and the end of non-refoulement" (2013) 20:2 *International Journal on Minority and Group Rights,* 307–335.

Seunghwan Kim, "Non-Refoulement and Extraterritorial Jurisdiction: State Sovereignty and Migration Controls at Sea in the European Context" (2017) *Leiden Journal of International Law* 30.

Silva Morgades-Gil, "The Discretion of States in the Dublin III System for Determining Responsibility for Examining Applications for Asylum: What Remains of the Sovereignty and Humanitarian Clauses after the Interpretations of the ECtHR and the CJEU?" (2015) 27:3 *International Journal of Refugee Law* 433–456.

Sophie H. Pirie, "Note: The Need for a Codified Definition of 'Persecution' in United States Refugee Law" (1986) 39:1 *Stanford Law Review* 187–234.

Stefano Montaldo, "On a Collision Course! Mutual Recognition, Mutual Trust and the Protection of Fundamental Rights in the Recent Case-Law of the Court of Justice" (2016) 1 *European Papers* 3, 965–996.

Terry Hutchinson, "The Doctrinal Method: Incorporating Interdisciplinary Methods in Reforming the Law" (2015) 8(3) *Erasmus Law Review* 130.

Terry Hutchinson and Nigel Duncan, "Defining and Describing What We Do: Doctrine Legal Research" (2012) 17:1 *Deakin Law Review* 83–119.

Theodor Meron, "Agora: The 1994 US Action in Haiti: Extraterritoriality of Human Rights Treaties" (1995) 89 *American Journal of International Law.*

Thomas David Jones, "Sale v. Haitian Centers Council, Inc." (1994) 88:1 *American Journal of International Law* 114–126.

Thomas Gammeltoft-Hansen and James C Hathaway, "Non-Refoulement in a World of Cooperative Deterrence" (2014) 53 *Columbia Journal of Transnational Law* 235.

Thomas Gammeltoft-Hansen and Nikloas Feith Tan, "Beyond the deterrence paradigm in global refugee policy" (2016) 39(3) *Suffolk Transnational Law Review,* 637.

Thomas Gammeltoft-Hansen and Nikolas Feith Tan, "The End of the Deterrence Paradigm? Future Directions for Global Refugee Policy" (2017) *Journal on Migration and Human Security* 28–56.

Volker T*ürk and Madeline Garlick, "From Burdens and Responsibilities to Opportunities: Comprehensive Refugee Response Framework and a Global Compact on Refugees" (2016) 28:4 International Journal of Refugee Law, 656–678.*

Yuval Shany, "Toward a General Margin of Appreciation Doctrine in International Law?" (2006) 16:5 *European Journal of International Law* 907–940.

A.6 Secondary Material: Other

A.6.1 Online Sources

Access to European Union Law, "The Principle of Subsidiarity", 3 September 2015.

"Admissibility, Responsibility and Safety in European Asylum Procedures", September 2016.

Agreement on the Withdrawal of the United Kingdom of Great Britain and Northern Ireland from the European Union and the European Atomic Energy Community, https://eur-lex.europa.eu/legal-content/EN/TXT/PDF/?uri=CELEX:12019W/TXT(02)&from=EN.

Amnesty International, "Hotspot Italy: How EU's Flagship Approach Leads to Violations of Refugee and Migrant Rights", 3 November 2016 https://www.amnesty.org/download/Documents/EUR3050042016ENGLISH.PDF.

Amnesty International, European Institutions Office, "The Proposed Dublin Reform", 25 November 2016, https://www.amnesty.eu/wp-content/uploads/2018/10/AI_position_paper_on_Dublin_IV_proposal.pdf.

Anja Palm, "The Italy-Libya Memorandum of Understanding: The baseline of a policy approach aimed at closing all doors to Europe?", 2 October 2017 http://eumigrationlawblog.eu/the-italy-libya-memorandum-of-understanding-the-baseline-of-a-policy-approach-aimed-at-closing-all-doors-to-europe/.

Annalisa Buscaini, "When Will the Time Be Ripe for a European Legal Migration Policy?", September 2018, https://eu.boell.org/en/2018/09/14/when-will-time-be-ripe-european-legal-migration-policy.

Anne Lagerwall, "Jus Cogens", *Oxford Bibliographies,* 28 May 2015 http://www.oxfordbibliographies.com/view/document/obo-9780199796953/obo-9780199796953-0124.xml.

Asylum Information Database, "Annex I—Transposition of the CEAS in National Legislation: Germany" http://www.asylumineurope.org/reports/country/germany/annex-i-%E2%80%93-transposition-ceas-national-legislation.

Asylum Information Database, "Common Asylum System at a Turning Point: Refugees Caught in Europe's Solidarity Crisis: Annual Report 2014/2015", September 2015, https://www.asylumineurope.org/sites/default/files/shadow-reports/aida_annualreport_2014-2015_0.pdf.

Asylum Information Database, "Country Report: Germany", March 2017, https://www.asylumineurope.org/sites/default/files/report-download/aida_de_2016update.pdf.

Asylum Information Database, "Country Report: Italy", December 2015, http://www.asylumineurope.org/reports/country/italy.

Asylum Information Database, "Country Report: United Kingdom", 2019 Update, https://www.asylumineurope.org/sites/default/files/report-download/aida_uk_2019update.pdf.

Asylum Information Database, "Dublin: Germany", http://www.asylumineurope.org/reports/country/germany/asylum-procedure/procedures/dublin.

Asylum Information Database, "National Country Report: Germany", May 2014, https://www.refworld.org/pdfid/5406c3ac4.pdf.

Asylum Information Database, "Not There Yet: An NGO Perspective on Challenges to a Fair and Effective Common European Asylum System" (Annual Report 2012–2013), https://www.ecre.org/wp-content/uploads/2016/06/not_there_yet_02102013.pdf.

Asylum Information Database, "Safe Third Country: Germany", http://www.asylumineurope.org/reports/country/germany/asylum-procedure/safe-country-concepts/safe-third-country.

Asylum Information Database, "Safe Third Country: UK", http://www.asylumineurope.org/reports/country/united-kingdom/asylum-procedure/safe-country-concepts/safe-third-country.

Asylum Information Database, "Short Overview of the Asylum Procedure: UK", https://www.asylumineurope.org/reports/country/united-kingdom/asylum-procedure/general/short-overview-asylum-procedure.

Asylum Information Database, "The Implementation of the Dublin III Regulation in 2018", March 2019, http://www.asylumineurope.org/sites/default/files/aida_2018update_dublin.pdf.

*Boldizs*ár Nagy, "Sharing the Responsibility or Shifting the Focus? The Responses of the EU and the Visegrad Countries to the Post-2015 Arrival of Migrants and Refugees", May 2017 *http://www.iai.it/sites/default/files/gte_wp_17.pdf.*

British Broadcasting Corporation, "Brexit: All You Need to Know About the UK Leaving the EU" http://www.bbc.co.uk/news/uk-politics-32810887.

British Broadcasting Corporation, "Syria Profile—Timeline", https://www.bbc.com/news/world-middle-east-14703995.

Bundesverfassungsgericht, "Court and Constitutional Organ" https://www.bundesverfassungsgericht.de/EN/Das-Gericht/Gericht-und-Verfassungsorgan/gericht-und-verfassungsorgan_node.html.

Bundesverfassungsgericht, "How to Lodge a Constitutional Complaint" https://www.bundesverfassungsgericht.de/EN/Homepage/_zielgruppeneinstieg/Merkblatt/Merkblatt.html.

Bundesverfassungsgericht, "International Perspectives" https://www.bundesverfassungsgericht.de/EN/Das-Gericht/Internationale-Perspektiven/internationale-perspektiven_node.html.

Bundesverfassungsgericht, "The Court's Duties" https://www.bundesverfassungsgericht.de/EN/Das-Gericht/Aufgaben/aufgaben_node.html.

Catherin Phuong, "Identifying States' Responsibilities towards Refugees and Asylum Seekers" *European Society of International Law Research Forum*, May 2005 at 2 http://www.esil-sedi.eu/sites/default/files/Phuong.PDF.

Cathryn Costello, "Policy Primer: The UK, the Common European Asylum System and EU Immigration Law", 2 May 2014, https://migrationobservatory.ox.ac.uk/wp-content/uploads/2016/04/PolicyPrimer-UK_EU_Asylum_Law.pdf.

Cathryn Costello, "The UK, the Common European Asylum System and EU Immigration Law", 2 May 2014, https://migrationobservatory.ox.ac.uk/resources/primers/the-uk-the-common-european-asylum-system-and-eu-immigration-law.

Commission of the European Communities, "Communication from the Commission to the European Parliament, the Council, the European Economic and Social Committee and the Committee of Regions: Policy Plan on Asylum", Brussels, 17 June 2008, COM(2008) 360 Final http://eur-lex.europa.eu/LexUriServ/LexUriServ.do?uri=COM:2008:0360:FIN:EN:PDF.

Council of Bars and Law Societies of Europe, "The European Court of Human Rights: Questions & Answers for Lawyers", 2014 https://www.echr.coe.int/Documents/Guide_ECHR_lawyers_ENG.pdf.

Council of Europe, "47 Member States", https://www.coe.int/en/web/portal/47-members-states.

Council of Europe, "A Convention to Protect Your Rights and Liberties" http://www.coe.int/en/web/human-rights-convention/.

Council of Europe, "Convention for the Protection of Human Rights and Fundamental Freedoms", https://www.coe.int/en/web/conventions/full-list/-/conventions/treaty/005.

Council of Europe, "European Court of Human Rights" http://www.coe.int/t/democracy/migration/bodies/echr_en.asp.

Council of Europe, "Our Member States", https://www.coe.int/en/web/about-us/our-member-states.

Council of Europe, "The Council of Europe in Brief", https://www.coe.int/en/web/about-us/do-not-get-confused.

Council of Europe, "Values: Human Rights, Democracy, and Rule of Law" http://www.coe.int/en/web/about-us/values.

Council of Europe, Migration and Human Rights "European Court of Human Rights" http://www.coe.int/t/democracy/migration/bodies/echr_en.asp.

Council of the European Union, "Proposal for a Regulation of the European Parliament and of the Council amending Council Regulation (EC) No 539/2001 listing the third countries whose nationals must be in possession of visas when crossing the external borders and those whose nationals are exempt from that requirement, as regards the withdrawal of the United Kingdom from the Union—Confirmation of the final compromise text with a view to agreement", 2018/0390 (COD), 2 April 2019, https://op.europa.eu/en/publication-detail/-/publication/eb734b75-e8e0-11e8-b690-01aa75ed71a1.

Council of the European Union, "Reform of the Common European Asylum System—The Safe Countries Concept", 8 May 2018, http://www.statewatch.org/news/2018/may/eu-council-safe-countries-concept-8735-18.pdf.

Court of Justice of the European Union, "Opinion of Advocate General Trstenjak delivered on 22 September 2011", Case C-493/10, M.E., A.S.M., M.T., K.P., E.H. v Refugee Applications Commissioner, Minister for Justice, Equality and Law Reform, http://www.statewatch.org/news/2011/sep/ecj-m-e-case-493-advocate-general-opinion.pdf.

Council of Bars and Law Societies of Europe, "The European Court of Human Rights: Questions & Answers for Lawyers", 2014, https://www.echr.coe.int/Documents/Guide_ECHR_lawyers_ENG.pdf.

Daniel Thym, "Beyond Dublin—Merkel's Vision of EU Asylum Policy", EU Immigration and Asylum Law and Policy, 26 October 2015.

Daria Davitti and Marlene Fries, "Offshore Processing and Complicity in Current EU Migration Policies: Parts 1 &2" *EJIL!Talk Blog,* https://www.ejiltalk.org/offshore-processing-and-complicity-in-current-eu-migration-policies-part-2.

Dartmouth College Library, "A Short Definition for Migration Studies", https://researchguides.dartmouth.edu/human_geography/migration.

Dartmouth College Library, "A Short Definition of Human Geography", https://researchguides.dartmouth.edu/human_geography/main.

Debra Long, "Guide to Jurisprudence on Torture and Ill-Treatment: Article 3 of the European Convention for the Protection of Human Rights", June 2002 https://www.apt.ch/content/files_res/Article3_en.pdf.

Deutscher Bundestag, *Basic Law for the Federal Republic of Germany,* last amended 28 March 2019, https://www.btg-bestellservice.de/pdf/80201000.pdf.

Durham University, "Are UK Courts bound by the European Court of Human Rights?", *Law School Research Briefing No 10,* https://www.dur.ac.uk/resources/law/research/AreUKCourtsboundbytheEuropeanCourtofHumanRights.pdf.

EMN Focussed Study 2017, "(Member) States' Approaches to Unaccompanied Minors Following Status Determination: Common Template for EMN Focussed Study 2017: Final Version", https://ec.europa.eu/home-affairs/sites/homeaffairs/files/29a_norway_unaccompanied_minors_2017_en_0.pdf.

"EU laws designed to deter refugees", *The New Humanitarian,* 27 January 2016, http://www.thenewhumanitarian.org/news/2016/01/27/eu-laws-designed-deter-refugees.

European Court of Human Rights, "Guide on Article 6 of the Convention—Right to a fair trial (criminal limb)", 31 August 2018, https://www.echr.coe.int/Documents/Guide_Art_6_criminal_ENG.pdf.

EUR-Lex, "Justice, Freedom and Security" http://eur-lex.europa.eu/summary/chapter/justice_freedom_security.html?root_default=SUM_1_CODED=23.

EUR-Lex, "Non-EU Nationals—Rules for Long-Term Residence", 23 August 2016 http://eur-lex.europa.eu/legal-content/EN/TXT/?uri=URISERV%3Al23034.

Europa, "EU Institutions and Other Bodies", 12 November 2016 https://europa.eu/european-union/about-eu/institutions-bodies_en.

Europa, "Regulations, Directives and Other Acts", 12 November 2016 https://europa.eu/european-union/law/legal-acts_en.

Europe in Strasbourg, "Member States of the European Union and the Council of Europe" http://en.strasbourg-europe.eu/member-states,44987,en.html.

European Agency for Fundamental Rights, "Access to Justice", https://fra.europa.eu/en/theme/access-justice.

European Agency for Fundamental Rights, "Handbook on European law relating to asylum, borders and immigration", https://www.europarl.europa.eu/greece/resource/static/files/handbook-on-european-law-relating-to-asylum–borders-and-immigration.pdf.

European Association for the Defence of Human Rights, International Federation for Human Rights, and EuroMed Rights, "Safe' Countries: A Denial of the Right of Asylum", May 2016, https://www.ohchr.org/Documents/Issues/MHR/ReportLargeMovements/FIDH2%20.pdf.

European Asylum Support Office, "An Introduction to the Common European Asylum System for Courts and Tribunals: A Judicial Analysis", August 2016 https://www.easo.europa.eu/sites/default/files/public/BZ0216138ENN.PDF.

European Asylum Support Office, "Judicial Analysis: Asylum Procedures and the Principle of *Non-Refoulement*", https://www.easo.europa.eu/sites/default/files/asylum-procedures-ja_en.pdf.

European Commission, "Applying EU Law" https://ec.europa.eu/info/law/law-making-process/applying-eu-law_en.

European Commission, "Common European Asylum System" http://ec.europa.eu/dgs/home-affairs/what-we-do/policies/asylum/index_en.htm.

European Commission, "Evaluation of the Dublin III Regulation: Final Report", 4 December 2015, https://ec.europa.eu/home-affairs/sites/homeaffairs/files/what-we-do/policies/asylum/examination-of-applicants/docs/evaluation_of_the_dublin_iii_regulation_en.pdf.

European Commission, "Evaluation of the Implementation of the Dublin III Regulation: Final Report", 18 March 2016, https://ec.europa.eu/home-affairs/sites/homeaffairs/files/what-we-do/policies/asylum/examination-of-applicants/docs/evaluation_of_the_implementation_of_the_dublin_iii_regulation_en.pdf.

European Commission, "FAQ on the EU Competences and the European Commission Powers", https://europa.eu/citizens-initiative/faq-eu-competences-and-commission-powers_en.

European Commission, "Presentation of ECtHR case Tarakehel vs. Switzerland and the relevant legal and jurisprudential context", https://ec.europa.eu/transparency/regexpert/index.cfm?do=groupDetail.groupMeetingDoc&docid=13083.

European Commission, "Types of EU Law", https://ec.europa.eu/info/law/law-making-process/types-eu-law_en.

European Commission, European Neighbourhood Policy and Enlargement Negotiations, "Acquis", https://ec.europa.eu/neighbourhood-enlargement/policy/glossary/terms/acquis_en.

European Commission, Migration and Home Affairs, "Hotspot Approach", https://ec.europa.eu/home-affairs/content/hotspot-approach_en.

European Commission, Migration and Home Affairs, "Procedural Guarantees", https://ec.europa.eu/home-affairs/content/procedural-guarantees_en.

European Commission, Migration and Home Affairs, "Safe Third Country", https://ec.europa.eu/home-affairs/what-we-do/networks/european_migration_network/glossary_search/safe-third-country_en.

European Commission, Migration and Home Affairs, "Schengen Area", 29 January 2016 http://ec.europa.eu/dgs/home-affairs/what-we-do/policies/borders-and-visas/schengen/index_en.htm.

European Commission, Migration and Home Affairs, "Subsidiary Protection", https://ec.europa.eu/home-affairs/what-we-do/networks/european_migration_network/glossary_search/subsidiary-protection_en.

European Commission, Migration and Home Affairs, "Third-Country National", https://ec.europa.eu/home-affairs/content/third-country-national_en.

European Commission of Human Rights, *The Greek Case*, App nos 3321/67, 3322/67, 3323/67 and 3344/67 (1969) *Yearbook of European Convention on Human Rights.*

European Committee for the Prevention of Torture and Inhuman or Degrading Treatment or Punishment, "Report to the Bulgarian Government on the visit to Bulgaria carried out by the European Committee for the Prevention of Torture and Inhuman or Degrading Treatment or Punishment (CPT) from 24 March to 3 April 2014", Strasbourg, 29 January 2015 http://www.cpt.coe.int/documents/bgr/2015-12-inf-eng.pdf.

European Committee for the Prevention of Torture and Inhuman or Degrading Treatment or Punishment, "Report to the Greek Government on the visit to Greece carried out by the European Committee for the Prevention of Torture and Inhuman or Degrading Treatment or Punishment (CPT) from 4 to 16 April 2013", Strasbourg, 16 October 2014 http://www.cpt.coe.int/documents/grc/2014-26-inf-eng.pdf.

European Council, "Note from the General Secretariat of the Council to Delegations, Conclusions of the European Council meeting on 28 June 2018", Brussels, https://www.consilium.europa.eu/media/35936/28-euco-final-conclusions-en.pdf.

European Council, "Statement of the EU Heads of State or Government", 7 March 2016, https://www.consilium.europa.eu/en/press/press-releases/2016/03/08/eu-turkey-meeting-statement.

European Council, "Timeline: Reform of EU Asylum Rules" http://www.consilium.europa.eu/en/policies/ceas-reform/ceas-reform-timeline/.

European Council on Refugees and Exiles, "Case Law Fact Sheet: Prevention of Dublin Transfers to Hungary", January 2016, http://statewatch.org/news/2016/jan/eu-ecre-factsheet-dublin-transfers-to-hungary-1-16.pdf.

European Council on Refugee and Exiles, "ECRE Comments on the Commission Proposal for a Dublin IV Regulation, COM(2016) 270", October 2016, http://www.ecre.org/wp-content/uploads/2016/10/ECRE-Comments-Dublin-IV.pdf.

European Council on Refugees and Exiles, "ECRE strongly opposes legitimising push-backs by declaring Turkey a 'safe third country', 29 January 2016, https://www.ecre.org/ecre-strongly-opposes-legitimising-push-backs-by-declaring-turkey-a-safe-third-country.

European Council on Refugees and Exiles, "Germany: Constitutional Court Strengthens Rights of Asylum Seekers Subject to Dublin", https://www.ecre.org/germany-constitutional-court-strengthens-rights-of-asylum-seekers-subject-to-dublin.

European Council on Refugees and Exiles, "Germany: Dublin Transfer to Denmark despite Church Asylum", https://www.ecre.org/germany-dublin-transfer-to-denmark-despite-church-asylum.

European Council on Refugees and Exiles, "Germany follows UNHCR call for suspension of Dublin transfers to Hungary", 14 April 2017, https://www.ecre.org/germany-follows-unhcr-call-for-suspension-of-dublin-transfers-to-hungary.

European Council on Refugees and Exiles, "Germany Steps Up Dublin Transfers Putting Asylum Seekers at Risk", 21 March 2019, https://www.ecre.org/germany-steps-up-dublin-transfers-putting-asylum-seekers-at-risk.

European Council on Refugees and Exiles, "Germany: Temporary Suspension of Dublin Returns Due to COVID-19", https://www.ecre.org/germany-temporary-suspension-of-dublin-returns-due-to-covid-10.

European Council on Refugees and Exiles, "Hungary: Dublin Transfers Suspended by Germany", https://www.asylumineurope.org/news/29-08-2017/hungary-dublin-transfers-suspended-germany.

European Council on Refugees and Exiles, "Italy: Vulnerable Dublin Returnees at Risk of Destitution", 14 December 2018, https://www.ecre.org/italy-vulnerable-dublin-returnees-at-risk-of-destitution.

European Council on Refugees and Exiles, "Our Work", https://www.ecre.org/our-work.

European Council on Refugees and Exiles, "The Dublin System in the First Half of 2019", https://www.asylumineurope.org/news/27-08-2019/dublin-system-first-half-2019.

European Court of Human Rights, "The ECHR in 50 Questions", February 2014, https://www.echr.coe.int/Documents/50Questions_ENG.pdf.

European Database of Asylum Law, "About EDAL European Database of Asylum Law", http://www.asylumlawdatabase.eu/en/content/about-edal-european-database-asylum-law.

European Database of Asylum Law, "ECtHR—M.S.S. v Belgium and Greece [GC], Application No. 30,696/09", 21 January 2011, https://www.asylumlawdatabase.eu/en/content/ecthr-mss-v-belgium-and-greece-gc-application-no-3069609.

European Database of Asylum Law, "ECtHR—Tarakhel v. Switzerland, Application No. 29,217/12", https://www.asylumlawdatabase.eu/en/content/ecthr-tarakhel-v-switzerland-application-no-2921712.

European Database of Asylum Law, "Germany—Administrative Court (of) Hannover, Case No. 1 B 5946/15, 7 March 2016" http://www.asylumlawdatabase.eu/en/case-law/germany-administrative-court-hannover-case-no-1-b-594615-7-march-2016.

European Database of Asylum Law, "Germany—Administrative Court of Justice Baden-Württemberg, 15 March 2017, A 11 S 2151/16" http://www.asylumlawdatabase.eu/en/case-law/germany-%E2%80%93-administrative-court-justice-baden-w%C3%BCrttemberg-15-march-2017-11-s-215116.

European Database of Asylum Law, "Germany—Administrative Court (of) Hannover, Case No. 1 B 5946/15, 7 March 2016", http://www.asylumlawdatabase.eu/en/case-law/germany-administrative-court-hannover-case-no-1-b-594615-7-march-2016.

European Database of Asylum Law, "Germany—Administrative Court of Magdeburg, Chamber, 26 January 2016, Case No 8 A 108/16" http://www.asylumlawdatabase.eu/en/case-law/germany-%E2%80%93-administrative-court-magdeburg-chamber-8-26-january-2016-8a-108-16.

European Database of Asylum Law, "Germany—Administrative Court of Minden, 2 October 2015, Case No. 10 L 923/15.A" http://www.asylumlawdatabase.eu/en/case-law/germany-administrative-court-minden-2-october-2015-case-no-10-l-92315a.

European Database of Asylum Law, "Germany—Administrative Court of Oldenburg, 12th Chamber, 2 October 2015, 12 A 2572/15" http://www.asylumlawdatabase.eu/en/case-law/germany-administrative-court-oldenburg-12th-chamber-2-october-2015-12-257215.

European Database of Asylum Law, "Germany—High Administrative Court Nordrhein-Westfalen, 27 March 2007, 8 A 4728/05.A" http://www.asylumlawdatabase.eu/en/case-law/germany-high-administrative-court-nordrhein-westfalen-27-march-2007-8-472805a.

European Database of Asylum Law, "UK: Upper Tribunal publishes new Country Guidance case on Eritrea", 10 October 2016 http://www.asylumlawdatabase.eu/en/content/uk-upper-tribunal-publishes-new-country-guidance-case-eritrea.

European Database of Asylum Law, "UK—The Queen on the application of Mr Mohsen Pourali Tabrizagh, Mr Tahir Syed, Mr Saeed Ali, Mr Ali Omar Mohammed, Mr Edmond Karaj, AB (Sudan) v Secretary of State for the Home Department", https://www.asylumlawdatabase.eu/en/case-law/uk-queen-application-mr-mohsen-pourali-tabrizagh-mr-tahir-syed-mr-saeed-ali-mr-ali-omar.

European Parliament, "An Area of Freedom, Security and Justice: General Aspects", http://www.europarl.europa.eu/ftu/pdf/en/FTU_4.2.1.pdf.

European Parliament, "Directorate-General for External Policies of the Union: Directorate B, Policy Department, Briefing Paper: Current Challenges for International Refugee Law, with a Focus on EU Policies and EU Co-Operation with the UNHCR", December 2013.

European Parliament, "Dublin Regulation on International Protection Applications: European Implementation Assessment", February 2020, https://www.europarl.europa.eu/RegData/etudes/STUD/2020/642813/EPRS_STU(2020)642813_EN.pdf.

European Parliament, "Fact Sheets on the European Union: The Maastricht and Amsterdam Treaties", October 2016 http://www.europarl.europa.eu/atyourservice/en/displayFtu.html?ftuId=FTU_1.1.3.html.

European Parliament, "The Common European Asylum System—Third Reform", 28 February 2017, http://www.europarl.europa.eu/RegData/etudes/PERI/2017/580866/IPOL_PERI(2017)580866_EN.pdf.

European Union, "Countries" https://europa.eu/european-union/about-eu/countries_en#the-28-member-countries-of-the-eu.

European Union, "Court of Justice of the European Union (CJEU)" https://europa.eu/european-union/about-eu/institutions-bodies/court-justice_en.

European Union, "EU Law", 28 January 2019, https://europa.eu/european-union/law_en.

European Union, "The History of the European Union", 18 November 2016 https://europa.eu/european-union/about-eu/history_en.

European Union, "Regulations, Directives and Other Acts", 24 May 2018, https://europa.eu/european-union/eu-law/legal-acts_en.

European Union, "Sources and Scope of European Union Law: Fact Sheets on the European Union—2016" http://www.europarl.europa.eu/ftu/pdf/en/FTU_1.2.1.pdf.

European Union, The Council, "Terms of reference of the High Level Working Group on Asylum and Migration; preparation of action plans for the most important countries of origin and transit of asylum-seekers and migrants", 13 January 1999 http://data.consilium.europa.eu/doc/document/ST-5264-1999-INIT/en/pdf.

European Union Agency for Fundamental Rights, "Fundamental Rights Implications of the Obligations to Provide Fingerprints for Eurodac", https://fra.europa.eu/sites/default/files/fra_uploads/fra-2015-fingerprinting-focus-paper_en.pdf.

European Union Agency for Fundamental Rights, "Scope of the principle of *non-refoulement* in contemporary border management: evolving areas of law", https://fra.europa.eu/sites/default/files/fra_uploads/fra-2016-scope-non-refoulement-0_en.pdf.

Eurostat, "Asylum and first time asylum applicants by citizenship, age and sex: Monthly data (rounded)", 5 May 2020, https://appsso.eurostat.ec.europa.eu/nui/show.do?dataset=migr_asyappctzm&lang=en.

Federal Office for Migration and Refugees, "Entitlement to Asylum", 1 October 2016, http://www.bamf.de/EN/Fluechtlingsschutz/AblaufAsylv/Schutzformen/Asylberechtigung/asylberechtigung-node.html;jsessionid=B5FDF16C53BC807E0861D803C0F4BCED.2_cid368.

Federal Office for Migration and Refugees, "Procedure Management and Quality Assurance" http://www.bamf.de/EN/Fluechtlingsschutz/VerfahrenssteuerungQualitaetssicherung/verfahrenssteuerung-node.html.

Federal Office for Migration and Refugees, "Refugee Protection", 1 October 2016, http://www.bamf.de/EN/Fluechtlingsschutz/AblaufAsylv/Schutzformen/Fluechtlingsschutz/fluechtlingsschutz-node.html.

Federal Office for Migration and Refugees, "The Authority" http://www.bamf.de/EN/DasBAMF/Aufgaben/Beh%C3%B6rde/die-behoerde-node.html.

Federal Office for Migration and Refugees, "Entitlement to Asylum", 1 October 2016, http://www.bamf.de/EN/Fluechtlingsschutz/AblaufAsylv/Schutzformen/Asylberechtigung/asylberechtigung-node.html.

Federal Office for Migration and Refugees, "The stages of the German asylum procedure", 2/2019, https://www.bamf.de/SharedDocs/Anlagen/EN/AsylFluechtlingsschutz/Asylverfahren/das-deutsche-asylverfahren.pdf?__blob=publicationFile&v=12.

Filippo Grandi, "Protecting Refugees in Europe and Beyond: Can the EU rise to the Challenge?", European Policy Centre, Brussels, 5 December 2016, https://www.unhcr.org/admin/hcspeeches/58456ec34/protecting-refugees-europe-beyond-eu-rise-challenge.html.

Free Movement, "What is the difference between refugee status and humanitarian protection?", https://www.freemovement.org.uk/what-is-the-difference-between-refugee-status-and-humanitarian-protection.

Gillian Brock, "Global Justice", *Stanford Encyclopedia of Philosophy,* 6 March 2015 https://plato.stanford.edu/entries/justice-global/#SomDefIss.

Glenda Garelli and Martina Tazzioli, "Beyond Detention: Spatial Strategies of Dispersal and Channels of Forced Transfer", *Society & Space,* 8 November 2016, https://www.societyandspace.org/articles/beyond-detention-spatial-strategies-of-dispersal-and-channels-of-forced-transfer.

Greater Manchester Immigration Aid Unit, "Briefing paper on the experiences of children from the Calais camp in the north west of England", March 2017, https://gmiau.org/briefing-paper-experiences-children-calais-camp-north-west-england.

Guy S. Goodwin-Gill, "Convention Relating to the Status of Refugees, Protocol Relating to the Status of Refugees", *United Nations Audiovisual Library of International Law,* https://legal.un.org/avl/pdf/ha/prsr/prsr_e.pdf.

Handbook Germany, "Dublin Procedure", https://handbookgermany.de/en/rights-laws/asylum/dublin-procedure.html.

Home Office, "Certification of protection and human rights claim under section 94 of the Nationality, Immigration and Asylum Act 2002 (clearly unfounded claims)", Version 4.0, 12 February 2019, https://assets.publishing.service.gov.uk/government/uploads/system/uploads/attachment_data/file/778221/certification-s94-guidance-0219.pdf.

House of Commons Library, "What is Dublin III Regulation? Will it be affected by Brexit?", https://commonslibrary.parliament.uk/home-affairs/immigration/what-is-the-dublin-iii-regulation-will-it-be-affected-by-brexit.

House of Lords, European Union Committee, "Brexit: Refugee Protection and Asylum Policy", 11 October 2019, https://publications.parliament.uk/pa/ld201719/ldselect/ldeucom/428/428.pdf.

Human Rights Watch, "'Diplomatic Assurances' against Torture—Questions and Answers", https://www.hrw.org/sites/default/files/related_material/ecaqna1106web.pdf.

Human Rights Watch, "Still at Risk: Diplomatic Assurances No Safeguard Against Torture", 15 April 2005, https://www.refworld.org/docid/42c3bd400.html.

Human Rights Watch, "Towards an Effective and Principled EU Migration Policy: Recommendations for Reform", June 2018, https://www.hrw.org/sites/default/files/supporting_resources/hrw_eu_migration_policy_memo_0.pdf.

InfoMigrants, "Seeking Asylum in Europe in 2019: Facts and Figures", https://www.infomigrants.net/en/post/21810/seeking-asylum-in-europe-in-2019-facts-and-figures.

International Commission of Jurists, "Procedural rights in the proposed Dublin IV Regulation", 27 September 2016, http://www.icj.org/wp-content/uploads/2016/09/EU-Dublin-IV-Regulation_Comment-Advocacy-Analysis-Brief-2016-ENG.pdf.

International Commission of Jurists, "Non-Refoulement in Europe after M.S.S. v. Belgium and Greece", July 2011 at 3–6,:http://www.icj.org/wp-content/uploads/2012/06/Non-refoulement-Europe-summary-of-the-workshop-event-2011-.pdf.

International Organization for Migration, "Key Migration Terms", https://www.iom.int/key-migration-terms.

International Protection Appeals Tribunal, Ireland, "About Us", http://www.protectionappeals.ie/website/rat/ratweb.nsf/page/about_the_tribunal-en.

"Chairperson's Guideline No: 2018/1: Application of 'Compelling Reasons' in the consideration of refugee status appeals originally submitted to the Tribunal pursuant to s.16(1) of the Refugee Act 1996, prior to the commencement of the International Protection Act 2015", http://www.protectionappeals.ie/website/rat/ratweb.nsf/page/MJOF-AXAA8J7595728-en/$File/IP%20Guideline%202018-1%20on%20Compelling%20Grounds.pdf.

International Protection Appeals Tribunal, Ireland, "Chairperson's Guideline No. 2019/1 on Taking Evidence from Appellants and Other Witnesses", http://www.protectionappeals.ie/website/rat/ratweb.nsf/page/MXKY-B9KK4514334220-en/$File/Guideline%202019-1%20on%20Taking%20Evidence%20from%20Appellants%20and%20Other%20Witnesses.pdf

International Protection Appeals Tribunal, Ireland, "Publications", http://www.protectionappeals.ie/website/rat/ratweb.nsf/page/Publications-en.

Izabella Majcher, "Border Securitization and Containment vs. Fundamental Rights: The European Union's 'Refugee Crisis'", *Georgetown Journal of International Affairs, Conflict & Security Blog,* 20 March 2017, https://www.georgetownjournalofinternationalaffairs.org/border-securitization-and-containment-vs-fundamental-rights-the-european-unions-refugee-crisis.

Jenny Poon, "ESIL Reflection: The EU Commission on 'Dublin IV': Sufficient Safeguards for Asylum Claimants?" (2016) 5:9 *European Society of International Law, Reflections* 1–10, http://esil-sedi.eu/wp-content/uploads/2016/10/ESIL-Reflections-Jenny-Poon-Nov-2016-Revision-20161109-clean_1.pdf.

Jenny Poon, "Is the Margin of Appreciation Accorded to European Union Member States Too Wide, Permitting Violations of International Law?" *Opinio Juris* Blog, 16 August 2016 http://opiniojuris.org/2016/08/16/emerging-voices-is-the-margin-of-appreciation-accorded-to-european-union-member-states-too-wide-permitting-violation-of-international-law.

Jenny Poon, "Libya-EU Memorandum of Understanding: Implications for Non-Refoulement and Compliance with International Human Rights Law?", *Cambridge Journal of International Law Blog,* 2 December 2017, http://cilj.co.uk/2017/12/02/libya-eu-memorandum-of-understanding-implications-for-non-refoulement-and-compliance-with-international-human-rights-law.

Jenny Poon, "Non-Refoulement as Lex Specialis?" (2017) *London School of Economics and Political Science Human Rights Blog*, https://blogs.lse.ac.uk/humanrights/2017/07/07/non-refoulement-as-lex-specialis.

Jenny Poon, "Non-Refoulement Obligations in EU Third Country Agreements", *European Database of Asylum Law Online Journal,* 28 March 2018, https://www.asylumlawdatabase.eu/en/journal/non-refoulement-obligations-eu-third-country-agreements.

Jenny Poon, "Non-Refoulement Obligations in the EU-Turkey Deal and Italy-Libya Memorandum of Understanding", *International Law Blog,* 20 June 2019, https://internationallaw.blog/2019/06/20/non-refoulement-obligations-in-the-eu-turkey-deal-and-italy-libya-memorandum-of-understanding.

Jenny Poon, "Non-Refoulement Obligations in Offshore Detention Facilities", *E-International Relations Blog,* 16 October 2018, https://www.e-ir.info/2018/10/16/non-refoulement-obligations-in-offshore-detention-facilities.

Jenny Poon, "Reframing Non-Refoulement as an Individual Right under International Law?", *Refugee Law Initiative Blog,* 18 July 2017, https://rli.blogs.sas.ac.uk/2017/07/18/reframing-non-refoulement-as-an-individual-right-under-international-law.

Jenny Poon, "Rethinking the Common European Asylum System: Protection or Containment?" (2020) *Rethinking Refuge,* University of Oxford, Department of International Development, Refugee Studies Centre, https://www.rethinkingrefuge.org/articles/rethinking-emergency-and-crisis.

Jessica Brandt and Claire Higgins, "Europe wants to process asylum seekers offshore—the lessons it should learn from Australia", *Brookings Institute, Order from Chaos,* 31 August 2018, https://www.brookings.edu/blog/order-from-chaos/2018/08/31/europe-wants-to-process-asylum-seekers-offshore-the-lessons-it-should-learn-from-australia.

Julian Lamont and Christi Favor, "Distributive Justice", 26 September 1997, *Stanford Encyclopedia of Philosophy*https://plato.stanford.edu/entries/justice-distributive/.

Katy Long, "No Entry! A Review of UNHCR's Response to Border Closures in Situations of Mass Refugee Influx", June 2010, http://www.unhcr.org/4c207bd59.pdf.

Kevin K. W. Ip, "Global Distributive Justice" (2017) *Oxford Research Encyclopedia of International Studies* 1–25.

Koen Lenaerts, "The Principle of Mutual Recognition in the Area of Freedom, Security and Justice", *Fourth Annual Sir Jeremy Lever Lecture,* 30 January 2015 https://www.law.ox.ac.uk/sites/files/oxlaw/the_principle_of_mutual_recognition_in_the_area_of_freedom_judge_lenaerts.pdf.

Library of Congress, "Refugee Law and Policy: European Union", 21 June 2016 https://www.loc.gov/law/help/refugee-law/europeanunion.php.

Madeline Chiam, "Monism and Dualism in International Law", 27 June 2018, http://www.oxfordbibliographies.com/view/document/obo-9780199796953/obo-9780199796953-0168.xml.

Marcello Di Filippo, "Dublin 'reloaded' or time for ambitious pragmatism?", 12 October 2016 http://eumigrationlawblog.eu/dublin-reloaded.

Maria Hennessy, "Vulnerability, the Right to Asylum and the Dublin System", 14 April 2015, http://www.reflaw.org/vulnerability-the-right-to-asylum-and-the-dublin-system.

Marion Smiley, "Collective Responsibility", *Stanford Encyclopedia of Philosophy,* 27 March 2017 https://plato.stanford.edu/entries/collective-responsibility/#CollRespDist.

Martina Tazzioli, "Rethinking Containment through the EU-Libya Migration Deal" *Völkerrechtsblog,* 23 October 2017, https://voelkerrechtsblog.org/rethinking-containment-through-the-eu-libya-migration-deal.

Marton Dunai, "Hungary says EU's Dublin rules 'dead'; won't leg migrants come back", Ruth Pitchford (ed), Thomson Reuters UK, 11 November 2015 https://www.reuters.com/article/us-europe-migrants-hungary/hungary-says-eus-dublin-rules-dead-wont-let-migrants-come-back-idUSKCN0T01LA20151111.

Memorandum of understanding on cooperation in the fields of development, the fight against illegal immigration, human trafficking and fuel smuggling and on reinforcing the security of borders between the State of Libya and the Italian Republic (English translated version), Odysseus Network, translated by: Sandra Uselli, revised by Marcello Di Filippo, Elena Marati, and Anja Palm, http://eumigrationlawblog.eu/wp-content/uploads/2017/10/MEMORANDUM_translation_finalversion.doc.pdf.

Merriam-Webster Online Dictionary, 10th Edition https://www.merriam-webster.com/.

Migrants At Sea, "NATO Expands Aegean Sea Migrant Patrols into Turkish and Greek Territorial Waters", https://migrantsatsea.org/tag/push-back-practice.

Migration and Home Affairs, "Common European Asylum System" https://ec.europa.eu/home-affairs/what-we-do/policies/asylum_en.

Migration and Home Affairs, "Country of First Asylum" https://ec.europa.eu/home-affairs/content/country-first-asylum_en.

Migration and Home Affairs, "Refugee in Orbit" https://ec.europa.eu/home-affairs/content/refugee-orbit_en.

Migration and Home Affairs, "Third-Country National" https://ec.europa.eu/home-affairs/content/third-country-national_en.

Minos Mouzourakis, "We Need to Talk about Dublin" https://www.rsc.ox.ac.uk/files/publications/working-paper-series/wp105-we-need-to-talk-about-dublin.pdf.

Nick Perre, Myrthe De Vries, Hannah Richards, and Mariana Gkliati, "Refugee Crisis: Three Perspectives on the Makings of a Crisis", 6 June 2018, https://rli.blogs.sas.ac.uk/2018/04/16/refugee-crisis-three-perspectives-on-the-makings-of-a-crisis.

Nicole Dicker and Joanna Mansfield, "Filling the Protection Gap: Current Trends in Complementary Protection in Canada, Mexico and Australia" (2012) *United Nations High Commissioner for Refugees, Policy Development and Evaluation Service*, Geneva http://www.unhcr.org/research/working/4fc872719/filling-protection-gap-current-trends-complementary-protection-canada-mexico.html.

Norwegian Refugee Council, "Q&A: What does the Turkish border situation mean for Europe?", https://www.nrc.no/news/2020/march/q–a-refugees-and-migrants-to-europe.

Olivia Sundberg Diez, "Diminishing safeguards, increasing returns: Non-refoulement gaps in the EU return and readmission system", 4 October 2019, https://www.epc.eu/en/publications/Diminishing-safeguards-increasing-returns-Non-refoulement-gaps-in-th~2b1d1c.

Oxfam, Belgrade Centre for Human Rights and Macedonian Young Lawyers Association, *A Dangerous 'Game': the Pushback of Migrants, including Refugees, at Europe's Borders*, 5 April 2017,

https://www-cdn.oxfam.org/s3fs-public/file_attachments/bp-dangerous-game-pushback-migrants-refugees-060417-en_0.pdf.

Oxfam, "Beyond 'Fortress Europe': Principles for a Humane EU Migration Policy", October 2017, https://d1tn3vj7xz9fdh.cloudfront.net/s3fs-public/file_attachments/bp-principles-humane-eu-migration-policy-111017-en.pdf.

Oxford English Dictionary, "Control", https://en.oxforddictionaries.com/definition/control.

Paul Weis, "The Refugee Convention, 1951: The Travaux Preparatoires Analysed with a Commentary by Dr Paul Weis" http://www.unhcr.org/protection/travaux/4ca34be29/refugee-convention-1951-travaux-preparatoires-analysed-commentary-dr-paul.html.

Paulina Tandiono, "The Extraterritoriality of the Principle of Non-Refoulement: A Critique of the Sale case and Roma case", https://blogs.lse.ac.uk/humanrights/2016/02/09/the-extraterritoriality-of-the-principle-of-non-refoulement-a-critique-of-the-sale-case-and-roma-case.

Ralph Wilde, "'Let Them Drown': Rescuing Migrants at Sea and the Non-Refoulement Obligation as a Case Study of International Law's Relationship to 'Crisis': Parts I and II", *EJIL!Talk* Blog, February 2017 https://www.ejiltalk.org/let-them-drown-rescuing-migrants-at-sea-and-the-non-refoulement-obligation-as-a-case-study-of-international-laws-relationship-to-crisis-part-i/.

Redress, "Mass Refugee Influxes, Refoulement and the Prohibition Against Torture", 3–50, https://www.refworld.org/pdfid/5800ecd14.pdf.

Robert Baratta, “EU Legislative Drafting: Views from those applying EU law in the Member States”, 19th Quality of Legislation Seminar, 2014, Brussels, https://ec.europa.eu/dgs/legal_service/seminars/20140703_baratta_speech.pdf.

Refworld, “Germany: Act Concerning the Entry and Residence of Aliens in the Territory of the Federal Republic (Aliens Act)”, 1 January 1991, https://www.refworld.org/docid/3ae6b55a0.html.

Refworld, “The Safe Third Country Concept (Article 27)”, https://www.refworld.org/cgi-bin/texis/vtx/rwmain/opendocpdf.pdf?reldoc=y&docid=4bab55e22.

Santhosh Persaud, “Protecting Refugees and Asylum Seekers under the International Covenant on Civil and Political Rights”, November 2006 at 5 http://www.unhcr.org/4552f0d82.pdf

Sarah Toucas, “Push and Pull Factors Towards and Against a Common European Migration Policy: France, Britain, and Their Approach to Irregular Migration”, December 2008, https://www.ifri.org/sites/default/files/atoms/files/cadbury1.pdf.

Selin Esen, “The Principle of Non-Refoulement as a Constitutional Right of Asylum Seekers in Turkey”, 26 July 2016, https://verfassungsblog.de/the-principle-of-non-refoulement-as-a-constitutional-eight-of-asylum-seekers-in-turkey.

Statewatch, “Analysis: The second phase of the Common European Asylum System: A Brave New World—or lipstick on a pig?”, 8 April 2013, http://www.statewatch.org/analyses/no-220-ceas-second-phase.pdf.

Stefan Trines, “Lessons From Germany’s Refugee Crisis: Integration, Costs, and Benefits”, https://wenr.wes.org/2017/05/lessons-germanys-refugee-crisis-integration-costs-benefits.

Steve Peers, “The Orbanisation of EU Asylum Law: The latest EU asylum proposals”, 6 May 2016 http://eulawanalysis.blogspot.ca/2016/05/the-orbanisation-of-eu-asylum-law.html.

The Guardian, “May Triggers Article 50 with Warning of Consequence for UK” https://www.theguardian.com/politics/2017/mar/29/theresa-may-triggers-article-50-with-warning-of-consequences-for-uk.

The Migration Observatory at the University of Oxford (analyzing Eurostat data), 8 November 2019, https://migrationobservatory.ox.ac.uk/resources/briefings/migration-to-the-uk-asylum/#kp7.

The Parliament of the United Kingdom, "Asylum: Applications: Written Question—220,305", 18 February 2019, https://www.parliament.uk/business/publications/written-questions-answers-statements/written-question/Commons/2019-02-12/220305.

Thomas Spijkerboer, "The Systemic Failure of the Common European Asylum System, as Exemplified by the EU-Turkey Deal", 18 March 2016 http://thomasspijkerboer.eu/thomas-blogs/the-systemic-failure-of-the-common-european-asylum-system-as-exemplified-by-the-eu-turkey-deal/.

Transnational Institute, "The shrinking space for solidarity with migrants and refugees" September 2018, https://www.tni.org/files/publication-downloads/web_theshrinkingspace.pdf.

United Nations, "Depositary: Status of Treaties—5. Protocol Relating to the Status of Refugees", https://treaties.un.org/pages/ViewDetails.aspx?src=TREATY&mtdsg_no=V-5&chapter=5&lang=en.

United Nations High Commissioner for Refugees, "2. Convention Relating to the Status of Refugees: Geneva, 28 July 1951", http://www.unhcr.org/protection/convention/3d9abe177/reservations-declarations-1951-refugee-convention.html.

United Nations High Commissioner for Refugees, "Asylum-Seekers", https://www.unhcr.org/asylum-seekers.html.

United Nations High Commissioner for Refugees, "Asylum Seeking Process", https://help.unhcr.org/germany/asylum-in-germany/asylum-seeking-process.

United Nations High Commissioner for Refugees, "Better Protecting Refugees in the EU and Globally", December 2016, http://www.europarl.europa.eu/cmsdata/114503/unhcr-better-protect.pdf.

United Nations High Commissioner for Refugees, "Beyond Proof—Credibility Assessment in EU Asylum Systems (May 2013)", https://www.unhcr.org/51a8a08a9.pdf.

United Nations High Commissioner for Refugees, "Desperate Journeys: Refugees and Migrants Arriving in Europe and at Europe's Borders", September 2018, https://data2.unhcr.org/en/documents/download/65373#_ga=2.259362563.824522296.1546209771-1257371235.1536847062.

United Nations High Commissioner for Refugees, "The Dublin Regulation: Asylum in Europe", https://www.unhcr.org/4a9d13d59.pdf.

United Nations High Commissioner for Refugees, "Fair and Efficient Asylum Procedures: A Non-Exhaustive Overview of Applicable International Standards", http://www.refworld.org/pdfid/432ae9204.pdf.

United Nations High Commissioner for Refugees, "Figures at a Glance", https://www.unhcr.org/figures-at-a-glance.html.

United Nations High Commissioner for Refugees, "Forced Displacement Worldwide at its Highest in Decades", http://www.unhcr.org/news/stories/2017/6/5941561f4/forced-displacement-worldwide-its-highest-decades.html.

United Nations High Commissioner for Refugees, "Guidance Note on Safeguards Against Unlawful or Irregular Removal of Refugees and Asylum-Seekers", https://www.refworld.org/pdfid/530afbd84.pdf.

United Nations High Commissioner for Refugees, "Legal Considerations regarding access to protection and a connection between the refugee and the third country in the context of return or transfer to safe third countries", April 2018, https://www.refworld.org/pdfid/5acb33ad4.pdf.

United Nations High Commissioner for Refugees, "Left in Limbo: UNHCR Study on the Implementation of the Dublin III Regulation: Recommendations", August 2017, https://www.refworld.org/docid/59d5dd1a4.html.

United Nations High Commissioner for Refugees, "Operational Portal: Refugee Situations", https://data2.unhcr.org/en/situations/syria.

United Nations High Commissioner for Refugees, "Procedural Safeguards for Refugee Status Determination under UNHCR's Mandate", https://www.unhcr.org/4317223c9.pdf.

United Nations High Commissioner for Refugees, "State Parties to the 1951 Convention relating to the Status of Refugees and the 1967 Protocol", https://www.unhcr.org/protection/basic/3b73b0d63/states-parties-1951-convention-its-1967-protocol.html.

United Nations High Commissioner for Refugees, "UNHCR Guidelines on Determining the Best Interests of the Child", https://www.unhcr.org/4566b16b2.pdf.

United Nations High Commissioner for Refugees, "UNHCR Note on Diplomatic Assurances and International Protection", August 2006, https://www.refworld.org/docid/44dc81164.html.

United Nations, Human Rights Office of the High Commissioner, "Human Rights Treaty Bodies—Individual Communications", https://www.ohchr.org/en/hrbodies/tbpetitions/Pages/IndividualCommunications.aspx.

United Nations Treaty Collection, "Chapter V: Refugees and Stateless Persons. 2. Convention Relating to the Status of Refugees", https://treaties.un.org/pages/ViewDetailsII.aspx?src=TREATY&mtdsg_no=V-2&chapter=5&Temp=mtdsg2&clang=_en.

United Nations Treaty Collection, "Chapter V: Refugees and Stateless Persons. 5. Protocol Relating to the Status of Refugees", https://treaties.un.org/Pages/ViewDetails.aspx?src=IND&mtdsg_no=V-5&chapter=5&lang=en.

United Nations Treaty Collection, "Convention Against Torture and Other Cruel, Inhuman or Degrading Treatment or Punishment", https://treaties.un.org/pages/ViewDetails.aspx?src=IND&mtdsg_no=IV-9&chapter=4&lang=en.

United Nations Treaty Collection, "International Covenant on Civil and Political Rights", https://treaties.un.org/Pages/ViewDetails.aspx?chapter=4&clang=_en&mtdsg_no=IV-4&src=IND.

UK Home Office, "Asylum Policy Instruction: Assessing Credibility and Refugee Status: Version 9.0", 6 January 2015, https://assets.publishing.service.gov.uk/government/uploads/system/uploads/attachment_data/file/397778/ASSESSING_CREDIBILITY_AND_REFUGEE_STATUS_V9_0.pdf.

UK Home Office, "Asylum Policy Instruction: Revocation of Refugee Status: Version 4.0" https://www.gov.uk/government/uploads/system/uploads/attachment_data/file/493918/revocation_of_refugee_status_v4_0_EXT.pdf.

UK Home Office, "Certification of Protection and Human Rights Claims under Section 94 of Nationality, Immigration and Asylum Act 2002 (clearly unfounded claims): Version 4.0" https://assets.publishing.service.gov.uk/government/uploads/system/uploads/attachment_data/file/778221/certification-s94-guidance-0219.pdf.

UK Home Office, "Dublin III Regulation, Version 1.0", 2 November 2017, https://www.gov.uk/government/publications/dublin-iii-regulation.

UK Home Office, "Humanitarian Protection" https://www.gov.uk/government/uploads/system/uploads/attachment_data/file/597377/Humanitarian-protection-v5_0.pdf.

UK Home Office, "Exclusion (Article 1 F) and Article 33(2) of the Refugee Convention" https://www.gov.uk/government/uploads/system/uploads/attachment_data/file/534985/exclusion_and_article_33_2__refugee_convention.pdf.

UK Home Office, "Immigration Bail: Version 5.0", 28 February 2020, https://assets.publishing.service.gov.uk/government/uploads/system/uploads/attachment_data/file/869352/Immigration-bail-v5.0ext.pdf.

UK Home Office, "Immigration Rules Part 11: Asylum" https://www.gov.uk/guidance/immigration-rules/immigration-rules-part-11-asylum.

UK Home Office, "Inadmissibility: EU grants of asylum, first country of asylum and safe third country concepts: Version 4.0", 1 October 2019, https://assets.publishing.service.gov.uk/government/uploads/system/uploads/attachment_data/file/835342/Inadmissibility-guidance-v4.0ext.pdf.

UK Home Office, "Restricted Leave" https://www.gov.uk/government/uploads/system/uploads/attachment_data/file/575522/Restricted-leave-v2.pdf.

UK Office of Visas and Immigration, "Appeal a Decision by the Immigration and Asylum Tribunal" https://www.gov.uk/upper-tribunal-immigration-asylum/the-tribunals-decision.

UK Office of Visas and Immigration, "Asylum Claims and the Dublin Regulations", https://www.gov.uk/government/collections/asylum-claims-and-the-dublin-regulations.

UK Office of Visas and Immigration, "Asylum Decision-Making" www.gov.uk/government/collections/asylum-decision-making-guidance-asylum-instructions.

United Kingdom Office of Visas and Immigration, "Asylum Policy", https://www.gov.uk/topic/immigration-operational-guidance/asylum-policy.

UK Office of Visas and Immigration, "Court of Appeal Civil Division" https://www.gov.uk/courts-tribunals/court-of-appeal-civil-division.

UK Office of Visas and Immigration, "First-Tier Tribunal (Immigration and Asylum)" https://www.gov.uk/courts-tribunals/first-tier-tribunal-immigration-and-asylum.

UK Office of Visas and Immigration, "What We Do" https://www.gov.uk/government/organisations/uk-visas-and-immigration.

UK Office of Visas and Immigration, "Our Priorities" https://www.gov.uk/government/organisations/uk-visas-and-immigration/about#our-priorities.

UK Office of Visas and Immigration, "Upper Tribunal (Immigration and Asylum Chamber)" https://www.gov.uk/courts-tribunals/upper-tribunal-immigration-and-asylum-chamber.

UK Refugee Council, "Quarterly Asylum Statistics", August 2019, https://www.refugeecouncil.org.uk/wp-content/uploads/2019/09/Asylum-Statistics-Aug-2019.pdf.

United Kingdom, Home Office, "Immigration Rules", https://www.gov.uk/guidance/immigration-rules.

UK Supreme Court, "How to Appeal" https://www.supremecourt.uk/procedures/how-to-appeal.html.

UK Supreme Court, "Role of the Supreme Court" https://www.supremecourt.uk/about/role-of-the-supreme-court.html.

Vladislava Stoyanova, "MN and Others v Belgium: no ECHR protection from refoulement by issuing visas", 12 May 2020, http://ejiltalk.org/m-n-and-others-v-belgium-no-echr-protection-from-refoulement-by-issuing-visas.

Wei Li, Emily Skop, Adriana Morken, "Geography of Migration", *Oxford Bibliographies,* 23 August 2017,

https://www.oxfordbibliographies.com/view/document/obo-9780199874002/obo-9780199874002-0038.xml.

World Refugee Council, "Mobilizing Political Will for Refugee Protection and Solutions: A Framework for Analysis and Action", *World Refugee Council Research Paper No 1,* June 2018

https://www.cigionline.org/sites/default/files/documents/WRC%20Research%20Paper%20no.1web.pdf.

A.6.2 Nongovernmental Organization Documents

Amnesty International, "Germany: Briefing to Committee Against Torture, October 2011", Index EUR 23/002/2011.

CAT Committee, "General Comment No. 4 (2017) on the implementation of article 3 of the Convention in the context of article 22" (2017), 9 February 2018.

Council of Europe, *Handbook on European Law relating to Asylum, Borders and Immigration* (Strasbourg: Council of Europe Publishing, 2014).

European Council on Refugee and Exiles, "ECRE Comments on the Commission Proposal for a Dublin IV Regulation, COM(2016) 270", October 2016.

European Council on Refugees and Exiles, "ECRE Comments on the Commission Proposal for a Qualification Regulation, COM(2016) 466", November 2016.

European Council on Refugees and Exiles, "ECRE Comments on the Commission Proposal for an Asylum Procedures Regulation, COM(2016) 467", November 2016.

European Council on Refugees and Exiles, "ECRE Comments on the Commission Proposal to recast the Reception Conditions Directive, COM (2016) 465", October 2016.

European Council on Refugees and Exiles, "ECRE Information Note on the Directive 2011/95/EU of the European Parliament and of the Council of 13 December 2011 on standards for the qualification of third-country nationals or stateless persons as beneficiaries of international protection, for a uniform status for refugees or for persons eligible for subsidiary protection, and for the content of the protection granted (recast)".

European Council on Refugees and Exiles, "Information Note on Directive 2013/32/EU of the European Parliament and of the Council of 26 June 2013 on common procedures for granting and withdrawing international protection (recast)", December 2014.

European Council on Refugees and Exiles, "Information Note on Directive 2013/33/EU of the European Parliament and of the Council of 26 June 2013 laying down standards for the reception of applicants for international protection (recast)", July 2015.

Inter-American Commission on Human Rights, "Report on the Situation of Human Rights of Asylum-Seekers within the Canadian Refugee Determination System", 28 February 2000.

International Commission of Jurists, "Procedural rights in the proposed Dublin IV Regulation", 27 September 2016.

International Law Commission, *Articles on the Responsibility of States for Internationally Wrongful Acts*, Supplement No 10 (A/56/10), Chapter IV.E.1, November 2001.

International Law Commission, "Fragmentation of International Law: Difficulties Arising from the Diversification and Expansion of International Law: Report of the Study Group of the International Law Commission: Finalized by Martti Koskenniemi", 13 April 2006, UN Doc A/CN.4/L.682.

Martti Koskenniemi, "International Law Commission, Study Group on Fragmentation: Fragmentation of International Law: Topic (a): The Function and Scope of *Lex Specialis* Rule and the Question of 'Self-Contained Regimes': An Outline".

Norwegian Refugee Council, "Non-Refoulement in the Context of Internal Displacement: The Case of IDPs in South Sudan's Protection of Civilians Sites", September 2017.

A.6.3 European Commission Documents

European Commission, "Communication from the Commission to the European Parliament and the Council towards a reform of the Common European Asylum System and enhancing legal avenues to Europe", Brussels, 6 April 2016, COM (2016) 197 final.

European Commission, "Communication from the Commission to the European Parliament, the Council, the European Economic and Social Committee and the Committee of the Regions: A European Agenda on Migration", COM(2015) 240 final, 13 May 2015.

European Commission, "Proposal for a Directive of the European Parliament and of the Council laying down standards for the reception of applicants for international protection (recast)", Brussels, 13 July 2016, COM(2016) 465 final.

European Commission, "Proposal for a Directive of the European Parliament and of the Council laying down minimum standards for the reception of asylum seekers (recast)", COM(2008) 815 final, 2008/0244 (COD), 3 December 2008 at explanatory memorandum.

European Commission, "Proposal for a Regulation of the European Parliament and of the Council establishing a common procedure for international protection in the Union and repealing Directive 2013/32/EU", COM(2016) 467 final, 13 July 2016.

European Commission, "Proposal for a Regulation of the European Parliament and of the Council establishing a crisis relocation mechanism and amending Regulation (EU) No 604/2013 of the European Parliament and of the Council of 26 June 2013 establishing the criteria and mechanisms for determining the Member State responsible for examining an application for international protection lodged in one of the Member States by a third country national or a stateless person", 2015/0208 (COD), Brussels, 9 September 2015.

European Commission, "Proposal for a Regulation of the European Parliament and of the Council establishing the criteria and mechanisms for determining the Member State responsible for examining an application for international protection lodged in one of the Member States by a third-country national or a stateless person (recast)", COM(2016) 270 final, 4 May 2016.

European Commission, "Proposal for a Regulation of the European Parliament and of the Council on the European Union Agency for Asylum and repealing Regulation (EU) No 439/2010", Brussels, 4 May 2016, COM(2016) final.

European Commission, "Proposal for Regulation of the European Parliament and of the Council on the establishment of 'Eurodac' for the comparison of fingerprints for the effective application of [Regulation (EU) No 604/2013 establishing the criteria and mechanisms for determining the Member State responsible for examining an application for international protection lodged in one of the Member States by a third-country national or a stateless person], for identifying an illegally staying third-country national or stateless person and on requests for the comparison with Eurodac data by Member States' law enforcement authorities and Europol for law enforcement purposes (recast)", COM (2016) 272 final, 4 May 2016.

European Commission, "Proposal for a Regulation of the European Parliament and of the Council on standards for the qualification of third-country nationals or stateless persons as beneficiaries of international protection, for a uniform status for refugees or for persons eligible for subsidiary protection and for the content of the protection granted and amending Council Directive 2003/109/EC of 25 November 2003 concerning the status of third-country nationals who are long-term residents", COM(2016) 466 final, 13 July 2016.

European Commission, "The Law and Practice on Safe Country Principles Against the Background of the Common European Asylum System and the Goal of a Common Asylum Procedure: Final Report", DG JAI-A2/2002/04.

A.6.4 UN Documents

Ad Hoc Committee on Statelessness and Related Problems, 1950 UN Doc E/AC.32/2 Annex.

Ad Hoc Committee on Statelessness and Related Problems, 1950 UN Doc E/AC.32/L.32.

Ad Hoc Committee on Statelessness and Related Problems, 1950 UN Doc E/AC.32/SR.20.

Ad Hoc Committee on Refugees and Stateless Persons, 1950 UN Doc E/AC.32/SR.40.

Committee Against Torture, "Concluding observations on the fifth periodic report of the United Kingdom, adopted by the Committee at its fiftieth session (6–31 May 2013)—Advance Unedited Version".

Committee Against Torture, "Conclusions and Recommendations of the Committee Against Torture concerning the Second Report of the United States of America", 25 July 2006, UN Doc CAT/C/USA/CO/2.

Committee Against Torture, "Convention Against Torture and Other Cruel, Inhuman or Degrading Treatment of Punishment: General Comment No 2", 23 November 2007, UN Doc CAT/C/GC/2/CRP.1/Rev.4.

Committee Against Torture, "Convention Against Torture and Other Cruel, Inhuman or Degrading Treatment or Punishment: General Comment No. 2", 24 January 2008, UN Doc CAT/C/GC/2.

Committee Against Torture, "General Comment No. 1: Communications concerning the return of a person to a State where there may be grounds he would be subjected to torture (article 3 in the context of article 22)", UN Doc A/53/44, annex IX at 52 (1998).

Committee Against Torture, "General Comment No. 4 (2017) on the implementation of article 3 of the Convention in the context of article 22", 9 February 2018.

Committee Against Torture, "List of issues to be considered during the examination of the fifth periodic report of Germany", 23 June 2011, UN Doc CAT/C/DEU/5.

Conference of Plenipotentiaries, 1951 UN Doc A/CONF.2/69.

Conference of Plenipotentiaries, 1951 UN Doc A/CONF.2/SR.35.

Human Rights Committee, "Concluding Observations on Barbados", 11 May 2007, UN Doc CCPR/C/BRB/CO/3.

Human Rights Committee, "Concluding Observations on Botswana", 24 April 2008, UN Doc CCPR/C/BWA/CO/1.

Human Rights Committee, "General Comment No 20", 1992.

Human Rights Committee, "General Comment No 29 on States of Emergency (Article 4)", 31 August 2001, UN Doc CCPR/C/21/Rev.1/Add.11.

Human Rights Committee, "General Comment No 31", 2003.

Jane McAdam, "The Refugee Convention as a Rights Blueprint for Persons in Need of International Protection" (2006) *UNHCR Research Paper No 125* http://www.unhcr.org/research/RESEARCH/44b7b7162.pdf.

Katy Long, "No Entry! A Review of UNHCR's Response to Border Closures in Situations of Mass Refugee Influx", June 2010 http://www.unhcr.org/4c207bd59.pdf.

League of Nations, "Russian Refugees: Report by Dr. Nansen, High Commissioner of the League of Nations", 1922 LNOJ.

League of Nations, "Supplementary Report: Submitted to the Twentieth Ordinary Session of the Assembly of the League of Nations by Sir Herbert Emerson, GCIE, KCSI, CBE, High Commissioner for Refugees", 20 October 1939, LN Doc A18(a).

Michael Blake and Patrick Taylor Smith, "International Distributive Justice" (2013) *Stanford Encyclopedia of Philosophy,* October 2013 https://plato.stanford.edu/entries/international-justice.

Statement by Chance (Canada) and Hoeg (Denmark), 1951 UN Doc A/CONF.2/SR.16.

UN, "Depositary: Status of Treaties—5. Protocol Relating to the Status of Refugees".

UN Commission on Human Rights, "Resolution 2005/80 on the Protection of Human Rights and Fundamental Freedoms while Countering Terrorism", 21 April 2005.

UN Commission on Human Rights, *Siracusa Principles on the Limitation and Derogation Provisions in the International Covenant on Civil and Political Rights,* 28 September 1984, UN Doc E/CN.4/1985/4.

UN Economic and Social Council, "Resolution 248 (IX) B of 8 August 1949".

UN Economic and Social Council, "Summary Record of the Twentieth Meeting: Ad Hoc Committee on Statelessness and Related Problems, First Session", UN Doc E/AC.32/SR.20, 1950.

UN General Assembly, "New York Declaration for Refugees and Migrants: Resolution 71/1", 3 October 2016.

UN General Assembly, "Resolution Adopted by the General Assembly: 52/103, Office of the United Nations High Commissioner for Refugees", 9 February 1998, UN Doc A/RES/52/103

United Nations General Assembly, "Resolution 60/148", 21 February 2006, UN Doc A/RES/60/148.

UN General Assembly, "Resolution 217 III".

UN General Assembly, "Resolution on the United Nations Millennium Declaration", UN Doc A/RES/55/2, 18 September 2000.

United Nations General Assembly, "Torture and other cruel, inhuman or degrading treatment or punishment: Note by the Secretary-General", 7 August 2015, UN Doc A/70/303.

United Nations General Assembly, "Torture and other cruel, inhuman or degrading treatment or punishment: Note by the Secretary-General", 30 August 2005, UN Doc A/60/316.

UN General Assembly, "X. Resolutions Adopted on the Report of the Third Committee", 12 February 1946.

UN Security Council, Resolution 1456 (2003), 20 January 2003; 1535 (2004), 26 March 2004; 1624 (2004), 14 September 2005.

UNHCR, "2. Convention Relating to the Status of Refugees: Geneva, 28 July 1951".

UNHCR, "Advisory Opinion on the Extraterritorial Application of *Non-refoulement* Obligations under the 1951 Convention Relating to the Status of Refugees and its 1967 Protocol", 26 January 2007.

UNHCR, "Asylum Procedures (Fair and Efficient Asylum Procedures)", 31 May 2001, UN Doc EC/GC/01/12.

UNHCR, "Background Paper", *High Commissioner's Dialogue on Protection Challenges: Protection at Sea,* 11 November 2018.

UNHCR, "Commentary on the Refugee Convention 1951, Articles 2–11, 13–37", October 1997.

UNHCR, "Guidelines on Applicable Criteria and standards relating to the Detention of Asylum-Seekers" (February 1999).

UNHCR, "Handbook and Guidelines on Procedures and Criteria for Determining Refugee Status under the 1951 Convention and the 1967 Protocol Relating to the Status of Refugees", December 2011.

UNHCR, "Implementation of the Dublin Convention: Some UNHCR Observations", May 1998.

UNHCR, "Introductory Note: By the Office of the United Nations High Commissioner for Refugees (UNHCR)".

UNHCR, "Moving Further Toward a Common European Asylum System: UNHCR's statement on the EU asylum legislative package" Bureau for Europe, June 2013.

UNHCR, "Note on Burden and Standard of Proof in Refugee Claims", 16 December 1998.

UNHCR, "Note on International Protection", 2 July 1997, UN Doc A/AC.96/ 882.

UNHCR, "Note on International Solidarity and Refugee Protection", 13 July 1988, UN Doc/EC/SCP/50.

UNHCR, "Note on the Principle of Non-Refoulement", November 1997.

UNHCR, "States Parties to the 1951 Convention Relating to the Status of Refugees and the 1967 Protocol".

UNHCR, "The Refugee Convention, 1951: The Travaux Preparatoires Analysed with a Commentary by Dr Paul Weis".

UNHCR, "UNHCR Annotated Comments to Directive 2013/33/EU of the European Parliament and Council of 26 June 2013 laying down standards for the reception of applicants for international protection (recast): To assist with transposition and implementation", April 2015.

UNHCR, "UNHCR comments on the European Commission's proposal for a Directive of the European Parliament and of the Council on minimum standards for the qualification and status of third country nationals or stateless persons as beneficiaries of international protection and the content of the protection granted (COM(2009)551, 21 October 2009)", July 2010.

UNHCR, "UNHCR Comments on the European Commission proposal for a Regulation of the European Parliament and of the Council establishing the criteria and mechanisms for determining the member state responsible for examining an application for international protection lodged in one of the Member States by a third-country national or a stateless person (recast)—COM(2016) 270", December 2016.

UNHCR, "UNHCR Note on Diplomatic Assurances and International Refugee Protection", August 2006.

UNHCR, Executive Committee, "Conclusion No. 22", 1981.

UNHCR, Executive Committee, "Conclusion No. 81", 1997.

UNHCR, Executive Committee, "Conclusion No. 82", 1997.

UNHCR, Executive Committee, "Conclusion No 87 (L)", 1999.

UNHCR, EU Bureau, "Fair and Fast: UNHCR Discussion Paper on Accelerated and Simplified Procedures in the European Union", May 2018.

A.6.5 Soft Law Policy Documents

UK Government, Home Office, "Asylum Policy Instruction: Assessing Credibility and Refugee Status", Version 9.0, 6 January 2015.

Glossary

Accelerated Procedure A fast track procedure for unfounded asylum claims or where there are serious national security or public order concerns in the claim by introducing shorter, but reasonable time limits for certain procedural steps

Area of Freedom, Security, Justice An area created by Article 67 TFEU which ensures the absence of internal border controls and which frames a common policy on asylum, immigration and external border control, based on solidary between Member States

Asylum Procedures Directive A key CEAS directive which determines the common procedure for granting and withdrawing international protection

Common European Asylum System A common European asylum policy aimed at enhancing efficiency and harmonizing asylum standards across the EU

Diplomatic Assurances An undertaking from the receiving State to the sending State to the effect that the person being transferred will be treated in accordance with relevant international human rights standards

Dublin III Regulation Mechanism and criteria for determining the Member State responsible for processing asylum applications

Dublin System The Dublin III Regulation along with key directives of the CEAS: the Qualification Directive, Asylum Procedures Directive, and the Reception Conditions Directive

Dublin Transfer Transfer of the claimant from one Member State to the Member State deemed responsible for examining the asylum application based on presumption of mutual trust

EUNAVFOR MED EU Naval Force Mediterranean

Eurodac Biometric database for fingerprint collection

FRONTEX EU's external border and coastguard agency

Irregular Movement In the EU context, refers to accessing Member State territories to seek asylum through means other than at authorized checkpoints such as at border crossings

J. Poon, *Counteracting Containment Policies in the EU*, European Union and its Neighbours in a Globalized World 31,
https://doi.org/10.1007/978-3-032-08351-7

Margin of Appreciation Deference given to Council of Europe Member States by the ECtHR in Member States' interpretation of international law and ECHR law obligations

Margin of Discretion Deference given to EU Member States by the Court of Justice of the EU, as distinguished from the 'margin of appreciation'

Member State Responsible EU Member State deemed responsible for processing asylum applications pursuant to Dublin III Regulation

Non-Entrée Non-admission policies which seek to deter claimants from reaching territory of States to access asylum

Presumption of Mutual Trust The presumption that EU Member States all comply with their relevant international and EU law obligations

Primacy of EU Law All EU law has absolute and unconditional precedence and should always be given precedence over all conflicting provisions of national law

Primary Legislation A source of EU law at the top of the hierarchy which consists of EU treaties and general principles of EU law

Principle of Mutual Recognition The recognition by each Member State of the decisions of courts from other Member States with minimum procedure and formality

Qualification Directive A key CEAS directive which determines the minimum standards for the qualification of international protection for Third Country Nationals and stateless persons

Reception Conditions Directive A key CEAS directive which determines the standards for reception of applicants for international protection

Responsibility-Sharing A legal principle binding upon all EU Member States which requires them to implement EU policies by sharing the responsibility for the implementation of such policies between the Member States

Safe Third Country A country which the applicant for international protection has passed through where they should have claimed for asylum but they did not. The onus is upon the claimant to prove on a rebuttable presumption that they do not have a connection with the 'safe third country' to prevent return.

Secondary Legislation A source of EU law superseded by primary legislation which consists of legislative acts, delegating acts, and implementing acts

Secondary Movement In the EU context, refers to activities such as smuggling and trafficking

Subsidiary Protection Complementary protection to the Refugee Convention that qualifies individuals who face a 'serious harm' upon return, but who do not meet the refugee definition

Suspensive Recourse Non-removal of an asylum claimant from the country of asylum pending the outcome of an appeal

Take Back Request A request by the sending Member State to the Member State responsible to take back the applicant who has withdrawn the application under examination or whose application has been rejected and made an application in another Member State. *Example*: When an applicant has already applied for asylum in another Member State

Take Charge Request A request by the sending Member State to the Member State responsible to take charge of the applicant who has lodged an application in a different Member State. *Example*: When an applicant has stayed in another Member State before entering the Member State which he/she first applied for asylum

Third-Country National A person who does not benefit from the right to freedom of movement within the EU and who is also not an EU citizen

www.ingramcontent.com/pod-product-compliance
Lightning Source LLC
Chambersburg PA
CBHW060215181125
35560CB00004BB/291
* 9 7 8 3 0 3 2 0 8 3 5 0 0 *